COGNITIVE DEVELOPMENT TO ADOLESCENCE

Cognitive Development to Adolescence
A Reader edited by Ken Richardson
and Sue Sheldon
at the Open University

Lawrence Erlbaum Associates, Publishers
in association with
The Open University

Lawrence Erlbaum Associates Ltd., Publishers
27 Palmeira Mansions
Church Road
Hove
East Sussex, BN3 2FA
U.K.

British Library Cataloguing in Publication Data

Cognitive development to adolescence: a
  reader.
  1. Cognition in children
  I. Richardson, Ken   II. Sheldon, Sue
  III. Open University
  155.4'13   BF723.C5

ISBN 0-86377-087-8
ISBN 0-86377-088-6 Pbk

Typeset by Multiplex Techniques Ltd., Orpington
Printed and bound by A. Wheaton & Co. Ltd., Exeter

Contents

Preface

This book of readings has been prepared to accompany the Open University third-level course, *Cognitive Development: Language and Thinking from Birth to Adolescence*. Because it aims to bring to the student the fundamental questions in the area at the present time, together with overviews of contemporary responses to those questions, it should also be of interest to students of this subject, generally. It covers the period, very broadly, from the immediate pre-school stage to about the onset of adolescence (around 12 years). Two accompanying Readers to the same course (Oates & Sheldon, 1987; Lock & Fisher 1984) cover the period of infancy, and language development, respectively.

Development to adolescence has long been recognised as one of the most important areas of scientific investigation. Part of this importance arises from the child's first contacts with the education system, the latter's statutory responsibility for the promotion of cognitive development, and what are usually seen as the long-term consequences of the schools' successes and failures, both for the remainder of education and for society generally. As such, there has been a long tradition of enquiry into child development motivated by the desire to improve the system of education. There is little doubt, in fact, that, because of this, the area has been among the most actively researched in the whole field of psychology. Moreover, because this enquiry covers a period when the child's cognitive processes appear to be more accessible, when the child can understand and answer questions meaningfully, when he or she is usually rather keen to participate in research projects, and cognitive developmental changes seem most patent and obvious, the research has been remarkably fruitful in the sense of richness of theorising and of sheer volume of empirical findings. Whether or not these command general agreement among psychologists, and therefore can stand as genuine progress, is, however, a different matter. In fact the *sources* of agreements and disagreements bring us to the heart of the matter in any scientific enquiry, in the sense that these are what you need to understand if you seriously want to "know" a particular area. This is what has primarily guided our selection of readings from what, in terms of abundance of literature, is a very overcrowded area indeed.

Because some agreements or disagreements have persisted over time, and others have changed dramatically, this updated Reader is both similar to, and different from, its predecessor (Floyd, 1979). Some things haven't changed. Piaget's theory still dominates the area. We are still preoccupied with descriptions of how differently children think at different ages or stages (rather than getting beyond that to the process of change itself). And what we can do in schools to promote development (especially in particular subject areas like scientific and mathematical thinking) is still close to our hearts and minds. But other things *have* changed. The grip of Piaget's theory has weakened in many ways, and a new critical tide is attempting to revise many Piagetian tenets. One of the issues, here, is the methodological one of how our research procedures may, themselves, constrain the child's *demonstration* of his or her true abilities. The realization of the influence of the research situation as a *social context* has led increasingly to a view of the child's knowledge and cognitive processes as inseparable from such contexts. Thus we have seen a growing sympathy with Vygotsky's theory of development, and the emergence of a new sub-area, *social cognition*, which attempts to take these social perspectives into account. There has also been a growing incursion of "information-processing" theories of cognition into the area of cognitive development. And new views of the persistent problems experienced in education over this period, and what we might be doing about them, have emerged.

All of these themes (and many more) are represented in this collection. The themes are, of course, dealt with in further detail in the Main Text of the course itself (Block 3, with the same title). But we hope the Reader will be generally useful, as it stands, in drawing out the major issues and trends at the present time. There may or may not be justification for using the old cliché that "these are exciting times" in the area. But we certainly hope that the understanding of the area which this collection is intended to furnish will help today's students to create exciting times in the future.

As usual, with a work of this kind, help and assistance has come from individuals too numerous to cite in detail. Apart from the contributors, many of whom offered guidance and suggestion well beyond the mere permission to use their material, and, of course, members of the course team, we would particularly like to acknowledge the valuable suggestions of George Butterworth, without which the collection would almost certainly have been less relevant and less circumspect.

Ken Richardson
Sue Sheldon

REFERENCES

Floyd, A. (Ed.) (1979). *Cognitive Development in the School Years*. London: Croom Helm.
Lock, A. & Fisher, E. (Eds.) (1984). *Language Development*. London: Croom Helm.
Oates, J. & Sheldon, S. (Eds.) (1987). *Cognitive Development in Infancy*. London: Lawrence Erlbaum Associates Ltd.

PERSPECTIVES

1 Extracts from Piaget's Theory

Jean Piaget

The following theory of development, which is particularly concerned with the development of cognitive functions, is impossible to understand if one does not begin by analyzing in detail the biological presuppositions from which it stems and the epistemological consequences in which it ends. Indeed, the fundamental postulate that is the basis of the ideas summarized here is that the same problems and the same types of explanations can be found in the three following processes:

a. The adaptation of an organism to its environment during its growth, together with the interactions and autoregulations which characterize the development of the "epigenetic system." (Epigenesis in its embryo-logical sense is always determined both internally and externally.)

b. The adaptation of intelligence in the course of the construction of its own structures, which depends as much on progressive internal coordinations as on information acquired through experience.

c. The establishment of cognitive or, more generally, epistemological relations, which consist neither of a simple copy of external objects nor of a mere unfolding of structures preformed inside the subject, but rather involve a set of structures progressively constructed by continuous interaction between the subject and the external world.

Source: Mussen, P.H. (1970). (Ed.) *Manual of child psychology.* London: John Wiley & Sons, pp. 703-732. Copyright 1970 John Wiley & Sons, Inc. Reprinted by permission of John Wiley & Sons, Inc.

We begin with the last point, on which our theory is furthest removed both from the ideas of the majority of psychologists and from "common sense."

THE RELATION BETWEEN SUBJECT AND OBJECT

1. In the common view, the external world is entirely separate from the subject, although it encloses the subject's own body. Any objective knowledge, then, appears to be simply the result of a set of perceptive recordings, motor associations, verbal descriptions, and the like, which all participate in producing a sort of figurative copy or "functional copy" (in Hull's terminology) of objects and the connections between them. The only function of intelligence is systematically to file, correct, etc., these various sets of information; in this process, the more faithful the critical copies, the more consistent the final system will be. In such an empiricist prospect, the content of intelligence comes from outside, and the coordinations that organize it are only the consequences of language and symbolic instruments.

But this passive interpretation of the act of knowledge is in fact contradicted at all levels of development and, particularly, at the sensorimotor and prelinguistic levels of cognitive adaptation and intelligence. Actually, in order to know objects, the subject must act upon them, and therefore transform them: he must displace, connect, combine, take apart, and reassemble them.

From the most elementary sensorimotor actions (such as pushing and pulling) to the most sophisticated intellectual operations, which are interiorized actions, carried out mentally (e.g., joining together, putting in order, putting into one-to-one correspondence), knowledge is constantly linked with actions or operations, that is, with *transformations*.

Hence the limit between subject and objects is in no way determined beforehand, and, what is more important, it is not stable. Indeed, in every action the subject and the objects are fused. The subject needs objective information to become aware of his own actions, of course, but he also needs many subjective components. Without long practice or the construction of refined instruments of analysis and coordination, it will be impossible for him to know what belongs to the object, what belongs to himself as an active subject, and what belongs to the action itself taken as the transformation of an initial state into a final one. Knowledge, then, at its origin, neither arises from objects nor from the subject, but from interactions – at first inextricable – between the subject and those objects.

Even these primitive interactions are so close-knit and inextricable that, as J. M. Baldwin noted, the mental attitudes of the infant are probably "adualistical." This means they lack any differentiation between an external world, which would be composed of objects independent of the subject, and an internal or subjective world.

Therefore the problem of knowledge, the so-called epistemological problem, cannot be considered separately from the problem of the development of intelligence. It reduces to analyzing how the subject becomes progressively able to know objects adequately, that is, how he becomes capable of objectivity. Indeed, objectivity is in no way an initial property, as the empiricists would have it, and its conquest involves a series of successive constructs which approximates it more and more closely.

2. This leads us to a second idea central to the theory, that of *construction*, which is the natural consequence of the interactions we have just mentioned. Since objective knowledge is not acquired by a mere recording of external information but has its origin in interactions between the subject and objects, it necessarily implies two types of activity – on the one hand, the coordination of actions themselves, and on the other, the introduction of interrelations between the objects. These two activities are interdependent because it is only through action that these relations originate. It follows that objective knowledge is always subordinate to certain structures of action. But those structures are the result of a *construction* and are not given in the objects, since they are dependent on action, nor in the subject, since the subject must learn how to coordinate his actions (which are not generally hereditarily programmed except in the case of reflexes or instincts).

An early example of these constructions (which begin as early as the first year) is the one that enables the 9- to 12-month-old child to discover the permanence of objects, initially relying on their position in his perceptual field, and later independent of any actual perception. During the first months of existence, there are no permanent objects, but only perceptual pictures which appear, dissolve, and sometimes reappear. The "permanence" of an object begins with the action of looking for it when it has disappeared at a certain point A of the visual field (for instance, if a part of the object remains visible, or if it makes a bump under a cloth). But, when the object later disappears at B, it often happens that the child will look for it again at A. This very instructive behavior supplies evidence for the existence of the primitive interactions between the subject and the object which we mentioned (¶ 1). At this stage, the child still believes that objects depend on this action and that, where an action has succeeded a first time, it must succeed again. One real example is an 11-month-old child who was playing with a ball. He had previously retrieved it from under an armchair when it had rolled there before. A moment later, the ball went under a low sofa. He could not find it under this sofa, so he came back to the other part of the room and looked for it under the armchair, where this course of action had already been successful.

For the scheme[1] of a permanent object that does not depend on the subject's own actions to become established, a new structure has to be constructed. This is the structure of the "group of translations" in the geometrical sense: (a) the translation $AB + BC = AC$; (b) the translations $AB + BA = O$; (c) $AB + O = AB$; (d) $AC + CD = AB + BD$. The psychological equivalent of this group is the possibility of behaviors that involve returning to an initial position, or detouring around an obstacle (a and d). As soon as this organization is achieved – and it is not at all given at the beginning of development, but must be constructed by a succession of new coordinations – an objective structuration of the movements of the object and of those of the subject's own body becomes possible. The object becomes an independent entity, whose position can be traced as a function of its translations and successive positions. At this juncture the subject's body, instead of being considered the center of the world, becomes an object like any other, the translations and positions of which are correlative to those of the objects themselves.

The group of translations is an instance of the construction of a structure, attributable simultaneously to progressive coordination of the subject's actions and to information provided by physical experience, which finally constitutes a fundamental instrument for the organization of the external world. It is also a cognitive instrument so important that it contributes to the veritable "Copernican revolution" babies accomplish in 12 to 18 months. Whereas before he had evolved this new structure the child would consider himself (unconsciously) the motionless center of the universe, he becomes, because of this organization of permanent objects and space (which entails moreover a parallel organization of temporal sequences and causality), only one particular member of the set of the other mobile objects which compose his universe.

[. . .]

3. What is already true for the sensorimotor stage appears again in all stages of development and in scientific thought itself but at levels in which the primitive actions have been transformed into *operations*. These operations are interiorized actions (e.g., addition, which can be performed either physically or mentally) that are reversible (addition acquires an inverse in

---

[1]Throughout this paper the term *scheme* (plural, *schemes*) is used to refer to *operational* activities, whereas *schema* (plural, *schemata*) refers to the figurative aspects of thought – attempts to represent reality without attempting to transform it (imagery, perception and memory). Later in this paper the author says, ". . . images . . ., however schematic, are not schemes. We shall therefore use the term schemata to designate them. A schema is a simplified image (e.g., the map of a town), whereas a scheme represents what can be repeated and generalized in an action (for example, the scheme is what is common in the actions of "pushing" an object with a stick or any other instrument)."

subtraction) and constitute set-theoretical structures (such as the logical additive "grouping" or algebraic groups).

A striking instance of these operational structurations dependent on the subject's activity, which often occurs even before an experimental method has been evolved, is *atomism*, invented by the Greeks long before it could be justified experimentally. The same process can be observed in the child between 4 to 5 and 11 to 12 years of age in a situation where it is obvious that experience is not sufficient to explain the emergence of the structure and that its construction implies an additive composition dependent on the activities of the subject. The experiment involves the dissolution of lumps of sugar in a glass of water. The child can be questioned about the conservation of the matter dissolved and about the conservation of its weight and volume. Before age 7 to 8 the dissolved sugar is presumed destroyed and its taste vanished. Around this age sugar is considered as preserving its substance in the form of very small and invisible grains, but it has neither weight nor volume. At age 9 to 10 each grain keeps its weight and the sum of all these elementary weights is equivalent to the weight of the sugar itself before dissolution. At age 11 to 12 this applies to volume (the child predicts that after the sugar has melted, the level of the water in the container will remain at its same initial height).

We can now see that this spontaneous atomism, although it is suggested by the visible grains becoming gradually smaller during their dissolution, goes far beyond what can be seen by the subject and involves a step-by-step construction correlative to that of additive operations. We thus have a new instance of the origin of knowledge lying neither in the object alone nor in the subject, but rather in an inextricable interaction between both of them, such that what is given physically is integrated in a logicomathematical structure involving the coordination of the subject's actions. The decomposition of a whole into its parts (invisible here) and the recomposition of these parts into a whole are in fact the result of logical or logicomathematical constructions and not only of physical experiments.
[. . .]

ASSIMILATION AND ACCOMMODATION

4. The psychological meaning of our previous points (¶ 1 to 3) is that the fundamental psychogenetic connections generated in the course of development cannot be considered as reducible to empirical "associations"; rather, they consist of *assimilations*, both in the biological and intellectual sense.

From a biological point of view, assimilation is the integration of external elements into evolving or completed structures of an organism. [. . .] Indeed, no behaviour, even if it is new to the individual, constitutes an absolute beginning. It is always grafted onto previous schemes and therefore amounts to assimilating new elements to already constructed structures (innate, as reflexes are, or previously acquired).

If assimilation alone were involved in development, there would be no variations in the child's structures. Therefore he would not acquire new content and would not develop further. Assimilation is necessary in that it assures the continuity of structures and the integration of new elements to these structures.

Biological assimilation itself, however, is never present without its counterpart, accommodation. During its embryological development, for instance, a phenotype assimilates the substances necessary to the conservation of its structures as specified by its genotype. But, depending on whether these substances are plentiful or rare or whether the usual substances are replaced by other slightly different ones, nonhereditary variations (often called "accommodates") such as changes in shape or height may occur. These variations are specific to some external conditions. Similarly, in the field of behavior we shall call accommodation any modification of an assimilatory scheme or structure by the elements it assimilates. For example, the infant who assimilates his thumb to the sucking schema will, when sucking his thumb make different movements from those he uses in suckling his mother's breast. Similarly, an 8-year-old who is assimilating the dissolution of sugar in water to the notion that substance is conserved must make accommodations to invisible particles different from those he would make if they were still visible.

Hence cognitive adaptation, like its biological counterpart, consists of an equilibrium between assimilation and accommodation. As has just been shown, there is no assimilation without accommodation. But we must strongly emphasize the fact that accommodation does not exist without simultaneous assimilation either. From a biological point of view, this fact is verified by the existence of what modern geneticists call "reaction norms" – a genotype may offer a more or less broad range of possible accommodations, but all of them are within a certain statistically defined "norm." In the same way, cognitively speaking, the subject is capable of various accommodations, but only within certain limits imposed by the necessity of preserving the corresponding assimilatory structure.

[. . .]

5. In the development of intelligence in the child, there are many types of equilibrium between assimilation and accommodation that vary with the levels of development and the problems to be solved.

[. . .]

Generally speaking, this progressive equilibrium between assimilation and accommodation is an instance of a fundamental process in cognitive development which can be expressed in terms of centration and decentration. The systematically distorting assimilations of sensorimotor or initial representative stages, which distort because they are not accompanied by adequate accommodations, mean that the subject remains centered on his own actions and his own viewpoint. On the other hand, the gradually emerging equilibrium between assimilation and accommodation is the result of successive decentrations, which make it possible for the subject to take the points of view of other subjects or objects themselves. We formerly described this process merely in terms of egocentrism and socialization. But it is far more general and more fundamental to knowledge in all its forms. For cognitive progress is not only assimilation of information; it entails a systematic decentration process which is a necessary condition of objectivity itself.

THE THEORY OF STAGES

6. We have seen that there exist structures which belong only to the subject (¶ 1), that they are built (¶ 2), and that this is a step-by-step process. We must therefore conclude there exist stages of development. Even authors who agree with this idea may use different criteria and interpretations of stage development. It therefore becomes a problem that requires discussion in its own right.

[. . .]

7. If we restrict ourselves to major structures, it is strikingly obvious that cognitive stages have a sequential property, that is, they appear in a fixed order of succession because each one of them is necessary for the formation of the following one.

If we now consider only the principal periods of development, one can enumerate three of them:

a. A sensorimotor period lasts until approximately 1½ years of age with a first subperiod of centration on the subject's own body (lasting about 7 to 9 months) followed by a second one of objectivization and spatialization of the schemes of practical intelligence.

b. A period of representative intelligence leads to concrete operations (classes, relations, and numbers bound to objects) with a first preoperational subperiod (there is no reversibility or conservation, but the beginnings of directional functions and qualitative identities), which begins around 1½ to 2 years of age with the formation of semiotic processes such as language and mental imagery. This is followed by a second subperiod (at about 7 to 8 years) characterized by the beginnings of operational groupings in their various concrete forms and with their various types of conservation.

c. Finally, there is the period of propositional or formal operations. This also begins with a subperiod of organization (11 to 13 years old) and is followed by a subperiod of achievement of the general combinatory and the group INRC of the two kinds of reversibilities.

If we now consider the preceding sequence, it is easy to observe that each one of these periods or subperiods is necessary to the constitution of its successor. As a first example, why do language and the semiotic function emerge only at the end of a long sensorimotor period where the only significates are indexes and signals, and where there are no symbols or signs? (If the acquisition of language were only dependent on an accumulation of associations, as is sometimes claimed, then it could occur much earlier.)
[. . .]

A second example of the sequential character of our periods and subperiods is the subperiod of ages 2 to 7, which itself results from the sensorimotor schemes elaborated in the ninth and tenth months and which prepares the concrete operations of ages 7 to 10. This subperiod is characterized by some negative aspects (lack of reversibility and absence of the concept of conservation), but it also evolves some positive achievements such as the directional functions. [*fonctions orientées* – mappings where $y = f(x)$ with unity of the value $f(x)$ for any (x) and the qualitative identity $a = a$.] In fact, these functions already play an extensive role in preoperational thought. Their one-way orientation explains the general primacy of the concept of order at this level, with its adequate aspects, but this also is the source of systematic distortions (e.g., "longer" understood as "going farther"; estimation of a quantity of water by taking only its level into account). The elementary functions are nothing other than the connections inherent in the schemes of action (which, before they become operational, are always oriented toward a goal) and therefore originate in the sensorimotor schemes themselves. Qualitative identity (the type of identity expressed by the child when he says: "It is the same water," even if the quantity of water changes) has its origin in the concept of permanent object, and in the notion that the subject's own body (as well as those of other subjects) maintains its identity both in time and in space; and these are three achievements of the sensorimotor stage. On the other hand, the one-way, directional functions and the identities they involve constitute the necessary condition for future operations. Thus we can see that the stages between 2 and 7 years are simultaneously an extension of the sensorimotor stages and the basis of the future concrete operations.

The propositional operations that appear between ages 11 and 15 with the INRC group and general combinatorial structures, all consist of applying operations to operations and transformations to transformations. It is therefore obvious that the existence of this last stage necessarily involves the acquisitions of the previous one (concrete operations, or operations to the first power).

8. Thus defined, the stages always appear in the same order of succession. This might lead us to assume that some biological factor such as maturation is at work. But it is certainly not comparable to the hereditary neurophysiological programming of instincts. Biological maturation does nothing more than open the way to possible constructions (or explain transient impossibilities). It remains for the subject to actualize them. This actualization, when it is regular, obeys the law of creodes, that is, of constant and necessary progress such that the endogenous reactions find support in the environment and in experience. It would therefore be a mistake to consider the succession of these stages as the result of an innate predetermination, because there is a continual construction of novelty during the whole sequence.

The two best proofs of this last point are the possibilities of deviations from the norm (with regulation by homeorhesis) and of variations in the time tally with the possibility of accelerations or delays. Deviations may be brought about by unforeseen experiences encountered by the activity of the child himself as well as by adult pedagogical interventions. Some pedagogical interventions can, of course, accelerate and complete spontaneous development; but they cannot change the order of the constructions. For example, educational programs rightly introduce the concept of metric proportions a long time after the elementary arithmetical operations, although a proportion seems to consist only of an equivalence between two divisions, as in 4:2 = 6:3. But there also exist untimely pedagogical interventions, such as those of parents who teach their children to count up to 20 or 50 before they can have any concept of number. In many cases, such premature acquisitions in no way affect the creode specific to the construction of integers. For instance, when two lines of m and n elements ($m = n$), respectively, are first put into visual one-to-one correspondence and their lengths changed by changing the spacing of the elements, the fact that the child of a certain age can count will not prevent him from saying that the longer line has more elements. On the other hand, when a pedagogical intervention has been successful or when the child obtains by himself a partial conquest in a specific operatory domain, the problem of the interactions between the various creodes remains still unsolved. In the case of classes or relations, for example, are the additive and multiplicative operations always synchronic – as they often seem to be – or can one follow the other, and in that event does the final synthesis remain unchanged (as is probably the case)?

9. In considering the problem of duration or rate of succession of the stages, we can readily observe that accelerations or delays in the average

chronological age of performance, depend on specific environments (e.g., abundance or scarcity of possible activities and spontaneous experiences, educational or cultural environment), but the order of succession will remain constant.

[. . .]

THE CLASSICAL FACTORS OF DEVELOPMENT

10. We have seen that there exist laws of development and that development follows a sequential order such that each of its stages is necessary to the construction of the next. But this fundamental fact remains to be explained. The three classical factors of development are maturation, experience of the physical environment, and the action of the social environment. The two last cannot account for the sequential character of development, and the first one is not sufficient by itself because the development of intelligence does not include a hereditary programming factor like the ones underlying instincts. We shall therefore have to add a fourth factor (which is in fact necessary to the coordination of the three others – equilibration, or self-regulation, *auto régulation*).

It is clear that maturation must have a part in the development of intelligence, although we know very little about the relations between the intellectual operations and the brain. In particular, the sequential character of the stages is an important clue to their partly biological nature and thus argues in favor of the constant role of the genotype and epigenesis. But this does not mean we can assume there exists a hereditary program underlying the development of human intelligence: there are no "innate ideas" (in spite of what Lorenz maintained about the a priori nature of human thought). Even logic is not innate and only gives rise to a progressive epigenetic construction. Thus the effects of maturation consist essentially of opening new possibilities for development, that is, giving access to structures which could not be evolved before these possibilities were offered. But between possibility and actualization, there must intervene a set of other factors such as exercise, experience, and social interaction.

[. . .]

11. A second factor traditionally invoked to explain cognitive development is *experience* acquired through contact with the external physical environment. This factor is essentially heterogeneous, and there are at least three categories and meanings of experience, among which we shall distinguish two opposite poles.

a. The first is simple *exercise*, which naturally involves the presence of objects on which action is exerted but does not necessarily imply that any knowledge will be extracted from these objects. In fact, it has been observed that exercise has a positive effect in the consolidation of a reflex or of a group of complex reflexes such as sucking, which noticeably improves with repetition during the first days of life. This is also true of the exercise of intellectual operations which can be applied to objects, although these operations are not derived from the objects. In contrast, the exercise of an exploratory perceptual activity or of an experiment can provide new exogenous information while consolidating the subject's activity. We can thus distinguish two opposite poles of activity in exercise itself: a pole of accommodation to the object, which is then the only source of the acquisitions based on the object's properties; and a pole of functional assimilation, that is, of consolidation by active repetition. In this second perspective, exercise is predominantly a factor of equilibration or autoregulation, that is, it has to do with structurations dependent on the subject's activity more than with an increase in the knowledge of the external environment.

As regards experience proper in the sense of acquisition of new knowledge through manipulations of objects (and no longer through simple exercise), we must again distinguish two opposite poles, which will correspond to categories (*b*) and (*c*).

b. There is what we call *physical experience*, which consists of extracting information from the objects themselves through a simple process of abstraction. This abstraction reduces to dissociating one newly discovered property from the others and disregarding the latter. Thus it is physical experience that allows the child to discover weight while disregarding an object's color, etc., or to discover that with objects of the same nature, their weight is greater as their volume increases, etc.

c. In addition to physical experience (*b*) and to simple exercise (*a*), there is a third fundamental category, which strangely practically never has been mentioned in this context. This is what we call *logicomathematical experience*. It plays an important part at all levels of cognitive development where logical deduction or computation are still impossible, and it also appears whenever the subject is confronted with problems in which he has to discover new deductive instruments. This type of experience also involves acting upon objects, for there can be no experience without action at its source, whether real or imagined, because its absence would mean there would be no contact with the external world. However, the knowledge derived from it is not based on the physical properties of these objects but on properties of the actions that are exerted on them, which is not at all the same thing. This knowledge seems to be derived from the objects because it consists of discovering by manipulating objects, properties introduced by action which did not belong to the objects before these actions. For example, if a child, when he is counting pebbles, happens to put them in a row and to make the astonishing discovery that when he counts them from the right to the left he finds the same number as when he counts from the left to the right, and again the same when he puts them in a circle, etc., he has thus discovered experimentally that the sum is independent of order. But this is a logicomathematical experiment and not a physical one, because neither the order nor even the sum was in the pebbles before he arranged them in a certain manner (i.e., ordered them) and joined them together in a whole. What he has discovered is a relation, new to him, between the action of putting in order and the action of joining together (hence, between the two future operations), and not, or *not only*, a property belonging to pebbles.

Thus we see that the factor of acquired experience is, in fact, complex and always involves two poles: acquisitions derived from the objects and constructive activities of the subject. Even physical experience (*b*) is never pure, since it always implies a logicomathematical setting, however elementary (as in the geometrical Gestalts of perception). This amounts to saying that any particular action such as "weighing" that results in physical knowledge is never independent of more general coordinations of action (such as ordering, joining together, etc.) which are a source of logicomathematical knowledge.

12. The third classical factor of development is the influence of the social environment. Its importance is immediately verified if we consider the fact that the stages we mentioned in the Section on the Theory of Stages are accelerated or retarded in their average chronological ages according to the child's cultural and educational environment. But the very fact that the stages follow the same sequential order in *any* environment is enough to show that the social environment cannot account for everything. This constant order of succession cannot be ascribed to the environment.

In fact, both social or educational influences and physical experience are on the same footing in this respect, they can have some effect on the subject only if he is capable of assimilating them, and he can do this only if he already possesses the adequate instruments or structures (or their primitive forms). In fact, what is taught, for instance, is effectively assimilated only when it gives rise to an active reconstruction or even reinvention by the child.

[. . .]

To conclude, ¶ 10, 11 and 12, it appears that the traditional factors (maturation, experience, social environment) are not sufficient to explain development. We must therefore appeal to a fourth factor, *equilibration*, and we must do this for two reasons. The first is that these three heterogeneous factors cannot explain a sequential development if they are not in some relation of mutual equilibrium, and that there must therefore exist a fourth organizing factor to coordinate them in a consistent, noncontradictory totality. The second reason is that any biological development is, as we now know, self-regulatory, and that self-regulating processes are even more common at the level of behavior and the constitution of the cognitive functions. We must thus consider this factor separately.

EQUILIBRATION AND COGNITIVE STRUCTURES

13. The main aim of a theory of development is to explain the constitution of the *operational* structures of the integrated whole or totality *opératoire d'ensemble*) and we believe only the hypothesis of progressive equilibration can account for it. To understand this we must first briefly consider the operational structures themselves.

[. . .]

We have therefore attempted to define and analyze the structures specific to intelligence, and they are structures involving operations, that is, involving interiorized and reversible actions such as addition, set-theoretic union, logical multiplication, or, in other words, composition of a multiplicity of classes or relations "considered simultaneously." These structures have a very natural and spontaneous development in the child's thought: to seriate, for instance (i.e., to order objects according to their increasing size), to classify, to put into one-to-one or one-to-many correspondence, to establish the multiplicative matrix, are all structures that appear between ages 7 and 11, at the level of what we call "concrete operations" which deal directly with objects. After ages 11 to 12 other structures appear, such as the four-group and combinatorial processes.

[. . .]

14. The problem then becomes that of understanding how the fundamental structures of intelligence can appear and evolve with all those that later derive from them. Since they are not innate, they cannot be explained by maturation alone. Logical structures are not a simple product of physical experience; in seriation, classification, one-to-one correspondence, the subject's activities add new relations such as order and totality to the objects. Logicomathematical experience derives its information from the subject's own actions (as we saw in ¶ 11), which implies an autoregulation of these actions. It could be alleged that these structures are the result of social or educational transmission. But as we saw (¶ 12) the child must still understand what is transmitted, and to do this the structures are necessary. Moreover, the social explanation only displaces the problem: how did the members of the social group acquire the structures in the first place?

[. . .]

15. Equilibration has explanatory value because it is founded on a process with increasing sequential probabilities. We can understand this better through an example. How can we explain the fact that when a spherical lump of clay is changed into the shape of a sausage in front of him, a child will begin by denying that the quantity of clay is preserved under this

transformation, and end by asserting the logical necessity of this conservation? To do this we must define four stages, each of which *becomes more probable*, not a priori, but as a function of the present situation or of the one immediately preceding it.

a. Initially the child considers only one dimension, for instance, length (say 8 times out of 10). He then says the sausage contains more matter because it is longer. Sometimes (say 2 times out of 10) he says it is thinner, but forgetting its greater length, he concludes the quantity of matter has decreased. Why does he reason thus? Simply because the probability of considering one dimension only is greater. If the probability for length is 0.8 and that for width is 0.2, that for length *and* width is 0.16, because they are independent occurrences as long as compensation is not understood.

b. If the sausage is made longer and longer, or if the child becomes weary of repeating the same argument, the probability of his noticing the other dimension *becomes* greater (though it was not initially) and he will fluctuate between the two.

c. If there is oscillation, the probability of the subject's noticing some correlation between the two variations (when the sausage becomes longer it becomes thinner) *becomes* greater (third stage). But as soon as this feeling of the solidarity existing between variables appears, his reasoning has acquired a new property: it does not rest solely on *configurations* any more but begins to be concerned with *transformations*: the sausage is not simply "long"; it can "lengthen," etc.

d. As soon as the subject's thought takes transformations into account, the next stage *becomes* more probable in which he understands (alternately or simultaneously) that a transformation can be reversed, or that the two simultaneous transformations of length and width compensate, because of the solidarity he has glimpsed [see stage (*c*)].

We can thus see that progressive equilibration has effective explanatory value. Stage (*a*) (which all those who checked our research have found) is not an equilibrium point because the child has noticed only one dimension: in this case the algebraic sum of the virtual components of work (to quote d'Alembert's principle on physical systems) is not zero since one of them, which consists of noticing the other dimension, has not been completed yet and will be sooner or later. The transition from one stage to another is therefore an equilibration in the most classical sense of the word. But since these displacements of the system are activities of the subject, and since each of these activities consists of correcting the one immediately preceding it, equilibration becomes a sequence of self-regulations whose retroactive processes finally result in operational reversibility. The latter then goes beyond simple probability to attain logical necessity.

What we have just said about an instance of operational conservation could be repeated about the construction of every operational structure. Seriation $A < B < C$, for example, when it becomes operational, is the result of coordinating the relations $<$ and $>$ (each new element in E in the ordered sequence having the property of being both $> D, C, B, A,$ and $< F, G, H, \ldots$ and this coordination is again the result of an equilibration process of increasing sequential probabilities of the kind we have described. Similarly for inclusion of classes, $A < B$ if $B = A + A'$ and $A' > O$ is obtained by an equilibration of the same type.

It is not therefore an exaggeration to say that equilibration is the fundamental factor of development, and that it is even necessary for the coordination of the three other factors.

[. . .]

CONCLUSION: FROM PSYCHOLOGY TO GENETIC EPISTEMOLOGY

[. . .]

16. In order to resolve the problem of what is knowledge (or its diversity of forms) it is necessary to formulate it in the following terms: How does knowledge grow? By what process does one pass from knowledge judged to be ultimately insufficient to knowledge judged to be better (considered from the point of view of science)? It is this that the proponents of the historicocritical method have well understood (see among others the works of Koyré and Kuhn). These critics, to understand the epistemological nature of a notion or a structure, look to see first how they were formed themselves.

[. . .]

In a word, the psychological theory of the development of cognitive functions seems to us to establish a direct, and even quite intimate, relationship between the biological notions of interactions between endogenous factors and the environment, and epistemological notions of necessary interaction between the subject and the objects. The synthesis of the notions of structure and of genesis that determines psychogenetic study finds its justification in the biological ideas of auto-regulation and organization, and touches on an epistemological constructivism which seems to be in line with all contemporary scientific work; in particular, with that which concerns the agreement between logicomathematical constructions and physical experience.

ACKNOWLEDGEMENTS

This paper was written in French and translated by Dr. Guy Gellerier of the University of Geneva and Professor Jonas Langer of the University of California at Berkeley. We are also grateful to Professors Bärbel Inhelder and Hermione Sinclair for their assistance in the translation.

AUTHOR'S NOTE

The present paper is, in part, the expansion of an article on my conceptions of development published in *Journal International de Psychologie*, a summary of previous publications, but it also takes into account recent or still unpublished work by the author or his collaborators and colleagues. As a matter of fact, "Piaget's theory" is not completed at this date and the author of these pages has always considered himself one of the chief "revisionists of Piaget".

2 Piaget's Contribution to Understanding Cognitive Development: An Assessment for the Late 1980s

Sara Meadows

INTRODUCTION

I can begin this assessment of Piaget's contribution to how we understand the thinking of school children with an indisputable fact. He was among the first people to deal seriously with children's thinking as a matter for scientific study and philosophical analysis, and as an important biological phenomenon: and by so doing, he enriched the field that I and many others now work in. Even if his work had been as worthy of dismissal as some critics have claimed, we would owe him thanks for pioneering efforts. But, as I argue in the rest of this paper, his work is far from negligible. Directly and indirectly it has probably influenced psychology as much as any other single person's work in any field. Much of what he said was wrong, some misleading. There are many gaps in the work – but who can be expected to deal with *every* aspect of highly complex issues? Still, his contribution over a wide range of matter and over a long period of years has been enormous.

This paper is concerned with the fundamental concepts which he developed throughout his career, particularly with those that dominated the latest stages of his work: the processes, structures and stages of development. Each is presented and evaluated in terms of the accumulated research and of the questions that remain to be dealt with. This enables me to draw some conclusions about the ways in which Piaget's model has been helpful or inadequate. Other papers in this collection discuss some of the alternative

Source: Meadows, S. (1987) – specially commissioned for this Reader.

approaches to cognitive development: readers may like to consider how far the points made about Piagetian theory apply to these too.

FUNDAMENTAL CONCEPTS

(i) Assimilation, Accommodation, Equilibration

Piaget's most fundamental concepts were that cognition is one form of the adaptation between organism and environment which is seen through all the living world, and that it proceeds by means of assimilation and accommodation. That cognition is adaptation, a biological process, is an assertion of his values, not an empirically-testable claim; believing this may have contributed to Piaget's tendency to underestimate the cultural aspects of cognition, but allowed him to draw very interesting analogies between aspects of biological development across species. The claim that assimilation and accommodation are the basic processes of cognition and of much other development was an important advance on the theories of learning which had pushed J. M. Baldwin's early assimilation-accommodation model into obscurity, and which dominated English language psychology through the earlier part of Piaget's career. Today's theorists seem to feel (e.g. Carey, 1986; Case, 1985; Flavell, 1985; Gelman & Baillargeon, 1983) that cognitive development is best described as a process of assimilation and accommodation; that we incorporate new information into the conceptual schemes we already have as far as it is possible for us to do, and also modify the conceptual schemes to cope with new information. It is also generally believed that conceptual schemes do become organised or "structured". However, there are still many obscurities in these "fundamental concepts" which need further discussion.

The first problem I want to mention is that we do not have a sufficiently detailed account of how assimilation and accommodation work. Piaget went into more detail about them in two books published in English in 1978a, b, distinguishing between different sorts of assimilation. He postulated that there is a sort of natural instinct to assimilate: "any scheme of assimilation tends to feed itself, that is, to incorporate outside elements compatible with its nature into itself" (Piaget, 1978a, p.7), thus driving development on. This happens at three levels. The first is assimilating objects to schemes, as the infant does when grasping a new object, or as scientists had to when a new planet's existence was discovered. The second is assimilation between different schemes, for example eye-hand coordination or the sort of alternation between writing and acting as reader of one's own writing which is achieved by the secondary school pupil. The third and highest level is assimilation between subschemes and the totality which integrates them into a coherent whole; the concept of "gravity" for example, is at the core of physicists' accounts of many quite different localised events from the motion of the planets round the sun to the falling of Newton's apple. These assimilations are said to involve the scheme "finding" or "distinguishing" characteristics which match the scheme or are near neighbours to it, as opposed to others which negate or contradict it, though these too must in the end be coordinated into the total scheme. Thus both affirmations and negations are important. A balance between affirmations and negations is necessary for development, just as a balance between assimilation and accommodation is.

While this account of assimilation and accommodation is of great interest, a number of problems arise. Some cluster around the "drive to assimilate". It is not clear to me at what point this drive would be satisfied. The model appears to imply that there could always be further assimilation and accommodation, that the "natural" state of cognitive development is progress towards a highly developed, subtle, sophisticated, intricately integrated cognitive system. Is this an empirical account of what is really done, or a rational reconstruction of ideal cognition? There is room for real doubt about whether most people really do go in for this sort of thorough thinking-out of everything (Boden, 1982; Mischel, 1971) – perhaps here Piaget was using himself as a prototype and forgetting that the rest of us are, probably, sloppier thinkers, content with localised understanding, not pushing its limits outwards, and quite capable of believing contradictory things?

There are problems also over the question of what is or can be assimilated to a scheme. What degree of match, on what dimensions, means that a new object or event affirms a pre-existing scheme? What mismatch negates it? Piaget's examples tend to be post hoc, and no one else has yet done better. We may also doubt whether affirmations and negations are equally readily dealt with by the thinker, as negations in logic, and in scientific theory building, seem to be so difficult to manage (e.g. Kuhn, 1962; Wason & Johnson-Laird, 1972). Further, in many areas it is extremely hard to see whether a new event affirms or negates a scheme. The concept is hard to apply in questions of moral or political judgment, for example, or in the visual arts. Russell (1978) argues that one of the important things we have to learn is, precisely, which kinds of knowledge have to be consistent and which do not.

These same problems apply also to the concept of "equilibration". Equilibration relies extremely heavily on the assumption of invariant regularities and consistencies in thought. It also involves seeing development as a progress from one state of equilibrium to a "better" one, more integrated and more differentiated and with more possibilities of interacting with a wider environment. It is obvious that adults do interact in more varied ways with their environment than infants do, and with more different aspects of it, and similarly that human-environment interactions are wider and more differentiated than amoeba-environment interactions. It should not be taken as obvious, however, that this makes humans or adults "better" or "better adapted to their environments" than amoebae or infants are (Midgley, 1985; Ruse, 1986). Nor is Piaget really justified in asserting that the progress of cognitive development is through one universal and invariant sequence. The cross-cultural evidence has illustrated a number of significant variations not just in rate but in whether formal operations and the later concrete operations develop, the sort of schooling provided and the sorts of concepts valued by the culture seem to be the determining factors (Dasen, 1977; Lab. for Comparative Human Cognition, 1983). It may well be that human cognitive development involves moving up a tree-like structure, as the evolution of species had done: Certain adaptations are developed but certain other possible adaptations remain as potential or are even given up. In this, experience of the demands of the environment is a crucial determining factor. Perhaps Bronfenbrenner's (1979, p27a) definition is useful:

> human development is the process through which the growing person acquires a more extended, differentiated and valid conception of the ecological environment, and becomes motivated and able to engage in activities that reveal the properties of, sustain or restructure that environment at levels of similar or greater complexity in form and content.

(ii) Structures and Procedures

Assimiliation, accommodation and equilibration give rise to cognitive "structures". Piaget's view of what structures were began in analogies with biological structures such as the stomach. It then developed an emphasis on formal characteristics, modelled on his modified versions of logical or mathematical systems. Towards the end of his career his interest moved to considerations of procedures. "Structures" are the timeless, abstract, universal laws of transformations and relations between objects or concepts, such as the mathematical system of real numbers. "Procedures" are the goal-directed behaviours which, occasion by occasion, we use. For example, commutativity ($8+2+7=7+2+8=2+7+8$, etc.) is part of the structure which underlies our successful procedures for adding up our bills, top to bottom or bottom to top, pence and pounds together or separately. In making this move, Piaget was transferring his interest somewhat from the generalised "epistemic subject" to the real and individual psychological subject such as may be seen in thirty or so subtly different examples in any classroom; a positive move as far as psychologists and teachers are concerned.

Part of the distinction between procedures and structures which Piaget made, and the Genevan school has developed since his death (Bullinger & Chatillon, 1983), is the description of two large and complementary cognitive systems. One is for *understanding* the world, it consists of representations and operations which are generalised and abstract, focussing on the underlying invariants and ignoring trivial variations. The other is for *succeeding* in the world, and involves much more procedural knowledge, though obviously representations and operations may both be involved. This distinction raises the very interesting issue of how what the child does is related to the means which are in principle available. Often children do not use principles or procedures which their behaviour in other contexts has shown they understand quite well. Bryant (1982), for example, found 6 year olds who could use a measuring stick to discover which hole was deeper but not to discover whether the tower on the floor was higher than the tower on the table. Procedures may be more successful than theory, as in the case of children whose early successful strategy was to balance an irregularly-weighted block by gradually nudging it into position and who later failed because they understood blocks to balance at their geometric centres (Karmiloff-Smith & Inhelder, 1975). "Knowing how" and "knowing why" are important concepts also in the new growth area of research on metacognition (Robinson, 1983). Although Piaget's interest moved from structures to procedures towards the end of his career, he did not altogether discard the stage model. Because of this, and because the question of stages is a fundamental part of the question of "what develops in cognitive development", and because it remains of interest to many researchers, some further discussion is needed.

(iii) Stages

In Piagetian theory the structures of thought are applicable to virtually any area of knowledge; they are seen as abstract content-free ways of reasoning. Piaget described them as fitting together into a succession of coherent and qualitatively different stages. The major ones are the sensori-motor, preoperational, concrete operational and formal operational stages, and there are sequences of substages within the sensori-motor stage and within areas of operational thought, such as conservation of quantity. The structure of each stage is such that thought at any given moment is relatively consistent in its level across different content areas. Consistency is especially to be expected at the times when concrete operations and, later, formal operations are fully developed, as both these stages are based on logical models. While logical systems are being constructed, temporary inconsistencies and fluctuations are to be expected, but an emphasis on differences between stages and similarities within them remains. In a child behaving according to the Piagetian model, performance on one test of, say, conservation predicts performance on other conservation tests and on other tests of concrete operations. Furthermore, the stage structure limits the possibilities of improving performance by instruction. The child cannot assimilate or accommodate to events which are too incompatible with his or her whole coherent system of understanding, and instruction can at best produce only a limited and possibly temporary advance isolated in the area being trained.

The sensori-motor stage develops over the first two years or so of the child's life and is therefore not relevant to a chapter on the school age child (but for an interesting review of it see Harris, 1983). The school years begin late in the "preoperational" period, cover "concrete operations", and end during "formal operations". It is therefore appropriate to provide a very brief account of each stage. The preoperational stage is described first as the period when children begin to use semiotic systems such as language and imagery but second as a time when they lack operational thought; that is flexible reversible reasoning which allows them to conserve, classify, seriate, coordinate perspectives, overcome misleading perceptual impressions, etc. Concrete operational children have these abilities. They can think much more systematically and quantitatively and their thinking is described in terms of formalized logical structures (the "groupings") relating to classifications and relations in quantity and in space. The final formal operations stage is a more integrated and more abstract development from concrete operations, less tied to content and more capable of dealing with hypothetical material. Formal operations receive a more abstract holistic and rigorous description from Piaget. Logicians as well as psychologists have queried the models given for both the concrete operations and the formal operations stages (Vuyk, 1981), and they remain controversial.

With this account of stages, Piagetian theory puts up a challenge which has attracted a good deal of research response. As I have said, direct evidence on the reality of assimilation, accommodation and equilibration has been hard to get. Testing the stage model has been somewhat easier, though not altogether unproblematic. Sequences of stages are fairly well confirmed, though there have been some suggestions that their order is logically necessary (e.g. Smedslund, 1980) and so of no empirical interest. Rate of progress through the sequence seems to vary somewhat between individuals, but this is far from crucial to Piagetian theory which is concerned with the idealised "normal" epistemic subject, not with individual differences. Rate also varies between cultures, degree of schooling and less formal educational experience being one of the main relevant variables. In some cultures there is little sign of formal operations. This finding is mildly embarrassing for a model which has been taken as claiming that formal operations is a universal high point of human cognition, but in fact Piaget's main account does not explicitly make such a claim (Inhelder & Piaget, 1958). The role of social and environmental experience in cognitive development is an important issue which needs more investigation.

The behaviours typical of different stages appear in a fairly constant order, then, if not at a constant rate. Their appearance can certainly be accelerated by training (Brainerd, 1983). Contrary to the predictions of the Piagetian account, training does produce improvement in performance which can be considerable, long-lasting and pervasive. A variety of training methods have been seen to succeed, and it is not the case that "neo-Piagetian" models which conjure up equilibratory mechanisms or provoke discovery are any more successful than methods involving initiation, didactic interaction, or the following of verbal rules. Initial stage level does not seem to predict the possibility of training or limit how effective it will be. Preschoolers have successfully been trained on the concrete operations tasks which they would not be expected to get right for another three or four years, and their performance after training appears as competent as that of untrained eight year olds (Brainerd, 1983; Gelman & Baillargeon, 1983). This has been interpreted as showing that there are minimal differences between the cognitive structures of preschool children and those of primary school children. It does seem to be clear that Piaget painted far too negative a picture of children's thinking in the pre-operational stage (Vuyk, 1981), and we might prefer a model of cognitive development which described more preschool competence and (perhaps) a less complete later stage competence, with a gradual consolidatory transition rather than a qualitative shift during the school years (Braine & Rumain, 1983; Donaldson, 1978). However, there seems at present to be some danger of arguing away a developmental change in cognition rather than carefully analysing the extent and nature of the change.

One of the differences between younger and older children is in the degree and type of within-stage consistency they show, or how many "decalages", that is slips in level of performance, there are. The question here is how the different areas fit together as structured stages. The usual research design has been the obvious one of seeing how children's performance correlates across a number of tasks which each involve the same logical principles (e.g. conservation) or belong to the same stage (e.g. measures of class inclusion, weight conservation and perspective-taking, which all belong to the concrete operations stage). It is not always altogether clear how large a correlation is required to support the theory of within-stage consistency, and the statistical complexities are considerable. If, accidentally, one test is slightly more difficult than another, for example, this may lead to misleading patterns of synchrony (Brainerd, 1978).

On the whole, research studies have found less consistency between different areas of concrete operations than a simple model of logical structures constructed quickly and underlying all tasks would suggest (Gelman & Baillargeon, 1983; Klausmeier & Sipple, 1982; Meadows, 1975). There have also been numerous inconsistencies between different measures of ostensibly the same operation, for example conservation tests using materials which seem obviously equivalent to the adult but produce obstinately different responses from children (e.g. Beard, 1963; Miller, 1982; Uzgiris, 1964). Some of these decalages are due to the "figurative aspect" of the test situation. For example, if the transformed material in a conservation test looks very different from the original, then children will be less likely to give a conserving response than if the change in appearance is slight. Similarly, various changes in the social situation or in the language used help young children to conserve or manage class inclusion (c.g. Light, Buckingham, & Robbins 1979; Siegel, McCabe, & Matthews, 1978).

Some decalages receive only a last resort explanation, that the objects involved offer more "resistance" to the thinker. Piaget never bothered to deal with the problem of decalages thoroughly. He was less interested in them than in how children managed the general principles underlying operational thought, for example how they had a feeling of certainty despite appearances which suggested otherwise. He thus had little to say about decalages except where they were common to all children, hence characteristic of his "epistemic subject". Recent work by Longeot (1978) starts to deal with this omission, and with some of the problems of low correlations within stages, with a model which predicts when consistencies and decalages will occur. He points again to the possibility that there may be discrepancies between the logico-mathematical structures of the epistemic subject and the natural thinking of children solving adaptive problems in real life; the distinctions between "knowing" and "doing" and between various degrees of "having a concept" that I mentioned earlier. This work has also shown that there may be alternative paths to the same outcome, and such individual differences need to be accounted for.

One possibility raised relates Piagetian concepts to psychometric ones: the suggestion is that there are different and partially independent sorts of intelligence (cf. Gardner, 1984). There is interest also in the possibility that cognitive development is domain-specific rather than, as in Piagetian theory, general across domains. Investigation here obviously requires detailed descriptions by domain and comparison between them; very much what Piaget and Inhelder did in the series of studies which are still acknowledged as brilliant investigative observation.

RESEARCH

To provide a full account of recent research in the areas Piaget studied and the new areas which have been opened up by subsequent workers would require far more space than is available here. I will, however, mention a few interesting studies in areas which look likely to show exciting developments in the near future. (Some of these are reviewed a little more fully in Meadows, 1986.)

Piaget was one of the pioneers of work on children's concepts of number (Piaget, 1952). He rightly argued that children may learn the names of numbers and the correct answers to simple sums without having an adequate understanding of the underlying mathematics. The latter he saw as much the more important, and as something which the child gradually constructed "independently and spontaneously" from his (sic) own experience. Thus the basic picture of children's use of number showed, consonant with Piagetian theory as a whole, young children who had little understanding of what they were doing developing through their own reflection on what they saw and did into older children who had a firm understanding of mathematical principles such as number conservation, class inclusion, commutativity, the effects of addition and subtraction, and so forth.

A great deal of research in the last ten years or so has resulted in modifications of this picture which are consonant with the sorts of modification which many aspects of Piagetian theory have undergone. One prominent change has been a greater appreciation of the competence of preschool children. Rochel Gelman and her colleagues, for example, (Gelman & Baillargeon, 1983; Starkey & Gelman, 1982), have found evidence that even three year olds have some understanding of counting and quantification and are not just reeling off rote-learned strings of number words. They can use their skills to count sets of objects in systematic ways which show some appreciation of how to count; they expect number to be invariant despite rearrangement of items if the set size is small; they try to use counting as a means to comparing numerical quantities, though they also use other strategies such as one-to-one matching of items in one set with items in the other or making perceptually-based judgments about the relative numbers in the sets. Young children in the number conservation test are of course faced with a situation where the counting strategy conflicts with the perceptual-spread strategy. As we all know, they commonly plump for the latter and give a non-conserving answer. In their excuse, it may be said that if you are, as yet, a shaky counter, the counting strategy may give you inconsistent results and no feeling of confidence in what you've done. A child in this situation may not be able to work out whether the number has really changed or whether something went wrong in the counting. It seems clear that Piaget underestimated the young child's possession of skills that can be used under favourable conditions through his insistence on studying children's performance under unfavourable conditions, but it is clear also that there are years of development between the young child's fragmentary skills and the adult's competence (see e.g. Ginsburg, 1983; Hughes, 1986; Meadows, 1986), though there are all too often distressing lacunae in adults' mathematical competence. Interestingly, one crucial part of the problem seems to be in the ability to translate between abstract rules and principles and real life performance; a translation which is not facilitated by the fear and hostility towards mathematics that many people feel. There are important implications for mathematics education in recent work.

Piaget's account of children's number concepts proposed that a proper understanding of number required an understanding of conservation and of class inclusion. Whether these are indeed prerequisites is not at all clear. As we have seen, there are many levels of competence on number tasks, on conservation and on class inclusion, and diagnosis is really very difficult. The *formal* relations between these different concepts – which implies which – may be quite different from the *functional* relations, the "understanding" and "succeeding" distinction I made earlier. A similar point can be made about children's (and indeed adults') use of logic. Braine and Rumain (1983) review recent work which suggests that the way young children handle logical problems bears a considerable resemblance to the way adults handle them: the same logical forms are easy or difficult, and the errors made are much the same. There seems to be, as I have said, rather little behavioural evidence for a *new* system of logic at the formal operations stage, rather at most a more principled and coordinated use of a pre-existing logic. This does not exclude age-related changes in, for example, children's understanding of logical necessity, their use of "disembedded" reasoning, and their ability to work through chains of inferences (Donaldson, 1978; Russell, 1978, 1982).

Here too there is substantial evidence to suggest that social experience in general and formal education in particular make a crucial and definitive contribution to children's cognitive development. Interesting work on literacy, done outside the Piagetian field, illuminates this point. The ways in which people come to use the skills associated with reading and writing seem to have quite specific effects on cognitive skills such as remembering and reasoning, and even their performance on Piagetian tasks (Brainerd, 1978; Cole & Griffin, 1980). Children taking part in the interpersonal world is a necessary condition of their cognition (Cox, 1986; Meadows, 1986).

In all of these areas cognitive development clearly involves the use of more knowledge more appropriately and more consistently. There has been much theoretical battling over this change, with "structural" models, such as Piaget's being opposed to "knowledge accumulation" models, such as learning theory – in Piaget's simplistic version of it. Although there are very important philosophical issues involved, the battle has not been productive of new understanding partly because in the normal course of using accumulated knowledge it becomes interpreted and organised. That is, it becomes structured. It is of more interest to examine what structuring and restructuring consist of. To do so involves mapping out the system of knowledge at successive points in its development. Attempts at maps, even in very limited domains such as a four year old's knowledge of dinosaurs (Chi

& Koeske, 1983), have not so far been altogether convincing, and there will clearly have to be further developments in theory and method. Carey (1986) argues that restructuring in development will involve changes in the relations between concepts, and the creation from these relations of new more abstract concepts which are at a superordinate level to the original basic concepts, but which can now be worked on as a basic level themselves.

I will use Piagetian content to illustrate this shift. In a class inclusion task involving "roses", "daisies" and "flowers", there might initially be precise, perceptually-based, concepts of "roses" and "daisies" and a less vivid concept of flowers, with a purely verbal appreciation that "flowers" includes the other two. That is, the concepts are weakly related and the child has trouble answering questions about the inclusion of the subordinate classes in the superordinate one. With development the concept of a superordinate class of "flowers" which includes and is necessarily bigger than the subordinates emerges, and the child has a new certainty about the relations between the classes.

Restructuring can also involve more radical change: new concepts, a change in the domain accounted for, change in the explanatory mechanisms used. This sort of restructuring leads to the emergence of new theories, through gradual emergence or as a revolutionary change (Kuhn, 1962). Carey argues that her data on children's ideas about living things show a development from a naïve psychology generalising from themselves out-wards to an autonomous theory of biological functioning applicable to themselves but also to all living things. A great deal more information is acquired and contained in this theory, via both formal and informal instruction, but the change is not just one from ignorance to encyclopedia, the knowledge is not just accumulated but is used, in theory and in practice. Carey sees this use as relatively domain-specific, although domains are not totally separate and, indeed, one may emerge out of another as the child's biology does from his or her psychology, and as modern psychology did from nineteenth-century biology and philosophy. She de-emphasises domain-general changes, pointing out the problems I have discussed in this paper of low consistencies between domains, the underestimation of young children's powers and the overestimation of older children's and adults'.

At present there is no clear verdict to be given on the question of whether an abstract and general model of cognitive development is to be preferred to more limited theory/domain ones. There is clearly a great deal of work to be done in providing good descriptions of development within domains. There is also work to be done in describing general mechanisms of cognitive change which are applied to and derived from behavioural changes (Sternberg, 1984). It seems likely that, as far as the school years are concerned, the difference between younger and older children will turn out to be that the former can do what the latter can; but only sometimes, only under favourable conditions, only with help, only without distractions, only up to a point, without so much efficiency, without so much self-control, without so much awareness of the implications, without so much certainty. It seems likely, also, that whatever it includes from our recently gained understanding of language and semantic networks, of information-processing and artificial intelligence, of social and educational interactions and their role in the learning and thinking of the individual child, our emergent theory of cognitive development will be proud to have Piaget's theory as an ancestor. Given the scope of his work, it will be several generations of thinkers yet before "new" ideas about cognitive development cannot be greeted by Piagetians with a true claim that "Piaget said that".

REFERENCES

Beard, R. (1963). The order of concept development: Studies in two fields. *Educational Review, 15.* 105–117, 228–237.

Boden, M. A. (1982). Is equilibration important? A view from artificial intelligence. *British Journal of Psychology, 73*, 165–73.

Braine, M. D. S. & Rumain, B. (1983). Logical reasoning. In J. H. Flavell & E. M. Markman (Eds.), *Handbook of Child Psychology, Vol. 3*, New York: Wiley.

Brainerd, C. J. (1978). *Piaget's theory of intelligence.* Englewood Cliffs, N. J.: Prentice Hall.

Brainerd, C. (1983). Modifiability of cognitive development. In S. Meadows (Ed.), *Developing Thinking*. London: Methuen.

Bronfenbrenner, U. (1979). *The ecology of human development*. Cambridge, Mass: Harvard University Press.

Bryant, P. E. (1982). The role of conflict and of agreement between intellectual strategies in children's ideas about measurement. *British Journal of Psychology, 73*, 243–252.

Bullinger, A. & Chatillon, J. F. (1983). Recent theory and research of the Genevan school. In J. H. Flavell & E.M. Markman (Eds.), *Handbook of Child Psychology, Vol. 3*. New York: Wiley.

Carey, S. (1986). *Conceptual change in childhood*. Cambridge, Mass.: MIT Press.

Case, R. (1985). *Intellectual development: Birth to adulthood*. New York: Academic Press.

Chi, M. T. H. & Koeske, R. D. (1983). Network representation of a child's dinosaur knowledge. *Developmental Psychology, 19*, 29–39.

Cole, M. & Griffin, P. (1980). Cultural amplifiers reconsidered. In D. R. Olson (Ed.), *The social foundations of language and thought*. New York: W. W. Norton.

Cox, M. V. (1986). *The child's point of view: The development of cognition and language*. Brighton: Harvester Press.

Dasen, P. (1977). Are cognitive processes universal? A contribution to cross-cultural Piagetian psychology. In N. Warren (Ed.), *Studies in cross-cultural psychology*. London: Academic Press.

Donaldson, M. (1978). *Children's minds*. London: Fontana.

Flavell, J. H. (1985). *Cognitive development*. Second edition. Englewood Cliffs, N.J.: Prentice Hall.

Gardner, H. (1984). *Frames of mind: The theory of multiple intelligence*. London: Heinemann.

Gelman, R. & Baillargeon, R. (1983). A review of some Piagetian concepts. In J. H. Flavell & E. M. Markman (Eds.), *Handbook of Child Psychology, Vol. 3*, New York: Wiley.

Ginsburg, P. L. (1983). *The development of mathematical thinking*. New York: Academic Press.

Harris, P. L. (1983). Infant cognition. In M. M. Haith & J. J. Campos (Eds.), *Handbook of Child Psychology, Vol. 2*, New York: Wiley.

Hughes, M. (1986). *Children and number: Difficulties in learning mathematics*. Oxford: Blackwell.

Inhelder, B. & Piaget, J. (1958). *The growth of logical thinking from childhood to adolescence*. New York: Basic Books.

Karmiloff-Smith, A. & Inhelder, B. (1975). If you want to get ahead, get a theory. *Cognition, 3*, 195–212.

Klausmeier, H. J. & Sipple, T.S. (1982). Factor structure of the Piagetian stage of concrete operations. *Contemporary Educational Psychology, 7*, 161–80.

Kuhn, T. S. (1962). *The structure of scientific revolutions*. Chicago: Chicago U.P.

Laboratory of Comparative Human Cognition. (1983). Culture and cognitive development. In W. Kessen (Ed.), *Handbook of Child Psychology* (Vol. 1,). New York: Wiley.

Light, P. H., Buckingham, N., & Robbins, A. H. (1979). The conservation task as an interactional setting. *British Journal of Educational Psychology, 49*, 304–310.

Longeot, F. (1978). *Les stades operatoires de Piaget et les facteurs de l'intelligence*. Grenoble: Press Universitaires de Grenoble.

Meadows, S. (1975). *The development of concrete operations: A short-term longitudinal study*. Unpublished Ph.D. thesis, University of London.

Meadows, S. (1986). *Understanding child development*. London: Hutchinson.

Midgley, M. (1985). *Evolution as a religion: strange hopes and stranger fears*. London: Methuen.

Miller, S. A. (1982). On the generalisability of conservation: A comparison of different kinds of transformation. *British Journal of Psychology, 73*, 221–30.

Mischel, T. (Ed.) (1971). *Cognitive development and epistemology*. New York: Academic Press.

Piaget, J. (1952). *The child's conception of number*. London: Routledge and Kegan Paul.

Piaget, J. (1978a). *The development of thought: Equilibration of cognitive structures*. Oxford: Blackwell.

Piaget, J. (1978b). *Success and understanding*. London: Routledge and Kegan Paul.

Robinson, E. J. (1983). Metacognitive development. In S. Meadows (Ed.), *Developing Thinking*. London: Methuen.

Ruse, M. (1986). *Taking Darwin seriously: A naturalistic approach to philosophy*. Oxford: Blackwell.

Russell, J. (1978). *The acquisition of knowledge*. London: Macmillan.

Russell, J. (1982). Propositional attitudes. In M. Beveridge (Ed.), *Children thinking through language*. London: Edward Arnold.

Siegel, L. S., McCabe, . A.E., & Matthews, J. (1978). Evidence for the understanding of class inclusion in preschool children: Linguistic factors and training effects. *Child Development, 49*, 688–693.

Smedslund, J. (1980). Analyzing the primary code: From empiricism to apriorism. In D. R. Olson (Ed.), *The social foundations of language and thought*. New York: W. W. Norton.

Starkey, P. & Gelman, R. (1982). The development of addition and subtraction abilities prior to formal schooling. In T. P. Carpenter, J. M. Moser, & T. A. Romberg (Eds.), *Addition and subtraction: A developmental perspective*. Hillsdale, N.J.: Lawrence Erlbaum Associates Inc.

Sternberg, R. J. (Ed.) (1984). *Mechanisms of cognitive development*. New York: Freeman.

Uzgiris, I. (1964). Situational generality of conservation. *Child Development, 35*, 831–841.

Vuyk, R. (1981). *Overview and critique of Piaget's genetic epistemology 1965–80. Vols. 1 and 2*. London: Academic Press.

Wason, P. C. & Johnson-Laird, P. N. (1972). *The Psychology of Reasoning*. London: Batsford.

3 The Course of Cognitive Growth

Jerome S. Bruner

I shall take the view in what follows that the development of human intellectual functioning from infancy to such perfection as it may reach is shaped by a series of technological advances in the use of mind. Growth depends upon the mastery of techniques and cannot be understood without reference to such mastery. These techniques are not, in the main, inventions of the individuals who are "growing up"; they are, rather, skills transmitted with varying efficiency and success by the culture – language being a prime example. Cognitive growth, then, is in a major way from the outside in as well as from the inside out.

Two matters will concern us. The first has to do with the techniques or technologies that aid growing human beings to represent in a manageable way the recurrent features of the complex environments in which they live. It is fruitful, I think, to distinguish three systems of processing information by which human beings construct models of their world: through action, through imagery, and through language. A second concern is with integration, the means whereby acts are organized into higher-order ensembles, making possible the use of larger and larger units of information for the solution of particular problems.

Let me first elucidate these two theoretical matters, and then turn to an examination of the research upon which they are based, much of it from the Center for Cognitive Studies at Harvard.

On the occasion of the One Hundredth Anniversary of the publication of Darwin's *The Origin of Species*, Washburn and Howell (1960, p.49) pre-

Source: Sears, P.S. (Ed.) (1971). *Intellectual development*. New York: John Wiley & Sons, Inc, pp. 255-282. Originally published 1964, *American Psychologist, 19*, 1, pp. 1-15. Copyright 1964 by the American Psychological Association. Reprinted by permission of the publisher and author.

sented a paper at the Chicago Centennial celebration containing the following passage:

> It would now appear . . . that the large size of the brain of certain hominids was a relatively late development and that the brain evolved due to new selection pressures *after* bipedalism and consequent upon the use of tools. The tool-using, ground living, hunting way of life created the large human brain rather than a large brained man discovering certain new ways of life. [We] believe this conclusion is the most important result of the recent fossil hominid discoveries and is one which carries far-reaching implications for the interpretation of human behaviour and its origins . . . The important point is that size of brain, insofar as it can be measured by cranial capacity, has increased some threefold subsequent to the use and manufacture of implements . . . The uniqueness of modern man is seen as the result of a technical-social life which tripled the size of the brain, reduced the face, and modified many other structures of the body.

This implies that the principal change in man over a long period of years – perhaps 500,000 – has been alloplastic rather than autoplastic. That is to say, he has changed by linking himself with new, external implementation systems rather than by any conspicuous change in morphology – "evolution-by-prosthesis", as Weston La Barre (1954) puts it. The implement systems seem to have been of three general kinds – *amplifiers of human motor capacities* ranging from the cutting tool through the lever and wheel to the wide variety of modern devices; *amplifiers of sensory capacities* that include primitive devices such as smoke signaling and modern ones such as magnification and radar sensing, but also likely to include such "software" as those conventionalized perceptual shortcuts that can be applied to the redundant sensory environment; and finally *amplifiers of human ratiocinative capacities* of infinite variety ranging from language systems to myth and theory and explanation. All of these forms of amplification are in major or minor degree conventionalized and transmitted by the culture, the last of them probably the most since ratiocinative amplifiers involve symbol systems governed by rules that must, for effective use, be shared.

Any implement system, to be effective, must produce an appropriate internal counterpart, an appropriate skill necessary for organizing sensorimotor acts, for organizing percepts, and for organizing our thoughts in a way that matches them to the requirements of implement systems. These internal skills, represented genetically as capacities, are slowly selected in evolution. In the deepest sense, then, man can be described as a species that has become specialized by the use of technological implements. His selection and survival have depended upon a morphology and set of capacities that could be linked with the alloplastic devices that have made his later evolution possible. We move, perceive, and think in a fashion that depends upon techniques rather than upon wired-in arrangements in our nervous system.

Where representation of the environment is concerned, it too depends upon techniques that are learned – and these are precisely the techniques that serve to amplify our motor acts, our perceptions, and our ratiocinative activities. We know and respond to recurrent regularities in our environment by skilled and patterned acts, by conventionalized spatioqualitative imagery and selective perceptual organization, and through linguistic encoding which, as so many writers have remarked, places a selective lattice between us and the physical environment. In short, the capacities that have been shaped by our evolution as tool users are the ones that we rely upon in the primary task of representation – the nature of which we shall consider in more detail directly.

As for integration, it is a truism that there are very few single or simple adult acts that cannot be performed by a young child. In short, any more highly skilled activity can be decomposed into simpler components, each of which can be carried out by a less skilled operator. What higher skills require is that the component operations be combined. Maturation consists of an orchestration of these components into an integrated sequence. The "distractability", so called, of much early behavior may reflect each act's lack of imbeddedness in what Miller, Galanter, and Pribram (1960), speak of as "plans". These integrated plans, in turn, reflect the routines and subroutines that one learns in the course of mastering the patterned nature of a social environment. So that integration, too, depends upon patterns that come from the outside in – an internalization of what Roger Barker (1963) has called environmental "behavior settings".

If we are to benefit from contact with recurrent regularities in the environment, we must represent them in some manner. To dismiss this problem as "mere memory" is to misunderstand it. For the most important thing about memory is not storage of past experience, but rather the retrieval of what is relevant in some usable form. This depends upon how past experience is coded and processed so that it may indeed be relevant and usable in the present when needed. The end product of such a system of coding and processing is what we may speak of as a representation.

I shall call the three modes of representation mentioned earlier enactive representation, iconic representation, and symbolic representation. Their appearance in the life of the child is in that order, each depending upon the previous one for its development, yet all of them remaining more or less intact throughout life – barring such early accidents as blindness or deafness or cortical injury. By enactive representation I mean a mode of representing past events through appropriate motor response. We cannot, for example, give an adequate description of familiar sidewalks or floors over which we habitually walk, nor do we have much of an image of what they are like. Yet we get about them without tripping or even looking much. Such segments of our environment – bicycle riding, tying knots, aspects of driving – get represented in our muscles, so to speak. Iconic representation summarizes events by the selective organization of percepts and of images, by the spatial, temporal, and qualitative structures of the perceptual field and their transformed images. Images "stand for" perceptual events in the close but conventionally selective way that a picture stands for the object pictured. Finally, a symbol system represents things by design features that include remoteness and arbitrariness. A word neither points directly to its referent here and now, nor does it resemble it as a picture. The lexeme "Philadelphia" looks no more like the city so designated than does a non-sense syllable. The other property of language that is crucial is its productiveness in combination, far beyond what can be done with images or acts. "Philadelphia is a lavender sachet in Grandmother's linen closet," or $(x + 2)^2 = x^2 + 4x + 4 = x(x + 4) + 4$.

An example or two of enactive representation underlines its importance in infancy and in disturbed functioning, while illustrating its limitations. Piaget (1954) provides us with an observation from the closing weeks of the first year of life. The child is playing with a rattle in his crib. The rattle drops over the side. The child moves his clenched hand before his face, opens it, looks for the rattle. Not finding it there, he moves his hand, closed again, back to the edge of the crib, shakes it with movements like those he uses in shaking the rattle. Thereupon he moves his closed hand back toward his face, opens it, and looks. Again no rattle; and so he tries again. In several months, the child has benefited from experience to the degree that the rattle and action become separated. Whereas earlier he would not show signs of missing the rattle when it was removed unless he had begun reaching for it, now he cries and searches when the rattle is presented for a moment and hidden by a cover. He no longer repeats a movement to restore the rattle. In place of representation by action alone – where "existence" is defined by the compass of present action – it is now defined by an image that persists autonomously.

A second example is provided by the results of injury to the occipital and temporal cortex in man (Hanfmann, Rickers-Ovsiankina, & Goldstein, 1944). A patient is presented with a hard-boiled egg intact in its shell, and asked what it is. Holding it in his hand, he is embarrassed, for he cannot name it. He makes a motion as if to throw it and halts himself. Then he brings it to his mouth as if to bite it and stops before he gets there. He brings it to his ear and shakes it gently. He is puzzled. The experimenter takes the egg from him and cracks it on the table, handing it back. The patient then begins to peel the egg and announces what it is. He cannot identify objects without reference to the action he directs toward them.

The disadvantages of such a system are illustrated by Emerson's (1931) experiment in which children are told to place a ring on a board with seven rows and six columns of pegs, copying the position of a ring put on an identical board by the experimenter. Children ranging from 3 to 12 were examined in this experiment and in an extension of it carried out by Werner (1948). The child's board could be placed in various positions relative to the experimenter's: right next to it, 90 degrees rotated away from it, 180 degrees rotated, placed face to face with it so that the child has to turn full around to make his placement, etc. The older the child, the better his performance. But the younger children could do about as well as the oldest so long as they did not have to change their own positions vis-à-vis the experimenter's board in order to make a match on their own board. The more they had to turn, the more difficult the task. They were clearly depending upon their bodily orientation toward the experimenter's board to guide them. When this orientation is disturbed by having to turn, they lose the position on the board. Older children succeed even when they must turn, either by the use of imagery that is invariant across bodily displacements, or, later, by specifying column and row of the experimenter's ring and carrying the symbolized self-instruction back to their own board. It is a limited world, the world of enactive representation.

We know little about the conditions necessary for the growth of imagery and iconic representation, or to what extent parental or environmental intervention affects it during the earliest years. In ordinary adult learning a certain amount of motoric skill and practice seems to be a necessary precondition for the development of a simultaneous image to represent the sequence of acts involved. If an adult subject is made to choose a path through a complex bank of toggle switches, he does not form an image of the path, according to Mandler (1962), until he has mastered and overpracticed the task by successive manipulation. Then, finally, he reports that an image of the path has developed and that he is now using it rather than groping his way through.

Our main concern in what follows is not with the growth of iconic representation, but with the transition from it to symbolic representation. For it is in the development of symbolic representation that one finds, perhaps, the greatest thicket of psychological problems. The puzzle begins when the child first achieves the use of productive grammar, usually late in the second year of life. Toward the end of the second year, the child is master of the single-word, agrammatical utterance, the so-called holophrase. In the months following, there occurs a profound change in the use of language. Two classes of words appear – a pivot class and an open class – and the child launches forth on his career in combinatorial talking and, perhaps, thinking. Whereas before, lexemes like *allgone* and *mummy* and *sticky* and *bye-bye* were used singly, now, for example, *allgone* becomes a pivot word and is used in combination. Mother washes jam off the child's hands; he says *allgone sticky*. In the next days, if his speech is carefully followed (Braine, 1963), it will be apparent that he is trying out the limits of the pivot combinations, and one will even find constructions that have an extraordinary capacity for representing complex sequences – like *allgone bye-bye* after a visitor has departed. A recent and ingenious observation by Weir (1962) on her 2½-year-old son, recording his speech musings after he was in bed with lights out, indicates that at this stage there is a great deal of metalinguistic combinatorial play with words in which the child is exploring the limits of grammatical productiveness.

In effect, language provides a means, not only for representing experience, but also for transforming it. As Chomsky (1957) and Miller (1962) have both made clear in the last few years, the transformational rules of grammar provide a syntactic means of reworking the "realities" one has encountered. Not only, if you will, did the dog bite the man, but the man was bitten by the dog and perhaps the man was not bitten by the dog or was the man not bitten by the dog. The range of reworking that is made possible even by the three transformations of the passive, the negative, and the query is very striking indeed. Or the ordering device whereby the comparative mode makes it possible to connect what is *heavy* and what is *light* into the ordinal array of *heavy* and *less heavy* is again striking. Or, to take a final example, there is the discrimination that is made possible by the growth of attribute language such that the global dimension *big* and *little* can now be decomposed into *tall* and *short* on the one hand and *fat* and *skinny* on the other.

Once the child has succeeded in internalizing language as a cognitive instrument, it becomes possible for him to represent and systematically transform the regularities of experience with far greater flexibility and power than before. Interestingly enough, it is the recent Russian literature, particularly Vygotsky's (1962) book on language and thought, and the work of his disciple, Luria (1961), and his students (Abramyan, 1958; Martsinovskaya, undated) that has highlighted these phenomena by calling attention to the so-called second-signal system which replaces classical conditioning with an internalized linguistic system for shaping and transforming experience itself.

If all these matters were not of such complexity and human import, I would apologize for taking so much time in speculation. We turn now to some new experiments designed to shed some light on the nature of representation and particularly upon the transition from its iconic to its symbolic form.

Let me begin with an experiment by Bruner and Kenney (in press) on the manner in which children between 5 and 7 handle a double classification matrix. The materials of the experiment are nine plastic glasses, arranged so that they vary in 3 degrees of diameter and 3 degrees of height. They are set before the child initially, as in Fig. 3.1, on a 3 × 3 grid marked on a large piece of cardboard. To acquaint the child with the matrix, we first remove one, then two, and then three glasses from the matrix, asking the child to replace them. We also ask the children to describe how the glasses in the columns and rows are alike and how they differ. Then the glasses are scrambled and we ask the child to make something like what was there before by placing the glasses on the same grid that was used when the task was introduced. Now we scramble the glasses once more, but this time we place the glass that was formerly in the south-west corner of the grid in the south-east corner (it is the shortest, thinnest glass) and ask the child if he can make something like what was there before, leaving the one glass where we have just put it. That is the experiment.

The results can be quickly told. To begin with, there is no difference between ages 5, 6, and 7 either in terms of ability to replace glasses taken from the matrix or in building a matrix once it has been scrambled (but without the transposed glass). Virtually all the children succeed. Interestingly enough, *all* the children rebuild the matrix to match the original, almost as if they were copying what was there before. The only difference is that the older children are quicker.

Now compare the performance of the three ages in constructing the matrix with a single member transposed. Most of the 7-year-olds succeed

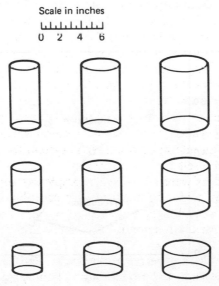

FIG. 3.1.   Array of glasses used in study of matrix ordering (Bruner & Kenney, in press).

in the transposed task, but hardly any of the youngest children. Figure 3.2 presents the results graphically. The youngest children seem to be dominated by an image of the original matrix. They try to put the transposed glass "back where it belongs", to rotate the cardboard so that "it will be like before", and sometimes they will start placing a few glasses neighboring the transposed glass correctly only to revert to the original arrangement. In several instances, 5- or 6-year-olds will simply try to reconstitute the old matrix, building right over the transposed glass. The 7-year-old, on the other hand, is more likely to pause, to treat the transposition as a problem, to talk to himself about "where this should go". The relation of place and size is for him a problem that requires reckoning, not simply copying.

Now consider the language children use for describing the dimensions of the matrix. Recall that the children were asked how glasses in a row and in a column were alike and how they differed. Children answered in three distinctive linguistic modes. One was *dimensional*, singling out two ends of an attribute – for example: "That one is higher, and that one is shorter". A second was *global* in nature. Of glasses differing only in height the child says, "That one is bigger and that one is little". The same words could be used equally well for diameter or for nearly any other magnitude. Finally, there was *confounded* usage: "That one is tall and that one is little", where a dimensional term is used for one end of the continuum and a global term for the other. The children who used confounded descriptions had the most difficulty with the transposed matrix (Fig.3.3). Lumping all ages together, the children who used confounded descriptions were twice as likely to fail on the transposition task as those who used either dimen-

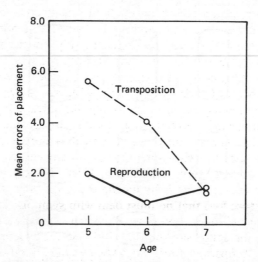

FIG. 3.2. Mean number of errors made by children in reproducing and transposing a 3 × 3 matrix (Bruner & Kenney, in press).

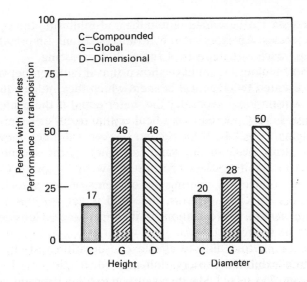

FIG. 3.3. Percentage of children (aged 5–7) using different language patterns who reproduced transposed matrix errorlessly (Bruner & Kenney, in press).

sional or global terms. *But the language the children used had no relation whatsoever to their performance in reproducing the first untransposed matrix.* Inhelder and Sinclair[1] in a recent communication also report that confounded language of this kind is associated with failure on conservation tasks in children of the same age, a subject to which we shall turn shortly.

The findings of this experiment suggest two things. First, that children who use iconic representation are more highly sensitized to the spatial-qualitative organization of experience and less to the ordering principles governing such organization. They can recognize and reproduce, but cannot produce new structures based on rule. And second, there is a suspicion that the language they bring to bear on the task is insufficient as a tool for ordering. If these notions are correct, then certain things should follow. For one thing, *improvement* in language should aid this type of problem solving. This remains to be investigated. But it is also reasonable to suppose that *activation* of language habits that the child has already mastered might improve performance as well – a hypothesis already suggested by the findings of Luria's students (e.g., Abramyan, 1958). Now, activation can be achieved by two means. One is by having the child "say" the description of something before him that he must deal with symbolically. The other is to take advantage of the remoteness of reference that is a feature of language, and have the child "say" his description in the absence of the things to be described. In this way, there would be less likelihood of a perceptual-

---

[1]Bärbel Inhelder and Mimi Sinclair, Personal Communication, 1963.

iconic representation becoming dominant and inhibiting the operation of symbolic processes. An experiment by Françoise Frank (in press) illustrates this latter approach – the effects of saying before seeing.

Piaget and Inhelder (1962) have shown that if children between ages 4 and 7 are presented two identical beakers which they judge equally full of water, they will no longer consider the water equal if the contents of one of the beakers is now poured into a beaker that is either wider or thinner than the original (Fig.3.4). If the second beaker is thinner, they will say it has more to drink because the water is higher; if the second beaker is wider, they will say it has less because the water is lower. Comparable results can be obtained by pouring the contents of one glass into several smaller beakers. In Geneva terms, the child is not yet able to conserve liquid volume across transformations in its appearance. Consider how this behavior can be altered.

Françoise Frank first did the classic conservation tests to determine which children exhibited conservation and which did not. Her subjects were 4, 5, 6, and 7 years old. She then went on to other procedures (Fig.3.5), among which was the following. Two standard beakers are partly filled so that the child judges them to contain equal amounts of water. A wider beaker of the same height is introduced and the three beakers are now, except for their tops, hidden by a screen. The experimenter pours from a

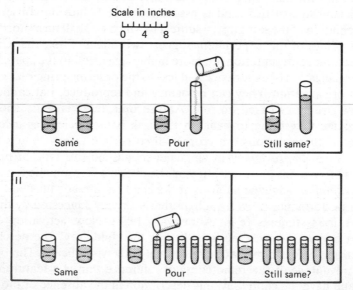

FIG. 3.4. Two Geneva tests for conservation of liquid volume across transformations in its appearance (Piaget & Inhelder, 1962).

standard beaker into the wider beaker. The child, without seeing the water, is asked which has more to drink, or do they have the same amount, the standard or the wider beaker. The results are in Fig.3.6. In comparison with the unscreened pretest, there is a striking increase in correct equality judgments. Correct responses jump from 0% to 50% among the 4s, from 20% to 90% among the 5s, and from 50% to 100% among the 6s. With the screen present, most children justify their correct judgment by noting that "It's the same water", or "You only poured it".

Now the screen is removed. All the 4-year-olds change their minds. The perceptual display overwhelms them and they decide that the wider beaker has less water. But virtually all of the 5-year-olds stick to their judgment, often invoking the difference between appearance and reality – "It looks like more to drink, but it is only the same because it is the same water and it was only poured from there to there", to quote one typical 5-year-old.

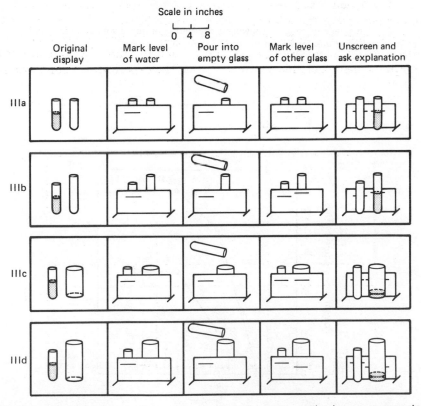

FIG. 3.5. One procedure used in study of effect of language activation on conservation (Frank, in press).

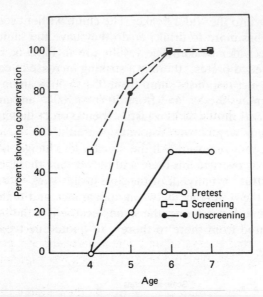

FIG. 3.6.   Percentage of children showing conservation of liquid volume before and during screening and upon unscreening of the displays (Frank, in press).

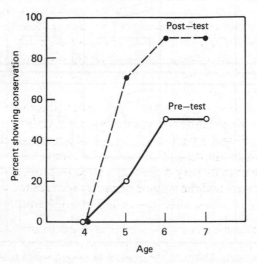

FIG. 3.7.   Percentage of children showing conservation of liquid volume in identical pre-test and post-test run after completion of experiment (Frank, in press).

And all of the 6s and all the 7s stick to their judgment. Now, some minutes later, Frank does a post-test on the children using a tall thin beaker along with the standard ones, and no screen, of course. The 4s are unaffected by their prior experience. None of them is able to grasp the idea of invariant quantity in the new task. With the 5s, instead of 20% showing conservation, as in the pre-test, 70% do. With both 6s and 7s, conservation increases from 50% to 90%. I should mention that control groups doing just a pre-test and post-test show no significant improvement in performance.

A related experiment of Nair's (1963) explores the arguments children use when they solve a conservation task correctly and when they do not. Her subjects were all 5-year-olds. She transferred water from one rectangular clear plastic tank to another that was both longer and wider than the first. Ordinarily, a 5-year-old will say there is less water in the second tank. The water is, of course, lower in the second tank. She had a toy duck swimming in the first container, and when the water was poured into the new container, she told the child that "The duck was taking his water with him".

Three kinds of arguments were set forth by the children to support their judgments. One is perceptual – having to do with the height, width, or apparent "bigness" of the water. A second type has to do with action. The duck took the water along, or the water was only poured. A third one, "transformational" argument, invokes the reversibility principle; if you poured the water back into the first container, it would look the same again.[2] Of the children who thought the water was not equal in amount after pouring, 15% used nonperceptual arguments to justify their judgment. Of those who recognized the equality of the water, two-thirds used nonperceptual arguments. It is plain that if a child is to succeed in the conservation task, he must have some internalized verbal formula that shields him from the overpowering appearance of the visual displays much as in the Frank experiment. The explanations of the children who lacked conservation suggest how strongly oriented they were to the visual appearance of the displays they had to deal with.

Consider now another experiment by Bruner and Kenney (in press) also designed to explore the border between iconic and symbolic representation. Children aged 5, 6, and 7 were asked to say which of two glasses in a pair was fuller and which emptier. "Fullness" is an interesting concept to work with, for it involves in its very definition a ratio or proportion between the volume of a container and the volume of a substance contained. It is difficult for the iconically oriented child to see a half-full barrel and a half-filled

---

[2] Not one of the 40 children who participated in this experiment used the compensation argument – that though the water was lower it was correspondingly wider and was, therefore, the same amount of water. This type of reasoning by compensation is said by Piaget and Inhelder (1962) to be the basis of conservation.

thimble as equally full, since the former looms larger in every one of the attributes that might be perceptually associated with volume. It is like the old riddle of which is heavier, a pound of lead or a pound of feathers. To make a correct judgment of fullness or emptiness, the child must use a symbolic operation, somewhat like computing a ratio, and resist the temptation to use perceptual appearance – that is, unless he finds some happy heuristic to save him the labor of such a computation. Figure 3.8 contains the 11 pairs of glasses used, and they were selected with a certain malice aforethought.

There are four types of pairs. In Type I (Displays 4, 9a, and 9b), the glasses are of unequal volume, but equally, though fractionally, full. In Type II (Displays 2, 7a, and 7b) again the glasses are of unequal volume, but they are completely full. Type III (Displays 3, 8a, and 8b) consists of two glasses of unequal volume, one filled and the other part filled. Type IV consists of identical glasses, in one case equally filled, in another unequally (Displays 1 and 5).

All the children in the age range we have studied use pretty much the same criteria for judging *fullness*, and these criteria are based on directly observable sensory indices rather than upon proportion. That glass is judged fuller that has the greater apparent volume of water, and the favoured indication of greater volume is water level; or where that is equated, then width of glass will do; and when width and water level are the same, then height of glass will prevail. But now consider the judgments made by the three age groups with respect to which glass in each pair is *emptier*. The older children have developed an interesting consistency based on an appreciation of the complementary relation of filled and empty space – albeit an incorrect one. For them "emptier" means the glass that has the largest apparent volume of unfilled space, just as "fuller" meant the glass that had the largest volume of filled space. In consequence, their responses seem logically contradictory. For the glass that is judged fuller also turns out to be the glass that is judged emptier – given a large glass and a small glass, both half full. The younger children, on the other hand, equate emptiness with "littleness"; that glass is emptier that gives the impression of being smaller in volume of liquid. If we take the three pairs of glasses of Type I (unequal volumes, half filled) we can see how the judgments typically distribute themselves. Consider only the errors. The glass with the larger volume of empty space is called emptier by 27% of the erring 5-year-olds, by 53% of the erring 6-year-olds, and by 72% of erring 7-year-olds. But the glass with the smallest volume of water is called emptier by 73% of the 5-year-olds who err, 47% of the 6s, and only 28% of the 7s. When the children are asked for their reasons for judging one glass as emptier, there is further confirmation. Most of the younger children justify it by pointing to "littleness" or "less water" or some other aspect of diminu-

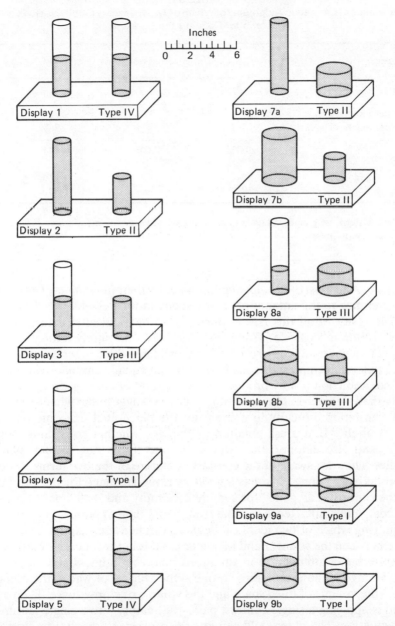

FIG. 3.8.   Eleven pairs of glasses to be judged in terms of which glass is fuller and which emptier (Bruner & Kenney, in press).

TABLE 3.1
Percentage of Erroneous Judgments of Which of Two Glasses is Emptier Based on Two
Criteria for Defining the Concept

Judgment	Age		
Criterion for "Emptier"	5	6	7
Greater empty space	27%	53%	72%
Smaller volume of liquid	73%	47%	28%
	100%	100%	100%
Percentage correct	9%	8%	17%
$N=$	30	30	30

Note. Criteria are greater volume of empty space and lesser volume of water. From Bruner and Kenney (in press).

tiveness. And most of the older children justify their judgments of emptiness by reference to the amount of empty space in the vessel.

The result of all this is, of course, that the "logical structure" of the older children seems to go increasingly awry. But surely, though Fig.3.9 shows that contradictory errors steadily increase with age (calling the same glass fuller and emptier or equally full but not equally empty or vice versa), the contradiction is a by-product of the method of dealing with attributes. How shall we interpret these findings? Let me suggest that what is involved is a translation difficulty in going from the perceptual or iconic realm to the symbolic. If you ask children of this age whether something can be fuller and also emptier, they will smile and think that you are playing riddles. They are aware of the contrastive nature of the two terms. Indeed, even the very young child has a good working language for the two poles of the contrast: "all gone" for completely empty and "spill" or "tippy top" for completely full. Recall too that from 5 to 7, there is perfect performance in judging which of two identical beakers is fuller and emptier. The difference between the younger and the older child is in the number of attributes that are being attended to in situations involving fullness and emptiness. The younger child is attending to one – the volume of water; the older to two – the volume of filled space and the volume of empty space. The young child is applying a single contrast pair – full-empty – to a single feature of the situation. The older child can attend to two features, but he does not yet have the means for relating them to a third, the volume of the container per se. To do so involves being able to deal with a relation in the perceptual field that does not have a "point-at-able" or ostensive definition. Once the

TABLE 3.2
Percentage of Children Who Justify Judgments of "Fuller"
and "Emptier" by Mentioning More Than a Single Attribute

Age	*"Fuller" Judgments*	*"Emptier" Judgments*	N
5	7.2%	4.1%	30
6	15.6%	9.3%	30
7	22.2%	15.6%	30

third term is introduced – the volume of the glass – then the symbolic concept of proportion can come to "stand for" something that is not present perceptually. The older child is on the way to achieving the insight, in spite of his contradictions. And, interestingly enough, if we count the number of children who justify their judgments of fuller and emptier by pointing to *several* rather than a single attribute, we find that the proportion triples in both cases between age 5 and age 7. The older child, it would seem, is ordering his perceptual world in such a way that, shortly, he will be able to apply concepts of relationship that are not dependent upon simple ostensive definition. As he moves toward this more powerful "technology of reckoning", he is led into errors that seem to be contradictory. What is particularly telltale is the fact, for example, that in the Type III displays,

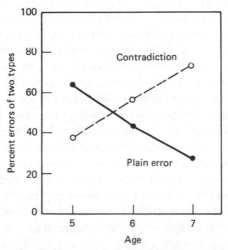

FIG. 3.9.   Percentage of children at three ages who make contradictory and plain errors in judging which of two glasses is fuller and which emptier. (A contradictory error is calling the same glass both fuller or emptier or calling them equally full but not equally empty or vice versa. A plain error is calling one glass fuller and the other emptier, but incorrectly. From Bruner & Kenney, in press.)

younger children sometimes seem to find the judgment easier than older children – pointing to the fuller by placing their finger on the rim of the full member and pointing to the emptier with the remark that "It is not to the top". The older child (and virtually never the younger one) gets all involved in the judgment of "fuller by apparent filled volume" and then equally involved in the judgment of "emptier by apparent empty volume" and such are his efforts that he fails to note his contradiction when dealing with a pair like Display 8b.

Turn now to a quite different experimental procedure that deals with the related concept of equivalence – how seemingly different objects are grouped into equivalence classes. In the two experiments to be cited, one by Olver (1961), the other by Rigney (1962), children are given words or pictures to sort into groups or to characterize in terms of how they are alike. The two sets of results, one for words, the other for pictures, obtained for children between 6 and 14, can be summarized together. One may distinguish two aspects of grouping – the first has to do with the features or attributes that children use as a criterion for grouping objects: *perceptual features* (the color, size, pattern, etc.), *arbitrary functional features* (what I can do with the objects regardless of their usual use: You can make noise with a newspaper by crumpling it and with a book by slamming it shut, etc.), *appropriate functional features* (potato, peach, banana, and milk are characterized "You can eat them"). But grouping behaviour can also be characterized in terms of the syntactical structure of the equivalence sets that the child develops. There are, first, what Vygotsky (1962) has called *heaps*; collections put together in an arbitrary way simply because the child has decided to put them together that way. Then there are *complexes*. The various members of a complex are included in the class in accordance with a rule that does not account uniformly for the inclusion of all the members. Edge matching is one such rule. Each object is grouped into a class on the basis of its similarity with a neighboring object. Yet no two neighboring pieces may be joined by the same similarity. Another type of complexive grouping is thematic. Here, objects are put together by virtue of participating in a sentence or a little story. More sophisticated is a key ring in which one organizing object is related to all others but none of those to each other. And finally, considerably more sophisticated than heaps and complexes, there are *superordinate concepts*, in which one universal rule of inclusion accounts for all the objects in the set – all men and women over 21 are included in the class of voters provided they meet certain residence requirements.

The pattern of growth is revealing of many of the trends we have already discussed, and provides in addition a new clue. Consider first the attributes or features of objects that children at different ages use as a basis for forming equivalence groups. As Fig.3.10 indicates, the youngest children rely more heavily on perceptual attributes than do the others. As they grow older, grouping comes to depend increasingly upon the functional properties of things – but the transitional phase is worth some attention, for it raises anew the issue of the significance of egocentrism. For the first functional groupings to appear are of an arbitrary type – what "I" or "you" can do to objects that renders them alike, rather than what is the conventional use or function to which objects can be put. During this stage of "egocentric functionalism", there is a corresponding rise in the use of first- and second-person personal pronouns: "I can do thus and so to this object; I can do the same to this one", etc. Gradually, with increasing maturity the child shifts to an appropriate and less egocentric form of using functional group-ings. The shift from perceptual to functional groupings is accompanied by a corresponding shift in the syntactical structure of the groups formed. Complexive groupings steadily dwindle; superordinate groupings rise, until the latter almost replace the former in late adolescence. It is difficult to tell which is the pacemaker in this growth – syntax or the semantic basis of grouping.

Rigney reports one other matter of some interest. Her young subjects formed groups of any size they wished, choosing pictures from a display board of several dozen little water colors. She observed that the most perceptually based groups and the ones most often based on complexive

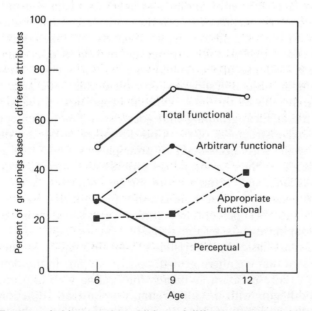

FIG. 3.10. Features of objects used by children of different ages as a basis for placing the objects in equivalence groups (Olver, 1961).

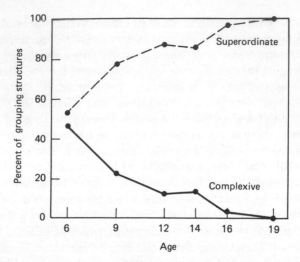

FIG. 3.11. The use of two rules of equivalence grouping found in children of different ages (Olver, 1961).

grouping principles were pairs. A count of these revealed that 61% of all the groups made by 6-year-olds were such pairs, 36% of those made by 8-year-olds, and only 25% of the groupings of 11-year-olds.

On the surface, this set of findings – Olver's and Rigney's alike – seems to point more to the decline of a preference for perceptual and iconic ways of dealing with objects and events, particularly with their grouping. But closer inspection suggests still another factor that is operating. In both cases, there is evidence of the development of hierarchical structure and rules for including objects in superordinate hierarchies. Hierarchical classification is surely one of the most evident properties of the structure of language – hierarchical grouping that goes beyond mere perceptual inclusion. Complexive structures of the kind described earlier are much more dominated by the sorts of associative principles by which the appearance of objects leads to their spontaneous grouping in terms of similarity or contiguity. As language becomes more internalized, more guiding as a set of rules for organizing events, there is a shift from the associative principles that operate in classical perceptual organization to the increasingly abstract rules for grouping events by the principles of inclusion, exclusion, and overlap, the most basic characteristics of any hierarchical system.

We have said that cognitive growth consists in part in the development of systems of representation as means for dealing with information. The growing child begins with a strong reliance upon learned action patterns to represent the world around him. In time, there is added to this technology a means for simultanizing regularities in experience into images that stand for events in the way that pictures do. And to this is finally added a technology of translating experience into a symbol system that can be operated upon by rules of transformation that greatly increase the possible range of problem solving. One of the effects of this development, or possibly one of its causes, is the power for organizing acts of information processing into more integrated and long-range problem solving efforts. To this matter we turn next.

Consider in rapid succession three related experiments. All of them point, I think, to the same conclusion.

The first is by Huttenlocher (in press), a strikingly simple study, performed with children between the ages of 6 and 12. Two light switches are before the child; each can be in one of two positions. A light bulb is also visible. The child is asked to tell, on the basis of turning only one switch, what turns the light on. There are four ways in which the presentations are made. In the first, the light is off initially and when the child turns a switch, the light comes on. In the second, the light is on and when the child turns a switch, it goes off. In the third, the light is on and when the child turns a switch, it stays on. In the fourth and final condition, the light is off and when the child turns a switch, it stays off. Now what is intriguing about this arrangement is that there are different numbers of inductive steps required to make a correct inference in each task. The simplest condition is the off-on case. The position to which the switch has just been moved is responsible for the light going on. Intermediate difficulty should be experienced with the on-off condition. In the on-off case, two connected inferences are required: The present position achieved is rejected and the original position of the switch that has been turned is responsible for lighting the bulb. An even larger number of consecutive acts is required for success in the on-on case: The present position of the turned switch is rejected, the original position as well and the present position of the *other* switch is responsible. The off-off case requires four steps: rejecting the present position of the turned switch, its original position, and the present position of the other switch, finally accepting the alternative position of the unturned switch. The natures of the individual steps are all the same. Success in the more complex cases depends upon being able to integrate them consecutively.

Huttenlocher's results show that the 6-year-olds are just as capable as their elders of performing the elementary operation involved in the one-step case: the on-off display. They, like the 9s and 12s, make nearly perfect scores. But in general, the more inferential steps the 6-year-old must make, the poorer his performance. By age 12, on the other hand, there is an insignificant difference between the tasks requiring one, two, three, or four connected inferences.

An experiment by Mosher (1962) underlines the same point. He was concerned with the strategies used by children from 6 to 11 for getting information in the game of Twenty Questions. They were to find out by "yes-no" questions what caused a car to go off the road and hit a tree. One may distinguish between connected constraint-locating questions ("Was it night-time?" followed up appropriately) and direct hypothesis-testing questions ("Did a bee fly in the window and sting the man on the eye and make him go off the road and hit the tree?"). From 6 to 11, more and more children use constraint-locating, connected questioning. Let me quote from Mosher's account (1962, p.6):

> We have asked children . . . after they have played their games, to tell us which of two questions they would rather have the answer to, if they were playing the games again – one of them a typical constraint-seeking question ("Was there anything wrong with the man?") and the other a typical discrete test of an hypothesis ("Did the man have a heart attack?"). All the eleven-year-olds and all the eight-year-olds choose the constraint-seeking question, but only 29% of the six-year-olds do.

The questions of the younger children are all one-step substitutes for direct sense experience. They are looking for knowledge by single questions that provide the answer in a finished form. When they succeed they do so by a lucky question that hits an immediate, perceptible cause. When the older child receives a "yes" answer to one of his constraint-locating questions, he most often follows up by asking another. When, on the rare occasions that a younger child asks a constraint question and it is answered "yes",

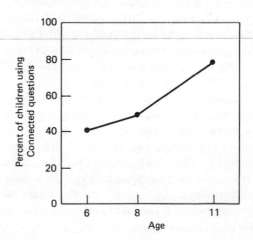

FIG. 3.12. The proportion of children at different ages who use connected questions in a Twenty Questions game (Mosher, 1962).

he almost invariably follows it up with a specific question to test a concrete hypothesis. The older child can accrete his information in a structure governed by consecutive inference. The younger child cannot.

Potter's (in press) study of the development of perceptual recognition bears on the same point. Ordinary colored photographs of familiar scenes are presented to children between 6 and 12, the pictures coming gradually into focus. Let me sum up one part of the results very briefly. Six-year-olds produce an abundance of hypotheses. But they rarely try to match new hypotheses to previous ones. "There is a big tower in the middle and a road over there and a big ice cream cone through the middle of the tower and a pumpkin on top." It is like a random collage. The 9-year-old's torrent of hypotheses, on the other hand, shows a sense of consistency about what is likely to appear with what. Things are in a context of likelihood, a frame of reference that demands internal consistency. Something is seen as a merry-go-round, and the child then restricts later hypotheses to the other things to be found in an amusement park. The adolescent operates under even more highly organized sequential constraints. He occasionally develops his initial hypotheses from what is implied by the properties of the picture, almost by intersection – "It is red and shiny and metallic. It must be a coffee-pot". Once such constraints are established, the order of hypotheses reflects even more the need to build up a consistent world of objects – even to the point of failing to recognize things that do not fit it.

What shall we make of these three sets of findings – that older children are able to cumulate information by asking questions in a directed sequence leading to a final goal, and that they are capable of recognizing visual displays in a manner governed by a dominating frame of reference that transcends momentary and isolated bits of information? Several points seem apparent. The first is that as children mature, they are able to use indirect information based on forms of information processing other than the act of pointing to what is immediately present. They seem, in short, to make remote reference to states and constraints that are not given by the immediate situation, to go beyond the information given. Second, and this is a matter that has already been discussed, they seem to be able to cumulate information into a structure that can be operated upon by rules that transcend simple association by similarity and contiguity. In the case of Twenty Questions, the rule is best described as impliction – that knowing one thing implies certain other things and eliminates still others. In the experiments with the light switches, it is that if the present state does not produce the effect, then there is a system for tracing back to the other states that cause the light to go on. Where perceptual recognition is concerned, the rule is that a piece of information from one part of the display implies what other parts might be. The child, in sum, is translating redundancy into a manipulable model of the environment that is governed by rules of implication. It is this model of the environment that permits him to go beyond the information before him. I would suggest that it is this new array of cognitive equipment that permits the child to transcend momentaneity, to integrate longer sequences of events.

Let me urge, moreover, that such a system of processing environmental events depends upon the translation of experience into symbolic form. Such a translation is necessary in order for there to be the kind of remoteness of reference as is required when one deals with indirect information. To transcend the immediately perceptual, to get beyond what is vividly present to a more extended model of the environment, the child needs a system that permits him to deal with the nonpresent, with things that are remote in space, qualitative similarity, and time, from the present situation. Hockett (1959), in describing the design features of language includes this feature as crucial. He is referring to human speech as a system of communication. The same point can be made about language as an instrument of thought. That humans have the *capacity* for using speech in this way is only part of the point. What is critical is that the capacity is *not* used until it is coupled with the technology of language in the cognitive operations of the child.

The same can be said for the models of the environment that the child constructs to go beyond present information. This is not to say that non-verbal animals cannot make inferences that go beyond the present stimulus. Anticipatory activity is the rule in vertebrates. But the models that the growing child constructs seem not to be anticipatory, or inferential, or probabilistic-frequency models. They seem to be governed by rules that can more properly be called syntactical rather than associative.

My major concern has been to examine afresh the nature of intellectual growth. The account has surely done violence to the richness of the subject. It seems to me that growth depends upon the emergence of two forms of competence. Children, as they grow, must acquire ways of representing the recurrent regularities in their environment, and they must transcend the momentary by developing ways of linking past to present to future – representation and integration. I have suggested that we can conceive of growth in both of these domains as the emergence of new technologies for the unlocking and amplification of human intellectual powers. Like the growth of technology, the growth of intellect is not smoothly monotonic. Rather, it moves forward in spurts as innovations are adopted. Most of the innovations are transmitted to the child in some prototypic form by agents of the culture: ways of responding, ways of looking and imaging, and most important, ways of translating what one has encountered into language.

I have relied heavily in this account on the successive emergence of action, image, and word as the vehicles of representation, a reliance based both upon our observations and upon modern readings of man's alloplastic evolution. Our attention has been directed largely to the transition between iconic and symbolic representation.

In children between 4 and 12 language comes to play an increasingly powerful role as an implement of knowing. Through simple experiments, I have tried to show how language shapes, augments, and even supercedes the child's earlier modes of processing information. Translation of experience into symbolic form, with its attendant means of achieving remote reference, transformation, and combination, opens up realms of intellectual possibility that are orders of magnitude beyond the most powerful image-forming system.

What of the integration of intellectual activity into more coherent and interconnected acts? It has been the fashion, since Freud, to see delay of gratification as the principal dynamism behind this development – from primary process to secondary process, or from assimilation to accommodation, as Piaget would put it today. Without intending to question the depth of this insight, let me suggest that delay of immediate gratification, the ability to go beyond the moment, also depends upon techniques, and again they are techniques of representation. Perhaps representation exclusively by imagery and perceptual organization has built into it one basic operation that ties it to the immediate present. It is the operation of pointing – ostensiveness, as logicians call it. (This is not to say that highly evolved images do not go beyond immediate time and given place. Maps and flow charts are iconic in nature, but they are images that translate prior linguistic and mathematical renderings into a visual form.) Iconic representation, in the beginning, is built upon a perceptual organization that is tied to the "point-at-able" spatioqualitative properties of events. I have suggested that, for all its limitations, such representation is an achievement beyond the earlier stage where percepts are not autonomous of action. But so long as perceptual representation dominates, it is difficult to develop higher-order techniques for processing information by consecutive inferential steps that take one beyond what can be pointed at.

Once language becomes a medium for the translation of experience, there is a progressive release from immediacy. For language, as we have commented, has the new and powerful features of remoteness and arbitrariness: It permits productive, combinatorial operations in the *absence* of what is represented. With this achievement, the child can delay gratification by virtue of representing to himself what lies beyond the present, what other possibilities exist beyond the clue that is under his nose. The child may be *ready* for delay of gratification, but he is no more able to bring it off than somebody ready to build a house, save that he has not yet heard of tools.

The discussion leaves two obvious questions begging. What of the integration of behavior in organisms without language? And how does language become internalized as a vehicle of organizing experience? The first question has to be answered briefly and somewhat cryptically. Wherever integrated behavior has been studied – as in Lehrman's (1955) careful work on integrated instinctive patterns in the ringdove, it has turned out that a sustaining external stimulus was needed to keep the highly integrated behavior going. The best way to control behavior in subhuman species is to control the stimulus situation. Surely this is the lesson of Lashley's (1938) classic account of instinctive behavior. Where animal learning is concerned, particularly in the primates, there is, to be sure, considerable plasticity. But it too depends upon the development of complex forms of stimulus substitution and organization – as in Klüver's (1933) work on equivalence reactions in monkeys. If it should seem that I am urging that the growth of symbolic functioning links a unique set of powers to man's capacity, the appearance is quite as it should be.

As for how language becomes internalized as a program for ordering experience, I join those who despair for an answer. My speculation, for whatever it is worth, is that the process of internalization depends upon interaction with others, upon the need to develop corresponding categories and transformations for communal action. It is the need for cognitive coin that can be exchanged with those on whom we depend. What Roger Brown (1958) has called the Original Word Game ends up by being the Human Thinking Game.

If I have seemed to underemphasize the importance of inner capacities – for example, the capacity *for* language or *for* imagery – it is because I believe that this part of the story is given by the nature of man's evolution. What is significant about the growth of mind in the child is to what degree it depends not upon capacity but upon the unlocking of capacity by techniques that come from exposure to the specialized environment of a culture. Romantic clichés, like "the veneer of culture" or "natural man", are as misleading if not as damaging as the view that the course of human development can be viewed independently of the educational process we arrange to make that development possible.

ACKNOWLEDGEMENT

The assistance of R. R. Olver and Mrs. Blythe Clinchy in the preparation of this paper is gratefully acknowledged.

REFERENCES

Abramyan, L. A. (1958). Organization of the voluntary activity of the child with the help of verbal instruction. Unpublished diploma thesis, Moscow University. Cited by A. R. Luria (1961). *The role of speech in the regulation of normal and abnormal behavior*. New York: Liveright.

Barker, R. G. (1963, September). *On the nature of the environment*. Kurt Lewin Memorial Address presented at American Psychological Association, Philadelphia.

Braine, M. D. (1963). On learning the grammatical order of words. *Psychological Review, 70*, 323–348.

Brown, R. (1958). *Words and things*. Glencoe, III.: Free Press.

Bruner, J. S., & Kenney, H. (In press). The development of the concepts of order and proportion in children. In J. S. Bruner (Ed.), *Studies in cognitive growth*. New York: Wiley.

Chomsky, N. (1957). *Syntactic structures*. S'Gravenhage, Netherlands: Mouton.

Emerson, L. L. (1931). The effect of bodily orientation upon the young child's memory for position of objects. *Child Development, 2,* 125–142.

Frank, F. (In press). Perception and language in conservation. In J. S. Bruner, *Studies in cognitive growth*. New York: Wiley.

Hanfmann, E., Rickers-Ovsiankina, M., & Goldstein, K. (1944). Case Lanuti: Extreme concretization of behavior due to damage of the brain cortex. *Psychological Monographs, 57,* (4, Whole No. 264).

Hockett, C.F., (1959). Animal "languages" and human language. In J. N. Spuhler, *The evolution of man's capacity for culture,* Detroit: Wayne State University Press. pp. 32–39.

Huttenlocher, J. (In press). The growth of conceptual strategies. In J. S. Bruner, *Studies in cognitive growth*. New York: Wiley.

Klüver, H. (1933). *Behavior mechanisms in monkeys*. Chicago: University of Chicago Press.

La Barre, W. (1954). *The human animal*. Chicago: University of Chicago Press.

Lashley, K. S. (1938). Experimental analysis of instinctive behavior. *Psychological Review, 45,* 445–472.

Lehrman, D. S. (1955). The physiological basis of parental feeding behavior in the ring dove (Streptopelia risoria). *Behavior, 7,* 241–286.

Luria, A. R. (1961). *The role of speech in the regulation of normal and abnormal behavior*. New York: Liveright.

Mandler, G. (1962). From association to structure. *Psychological Review, 69,* 415–427.

Martsinovskaya, E. N. (Undated). Research into the reflective and regulatory role of the second signalling system of pre-school age. Collected papers of the Department of Psychology, Moscow University. Cited by A. R. Luria (1961). *The role of speech in the regulation of normal and abnormal behavior*. New York: Liveright.

Miller, G.A. (1962). Some psychological studies of grammar. *American Psychologist, 17,* 748–762.

Miller, G. A, Galanter, E, & Pribram, K. H. (1960). *Plans and the structure of behavior*. New York: Holt.

Mosher, F. A. (1962). *Strategies for information gathering*. Paper read at Eastern Psychological Association, Atlantic City, N.J.

Nair, P. (1963). An experiment in conservation. In *Center for Cognitive Studies, Annual Report*. Cambridge, Mass.

Olver, R. R. (1961). *A developmental study of cognitive equivalence*. Unpublished doctoral dissertation, Radcliffe College.

Piaget, J. (1954). *The construction of reality in the child*. (Trans. by Margaret Cook) New York: Basic Books.

Piaget, J. & Inhelder, B. (1962). *Le développement des quantités physiques chez l'enfant*. (2nd rev. ed.) Neuchâtel, Switzerland: Delachaux & Niestlé.

Potter, M. C. (in press). The growth of perceptual recognition. In J. S. Bruner, *Studies in cognitive growth*. New York: Wiley.

Rigney, J. C. (1962). *A developmental study of cognitive equivalence transformations and their use in the acquisition and processing of information*. Unpublished honors thesis, Radcliffe College, Department of Social Relations.

Vygotsky, L. S. (1962). *Thought and language*. (Ed. & trans. by E. Hanfmann & G. Vakar) New York: Wiley.

Washburn, S. L. & Howell, F. C. (1960). Human evolution and culture. In S. Tax, *The evolution of man*. Vol. 2. Chicago: University of Chicago Press.

Weir, R. H. (1962). *Language in the crib*. The Hague: Mouton.

Werner, H. (1948).*Comparative psychology of mental development*. (Rev. ed.) Chicago: Follett.

4 The Genesis of Higher Mental Functions

L.S. Vygotsky

[. . .]

The third aspect of our investigation is most closely concerned with our historical way of viewing higher forms of behavior. The analysis of higher mental processes aids us in understanding fundamental problems of the child's cultural development. It allows us to analyze the genesis of higher behavioral forms, i.e., the mental forms that constitute the object of our study.

According to Hall, psychology produces a genetic explanation of a higher form of logic; it is concerned with the question of where a given phenomenon is going and from whence it came. It is also concerned with the results of future transformations.

For the developmental psychologist the historical form of explanation is the highest possible. In order to answer the question of what a form of behavior represents, he/she finds it necessary to discover its origin and the history of its development up to the present. In Blonsky's words, behavior can be understood only as the history of behavior.

But before turning to the genesis of higher forms of behavior, we must elucidate the very concept of development, as we have done in the chapters [of our book] on the analysis and structure of higher mental processes. The fact is that because of the crisis in psychology, all concepts have become meaningless and vague. They change depending on the investigator's point of view. In different systems of psychology based on different methodolog-

Source: Wertsch, J.V. (Ed.) (1981). *The concept of activity in Soviet psychology*. New York: M.E. Sharpe, Inc., pp. 144-188. Reprinted by permission of M.E. Sharpe, Inc., Armonk, New York 10504.

ical principles, all the fundamental categories of research, including that of genesis, acquire different meanings.

A second consideration that compels us to look at the genetic problem is that contemporary psychologists have not yet come to appreciate the unique nature of the development of the higher forms of behavior that are the object of our research. The child's cultural development, as we have already tried to establish, represents a completely new level of development, which not only is insufficiently studied but is usually not even distinguished in child psychology.

If we turn to the concept of development as it is used in modern psychology, we see that it still contains many problems that must be overcome. The first such problem, a regrettable vestige of prescientific thought in psychology, is latent, residual performism in the theory of child development. Old ideas and mistaken theories that disappear from science leave traces and remnants in the habits of thought. In spite of the fact that we long ago rejected the view that children are distinguished from adults only by the proportions of their bodies – in scale and size – this idea continues to exist in subtle form in child psychology. No essay in this field can now openly repeat the long-rejected falsehood that the child is an adult in miniature, but this view is nevertheless retained to this day in hidden form in almost every psychological investigation.

It is sufficient to say that the most important aspects of child psychology, such as study of memory, attention, and thought, are, in our estimation, only beginning to escape from this dead end and to recognize the process of psychological development in all its real complexity. But in the vast majority of cases, scientific research latently continues to maintain a view that would explain the child's development in purely quantitative terms.

Such a view was once adhered to in embryology. A theory based on this view is called "preformism" or a "theory of preformation". Its essence consists of the doctrine that the embryo contains an organism that is completely finished and formed in advance. The only difference is that it is of a smaller size. For example, according to this theory, the entire oak tree with its roots, trunk, and branches is contained in the acorn, the only difference being that it is an oak in miniature. With regard to humans, it is assumed that the fully formed human organism, in a much smaller form, is contained in the human seed.

From this point of view, the whole developmental process can be represented very simply: it consists purely of a quantitative increase in the size of what exists from the very beginning in the embryo. The embryo gradually grows and in this manner is converted into a mature organism. This point of view was abandoned long ago in embryology, and is of only historical interest. Meanwhile, in psychology it continues to exist in practice despite the fact that in theory it was long ago abandoned in this discipline as well.

From a theoretical standpoint, psychology long ago gave up the idea that the child's development is a purely quantitative process. Everyone agrees that the process is much more complex, and is not confined to quantitative changes alone. But in practice psychology still has not discovered the complex process of development in all its real fullness and has not identified all the qualitative changes and conversions involved in the child's development.

Claparède is quite correct when he says in his preface to Piaget's research that the problem of the child's thought is usually posed in purely quantitative terms in psychology and that only new work will permit us to redefine it as a qualitative problem. He points out that former analyses of the child's intellectual development usually relied on several additions and subtractions, the growth of new experience, and liberation from some mistakes. Modern investigations reveal to us that the very nature of the child's intellect gradually changes.

If we wanted to characterize in one general principle the basic requirement the problem of development poses for modern research, we would say that this requirement is that one must study the positive aspects of the child's behavior. This notion is in need of some further clarification.

Up to the present, all the psychological methods applied to the investigation of the normal and abnormal child's behavior, despite all the great variation and differences that exist among them, have one feature in common: negative characterization of the child. All of these methods tell us about what the child does not have or what is lacking in the child compared with the adult. In the abnormal child these deficiencies are specified in terms of the normal child. We are always confronted with a negative picture of the child. This does not tell us anything about the positive features that distinguish the child from the adult and the abnormal from the normal child.

Psychology is now confronted with the problem of how to capture these features in the child's behavior in all their richness and how to give a positive picture of the young individual. But this positive picture becomes possible only if we change our idea of child development in a fundamental way and if we take into consideration the fact that it represents a complex, dialectical process characterized by a multifaceted, periodic timetable, by disproportion in the development of various functions, by metamorphoses or qualitative conversion of one set of forms into others, by complex combinations of the processes of evolution and involution, by complex mixing of external and internal factors, and by the process of adaptation and surmounting difficulties.

The second feature that must be overcome in order to clear the way for modern genetic research is latent evolutionism, which even now continues to rule in child psychology. Evolution, or the development by means of gradual and slow accumulation of various changes, continues to be considered the only form of child development to account for all the known

CDA—C*

processes that enter into the composition of this general concept. In discussions of child development there is a latent analogue with processes of plant growth.

Child psychology does not want to know about the sudden, violent, and revolutionary changes that appear throughout ontogenesis and that are so often encountered in the history of cultural development. To naïve observers, revolution and evolution do not appear to coincide. Historical development seems to proceed along a straight path. When a revolution, the rupture of the historical fabric, or a leap occurs, naïve observers see nothing but catastrophe, gaps, and precipices. For them, historical progression stops at this point until it alights anew on a straight and smooth path.

Scientific observers, on the other hand, consider revolution and evolution as two mutually connected forms of development that presuppose one another. They see the sharp changes in the child's development that occur simultaneously with other, similar changes as the determining point in the whole line of development.

This position has special significance for the child's cultural development. As we shall see later, cultural development to a large degree results from such critical and uneven changes that arise in the child's development. The very essence of cultural development is in the collision of mature cultural forms of behavior with the primitive forms that characterize the child's behavior.

The immediate outcome of this is a change in the usual point of view about children's mental development and a change in the idea of the nature of its structure and flow. Usually, all the processes of child development are represented as smoothly flowing processes. In this sense embryological development is considered to be the standard form or model with which all other forms are compared. This type of development depends heavily on the external environment. The word *development* in its literal sense can be related most correctly to this, i.e., the unfolding of the possibilities contained in the undeveloped embryo. But, embryological development cannot be considered the model of any process of development, in the strict sense of the word; it could more readily be presented as its result or sum. It is already a settled, finished process that proceeds more or less smoothly.

One needs only to compare, as Darwin did, the evolution or emergence of animal species with embryological development to see the fundamental distinction between the one type of development and another. Species have emerged and have become extinct; they have undergone modification and have developed in the struggle for existence during the process of adapting to the surrounding environment. If we wanted to draw an analogy between the process of child development and some other process of development, we would be more likely to choose the evolution of animal species than embryological development. Child development is least of all like a smooth process sheltered from external influences. The child develops and changes in his/her active adaptation to the external world.

New forms emerge in this process, which does not simply involve a stereotyped reproduction of chains formed in advance. Any new stage in the development of the embryo, which is already contained in potential form in the preceding stage, arises as the unfolding of these inner potentialities. This is not so much the process of development as a process of growth and maturation. This type of process is also represented in the child's mental development. But in the history of cultural development, a second type of process occupies a much larger place. This process consists of having a new stage arise not from the unfolding of potentials contained in the preceding stage, but from actual collision of the organism and the environment and from active adaptation to the environment.

In modern child psychology we have two basic points of view on the process of child development. One of these goes back to Lamarck; the other, to Darwin. Bühler correctly says that one must view Koffka's book on the psychology of child development as an attempt to give Lamarck's idea modern psychological expression. The essence of this point of view is that in explaining lower forms of behavior we should use a principle that we usually use to explain higher forms of behavior, whereas, until now, psychologists have relied on principles used to explain primitive behavior to analyze a higher level. But the author states that this method has nothing in common with anthropomorphism. One of the important methodological achievements of modern psychology is the establishment of the extremely important difference between naïve and critical anthropomorphism.

While the naïve theory equates the functions at various levels of development, critical anthropomorphism begins with higher forms we know about in humans and traces the same psychological structure and its development further down the ladder of psychological development. The works of Köhler and Koffka are examples of this latter approach. These important exceptions notwithstanding, present theories simply transfer the explanatory principle found in the investigation of higher forms of behavior to the study of lower ones.

In contrast to this, Bühler looks on his work in child psychology as an attempt to continue Darwin's idea. Although Darwin knew only one area of development, Bühler points out two new areas that, in his opinion, corroborate Darwin's principle of selection. True, Bühler tries to combine Darwin's point of view with Lamarck's, using Hering's words:

From two theories – Lamarck's and Darwin's – developed with ingenious unilaterality, one general picture of the history of the development of all living things emerged for me. What happened with me was what happens when looking through a stereoscope. At first, one receives two impressions, which cross and contend with one another. Initially, they do not suddenly unite into one clear figure in three dimensions.

Continuing this simile, Bühler says:

Neo-Darwinism without Lamarck is too blind and immobile; but without Darwin, Lamarck does not arrive at the diversified richness of living forms. The theory of development will make a genuine step forward when it becomes more evident than it has up to now in child psychology how these two investigators are connected with one another.

Thus, we see that there is no unified concept of child psychology in the minds of various investigators. In Bühler's study it seems to us that his idea of different areas of development is extremely fruitful. Darwin himself said that he knew essentially only one area, but Bühler pointed out three distinct areas. In Bühler's opinion, the development of behavior goes through three basic stages and consists of the fact that there is "a change in the place of selection". Darwinian adaptation is accomplished by the elimination of less favorably organized individuals. Here we are talking about life and death. Adaptation by training is completely internal to the individual. It sorts out old modes of behavior and creates new ones. Its field of action is the area of bodily activity; and its cost is no longer life, but surplus body movements that are dissipated by the same means as in nature.

Bühler points out the futher possibility of development. If bodily movements are still too costly or for some reason insufficient, the field of action selection must be transferred to the area of representation and thoughts. Bühler writes:

It is necessary to reduce both higher forms of human invention and discovery and the most primitive ones with which we are acquainted in the child and the chimpanzee to one common denominator and to understand their equivalence.

Hence, the concept of internal probing or probes in thought, which are equivalent to a probe of an object itself, allows Bühler to extend Darwin's formula for selection to the whole field of human psychology. The emergence of the principle of selection, which is useful in three different spheres (instinct, training, and intellect) or fields of action, is explained by starting from one principle. This idea, in my opinion, is a consistent extension of the modern theory of development in the Darwinian tradition.

I should like to dwell in a bit more detail on this theory of three stages in the development of behavior. It really includes all of the most important forms of behavior, distributing them in accordance with three stages on the evolutionary ladder. Instinct, or the innate, inherited fund of behavioral modes, forms the first stage. The second stage consists of what Bühler called the stage of training or the stage of habits or conditioned reflexes, i.e., conditioned reflexes mastered and acquired in personal experience. Finally, and still higher, we have the third stage, the stage of intellect or intellectual responses that fulfill the function of adaptation to new conditions. In Thorndike's words, these constitute the organizing hierarchy of habits used for solving new problems.

The third step in this scheme has up to now remained debatable. It is the most complex and the least studied. Many authors try to limit the whole scheme of development to two stages, arguing that intellectual responses can be considered as especially complex forms of habits and therefore should not be isolated as a special class. It seems to me that contemporary experimental research provides solid foundations for considering this argument settled in favor of recognizing a third class. The intellectual response, characterized by several essential features in origin and functioning, even in the area of animal behavior, as Köhler's research showed, cannot be put in the same class as the mechanical formation of habits resulting from trial and error.

True, we must not forget that the stage of intellectual responses is very closely connected with the second stage in the development of behavior and relies on it. But this is a general phenomenon that applies equally to the second stage in the development of behavior.

In my opinion, one of the most fruitful theoretical ideas genetic psychology has adopted is that the structure of behavioral development to some degree resembles the geological structure of the earth's core. Research has established the presence of genetically differentiated layers in human behavior. In this sense the geology of human behavior is undoubtedly a reflection of "geological" descent and brain development.

If we turn to the history of brain development, we see what Kretschmer calls the law of stratification in the history of development. In the development of higher centers:

> . . . older, lower centers do not simply fall by the wayside. Rather, they work further in the general union as subordinated centers under the direction of higher ones so that, in the undamaged nervous system, it is usually impossible to define them separately.

The second pattern in brain development is what can be called the transition of functions from below upward:

> The subordinated centers do not fully retain their original type of functioning. Rather, they relinquish an essential part of their former functions to the new centers above them.

Only when the higher centers are damaged or their functioning is weakened does the "subordinated structure become independent and show us elements of its former type of functioning that have been retained".

Thus, we see that the lower centers are retained as subordinated structures in the development of higher ones and that brain development proceeds in accordance with the laws of stratification or construction of new levels on old ones. The old level does not die when a new one emerges, but is copied by the new one and dialectically negated by being transformed into it and existing in it. Instinct is not destroyed, but "copied" in conditioned reflexes as a function of the ancient brain, which is now to be found in the new one. Similarly, the conditioned reflex is "copied" in intellectual action, simultaneously existing and not existing in it. Two equally important problems confront science: it must be able to distinguish the lower stages in the higher, but it must also be able to reveal how the higher stages mature out of lower ones.

Werner has recently proposed that the behavior of the modern, cultural, adult human can be understood only "geologically", since various genetic layers, which reflect all the stages through which humans have traveled in their psychological development, are preserved in it. He says that psychological structure is characterized by not one, but several layers deposited on one another. Therefore, in a genetic examination even the individual displays certain phases in behavioral development that have already been completed genetically. Only a psychology based on elementary units sees human behavior as a united, closed sphere. Contrary to this, modern psychology is establishing that humans display various genetic states in their behavior. Werner sees the disclosure of this genetic, multilayered behavior as the main problem for modern research.

Blonsky's entire book *Psychological essays* is based on such a genetic analysis of human behavior. The new idea included in it is that everyday human behavior can be understood only by disclosing the presence of four general fundamental genetic stages through which behavioral development passes. Blonsky distinguishes sleeping life as the primitive state of life, primitive awakening life, life of incomplete awakening, and fully awakened life. This unified genetic scheme embraces both everyday human behavior and the history of its development, which spans many thousands of years. It would be more accurate to say that it considers everyday human behavior from the point of view of this long history. In this regard it provides a splendid picture of it since the historical point of view can be applied to general psychology, to the analysis of the behavior of modern humans.

The history of signs, however, brings us to a much more general law governing the development of behavior. Janet calls it the fundamental law of psychology. The essence of this law is that in the process of development, children begin to use the same forms of behavior in relation to themselves that others initially used in relation to them. Children master the social forms of behavior and transfer these forms to themselves. With regard to our area of interest, we could say that the validity of this law is nowhere more obvious than in the use of the sign. A sign is always originally a means used for social purposes, a means of influencing others, and only later becomes a means of influencing oneself. Many factual connections and dependencies formed in this way have been found in psychology. For example, we could point out what Baldwin discussed in his time and what Piaget has developed more recently in his research. This research has shown that there definitely is a genetic tie between a child's argumentation and his/her reflections. The child's logic corroborates this tie. Logical argumentation first appears among children and only later is united within the individual and internalized. Child logic develops only along with the growth of the child's social speech and whole experience. In connection with this it is interesting to note that in the child's behavioral development, the genetic role of the collective changes. The higher functions of child thought at first appear in the collective life of children in the form of argumentation and only later develop into reflection for the individual child. Piaget established that it is the emerging transition from preschool to school age that results in the change in the forms of collective activity, and that on this basis the very thought of the child is altered. He writes:

> Reflection can be viewed as internal argumentation. One needs only to remember speech, which initially is a means of social interaction and only later a means of thought (in the form of inner speech), in order for the applicability of this law to the history of the child's cultural development to become quite clear.

Nevertheless, we would have said very little about the significance of this law if we were unable to show the concrete forms in which it is manifested in cultural development. Here let us link the action of this law with the four stages in behavioral development mentioned earlier. If we take this law into consideration, it becomes quite clear why everything that is internal to higher mental functions was at one time external. If it is correct that the sign initially is a means of social interaction and only later becomes a means of behavior for the individual, it is quite clear that cultural developmcnt is bascd on thc usc of signs and their inclusion in a general system of behavior that initially was external and social. In general, we could say that the relations among higher mental functions were at some earlier time actual relations among people. I shall relate to myself as people relate to me. Just as verbal thought is the transferal of speech to an internal level, and just as reflection is the transferal of argumentation to an internal level, the mental function of the word,[1] as Janet demonstrated, cannot be explained, except through a system extending beyond individual humans. The words first function is its social function; and if we want to trace how it functions in the behavior of an individual, we must consider how it used to function in social behavior.

I shall not evaluate the validity of the main body of Janet's theory of speech. I want only to say that the research method he proposes is indisputably correct from the point of view of the history of the child's development. According to Janet, the word initially was a command to others and then underwent a complex history consisting of imitations, changes of functions, etc. Only gradually was it separated from action. According to Janet, it is always a command, and that is why it is the basic means of mastering behavior. Therefore, if we want to clarify genetically the origins of the voluntary function of the word and why the word overrides motor responses, we must inevitably arrive at the real function of commanding in both ontogenesis and phylogenesis. Janet says that behind the word's power over mental functions lies the real power of the supervisor over a subordinate. Relations among mental functions genetically must be linked to the real relations among people. Regulation of others' behavior by means of the word gradually leads to the development of verbalized behavior of the people themselves.

Speech plays a central role in the individual's social ties and cultural behavior. Therefore, the individual's history is especially instructive, and the transition from the social to the individual function emerges with particular clarity. It is no coincidence that Watson sees the essential distinctions between inner and external speech as being that inner speech is for individual rather than social forms of adaptation.

If we turn our attention to types of social connection, we discover that even relations among people are of two types. It is possible to have direct

---

[1]Throughout this section Vygotsky consistently uses the term *word* [*slovo*] where it may appear to many readers that *speech* [*rech'*] would be more appropriate. Since Vygotsky's emphasis here is on how signs mediate social and individual activity rather than on the process of speech activity, it would seem that his use of *word* rather than *speech* is significant. Therefore, I have maintained this distinction in my translation. It should be noted, however, that one should not take the term *word* too literally. Since it is used in connection with Vygotsky's general concern with sign mediation, it does not refer solely to morphological units; rather, phrases, sentences, and entire texts fall under this category as well. – J.V.Wertsch

and mediated relations among people. Direct relations are those based on instinctive forms of expressive movement and action. When Köhler describes how apes wishing to get other apes to go with them somewhere look the other ones in the eyes, push them, and start the very action toward which they want to persuade their friends, we have a classic case of a direct social bond. It may be noted that all descriptions of chimpanzees' social behavior abound in examples of this type. One animal influences another either by means of actions or by means of instinctive, automatic, expressive movements. Contact is established through touching, cries, or gazes. The entire history of early forms of social contact in the child is full of examples of this type. We see contact here established by means of a cry, seizing with the hands, and gazes.

At a higher level of development, however, mediated relations among people emerge. The essential feature of these relations is the sign, which aids in establishing this social interaction. It goes without saying that the higher form of social interaction, mediated by the sign, grows from natural forms of direct social interaction, yet is distinguished from it in an essential way.

Thus, the imitation and division of functions among people are a basic mechanism for the modification and transformation of the individual's functions. If we examine the initial forms of labor activity, we see that the function of execution of orders and the function of giving directions are separate. A major step in the evolution of labor is that the work of the supervisor and that of the slave are united in one person. As we shall see below, this is the fundamental mechanism of voluntary attention and labor.

In this sense, the child's entire cultural development goes through three basic stages, which, using the breakdown introduced by Hegel, we can describe as follows.

As an example, let us consider the history of the development of the indicatory gesture. We shall see later that it plays an extremely important role in the development of the child's speech and in general is largely the historic basis of all higher forms of behavior. In investigating its history we notice that at first the indicatory gesture is simply an unsuccessful grasping movement directed at an object and designating a forthcoming action. The child tries to grasp an object that is too far away. His/her hands, reaching toward the object, stop and hover in midair. The fingers make grasping movements. This is the initial situation for all further development; it is the first point where we see movements we have a right to call indicatory gestures. Here we have a child's movements that do nothing more than objectively indicate an object.

When the mother comes to the aid of the child and comprehends his/her movement as an indicator, the situation changes in an essential way. The indicatory gesture becomes a gesture for others. In response to the child's unsuccessful grasping movement, a response emerges not on the part of the object, but on the part of another human. Thus, other people introduce the primary sense into this unsuccessful grasping movement. And only afterward, owing to the fact they have already connected the unsuccessful grasping movement with the whole objective situation, do children themselves begin to use the movement as an indication. The functions of the movement itself have undergone a change here: from a movement directed toward an object it has become a movement directed toward another human being. The grasping is converted into an indication. Thanks to this, the movement is reduced and abbreviated, and the form of the indicatory gesture is elaborated. We can now say that it is a gesture for oneself. However, this movement does not become a gesture for oneself except by first being an indication, i.e., functioning objectively as an indication and gesture for others, being comprehended and understood by surrounding people as an indicator. Thus, the child is the last to become conscious of his/her gesture. Its significance and functions first are created by the objective situation and then by the people surrounding the child. The indicatory gesture initially relies on a movement to point to what others understand and only later becomes an indicator for the child.

We could therefore say that it is through others that we develop into ourselves and that this is true not only with regard to the individual but with regard to the history of every function. The essence of the process of cultural development also consists of this. This cultural development is expressed in a purely logical form. The individual develops into what he/she is through what he/she produces for others. This is the process of the formation of the individual. For the first time in psychology, we are facing the extremely important problem of the relationship of external and internal mental functions. As has already been said, it becomes clear here why it is necessary that everything internal in higher forms was external, i.e., for others it was what it now is for oneself. Any higher mental function necessarily goes through an external stage in its development because it is initially a social function. This is the center of the whole problem of internal and external behavior. It is true that many authors long ago pointed out the problem of internalization or the transferal of behavior to an internal level. Kretschmer viewed the law of nervous activity in terms of this process. Bühler reduces the whole evolution of behavior to the fact that the selection of useful actions is internalized.

But this is not what we have in mind when we speak of the external stage in the child's cultural development. When we speak of a process, "external" means "social". Any higher mental function was external because it was social at some point before becoming an internal, truly mental function. It was first a social relation between two people. The means of influencing oneself were originally means of influencing others or others' means of influencing an individual.

In the child we may follow the steps in the changes of these three basic forms of development in speech functions. First, a word must have sense, i.e., a relation to an object. There must be an objective bond between the word and what it signifies. If this does not exist, further development of the word is impossible. Moreover, this objective bond between the word and the object must be used functionally by the adult as a means of social interaction with the child; only then does the word acquire significance for the child. Hence, a word's meaning first exists objectively for others and only subsequently begins to exist for the child. All the basic forms of the adult's verbal social interaction with the child later become mental functions.[2]

We could formulate the general genetic law of cultural development as follows: Any function in the child's cultural development appears twice, or on two planes. First it appears on the social plane, and then on the psychological plane. First it appears between people as an interpsychological category, and then within the child as an intrapsychological category. This is equally true with regard to voluntary attention, logical memory, the formation of concepts, and the development of volition. We may consider this position as a law in the full sense of the word, but it goes without saying that internalization transforms the process itself and changes its structure and functions. Social relations or relations among people genetically underlie all higher functions and their relationships. Hence, one of the basic principles of volition is that of the division of functions among people, the new division into two parts of what is now combined into one. 'It is the development of a higher mental process in the drama that takes place among people. Therefore, the sociogenesis of higher forms of behavior is the basic goal toward which the child's cultural development leads us.

The word *social* when applied to our subject has great significance. Above all, in the widest sense of the word, it means that everything that is cultural is social. Culture is the product of social life and human social activity. That is why just by raising the question of cultural development of behavior we are directly introducing the social plane of development. Further, one could point to the fact that the sign, like the tool, is separate from the individual and is in essence a social organ or a social means. We

---

[2]In order to be consistent with the translation practices first adopted in Vygotsky's book *Thought and language*, I have used the words *sense* [*smysl*] and *meaning* [*znachenie*] here. It seems that in this paragraph, however, Vygotsky is using the term *sense* to deal with a problem of reference. In general, the reader should note that in the translations of Vygotsky's writings, these terms are not used in the way they are generally used in contemporary linguistics and language philosophy in the West. Since the translation of Frege's writings into English, the term *sense* has been used in the West to signify what Vygotsky termed *meaning* [*znachenie*]. The potential confusion is compounded by the fact that some writings in English use the term *meaning* to signify what Vygotsky meant by *sense* [*smysl*]. Vygotsky's final and most authoritative analysis of sense and meaning may be found in the last chapter of *Thought and language*. – J.V. Wertsch.

may even go further and say that all higher functions are not developed in biology and not in the history of pure phylogenesis. Rather, the very mechanism underlying higher mental functions is a copy from social interaction; all higher mental functions are internalized social relationships. These higher mental functions are the basis of the individual's social structure. Their composition, genetic structure, and means of action – in a word, their whole nature – is social. Even when we turn to mental processes, their nature remains quasi-social. In their own private sphere, human beings retain the functions of social interaction.

To paraphrase a well-known position of Marx's, we could say that humans' psychological nature represents the aggregate of internalized social relations that have become functions for the individual and forms of his/her structure. We do not want to say that this is the meaning of Marx's position, but we see in this position the fullest expression of that toward which the history of cultural development leads us.

In the ideas developed here we have tried to convey in summary form the basic pattern we have observed in the history of cultural development. They are directly connected with the problem of the child collective. On their basis we have seen that higher mental functions, such as the function of the word, are first divided and distributed among people, and then become functions of the individual. If we analyzed only the individual's behavior, it would be impossible to expect anything like this. Formerly, psychologists tried to derive social behavior from individual behavior. They investigated individual responses observed in the laboratory and then studied them in the collective. They studied how the individual's responses change in the collective setting. Posing the problem in such a way is, of course, quite legitimate; but genetically speaking, it deals with the second level in behavioral development. The first problem is to show how the individual response emerges from the forms of collective life. In contrast to Piaget, we hypothesize that development does not proceed toward socialization, but toward the conversion of social relations into mental functions. Therefore, the psychology of the collective in child development emerges in an entirely new light. Usually, the question has been asked, How does one or another child behave in the collective? We ask how the collective creates higher mental functions in the child. It has been suggested that a function is in the individual's head in a semiprepared or rudimentary form and that it matures in the collective, is made more complex, is raised to a higher level and enriched or, conversely, is impeded, neutralized, etc. We now have grounds for thinking that with regard to higher mental functions, just the opposite is true. Functions are first formed in the collective as relations among children and then become mental functions for the individual. In particular, it was formerly thought that each child was able to reflect on, give reasons for, construct proofs for, and search for the foundations of any position. An argument was spawned out of the clash of such reflections. But, in fact, matters stand otherwise. Research shows that reflection is spawned from argument. The study of all the other mental functions leads us to the same conclusion.

[. . .]

Let us now turn to some concrete problems in the development of higher mental functions. By examining them we will be able to understand better the data from the psychology of education and the child.

In general, can we apply the concept of development to the changes that concern us? After all, when we speak of the idea of development, we have in mind a very complex process that is defined by a number of features. The first feature of this process is that with any change, the substratum at the basis of the developing phenomenon remains the same. The second feature is that, to a large extent, any change has an internal character. We should not label as development a change that was completely unconnected with an internal process in the organism and is a form of an activity. Thus, the second basic feature that characterizes the concept of development is the unity of the entire process of development, the internal connection between a past stage of development and the emerging change.

With this in mind, we must point out that for a very long time, investigators in child psychology refused to consider the child's cultural experience as an act of development. It was usually said with respect to this: what can be labeled development is what proceeds from the inside out. What goes from outside in is schooling, because we never find a child who would naturally develop arithmetic functions in nature; but as soon as the child attains, say, school age, or somewhat earlier, he/she grasps a number of arithmetic concepts and logical operations in their outer form from surrounding people. It would seem, therefore, that we cannot say that the eight-year-old's acquisition of addition and subtraction and the nine-year-old's acquisition of multiplication and division are natural results of the child's development. These are external changes coming from the environment and are not in any way a process of internal development.

However, deeper study of how the child's cultural experience is accumulated has shown that several of the most important features necessary for applying the concept of development are present in this case.

As research has demonstrated, the first feature is that any new form of cultural experience does not simply come from outside, independently of the state of the organism at a given point of development. The fact is that the organism that is mastering external influences masters a number of forms of behavior or assimilates these forms depending on its level of mental development. Something similar to what is called nourishment in the field of physical growth occurs – that is, the child masters certain external things. However, these external materials are reprocessed and assimilated in the organism.

For example, let us assume that a child who does not yet know the cultural forms of arithmetic enters school and begins to learn the four arithmetic operations. The question arises: Can one demonstrate that this mastery of the four arithmetic operations occurs as a process of development, i.e., is determined by the presence of (a certain) knowledge of arithmetic with which the child entered school?

It turns out that such is indeed the case. This provides a foundation for knowing what to teach at different ages and at different levels of instruction and explains the fact that during the seventh to eighth year it becomes possible for the child to master these operations for the first time, because the development of knowledge about arithmetic has occurred in the child. If we examine children in grades one through three in elementary school,[3] we find that for two to three years the child still displays traces of the preschool, natural arithmetic with which he/she entered school. Likewise, it turns out that when the child is learning various operations in school in what would appear to be purely external form, in reality he/she is mastering any new operation as a result of the process of development.

I shall try to show this at the end of the paper, when I analyze the concepts of mastery, invention, and imitation, i.e., all the means with the help of which new forms of behavior are mastered. I shall attempt to show that even when it would seem that the behavioral form is mastered by pure imitation, one cannot exclude the possibility that it arose as a result of development, not simply by imitation.

In order to be persuaded of this, it is sufficient to demonstrate in an experiment that any new form of behavior, even one mastered from outside, has various features. It is natural that such a form is built on the preceding one and that it becomes possible only on the basis of the preceding one. If someone were to succeed in showing experimentally that it was possible to master some cultural operation directly in its most developed stage, it would have been demonstrated that we were not dealing with development in this case, but rather with a superficial mastery, i.e., with some kind of change by virtue of purely superficial influences. However, studies have shown us that every external action is the result of an internal genetic pattern. On the basis of experiments we can say that the child – even the prodigy – can never master the last stage in the development of operations immediately or any earlier than by going through the first two stages. In other words, the inculcation of a new cultural operation is broken down into a series of links or stages that are internally connected with one another and follow one another. Once we realize this, we have the basis for applying

---

[3]In the Soviet Union children enter first grade at age seven. – J.V.Wertsch.

the concept of development to the accumulation of internal experience. This is the second feature we spoke of earlier.

It is clear that this will be a completely different kind of development from the development studied in the emergence of the child's elementary functions. This is an essential distinction. We know that in the development of fundamental forms of human adaptation, in the human struggle with nature, the essential distinction between zoological and historical human development is that in the first case, anatomical changes occur in the organism and the biological development takes place in the living organism on the basis of the structure's organic changes. In the second type, extensive adaptation to nature occurred in human history without such organic changes.

Finally, one must point to the connection between the child's natural behavioral development based on organic maturation and the types of development we have dealt with. This connection has a revolutionary rather than an evolutionary character. Development does not take place by means of gradual alteration or change, by the accumulation of small increments, the sum of which finally provides some kind of essential change: From the very beginning we observe a revolutionary type of development. In other words, we see sharp and fundamental changes in the very type of development, in the motivating factors of this process. It is well known that this mix of revolutionary and evolutionary changes does not exclude the possibility of applying the concept of development to this process.

[. . .]

Any development in children's arithmetic development must first go through a natural or primitive stage. Simply by looking at two groups of objects, can three-year-olds decide which group of objects – three or seven apples – is larger? They can. And in the case of a more complex differentiation – one group contains 16 and the other 19 apples – can children give the same answer? No, they cannot. In other words, first we have a natural stage, operating purely by natural laws, when children simply compare the necessary quantity by sight. However, we know that children very quickly and quite imperceptibly move from this stage to another. At this later stage, when they must ascertain where more objects are, most children in a cultural situation begin to count. Sometimes they do this even before they understand what counting is. They count, "One, two, three . . ." and so on despite the fact that they do not yet understand genuine counting. Shtern's observations verify that many children begin to count before understanding what they are doing. For example, if we ask such a child, "How many fingers are on your hand?" he/she counts the ordinal series and says, "Five". If we say to him/her, "How many do I have? Count again!" the child replies, "No. I can't". This means the child can apply this series only to his/her own fingers, not to the fingers of others.

Another example from Shtern is that the child counts fingers: "One, two, three, four, five". When asked, "How many do you have in all?" he/she answers, "Six". The child is asked "Why six?" He/she answers, "Because this is the fifth, and in all there are six". the child has no clear concept of the sum. In other words, he/she masters this operation in a purely external, "magical" way, without yet knowing its inner relationships.

Finally, from this stage children move on to genuine counting. They begin to understand what it means to count their fingers; but nevertheless, they still count by means of external signs. At this stage children count mainly with their fingers. For example, when given the problem "Here are seven apples. If we take two away, how many remain?" – children must switch from apples to fingers. In this case fingers play the role of signs: children put seven fingers up and then take two away, and five remain. In other words, they solve the problem with the help of external signs. It is interesting to observe what happens when children are prohibited from moving their hands. It turns out that they are unable to carry out the corresponding operations.

But we know quite well that children move very quickly from counting on their fingers to counting mentally. If older children need to subtract two from seven, they no longer count on their fingers, but mentally. In this case children display two basic types of rooting. On the one hand, counting in one's head is undifferentiated rooting. Children have rooted the undifferentiated external series (for example, counting to oneself: one, two, three, etc.) internally. On the other hand, children display rooting of the juncture type. This takes place if they have practiced and then say, finally, that there is no need for an intermediate operation and come up with the result directly. This occurs with any calculation or figuring with "tables". In this instance, all mediating operations are dropped, and the stimulus produces the needed result directly.

Another example is in children's language development. At first children are at the natural, primitive, or, properly speaking, preverbal stage. They scream and utter identical sounds in different situations. This is purely external action. At this stage, when they need something they resort to natural means, using immediate or conditioned reflexes. Then a new stage emerges. It consists of children's discovering the basic external laws or outer structure of speech. They notice that every object has its word and that a given word is the conventional signification for a particular object. For a long time children consider this word to be one of the qualities of the given object. Research conducted with older children has shown that this relationship in which words are treated as inherent features of objects persists for a very long time.

There is an interesting philological anecdote that demonstrates the kind of relationship primitive people have to their language. Consider the story in Fedorchenko's book about how a soldier argued with a German about what language was the best and most correct. The Russian argues that Russian is the best and says in this connection: "For instance, let us take a knife [*nozh*]: it will be *messer* in German, *couteau* in French, and *knife* in English. But in fact, it is a *nozh* after all, and this means that our word is the most correct". In other words, it is assumed that a thing's name is the expression for its true essence.

Shtern's second example concerning the child who speaks two languages reflects the same situation. When the child is asked which language is correct, he/she says that German is correct because *wasser* is what can be drunk, not what is called *l'eau* in French. Thus, we see that children create a connection between a thing's name and the thing itself and consider an object's name one of its qualities along with other qualities. In other words, the external connection of stimuli or the connection of things is accepted as the psychological connection.

It is well known that such a magical relationship to words exists among primitive people. For example, among people who have grown up under the influence of religious prejudices, such a magical relationship toward words exists: there are words that must not be spoken. If one must talk about something, say, about a deceased person, then the following words are added to this: "Don't talk about that in your home". It is forbidden to name the devil because if he is mentioned, he himself will appear. The same applies with regard to words that designate shameful things: they acquire tinges of these shameful things, and it becomes shameful to pronounce them. In other words, this is a remnant of the transference of the qualities of the object designated by signs to the conventional signs themselves.

From this stage in which the word is considered to be an inherent property of the object, children move very quickly to the conventional signification of the word, i.e., they use words as signs, especially in the stage of "egocentric" speech, about which we have already spoken – the stage at which children can use speech to plan the most complex operations they must accomplish. Finally, we know that from this stage children go on to the last stage; this is the stage of inner speech, in the proper sense of the word.

Thus, in children's speech development we have identified these stages: the natural stage or "magical" stage, in which they see the word as a property of the object; the external stage; and then inner speech. This last stage is thought itself.

One can speak separately about all these examples. However, in light of everything that has been said, we accept the notion that the basic stages in the formation of memory, volition, arithmetic, and speech are the same stages we have described and the stages through which children develop with respect to all higher mental functions.

II WHAT DEVELOPS?

5 On the Structure-Dependent Nature of Stages of Cognitive Development

Frank C. Keil

In the last several years there has been a strong trend in cognitive development research raising serious questions about the reality of stages in cognitive development. In increasing numbers, investigators are challenging stage theories such as those of Piaget, Bruner, and Vygotsky. The pattern has been to question whether young children really lack a certain type of competence that older children have; and the studies have generally argued that, if careful enough tasks are used, young children are not qualitatively different from older ones. Of course, if they are not qualitatively different, then there can be no stages of cognitive development for that type of knowledge.

One of the most influential critiques along these lines was Fodor's (1972) retrospective review of Vygotsky's (1934/1962) *Thought and Language* which argued that there has been little evidence for general representational shifts in the course of development. Instead, Fodor suggested that roughly the same computational and representational systems are shared by individuals of all ages and that what develops is an increasing ability to use these systems in a wider and wider range of tasks.

Rozin (1976) echoed this notion when he argued for increasing access to underlying competencies as one of the main mechanisms of developmental change. In his view, children may not differ from adults in terms of basic underlying abilities or competencies but more in how easily they can apply those abilities to a wide range of potentially relevant tasks.

These theoretical proposals have been supported by a number of different

Source: Levin, I. (Ed.) (1986). *Stage and structure: Reopening the debate*. New Jersey: Ablex, pp. 144–163.

research programs that seem to argue against qualitative changes in either mode of representation or of processing. For example, in contrast to the Piagetian accounts of number conservation, Gelman and her associates (e.g., Gelman & Gallistel, 1978) have found that preschoolers are able to conserve number, if certain task factors irrelevant to the conservation paradigms are controlled. Thus, if the size of the numerical display is made small enough and if the two displays to be compared are presented in an appropriate manner, 3-year-olds are able to show the hallmarks of conservers. Gelman argues that these children normally fail on the traditional Piagetian tasks, not because they are unable to engage in concrete operational thought, as the Piagetian account would hold, but because memory limitations and other irrelevant factors interfere with the application of their basic competencies.

A different example is research on classification, where researchers have again argued that very young children can engage in types of cognition that meet all the criteria of concrete operational thought. Rosch, Mervis, Gray, Johnson, and Boyes-Braem (1976), for example, showed that the same child who seemed to classify in a completely preoperational way for some classes of objects could behave in a concrete operational manner with other objects that used the more salient differences between members of basic level categories. Similarly, Markman (Markman & Siebert, 1976) has shown that the ability to apprehend subset/superset relations is present in preschoolers, if the classes are united by certain concepts that make them be viewed as collections rather than classes. A group of blue blocks is judged correctly to be less than all of the blocks present, if all of the blocks are referred to as "the pile of blocks" and not if referred to as "blocks".

The same sort of account has been repeated in several other domains as well. One final example is causal knowledge, where a number of investigators such as Bullock, Gelman, and Baillargeon (1982) argue that young preschoolers, if assessed carefully enough, show almost all the aspects of mature causal knowledge. Bullock et al. describe a series of studies concerned with three separate principles that adults use to understand causal relations: determinism (physical events must have causes), priority (causal events must precede effects), and mechanism (causes bring about effects by a kind of transfer of "causal impetus"). In contrast to earlier work suggesting dramatic qualitative shifts in the nature of causal thinking, they describe a series of studies showing that children as young as 3 years adhere to each of these principles. They conclude (p. 251) that

> This means that the development of causal understanding is more a process of learning where, when, and how to apply the rules of reasoning than figuring out what those rules might be . . . The differences that exist [between pre-

schoolers' causal thinking and that of adults, F. Keil] arise not because the child and adult think about things in fundamentally different ways, but because the child's thought is more constrained by context, complexity and verbal demands, limiting the scope and flexibility with which the child can apply his or her knowledge.

What develop, according to these accounts (e.g., Fodor, 1972; Gelman & Gallistel, 1978; Rozin, 1976), are a variety of factors, none of which strongly suggests qualitative change. Thus, there is increasing access to the same competence, enabling its use in an ever broadening range of tasks. There is also the adoption of new strategies, which represent not so much a change in competence as of choice. Finally, there is increasing differentiation and complexity of knowledge, but not necessarily any change in its fundamental nature.

Elsewhere (Keil, 1981) I have interpreted research along these lines as suggestive of a constraints-oriented view of cognitive development of the sort that Chomsky (1980) has proposed in linguistic theory. Under this view, acquiring complex knowledge would be impossible, if all of us did not share certain a priori constraints that restrict the range of hypotheses to be made about the structure of what is learned. Throughout development, the child is guided by sets of constraints that represent a kind of competence that is always present, namely, the set of possible, or natural, knowledge structures in a domain. In this account the main phenomena of development are increasing differentiation and increasing access. If our knowledge structures and procedures in various domains are always guided by constraints, then little qualitative change would appear possible.

To summarize, one line of recent research in cognitive development argues that, whereas children may differ from adults, they do not differ in any qualitative way that suggests general stages of mental representation or processing. This perspective might nonetheless be regarded as structuralist in that much of the work is devoted to uncovering structural descriptions of the basic competencies and constraints in various domains of cognition. One can be interested in the structural principles of mind without being a stage theorist. The converse, being a stage theorist without being a structuralist, does not seem possible. The very notion of a cognitive stage would seem to require structural descriptions of knowledge at various points in development. Without such descriptions it is difficult to know how to evaluate whether the developmental differences are qualitative versus quantitative.

I still embrace the constraints perspective; it represents a fundamental component of any account of knowledge acquisition. It is incorrect, however, to assume that this perspective and the above trends in cognitive development research imply that there cannot be clear, qualitative, stagelike changes in development as well. Demonstrations of core competencies in surprisingly young children are not the entire story; nor are increasing access and gradual differentiation along the strict guidelines of a priori constraints the only types of change. While each of these undoubtedly exists, and while the previously described studies do suggest that there is very little evidence for across the board developmental shifts in manner of representation or processing, there are other types of change that do not fit into the patterns just described.

CASES WHERE QUALITATIVE SHIFTS DO OCCUR

Some types of conceptual change have traditionally been used as support for the idea of global representational shifts in development. Consider, for example, a pattern of change in conceptual structure that has led developmental theorists over the years to propose general shifts from the holistic to the analytic, or from the concrete to the abstract, or from the perceptual to the conceptual (e.g., Anglin, 1984; Bruner, Olver, and Greenfield, 1966; Werner, 1948).

Each of these theories has been grounded in robust observations about the sorts of errors that children seem to make in using and talking about concepts; however, each of them has also failed to recognize how closely the shifts are tied into the particular concepts involved. My students and I have been investigating a shift in conceptual structure for word meanings that appears to reflect the same phenomenon that motivated these theories. We have described it as a shift from representations based on features that are merely characteristic of an entity to representations that emphasize defining features. There are numerous instances from past literature that illustrate the idea. For example, many investigators have noted that young children seem to represent the meanings of kinship terms solely in terms of the properties of typical examples or symptoms (e.g., Piaget, 1928; Vygotsky, 1962; Haviland & Clark, 1974; Landau, 1982). Thus a grandmother might be initially represented as an elderly woman with a certain set of behavioral dispositions. Only later does the child begin to realize that these characteristic features are only characteristic and that what really counts for someone to be a grandmother are the various kinship relations that define the concept.

We (Keil & Batterman, 1984) have documented repeatedly the occurrence of such a shift by using stories that have either all the defining features of a concept but highly uncharacteristic ones, or vice versa. Thus a child will first state that the story with highly characteristic features but incorrect defining ones describes a valid instance, while rejecting the one with correct defining features but highly uncharacteristic ones. An older child will do the opposite. The +characteristic/−defining (+c/−d) story for "uncle" described a fellow "roughly the age of your father who brought you presents on your brithday, visited a lot on weekends and watched football with your dad, but who wasn't related to anyone in the family". The −c/+d story described "a 2-year-old infant who was your father's brother". For almost all terms studied, one sees crossovers from an emphasis on defining features to an emphasis on characteristic ones, as shown in Fig.5.1.

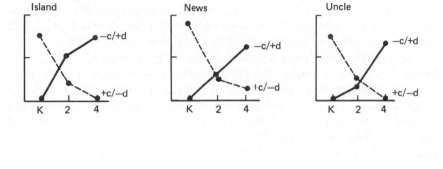

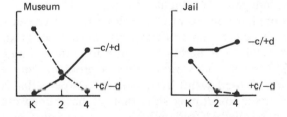

FIG. 5.1. Examples of the characteristic-to-defining shift for five terms; the Y-axis represents extent to which children judge story to be valid instance of concept.

These results might at first be interpreted as evidence for a general stagelike transition in cognitive development from characteristically based concepts to more definitionally based ones. There is an additional finding, however, that challenges such an interpretation: the shift can occur at radically different times for different concepts. Thus, most preschoolers may have already made the shift for some concepts, while 12-year-olds still have not made it for others. It is difficult to argue that such a shift represents merely a horizontal décalage for a general stage, when the stage seems to cover such a large age range. This is especially true, given that comparable shifts occur in most adults, as will be described later. If one does wish to call it a décalage, then the décalage becomes the entire developmental phenomenon and the general stage becomes irrelevant.

This claim that the occurrence of the shift is dependent on local knowledge structures gains further support from two additional lines of research: work with terms from different semantic fields and demonstrations that the shift occurs between novice and expert adults. In a follow-up study, we have looked at how and when such shifts occur for closely related sets of terms that form what are normally known as semantic fields (cf. Lehrer, 1978). These would include kinship terms (e.g., aunt, uncle, grandmother), cooking terms (e.g., boil, bake, fry), and moral act terms (e.g., lie, steal, cheat). In all cases we had two stories, one that described an entity or activity that had many of the most salient characteristic features of a word, but incorrect defining ones, and one that had the opposite.

The results support the claim that the shift is structure dependent, because it occurs at roughly the same time for terms within each field but at widely differing times for the sets of terms across fields. Thus, children generally shifted at a much earlier age for moral act terms than they did for cooking terms. Figure 5.2 illustrates how the shift occurred at different ages depending on the concepts involved. The crossover points on each graph can be construed as roughly the ages at which the shift occurred. This pattern of results does not fit well with the proposal that there is a general-content independent stagelike change.

A second example comes from Chi, Feltovich, and Glaser (1981), who examined differences between adult experts and novices in knowledge of classical physics. While their method was quite different and simply involved having the subjects sort out various physics problems into equivalence classes, the results showed a shift from novices to experts that is very much like the characteristic-to-defining shift that we have uncovered. Novices tended to classify problems based on highly characteristic features that had little to do with underlying principles of physics. Thus they would sort all the ramp problems in one pile and all the pendulum ones in another, and so on. The experts sorted on a completely different basis that involved reference to basic laws of physics such as Newton's Force laws, Conservation of Energy, etc. The occurrence of such shifts in adults again argues against an across-the-board developmental shift. The expert/novice contrast is not in itself a complete description of child/adult differences, but it does illustrate the limitations of a general stage theory explanation for the characteristic-to-defining shift.

A final example of the characteristic-to-defining shift comes from a training study that we are just now transcribing and analyzing. It is particularly relevant because of the major role that training studies have played in discussions of general stages of cognitive development. In essence, we attempted to teach children the meanings of novel words that come from

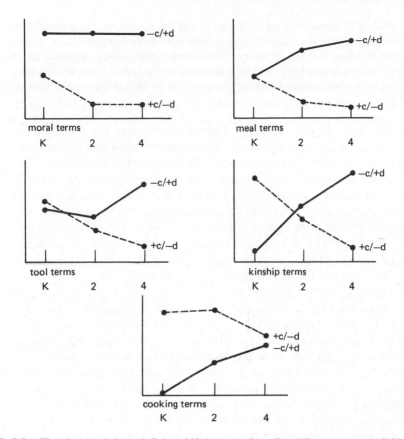

FIG. 5.2. The characteristic-to-defining shift in terms from five different semantic fields.

various semantic fields. For example, we taught children the meanings of new cooking terms (e.g., sauté, baste) and new agricultural terms (e.g., mulch, irrigate) by giving them explanations that included clear definitions as well as several typical examples. The following two passages illustrate the explanations we gave, including the special care we took to present the defining properties twice, once at the beginning and once at the end of the story:

> *Baste:* To baste is to wet a food with something while it's cooking. For example, at Thanksgiving, your mom probably basted your turkey by brushing on melted butter and meat juices every half hour so the meat would stay moist.
>
> So to baste is to wet something every so often with a liquid while you're cooking it.

Mulch: To mulch is to put something over the land so that things will grow better on it. I'm sure you've seen people mulch the land in Ithaca. People often put lots and lots of wood chips around rose bushes or young plants here in the winter to keep them from freezing and to keep the water in the soil.

So mulching is when you cover the ground to help things you've planted there grow better.

After making sure that the children understood the explanations for these novel words, we followed the procedure used in prior studies and asked them whether +characteristic/−defining and −characteristic/+defining stories described valid instances. We had two hypotheses, and it looks as if both will be supported. The first was that, even when given an explanation with a clear definition, young children may nonetheless tend to represent the meaning in terms of characteristic features. Based on preliminary scoring, there is a significant main effect of age with an increasing reliance on defining features in older children. A second expected pattern was that the shift would not occur at the same time for all concepts; and this too, appears to be happening. Children tended to shift at an earlier age for the cooking terms than they did for the agricultural terms, although the effect is not as strong as in the semantic field study described previously.

This study illustrates that the effectiveness of training may depend not so much on a general cognitive awareness afforded by a particular stage of cognitive development as it does on the degree of knowledge in the domain in which the novel concept is being taught. Only when a child is beginning to master several more familiar cooking terms does s/he begin to develop an understanding of what the underlying dimensions are that are relevant to the various cooking verbs and what sorts of relations are likely to be defined when learning new ones. More generally, success and failure in training studies should not necessarily be regarded as evidence for a general stage of cognitive development when a more local knowledge specific explanation will suffice.

The characteristic-to-defining shift is only one case of several where a general stagelike phenomenon has been shown to be more dependent on specific knowledge structures than was previously thought. Much of the classical developmental literature assumed that younger children had qualitatively different memories and memory procedures that reflected a general change in representation and/or processing. Recent studies, however, suggest an alternative account. For example, Chi (1978) and others have used the expert/novice distinction to show that expert kindergarteners can show adultlike performance on tasks involving their own expertise and childlike performance with less familiar domains, whereas adults who are novices in the children's area of expertise might show the opposite pattern. Consequently, differences in memory performance reflect not so much changes in underlying competence as they do the increasing enrichment of knowledge in different domains.

The discussion up to this point leaves us with several loose ends. One concerns the relations between the two views that have been used to criticize the stage theories, the early competency view and the knowledge enrichment view. How do these two views fit with each other? Can they be put together into one theory or must one flourish at the expense of the other?

A second issue concerns interactions between various domains of cognition. What happens when a qualitative shift occurs in one particular domain that is used in a wide range of cognitive tasks? Do such cases exist, and if so do they not in effect result in general stages of cognitive development? Second, to what extent are there interdependencies between domains such that knowledge must reach a certain form in one before a shift can occur in the other?

A third and related issue asks what else there is beyond expert/novice differences to qualitative changes in development. It is unsatisfying to assume that children simply acquire knowledge in the same manner that adults become experts. Common sense suggests that children often go about acquiring knowledge in fundamantally different ways than adults and that one cannot simply map the adult model in its entirety onto children.

RECONCILING THE EARLY-COMPETENCY AND KNOWLEDGE-ENRICHMENT VIEWS

I have argued that two lines of research raise questions about the validity of general stages of cognitive development; but each does so in very different ways. The early competence view argues that the basic properties of knowledge are the same throughout development. Thus the formal structural properties of knowledge in each domain show very little qualitative change. The constraints version of this view argues that knowledge structures at all points in development honor fundamentally the same sets of constraints. The main types of change are increasing access to the same underlying structures and increasing differentiation of present structures along the guidelines of constraints. The increasing access may result in what look like qualitative changes in representation but which are not; and the increasing differentiation presumably does not even appear to be qualitative. This view on its own, therefore, not only argues against general stages of cognitive development but also against stages specific to local domains. Other early competence views might not put as explicit an emphasis on constraints, but the general critique of stage theories remains the same.

The knowledge enrichment view makes few commitments either way about stagelike changes, but the described examples suggest that, whenever stagelike changes do occur, they are functions of local knowledge systems and the particular properties of what is being learned, not general, more endogenous changes in cognition.

What these two views have in common, therefore, is a questioning of developmental patterns that purportedly show changes in cognitive structures that are global in nature. Where they differ is that an absolute constraints view disallows any sort of qualitative change while the knowledge view is more noncommittal.

Not surprisingly, I will suggest that both views are needed for an adequate account of cognitive development. It is difficult to doubt that there are universal constraints on knowledge that seem to guide how that knowledge is acquired and the structure it takes even in very young children. It is equally difficult to doubt that local expertise can sometimes result in dramatic changes in the nature of specific knowledge structures.

The system I envision consists of a conceptual core or core competency that is defined by sets of rigorous constraints and which is supplemented by periphery that is governed much more loosely by more domain-general (i.e., content-independent) constraints. Obviously, the relative proportions of core and periphery vary greatly depending on the type of knowledge involved, but virtually all natural learning situations involve elements of both.

The conceptual core lays down a skeletal framework within which the periphery differentiates. Thus, the constraints are rarely if ever overridden by the periphery; nonetheless dramatic shifts can occur in the periphery, provided they honor the general boundaries of the skeleton. Because this core is only a skeletal framework, it does not completely constrain the structures within it and therefore allows changes that might be called qualitative. Initially, the patterns of learning in the periphery and the resultant representations might be surprisingly homogeneous across domains and may use many common types of learning procedures. But as the learner becomes more and more knowledgeable in each domain, the particular properties of each domain begin to dominate and the knowledge representations begin to diverge, so that there is an increasing plurality of representational types with increasing knowledge. Put differently, at the level of the periphery, development consists of a gradual divergence of knowledge structures, as the particular properties of what is learned in each domain begin to have dominance over the earlier influences of general learning procedures.

This model can be illustrated more concretely with examples from the characteristic-to-defining shifts. At the periphery virtually all word meanings start off being represented in roughly the same manner: namely, sets of characteristic features, perhaps arising out of familiar exemplars. Repeatedly, for a wide range of terms we have found that the earliest stage of knowledge seems to be represented in terms of some sort of typicality structure. This is true for many different types of nouns as well as verbs and adjectives. Nouns as different as artifact and natural-kind terms both start out being represented by lists of their most typical properties. Similarly verbs ranging from "lie" to "boil" to "irrigate" are initially construed as applying to events that have all the characteristic features of those words. Finally, adjectives such as "tall" are initially understood in terms of characteristically tall things (Keil & Carroll, 1980).

As children learn more about each of these concepts, their knowledge structures show a shift away from characteristic features. For some terms the shift is toward what seem to be necessary and sufficient features. These are words that have been discussed so far and include kinship terms, terms referring to social conventions, and the like. They also include artifacts, although here the shift is to a definition that corresponds to the function intended by the creator of the artifact.

Even with these words with clear definitions, the final adult-knowledge structures may differ substantially from domain to domain, because the sorts of relations necessary to describe each can be intrinsically different. Thus, the kinds of relations describing various cooking terms are likely to be very procedural in nature while, in the case of kinship terms, the relevant procedures (i.e., those of reproduction) are referred to in only the most fleeting manner. Moreover, the differences between terms across the various syntactic categories may also cause different sorts of representations such as the noun/verb differences described by Gentner (1981).

The differences in final knowledge structures are more dramatic, if one considers the natural-kind terms. As philosphers of language have now argued for some time, these terms do not seem to have simple definitions or anything close to a set of necessary and sufficient features (cf. Kripke, 1972; Putnam, 1975). In more recent work we have demonstrated that children also start off with instance-bound representations for natural-kind terms and shift away from them; but they shift to a very different sort of knowledge structure than for artifacts. One research paradigm that we have used extensively consists of describing to children certain transformations on objects that change many of the most salient characteristic features and nothing else. Thus a lion might have various parts of its body shaved and then be dyed with stripes. The child is asked whether the end product is a lion or a tiger. (Photographs of the before-and-after states are shown to the children and are, in fact, photographs of a real tiger and a real lion.)

We find that young children will often assume that changes in characteristic features cause changes in identity, whereas older children do not; and this is true, not just for natural kinds that are animals, but also for plants and minerals. The older children do not shift to a belief in simple definitions, however, but rather to a belief in complex theories of a more causal nature.

They move away from representing the meaning merely in terms of typical properties to an underlying causal theory and often a theory that explains the origins of the natural kind. For example, for animals, older children and adults often refer to the animal's parents as the basis for its identity.

We have compared the same children's responses to stories about artifacts and find that, while in the early stages both sorts of terms are represented in roughly the same manner, they diverge dramatically in how they are represented in older children and adults.

More generally, characteristic features or other sorts of representations based on typicality information seem to be very pervasive in the early stages of knowledge acquisiton, not just for the meanings of words but also for syntactic categories (Maratsos, 1983) and perceptual patterns (Kemler, 1983). There are probably several other general representational strategies and types that are employed in the early stages of knowledge acquisition and which give way to more local structural influences with increasing knowledge. The important point here is that when qualitative change occurs, it is of a certain sort – from representations that are initially set up with relatively little attention to the peculiarities of what is learned to representations where these peculiarities dominate. This few-to-many mapping of representational types may be the primary way in which qual-itative changes occur. Thus, early in concept acquisition when general strategies predominate, concepts from a wide range of domains may show many representational properties that are derivative from those strategies. Later, however, the concepts tend to diverge more and more from each other in terms of their particular structural properties.

Above and beyond these qualitative shifts, however, there is a conceptual core that exerts constraints on the knowledge at any point in its develop-ment. Again, the case of word meaning acquisition provides a useful illust-ration. While young children will frequently assume that merely changing the characteristic features of natural kinds can change them into a different natural kind, they do not allow just any changes to do so. They are perfectly willing to let one animal be changed into another animal, or a plant to be changed into another plant, or an artifact into another artifact; but they are unwilling, for example, to say that a toy mouse that acquires all the characteristic features of a real mouse has been changed into a real mouse. This is the case, even though the photographs of the toy mouse and the real mouse might be more perceptually similar than other within-category picture pairs such as the tiger and the lion. The children appear to have some basic principled categorical distinctions such as those between artifacts, animals, and plants that overrule characteristic features. Within each of these categories, children frequently judge changes of characteristic features to change identity; but they are very reluctant to have changes in characteristic features move an object into a different category. These broad categories are the same ones that I have focused on at length in other work and have been called *ontological categories* or *basic categories* of *existence* (Keil, 1979). One of the most important aspects of that knowledge is that it seems to obey certain structural constraints from even the earliest ages.

One can find evidence for constrained cores in other natural domains such as natural language syntax (Chomsky, 1980), visual pattern perception (Marr, 1982), and causal reasoning (Bullock et al, 1982). With other domains that are more artifical – such as knowledge of chess – it is clear that there will be no constraints specific to the domain. Our knowledge of chess may be indirectly constrained, however, by constraints on cognitive faculties used in chess such as spatial maps and causal thinking.

DOMAINS AND CONSTRAINTS: SOME ESSENTIAL DISTINCTIONS

There are a number of different senses that the terms *domain* and *constraint* can take, and it is essential, before proceeding any further, to draw some distinctions between these various senses. As with so many other terms in psychology such as schema, stage, and competence, these terms have come to mean different things to different people. Each of these senses has value, but it is all the more important to know what they are.

There are at least three different ways in which knowledge can be constrained, and these different types of constraints lead us naturally into making distinctions among different senses of *domain*. One sense of constraint, the sense that I have emphasized here, is the domain-specific a priori. These are the sort of constraints that set up the core competencies discussed above. They demarcate broad areas of cognition such as moral reasoning, language, knowledge of spatial layout, causal reasoning, visual pattern perception, and the like. They are specifically applicable to one, and only one, of these broad areas and are often instrumental in defining the scope of these areas. They are called domain-specific with a sense of domain that refers to these broad areas of cognitive competence. A priori domain-specific constraints are either present throughout development or emerge at certain points in a maturational fashion relatively independent of experience, just as beards emerge in men. Some of the universal constraints on syntax may emerge in this fashion (cf. Gleitman, 1981).

Domain-general, a priori constraints apply across many different sorts of knowledge, if not all types, and because they apply to such a wide range of knowledge types, they tend to be less restrictive. The more general the range of application, the more flexible and diluted a constraint is likely to be. The sorts of constraints that arise here appear to be more closely linked to learning procedures or patterns of processing and might include the general tendency to form prototypes or similar representations based on typicality information, the limits of short-term memory (if that is a unified concept), patterns of memory interference between related types of knowledge, and properties of general associative models. It is suggested that these constraints are almost invariably present from the earliest stages of concept acquisition and that they play an important role in structuring the "periphery" in initial periods of acquisition of natural concepts and in structuring the entire concept in the intitial stages for more artificial sorts of knowledge. If these domain-general constraints were more restrictive and showed dramatic change at various points in development, they might be responsible for across-the-board stagelike changes. It is suggested, however, that this does not occur.

Expertise-specific, post priori constraints are perhaps the most obvious. What you learn influences or exerts constraints upon what you will learn next, not only in terms of the process of learning itself but in terms of how it comes to be represented. If one has a rich knowledge of cooking terms, for example, then one will have different representations of novel cooking terms than a novice, differences that may be striking and qualitative in nature. These constraints are products of the structure of what is learned, and their restrictiveness and generality depend on the knowledge involved. It is assumed here that the various areas of expertise that exist in our world have many unique structural properties that become all the more pronounced with increasing expertise. Thus novice-to-expert transitions may frequently represent qualitative shifts in manner of processing and representation.

These different types of constraints illustrate at least two important senses of domain. The domains that are demarcated by a priori, domain-specific constraints are relatively small in number and represent broad areas of competency for which humans have evolved special structural predispositions. The expertise domains are potentially unlimited in number because they are dependent on the varieties and intensities of human experiences. They tend to be much more local and can subdivide into finer and finer distinctions as demands on more and more local areas of expertise increase. There are countless examples of these sorts of differentiating areas of expertise in the history of technology. Computer science and its various subdisciplines are an excellent example.

All these sorts of constraints and both senses of domain are involved in virtually any learning situation, and it thus becomes very easy for theorists from different perspectives to end up talking at cross-purposes, because they may be talking about different things. In addition, depending on the type of knowledge to be acquired and depending on the degree to which the learner has mastered that knowledge, there will be dramatically different weights put on each of those components.

I interpret Turiel and Davidson's work (1986) as particularly relevant to the domains issue. They argue that there are seemingly paradoxical trends of not only homogeneity and consistency but also heterogeneity and inconsistency in the development of social concepts, and they suggest that the solution to this contradiction is the recognition of different domains of social judgement. The heterogeneity comes from the differences between such domains as social conventions, morality, and psychological concepts. The homogeneity arises from the internal coherence of each domain resulting from shared organizing principles and the like. This heterogeneity/homogeneity compromise results in a level of domain organization that may be comparable with the domains demarcated by the domain-specific, a priori constraints that I have discussed here and elsewhere (e.g., Keil, 1981). As Turiel and Davidson state:

> The domain-specific proposition is that there is neither a general structure of mind as a whole to be identified nor that there are so many domains of knowledge that we are left with a series of elements with no systems of organization.

Broad domains such as social conventions, morality, and psychological concepts might have each been of sufficient importance in evolution and sufficiently different from one another in basic structure that humans have developed specific predispositions to process and represent each in qualitatively different ways. The optimal or most efficient representations and methods of learning for each type of concept might differ considerably and thus, as demands were placed on skills in these areas, these manners of learning and representation may have become increasingly divergent.

An additional claim made here is that clear qualitative shifts are only likely to be observed in the more local expertise domains within each of these broader social domains. It is not clear if Turiel and Davidson would endorse this claim as well, but it at least seems consistent with their account. Thus, there may not be stagelike changes for the broad field of social conventions, but within more local areas of expertise such as table manners and traffic rules there might be much more stagelike changes (cf. Lockhart, 1980).

INTERACTIONS BETWEEN DOMAINS

If my account is correct, then qualitative changes will be observed only in certain well-specified situations, namely, where a child is moving from a general representational format to more detailed knowledge structures that reflect the particular properties of a given domain. A necessary corollary is that the qualitative shift is always restricted to specific knowledge domains and that there are no general stages of cognitive development constituting across-the-board shifts in representation or manner of thinking. It is now necessary to show how such knowledge specific shifts might nonetheless occasionally give the appearance of much more general shifts by means of interactions between domains.

Consider the situation where a child gains a new level of mastery of some particular domain of knowledge that is crucially involved in a wide range of cognitive tasks. As soon as the child gains mastery in that one domain, it might result in qualitative shifts across all the various domains that use that knowledge. So, at least in principle, it is possible for a qualitative shift in a particular type of knowledge to result in dramatic changes for a much broader group of cognitive domains. The problem is trying to find clear cut examples of such a phenomenon. If one believes that a certain set of logical operations are crucially involved in successful performance of a wide range of cognitive tasks as Piaget did, one might argue that shifts in the nature of such logical operations can have far-reaching effects on virtually all cognitive tasks. This particular example, however, has been quite controversial (see Osherson, 1974; Brainerd, 1978), and it is not clear that one universal logical competence is responsible for success on as wide a range of tasks as conservation, classification, and seriation. Moreover, even if such a competence is implicated in all these tasks, it is even less clear whether it changes in fundamental qualitative ways in the course of development (Osherson, 1974; Brainerd, 1978).

There are probably no cases where a domain that itself undergoes qualitative shifts is an indispensable component in all other cognitive tasks. On a smaller scale, however, there are many cases where local knowledge structures can cause changes in performance in at least a few other domains. Thus, the child's emerging arithmetic abilities will obviously enhance any task requiring such competence; but it is not clear if dramatic qualitative shifts are observed in the development of arithmetic abilities. Moreover, even if there were qualitative changes in arithmetic knowledge, it does not necessarily follow that these changes would cause qualitative shifts in performance on tasks that required such knowledge.

One clearer case involves the ability to comprehend metaphors. In some recent work (Keil, 1985) we have shown that the ability to comprehend metaphors is again largely a function of the sophistication of knowledge one has in various cognitive domains. Thus, if two domains are used in which young children are knowledgeable, they will readily comprehend metaphors between those two domains such as metaphors about animal functions being applied to automobiles (e.g., the car is hungry, the car is thirsty, the car is tired, etc.). If their knowledge is not well articulated in one or both of the domains in a metaphor, then the children will often only understand the literal meaning.

On occasion, increasing maturity of knowledge in one domain might have more far-reaching effects, because that domain interacts with several others. One example is human personality traits which have been used metaphorically with cars, books, plants, computers, and weather conditions, among others. If the child's knowledge in the personality domain undergoes a dramatic shift, then metaphorical competence in general might show a dramatic change, because it is now possible to map relations from personality traits onto several other domains that have already been well articulated in their own right. In our own work, we saw some indications of such an effect for terms referring to human feelings and personality.

A different example of how a local shift can have broader effects is seen in children's emerging awareness of the nature of nonphysical entities, in particular, mental entities. I have argued elsewhere (Keil, 1983) that early on, children have little or no awareness that there are things that exist in the world that are not in themselves physical objects such as events, mental entities, and various other abstractions. Their knowledge of the ontological category of nonphysical objects appears to emerge rather suddenly and dramatically (see Keil, 1983, for details). This initial awareness is confined to ontological knowledge; but once the insight occurs, it can influence a wide range of tasks that benefit from an awareness of categories other than the physical. Thus, any of the mental abilities known as metacognitive skills (e.g., metamemorial, metalinguistic, meta-attentional) cannot develop until the child is aware that there is such a thing as memory, or language, or attention. More important, the various metacognitive strategies (such as memory heuristics) that arise out of these abilities and greatly enhanced task performance may also be dependent on such an awareness. In this manner, the child's very specific awareness that there are mental entities can have a dramatic impact on a wide range of tasks.

I suspect that such cases where a local insight or change has broader effects are not uncommon. I doubt that the influence is ever as sweeping as the proposed role of logical operations, but it could nonetheless give an illusion of a much broader cognitive change than actually occurred. Even as adults, we are often surprised with how some new local expertise helps us better understand many other more familiar phenomena. One example is knowledge of the basic principles of operation of the computer. People who acquire such expertise often use it to make conjectures about the nature of human cognition, social organizations, biological models, and the like. Metaphorical extensions are particularly relevant here; for if a new domain has within it relationships that give new insight into the nature of other more familiar domains, then metaphorical extensions from that new domain into the old ones have a strong impact on thinking in those domains.

Domain interactions can also mask developmental patterns. Thus, Turiel and Davidson (1986) describe how different subjects can perceive the same task as drawing on different domains of knowledge, such as moral versus conventional knowledge. Depending on which domain they choose to access to make a judgement or decision, they may show very different patterns of responses. Similarly, in development children may shift in which domain they predominantly access to solve a problem and give the resulting appearance of a stagelike shift in competence, while in actual fact, they possess both competencies throughout. This then is a modified version of Rozin's (1976) proposal about increasing access and development, one that can mimic stages.

In sum, if one grants the existence of cognitive domains with unique organizing principles, patterns of representation, and modes of processing, those domains can closely approximate behaviors that have been taken as evidence for broad stagelike changes. Moreover, beyond the mere plausibility of such accounts, this may be the favored alternative given the empirical difficulty of finding support for general stages.

BEYOND EXPERTISE: SOME DIFFERENCES BETWEEN EXPERTS AND NOVICES AND ADULTS AND CHILDREN

It seems strongly counterintuitive to suggest that the major qualitative changes in childhood are no different from changes that occur between adult novices and experts. We are all uncomfortable with the notion that development and learning are simply the same thing. Moreover, a little reflection reveals that there are important differences between the two. One of the most important is that the child is much closer to being a universal novice, something that no adult ever could be; and because of this, to the extent that there are well-articulated domains and rich interactions between them, there will be strong differences between children and adult novices.

An adult who is a novice in one domain has considerable expertise in others and, if any of these are relevant to performance or learning in the novel domain, the adult is likely to exhibit a very different pattern of learning than the young child. To use the metaphor example again, an adult who is a complete novice about cognitive psychology might nonetheless find it considerably easier to learn about than a young child because of all the other knowledge domains that help one understand cognition better, such as knowledge of how computers work, for example. It is clear that much of the formal instruction to adults relies on comparisons to related concepts from other domains of greater expertise.

In general, adults have a much richer cognitive context within which they can learn about new concepts. It is this context that often enables them to learn more efficiently than young children. Their acquisition patterns should more closely approximate those of children in situations where what they are learning is both novel and relatively autonomous (that is, not connected to other sorts of knowledge) and cannot benefit from analogies to other domains. Knowledge of chess and dinosaurs might be two such examples, and this may be why Chi chose them in her work with expert children and novice adults.

This broader cognitive context created by rich knowledge in other domains is clearly an important difference between expert and novice adults and children and adults and is most relevant to the concerns of this chapter. There are other differences as well, however, that at least deserve mention. Adults may develop new general learning strategies that help them acquire knowledge in a wide variety of domains such as general studying or reasoning skills. Many of these may be a reflection of an emerging metacognitive awareness that enables them to develop and use strategies. Strategies may also become more robust with increasing age, and the older child or adult may become more able to apply them across a wider range of situations, that is, they become less task- and content-bound (cf. Brown, Bransford, Ferrara, & Campione, 1983). Thus, while many strategies emerge and continue to operate in experts in a fully content-dependent manner, some do become increasingly detached from the original domain of acquisition. Adults may also learn differently from children because certain basic processes that they share with children become more efficient (cf. Brown et al., 1983). While not the same as a capacity difference, this could have essentially the same effect, as Case et al. (1986) have argued.

It is not clear how independent either of these alternatives (strategies and efficiency of basic processes) can be from expertise in local domains, and Brown et al. (1983) argue that, to a certain extent, they must be intertwined. Nonetheless, at least in principle, they represent two other reasons to distinguish between expert/novice differences and developmental ones.

CONCLUSIONS

I have tried to sketch out some ways in which qualitative changes are and are not likely to occur in cognitive development. The qualitative/quantitative issue can be overemphasized, because there are many indeterminate cases. Nonetheless, people who spend a lot of time with children frequently

have strong intuitions that dramatic restructurings of knowledge are occur-
ing, and these intuitions need to be explained. I have argued that two
recent research trends in development, reflecting the early competency
view and the knowledge-enrichment view, both raise serious challenges to
the notion of across-the-board stages of cognitive development. I have
interpreted them as also raising challenges to changes in representation
that are purely endogenous, as if the child simply goes through certain
stages that then have dramatic impacts on all aspects of their interactions
with the world. Instead, qualitative shifts mostly occur as the child goes
beyond general representational schemes such as collections of characteristic features to learn more about the particular properties of each domain.
At the same time, however, the early competency view is involved in that
there are constraints on cognitive domains that restrict the nature of the
resulting knowledge structures in a more skeletal fashion.

Perhaps the most important theme that these two approaches share is
an emphasis on cognitive content and structure rather than on content-independent procedures and heuristics that apply indiscriminately to all types
of knowledge. Such processes may only be seen at the earliest stages of
acquisition of knowledge and, even then, they are likely to be heavily
influenced by constraints if the domain is a cognitively natural one. For
more artificial domains such as chess, the primary shift is from general
representational formats to those reflecting the properties of chess, with
little reference to universal constraints. Attempts to explain stagelike transitions in terms of general formal structural or procedural properties that
are imposed on all types of knowledge are not likely to succeed. The most
powerful constraints are almost always domain-specific and inapplicable to
other domains; and expert knowledge in different domains reflects much
more the unique properties of each domain than it does general principles
of representation or processing. Because the structures of each of our
mental faculties tend to be so different from each other, and because the
structures of the types of things there are in the world vary so greatly,
developmental change is extremely sensitive to these differences and cannot
be modeled in terms of vast homogeneous modes of thought that ignore
this rich diversity of structure in both the mind and the world.

ACKNOWLEDGEMENTS

Preparation of this paper and much of the research described herein was supported
by National Science Foundation grants BNS-81-02655 and BNS-78-06200. Many
thanks to Sydney Strauss, Iris Levin, Michael Kelly, Tammy Globerson, Ruth Ber-
man, and Barbara Bauer for making very helpful comments on this manuscript.

REFERENCES

Anglin, J. M. (1984). The child's expressible knowledge of word concepts: what preschoolers can say about the meanings of some nouns and verbs. In K. E. Nelson (Ed.), *Children's language* (Vol. 5). Hillsdale, N. J.: Lawrence Erlbaum Associates Inc.

Brainerd, C. J. (1978). The stage question in cognitive developmental theory. *Behavioral and Brain Sciences, 1,* 173–182.

Brown, A. L., Bransford, J. D., Ferrara, R. A., & Campione, J. C. (1983). In J. H. Flavell & E. M. Markman (Eds.), *Handbook of child psychology: Vol. 3. Cognitive development.* New York: John Wiley.

Bruner, J. S., Olver, R. R., & Greenfield, P. M. (1966). *Studies in cognitive growth.* New York: John Wiley.

Bullock, M., Gelman, R., & Baillargeon, R. (1982). The development of causal reasoning. In W. F. Friedman (Ed.), *The developmental psychology of time.* New York: Academic.

Case, (1986). In I. Levin, (Ed.), *Stage and Structure: Reopening the Debate, Chap 1,* New Jersey: Ablex.

Chomsky, N. (1980). *Rules and representations.* New York: Columbia University Press.

Chi, M. T. H. (1978). Knowledge structures and memory development. In R. S. Siegler (Ed.), *Children's thinking: What develops?* Hillsdale, N.J.: Lawrence Erlbaum Associates Inc.

Chi, M. T. H., Feltovich, P. J., & Glaser, R. (1981). Categorization and representations of physics problems by experts and novices. *Cognitive Science, 5,* 121–152.

Fodor, J. (1972). Some reflections on L. S. Vygotsky's *Thought and language. Cognition, 1,* 83–95.

Gelman, R. & Gallistel, C. R. (1978). *The child's understanding of number.* Cambridge, MA:Harvard University Press.

Gentner, D. (1981). Verb semantic structures in memory for sentences: Evidence for componential representation. *Cognitive Psychology, 13,* (1), 56–83.

Gleitman, L. (1981). Maturational determinants and language growth. *Cognition, 10,* 105–113.

Haviland, S. & Clark, E. (1974). This man's father is my father's son: A study of the acquisition of kin terms. *Journal of Child Language, 1,* 23–47.

Keil, F. C. (1979). *Semantic and conceptual development: An ontological perspective.* Cambridge, MA: Harvard University Press.

Keil, F. C. (1981). Constraints on knowledge and cognitive development. *Psychological Review, 88,* (3), 197–227.

Keil, F. C. (1983). On the emergence of semantic and conceptual distinctions. *Journal of Experimental Psychology: General, 112*(3), 357–385.

Keil, F. C. (1985). *Semantic fields and the acquisition of metaphor.* Unpublished manuscript.

Keil, F. C. & Batterman, N. (1984). A characteristic-to-defining shift in the development of word meaning, *Journal of Verbal Learning and Verbal Behavior, 23,* 221–236.

Keil, F. C. & Carroll, J. J. (1980). The child's conception of "tall": Implications for an alternative view of semantic development. *Papers and Reports on Child Language Development, 19,* 21–28.

Kemler, D. G. (1983). Exploring and reexploring issues of integrality, perceptual sensitivity, and dimensional salience. *Journal of Experimental Child Psychology, 36,* 365–379.

Kripke, S. (1972). Naming and necessity. In D. Davidson & G. Harman (Eds.), *Semantics of natural language.* Dordrecht, Holland: Reidel.

Landau, B. (1982). Will the real grandmother please stand up? The psychological reality of dual meaning representations. *Journal of Psycholinguistic Research, 11,* (1), 47–62.

Lehrer, A. (1978). Structure of the lexicon and transfer of meaning. *Lingua, 45,* 95–123.

Lockhart, K. L. (1980). *The development of knowledge about uniformities in the environment: A comparative analysis of the child's understanding of social, moral, and physical rules.* Unpublished doctoral dissertation, University of Pennsylvania.

Maratsos, M. (1983). Some current issues in the study of the acquisition of grammar. In J. H. Flavell & E. M. Markman (Eds.), *Handbook of child psychology: Vol, 3, Cognitive development.* New York: Wiley.

Markman, E. M., & Siebert, J. (1976). Classes and collections: Internal organization and resulting holistic properties. *Cognitive Psychology, 8,* 561–577.

Marr, D. (1982). *Vision.* San Francisco: Freeman.

Osherson, D. N. (1974). *Logical abilities in children,* Vol. 1. Hillsdale, N. J.: Lawrence Erlbaum Associates Inc.

Piaget, J. (1928). *Judgment and reasoning in the child.* London: Routledge & Kegan Paul.

Putnam, H. (1975). *Mind, language and reality.* New York: Cambridge University Press.

Rosch, E., Mervis, C. B., Gray, W. D., Johnson, D., & Boyes-Braem, P. (1976). Basic objects in natural categories. *Cognitive Psychology, 8,* 382–439.

Rozin, P. (1976). The evolution of intelligence and access to the cognitive unconscious. In J. M. Sprague & A. A. Epstein (Eds.), *Progress in psychobiology and physiological psychology.* New York: Academic Press.

Turiel, E. & Davidson, P. (1986). In I. Levin (Ed.), *Stage and Structure: Reopening the Debate, Chap 5,* New Jersey: Ablex.

Vygotsky, L. S. (1962). *Thought and language* (E. Hanfmann & G. Vakar, Trans.). Cambridge, MA: MIT Press. (Original work published 1934).

Werner, H. (1948). *Comparative psychology of mental development* (2nd ed.). New York: International Universities Press.

6

Are Children Fundamentally Different Kinds of Thinkers and Learners Than Adults?

Susan Carey

The task set for me was to debate, with special attention to Piaget's position, the following propositions: (1) that children are fundamentally different kinds of thinkers and learners from adults, and (2) that children differ from adults only in accumulation of knowledge.

Quite obviously, this issue cannot be joined until we have agreed what is meant by *fundamentally different kinds of thinkers and learners*. There are five quite different interpretations of the first proposition, and textual evidence from Piaget's writings (that are not presented here) for all five can be provided. I argue that it is important to keep these interpretations clear and separate, for under some interpretations the claim is clearly true and under others it is clearly false. Also, the educational implications vary with each interpretation of the claim.

Table 6.1. shows the five interpretations that are considered here. The most radical is the first: that children differ from adults in the kinds of concepts they can represent mentally, and/or in the logical operations that can be computed using their mental representations. I call either type of difference one of *representational format;* in the developmental literature such changes are often called structural.[1] Several current metaphors provide

---

[1] Whereas putative developmental changes in representational format (e.g., the shift from preoperational to concrete operational thought) clearly involve structural change, so do important classes of conceptual change that do not involve any changes in representational format. Theory change, for example, is structural in that it involves simultaneous adjustments of many different concepts and the relations among them, but one is not tempted to think of later scientists (e.g., Einstein) as possessed of different mental machinery than earlier scientists (e.g., Newton), except with regard to physics itself.

Source: Chipman, S.F., Segal, J.W., and Glaser, R. (Eds). (1985) *Thinking and learning skills*, Vol 2, 'Research and open questions'. Hillsdale, N.J.: Lawrence Erlbaum Associates Inc., pp 485–517.

TABLE 6.1
Five Interpretations of "Fundamentally Different Kinds of Thinkers and Learners"

1. Representational format: The data structures for the representation of information and/or processes that manipulate these structures differ between children and adults.

2. Metaconceptual knowledge: Unlike adults, children cannot think *about* their mental representations and inferential processes.

3. Foundational concepts: Children differ from adults in certain concepts fundamental to many domains of knowledge, such as causality.

4. Tools of wide application: Children lack specific tools that apply broadly, such as mathematical tools.

5. Domain-specific knowledge: Children's theories of the world differ from adults'.

the flavor of a developmental difference in representational format. One computer metaphor, for example, might say that young children do not have some higher order compiled language (such as LISP) that older children and adults do have. Or, in the language-of-thought metaphor, differences in the power of the syntax or semantics of *mentalese* would also constitute a difference in representational format (see Fodor, 1975). Developmental changes in representational format would be the most fundamental differences in thinking or learning possible.

Piaget's work on operational thinking has often been seen as an attempt to formalize developmental changes in the logic of the child's conceptual system. Inhelder and Piaget (1964) claimed that children before age 6 or 7 are not capable of carrying out certain deductive inferences (those dependent on class inclusion relations or those dependent on the transitivity of relations such as *shorter than*). Inhelder and Piaget (1958) also claimed that before ages 13 to 15, young children neither entertain hypotheses nor have available the logic of confirmation that is part of learning in science. The putative differences in representational format between children and adults extend beyond limitations in the operations the young child can perform over mental representations; Piaget (Inhelder & Piaget, 1964) and others (Vygotsky, 1962; Bruner, Olver, & Greenfield, 1966) also claim that preschool children cannot represent true concepts, being limited to *complexes* instead. That the complex/concept shift was thought to occur at the level of representational format was most explicit in the case of Vygotsky. Vygotsky argued that if it is assumed that word meanings are concepts, and if there are limitations on the types of concepts children can represent, then it follows that children's word meanings are fundamentally different in kind from adults'.

Many would argue that in his work on operational development, Piaget did not intend the claim that children differ from adults at the level of representational format. With respect to classes, for example, Inhelder and Piaget sometimes emphasize the child's developing ability to become conscious of the basis of their categorization. And certainly much of the work on formal operations was intended to be about metaconceptual development, e.g., although the young child clearly represents propositions, only in adolescence does the child become able to consciously scrutinize the proposition. In Piaget's writings, the distinction between metaconceptual change and format level change is not clearly drawn. Format level changes are considered at length in this reading for three reasons. First, even if Piaget did not intend this interpretation of operational change, he himself slipped into it occasionally, and others have certainly interpreted *fundamentally different kinds of thinkers and learners* in this way. Second, this is the only interpretation of the first proposition that I consider that actually contrasts with the second (children differ from adults only in the accumulation of knowledge). Third, the implications for education of the existence of format level changes in development are gloomy, because such changes would not be amenable to instructional manipulation. Given a hypothesis-testing model of learning, the child cannot possibly learn something he cannot represent. Therefore, he cannot be taught to represent something that he cannot at that time represent (see Fodor, 1972).

As important as the distinction between thinking differently or merely knowing more is the distinction between two kinds of knowledge – domain-specific and domain-independent knowledge. By domain here I mean what Dudley Shapere, a philosopher of science, meant. He characterized a domain as encompassing a certain set of real-world phenomena, a set of used to represent those phenomena, and the laws and other explanatory mechanisms that constitute an understanding of the domain. Domain here is roughly synonymous with theory (in the philosophy of science, however the word theory is often reserved for a slightly narrower usage). One cannot know a priori what phenomena constitute the subject of a domain – the first step in the development of any new theory is the recognition of a new domain.

Some domain-independent knowledge, some skills, some stances toward learning might be so basic and have such far-reaching consequences that developmental differences in these might qualify as fundamental differences in thinking or learning. Any candidate who seeks such a qualification should satisfy two criteria: (1) the developmental change must affect knowledge acquisition and understanding in all conceptual domains – or at least in a very wide variety of different domains; that is, it should *be* domain independent; (2) the developmental change must somehow involve reasoning or problem-solving skills. I mean to rule out, for the purposes of the present reading, such overwhelmingly important developmental changes as learning to talk and learning to read, although these changes certainly meet the first criterion.[2]

Developmental differences in metaconceptual skills concerning memory, problem solving, learning, reasoning, the doing of science, and so on would meet these criteria. Piaget has pointed out that some of what distinguished Aristotelian mechanics, on the one hand, and post-Galilean mechanics, on the other, involves some of the same metaconceptual developments that characterize the shift to formal operational thought. It is certainly true that Aristotelian physics was not experimental in the ways that science was to become in the 16th century and thereafter. Thus, a second interpretation of the fundamental-differences proposition to be considered here is that children acquire metaconceptual skills that affect learning and thinking in a very wide variety of domains.

The third class of possible differences between children's and adults' thinking to be considered here is closely related to the second. In his early work, Piaget (e.g., 1972) concentrated on domain-independent developmental changes that were not changes in metaconceptual skills involved in conscious hypothesis formation and testing. Rather, in this early work, he concerned himself with such changes as the shift away from egocentricity, the growing appreciation of the distinction between appearance and reality, changes in content of such basic concepts as causality, and so forth. In Piaget's treatment of such changes, they were certainly domain independent – becoming less egocentric was reflected in such diverse domains as language acquisition (Piaget, 1926), moral reasoning (Piaget, 1932), and spatial representations (Piaget & Inhelder, 1967); similarly, the young child's putative failure to distinguish intentional, purposeful causality from mechanical, physical causality is at the root of the child's animistic reasoning about many different aspects of the physical world. I call this third class of putative differences *foundational* because almost every particular scientific advance involves interalia some distinction between relatively surface appearance and some deeper reality and some changes in the causal mechanisms

---

[2]Learning to talk and learning to read each opens the child to vast new sources of information. This alone must have a large effect on the child's learning. Each development might well have other influences on learning and thinking – e.g., learning to read both requires and fosters metalinguistic skills. Although I do not argue the point here, I believe that all effects of learning to read (or talk) can be classified in one of the categories in Table 6.1.

believed to apply in the world. The failure to grasp the distinction between appearance and reality or that between animate and purposeful causality as opposed to mechanical causality would certainly affect learning in a wide variety of domains.

There are some tools that affect science very broadly. For example, calculus proved invaluable not only for its original applications in mechanics, but also for most of physical science. Unlike the concept of causality, or the distinction between appearance and reality, a tool like calculus is not a foundational concept necessary to all theories, and its moment of invention can at least roughly be pinpointed. There may be analogous developments during childhood such that children who have some tool can be said to be fundamentally different learners than younger children who lack that tool. This is the fourth interpretation of the funda-mental-differences proposition that I consider.

Notice that interpretations 2, 3, and 4 of this proposition do not contrast with the second proposition which states that children differ from adults merely in the accumulation of knowledge. On these three interpretations, the child thinks or learns differently because he or she has acquired some knowledge whose domain cross-cuts other domains. For example, metacon-ceptual knowledge has mental phenomena as its domain and its acquisition does not differ in kind from knowledge whose domain encompasses, say, biological phenomena or mechanical phenomena. However, having explicit views about problem solving and hypothesis formation and testing could affect learning and thinking in many diverse domains.

Historians of science (e.g., Hanson, 1961; Kuhn, 1962) often used the locution think differently to refer to scientists working within two theoretical frameworks. By this they mean adherents of competing theories accept different explanatory constructs and different characterizations of basic reality. This is the fifth interpretation of the first proposition that I consider. On this final interpretation, the distinction between the first and second propositions *totally* collapses. Theory change is a paradigm example of knowledge acquisition; indeed, it is the most challenging case. Also, a little reflection dictates that on this fifth interpretation, it is a truism that children are fundamentally different thinkers and learners from adults. Children are novices in a multitude of domains where adults are experts.

The question for us in this reading, then, is whether the fundamental-dif-ferences proposition is true on any of the other four interpretations. To limit the discussion, I consider the developmental period from roughly age 3 to adulthood. I present my argument in terms of particular proposals that have been made for developmental changes of each type – in each case I evaluate the evidence that has been offered in support of that prop-osal. My conclusions are necessarily limited – there can be no general argument, for example, that there *cannot* be developmental changes in representational format. Rather, all one can do is submit actual proposed developmental changes in thinking or learning to close scrutiny.

THE FORMAT-LEVEL INTERPRETATION

In his work on logical development, Piaget described two major shifts – that between preoperational and concrete operational thinking (occurring around age 6) and that between concrete operational and formal operational thinking (occurring in early adolescence). He attempted to formalize the logical structures that become available to the child with each transition (the groupings of concrete operational thought and the 16 binary operations, plus the INRC group, of formal operations; see Flavell, 1963, for a clear exposition of these formal systems; see Osherson, 1974, and Parsons, 1960, for criticisms of Piaget's formal work). I have chosen two cases for brief exposition – one from each of these two putative developmental stages.

Case 1: Classes and Class Inclusion

As mentioned earlier, many developmental psychologists once held that preschool children cannot represent true concepts. According to Inhelder and Piaget (1964), this limitation took form in preoperational children's inability to represent classes, a limitation overcome with the development of concrete operations in the early elementary years. Similarly, Bruner et al. (1966) and Vygotsky (1962) saw the limitation in the context of broad changes in these years, when children switch from Bruner et al.'s iconic to symbolic thinking, and from Vygotsky's intuitive to scientific thought. All three research teams agreed on the characterization of adult concepts. All held a version of the classical empiricist view, in which a concept's intension is a Boolean function[3] over some primitive base. The extension of a concept is the class of real-world objects (or events, or actions, or whatever one's ontology allows) to which the concept applies. The properties represented in the concept's intension provide necessary and sufficient conditions for category membership; intensions determine extensions. All three research teams also agreed that complexes (young children's concepts) differed from true concepts in that intensions do not contain properties common to all the extensional members. Rather, the criteria for category membership shift from member to member, with some overlap among different subgroups of the set (see Bruner et al., 1966, for a discussion of complexes with different kinds of structures).

---

[3]The combinatorial syntax of Boolean functions is limited to the operators "and," "or," and "not." Thus, typical concepts on this view would be "animal or plant" (equals living thing); "not green," "tables and chairs," "not red or green," and so on.

Evidence for the complex/concept shift is of three sorts: the wild over-generalizations in production found in very early speech, the results from the Vygotsky block concept attainment tasks, and the results from studies of free classification. Let us consider these three types of evidence.

Vygotsky was aware of the striking examples from diary studies of apparent complexes in early speech (e.g., "dog" being used to refer to dogs, fur pieces, hour glasses, thermometers, mantel clocks . . .). But diary studies certainly do not demonstrate a stage in the acquisition of the lexicon where all words are mapped onto complexes rather than adult-type concepts. Such striking complexes are found only in earliest speech production, even then they do not characterize all the child's lexicon. Many children never produce them at all. Further, some writers have recently questioned the assumption that in such utterances the child is trying to refer to the particular object; rather, the child might be trying to indicate that the fur piece, for example, is like a dog in some respects (e.g., Winner, 1976). In sum, the diary data will not do the work Vygotsky wanted it to.

That there is systematic developmental change on the Vygotsky block problems, in contrast, is not in doubt. Vygotsky set up for children typical concept-attainment problems in which the child has to discover that a new word refers to something like *large, red or blue, block*. He found developmental differences revealed by the children's guesses about which blocks the new word referred to. Young preschool children kept changing their bases of categorization in a complex-like manner (Vygotsky, 1962). However, for such changes to support a complex/concept shift in development, these tasks must in fact model concept attainment. For this, the classical view of adult concepts as Boolean functions of attributes must be correct. As is well known, the empiricist view is under heavy attack. There are three major lines of criticism – Rosch's, Fodor's, and Kripke's (see Carey, 1982, for a brief review of all three). Although all three critics have different views of the nature of concepts, all three agree that adult concepts, for the most part, are nothing like *round, red or blue, block*. Even modern adherents to the classical view (e.g., Katz, 1972) agree this is so, because the syntax of combinations of primitive concepts into complex concepts must be more powerful than Boolean functions. If adult concepts do not resemble those aspired to in the Vygotsky block-problems, then developmental changes on these problems cannot support claims for a format level change in the very kinds of concepts that can be represented (see Fodor, 1972). Indeed, if Rosch's line of attack on classical concepts is correct, then adult concepts as well as children's are complexes (see E. E. Smith & Medin, 1981, for a review of psychological research that undermines the classical view).

Parallel results are found when the child is merely asked to group objects according to similarity – a free classification task. After the earliest stage of *graphic collections*, where the child makes pictures out of materials, there is a period where complex-like collections are produced, in which the bases of similarity among members of the collections keep shifting. Adult taxonomic grouping is not achieved until age 7 (Inhelder & Piaget, 1964). As in the Vygotsky block case, the relevance of these data to the claim of a change in the nature of concepts is doubtful. But another point can be made with regard to the free classification results. if the task is simplified (e.g., fewer items to sort) and if basic level categories (e.g., "dog," "cat," rather than "animal," see Rosch, Mervis, Gray, Johnson, & Boyes-Braem, 1976) are used, young preschoolers perform in an adult manner. Data from the habituation paradigm indicate that even 12, 18, and 24 month-olds categorize different kinds of food, different animals, and different kinds of furniture together (Ross, 1980).

Why children do not group objects according to taxonomic categories in the Piagetian free classification task is an interesting developmental question (see Markman & Callanan, 1983, for an excellent review). However, as long as there is positive evidence that children represent the very concepts in question, their failure to group taxonomically cannot be the result of format limitations on the very nature of concepts that are represented by young children.

The Piagetian claims for changes at around age 6 in representation of classes go far beyond the complex/concept shift. Piaget also claimed that preoperational children could not represent the relation of class inclusion and therefore could make no deductive inferences that depend on inclusion. In contrast to the paucity of evidence for the putative complex/concept shift, evidence for the young child's problems with class inclusion is forthcoming from many different sources.

Most problems emerge when the child must make use of the asymmetry of the inclusion relation. For example, Inhelder and Piaget (1964) presented preschool children with arrays such as that in Fig. 6.1 and asked questions like, "Are all the dotted ones square?" A common error was the answer, "No, some squares are striped". A question about the inclusion of dotted ones in the class of square ones seems to have been interpreted as a question of equivalence. Similarly, C. Smith (1979) found poor performance by 4- to 6-year-olds when asked questions about natural language hierarchies, such as, "Are all animals lions?" and "Are all lions animals?" Children often said yes to both questions, suggesting a failure to appreciate the asymmetry of the relation. Another reflection of difficulty with inclusion is found on what is often referred to as Inhelder's and Piaget's class-inclusion task. The child must evaluate arrays such as that in Fig. 6.2 to answer such questions as "Are there more animals or squirrels?" The child answers, "more squirrels," comparing squirrels and cats rather than squirrels and all the animals. Markman (1978) recently extended this work in an ingenious way. She showed that many 6- to 11-year-old children, who *could* pass the

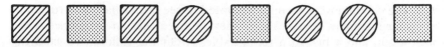

FIG. 6.1. Stimuli from Piagetian classification task.

FIG. 6.2. Stimuli from Piagetian class-inclusion task.

Piaget class-inclusion task, did not appreciate the necessity of there being more animals than squirrels. For example, they did not know whether or not by adding more squirrels to the array one could make it so that there were more squirrels than animals! A third class of results concerns inferences, where appreciation of the asymmetry of the relation again comes to the fore. Harris (1975) taught 4-to 6-year-old children that all birds had some new property and found that the children correctly inferred that all robins have the property. But, when taught that all robins have some property, children of this age are also likely to conclude that all birds do! C. Smith (1979) pointed out that the second question has no determinate answer; from what the child had been told, it is *possible* that all birds might have the property. She changed Harris' procedure by adding the words "have to" to the question: "All birds have X, do all robins have to have X?" "All robins have X; do all birds have to have X?" The 4- to 6-year-old children continued to perform badly on the task. Finally, Markman, Horton, and McLanahan (1980) have added still one more phenomenon to the battery that indicates problems with class inclusion. They presented 6- to 11-year-old children with arrays such as Fig. 6.3 and told them that the As were zugs, the Bs were laks, and the Cs (indicating all the animals) were

FIG. 6.3. Stimuli from Markman's class-inclusion collection task.

bivs. The children were then interrogated to see if they had constructed an inclusion hierarchy, specifically if they realized that an individual A was both a zug and a biv. To a remarkable extent the children resisted this interpretation. They preferred to think of biv as referring to the entire collection of C's, as if it were a word like forest rather than a word like tree.

These results leave no doubt that the young child differs from the adult in ability to impose inclusion hierarchies on new materials and in ability to make various deductive inferences that depend on inclusion. One explanation for these difficulties may be that the representational-format interpretation of the fundamental-differences proposition is correct: the child simply is unable to mentally represent the inclusion relation or is unable to make inferences over it. However, other explanations are hinted at by the data briefly summarized previously. First of all, there are particular problems afforded by each task that could result in failure despite no format differences. For example, the syntax of quantification may pose difficulties independent from the representation of inclusion relations, the question, "Are there more flowers than daisies?" may violate certain conversion maxims, knowledge of the particular hierarchies used in these tasks may sometimes be limited, and so on. (See Gelman & Baillargeon, 1983, for a review.) Secondly, the child very probably lacks metaconceptual awareness of the inclusion relation (see later section). Representing the inclusion relations among concepts is quite a different matter from being aware of that relation. For example, it is quite possible that a child might know that all robins are birds and that not all birds are robins, but that same child might not be able to learn to classify pairs of concepts according to whether the inclusion relation holds, to state formal properties such as transitivity, or to classify various relations according to their formal logical properties. It is possible that lack of metaconceptual awareness of the inclusion relation precludes the child's appreciation of the necessity of various consequences of inclusion (as Markman, 1978 and C. Smith, 1979, both demonstrated). It is also possible that metaconceptual awareness of the inclusion relation would help the child in others of the tasks that are failed at this age. This possibility is returned to later.

Any unequivocal evidence that the child does represent inclusion relations and can make deductive inferences over them militates against the representational-format interpretation of these results. C. Smith (1979) provides such evidence. She devised an inference problem that was determinate and also did not require an appreciation of the necessity of the inference (no modal like "have to" was needed). She also probed the child's knowledge of the vocabulary in the problems beforehand, constructing inference problems with three level hierarchies each child knew. She contrasted two inference types: "A pug is a kind of animal, but not a dog. Is a pug a poodle?" (No) and "A pug is a kind of animal, but not a poodle.

Is a pug a poodle?" (Yes). Answering both types correctly required deductive inferences and an appreciation of the asymmetry of inclusion. Children as young as 4 had no trouble, justifying their answers with such statements as "You said it wasn't a dog, and poodles are dogs" or, "You said it was a dog and all dogs are animals". Smith also showed that young children's problems with strings of questions such as "Are all dogs animals?" and "Are all animals dogs?" are due to surface strategies in the face of repeated questioning. In a test with just eight questions (four yes and four no), every 4-year-old showed the adult pattern, again reflecting the representation of the inclusion relations and an appreciation of a quantificational consequence of the asymmetry of inclusion. Smith presented a third analysis with the same lesson. Three tasks on which 4- to 6-year-olds do badly were given to each of several children in this age range. If lack of success was due to failure to represent inclusion relations, then the children who fail should fail at all three tasks, because each task depends on this relation. If, however, lack of success in each case was due to reasons idiosyncratic to the task, one might expect children succeeding on one or two of the tasks. The latter pattern was observed. An adult pattern of responses on only one of the tasks is all that is required to demonstrate that the child's representational format is capable of representing inclusion, and this is what was found, even among the 4-year-olds. Finally, Markman et al. (1980) included a condition in which children were told, after being taught about laks, zugs, and bivs as described earlier, that "Zugs and laks are kinds of bivs". With the addition of this sentence, children then imposed an inclusion hierarchy on the materials. Note that in the task Smith found solved correctly by 4-year-olds, inclusion was flagged by "kind of" as well. This locution may be necessary for children and not for adults, but the results such as Markman's and Smith's show that the failure to impose inclusion hierarchies in so many situations cannot be due to a format limitation that *precludes* such an organization among concepts.

In sum, there is no compelling evidence that the child's basic representational format differs from the adult's in type of concepts, capacity to represent class-inclusion hierarchies, or ability to recognize at least some quantitative and deductive consequences of inclusion. Nonetheless, in many different situations the child fails to deal with classes and class-inclusion hierarchies as would an adult. Although the child is able to represent class-inclusion hierarchies, this organizational principle is less salient than others and therefore not always invoked. A very important question for developmental psychologists is why this is so. One important factor in the problems children have with inclusion is lack of knowledge of particular hierarchies. A series of my own studies shows the role played by acquisition of biological knowledge in the construction of the hierarchy of plants and animals, on one level, and living things, on the next (Carey, in press).

Another important factor, as already suggested, is the young child's lack of metaconceptual awareness of the relation of inclusion. It is likely, then, that acquisition of two kinds of knowledge – metaconceptual knowledge and domain specific knowledge – underlies much of the developmental change in handling class inclusion.

Markman (1981) has supplied another piece of the puzzle – an account of why the class-inclusion relation is so hard for the child to handle, compared to a very similar relation, the part-whole inclusion relation. She has systematically compared class-inclusion hierarchies (e.g., oak, tree) with part-whole hierarchies (e.g., oak, forest). In many different tasks, from Piaget's class-inclusion problems, to number conservation, to her own studies of the child's appreciation of the necessity for more members in the superordinate than the subordinate category, she has found that children solve the problem much earlier in the case of part-whole hierarchies than in inclusion hierarchies. Her interpretation is that the superordinate concepts in part-whole hierarchies have an internal structure lacking in the case of class-inclusion hierarchies. This internal structure helps the child with two problems – keeping the levels of the hierarchy separate and keeping the relations between subordinate and superordinate straight. To understand Markman's hypothesis, consider the relation of oak to forest. For forest to be superordinate to oak, the oaks in the forest must be in a certain relation to each other (in this case spatial). Similarly, for family to be superordinate to child, the people in the family must have a particular structure (in this case social). Such differences between the two levels of the hierarchy are not present in the case of inclusion relations – there are no relations among people necessary for children to be people. Markman's hypothesis is that this difference between class-inclusion hierarchies and part-whole hierarchies makes the latter more salient and more accessible to metaconceptual awareness.

In Case 1, I have reviewed the literature on two claims concerning format-level differences between preschool children and early elementary-age children. With respect to both, important differences between the two age groups are found, but I have argued that these differences do not support the claims for limitations of the young child's basic representational capacities. In my next section, Case 2 develops parallel arguments for an aspect of formal operational thought.

Case 2: Hypothesis Formation and Testing

Inhelder and Piaget (1958) claim that before ages 13 to 15, young children do not entertain hypotheses nor do they have available to them the logic of confirmation that characterizes scientific learning. If these claims are true, then children certainly are fundamentally different kinds of learners than adults.

Representational theories of mind presuppose hypothesis-testing theories of learning. In explaining the acquisition of any body of knowledge, one must specify the class of hypotheses the organism entertains, the evidence that is taken as relevant to decisions among the hypotheses, and evaluation metrics for that evidence (see Fodor, 1967, and Pinker, 1979, on hypothesis-testing theories of syntax acquisition). If the child is not a hypothesis generator, then representational theories of mind are false, and cognitive psychology is in trouble. My argument here, of the this-is-the-only-theory-you've-got variety, is that given basic assumptions shared by all cognitive psychology there could not be developmental differences at the format level, such that inductive theories of learning do not describe the young child's acquisition of knowledge as well as the adult's.

In their rich book, *The Growth of Logical Thinking from Childhood to Adolescence* (1958), Inhelder and Piaget present 15 experiments, each of which illustrates an aspect of the development of formal operational thought; that is, each chapter focuses on one particular skill supposedly acquired with formal operations. Each chapter also is used to illustrate the acquisition of hypothetical reasoning in general. One skill they examined was the capacity to separate variables in establishing causal relations. A general claim they made was that the child does not reason hypothetically (a better word might be theoretically), considering cases he or she has not yet encountered, and therefore cannot plan observations to confirm or disconfirm hypotheses. The bending rods experiment (Inhelder & Piaget, 1958, Chapter 3) presented evidence for developmental changes of both kinds. The child was shown rods varying along four dimensions (material, length, thickness, cross-sectional form) and was asked to find out which variables affect whether or not the rods will bend enough to touch the water when they are weighted at one end. A fifth variable was the size of the weights. In fact, all these variables are relevant, and Inhelder and Piaget were interested in the child's ability to systematically show this. Whereas they grant that children in the concrete operations stage are capable of registering the raw data and drawing the correct conclusions, Inhelder and Piaget claim that children at this stage are unable to verify the effect of one factor by leaving all the other known factors constant. Also typical of preformal operational children is an incomplete solution of the problem – only two or three of the relevant factors will be discovered. Piaget and Inhelder argue that this results from the lack of a consciously systematic approach to the task.

These are fascinating and important results. However, Inhelder and Piaget's descriptions themselves belie a representational format interpretation of these changes. The ability to separate variables and entertain hypotheses underlies the success 7- and 8-year-old children *do* have on this task. Without these abilities, children could not register the relevant data and draw correct conclusions. In another book, Inhelder and Piaget (1964) also show children of 7 or 8 who succeed in separating variables. In this task, one of three variables (size, weight, and colour) is relevant to making a ball appear when boxes varying in these three dimensions are placed on a pan on top of an apparatus. Not only are 7- and 8-year-olds able to isolate weight as the relevant variable, they understand that to prove that size and colour are not relevant they must show a large box that does not make the ball appear, and a red (or blue) box that does not as well. They also understand that to show that weight does matter, they must hold other variables constant!

Case (1974) gave 6- and 8-year-olds about 1 hour of teaching on the control-of-variables scheme, using materials unrelated to the bending rods apparatus. Field independent 8-year-olds (as assessed by performance on the WISC blocks test) were able to do the bending rods test (able to produce proofs for the effects of each variable and to indicate and explain when the experimenter produced an inadequate demonstration). If the experimenter picked a long aluminium rod and a short brass rod, showed that the long rod bent more, and argued that this proved that longer rods bend more, these children maintained that the proof was flawed because it could be the material that makes the difference! Over half of a control group of field independent 8-year-olds who received no prior training also showed considerable facility with the task. Thus, at least some 8-year-olds are able to do Inhelder and Piaget's bending rods task well before they could be "formal-operational".

Clearly, the 8-year-old child can separate variables and does understand that other variables must be controlled in order to demonstrate the effect of any one. What accounts for the lack of success until age 15 on the Inhelder and Piaget bending rods test? In Inhelder and Piaget's version, the child is not credited with success unless he or she systematically discovers for himself or herself the effect of all the variables, whereas in Case's version the experimenter structured the task so the child considered only one variable at a time. No doubt there are metaconceptual changes of great importance concerning such notions as hypothesis and proof. Although the child's inductive practices, like anybody's, require that he or she disentangle variables, the child need not be fully aware of doing so. Note that the performances of the 8-year-olds in Inhelder and Piaget (1964) and Case (1974) show *some* metaconceptual command of these notions, for the children are able to explain what they are doing. Systematic, self-conscious planning may require further metaconceptual development. Indeed, Inhelder and Piaget's (1958) work on formal operational thought is often interpreted as being *about* metaconceptual change. My argument is that the format interpretation (i.e., claims about the logic of confirmation available to the child) and the metaconceptual interpretation (i.e., claims about the child's beliefs about learning and knowledge) are not clearly distinguished in the literature, and that the data do not support Piaget's claims if interpreted as pertaining to representational format.

In the studies just cited (Inhelder & Piaget, 1958, 1964; Case, 1974), the behaviour of children younger than 7 or 8 appeared incoherent and self-contradictory in their unsuccessful attempts at finding and justifying the relevant variables. Perhaps the changes Inhelder and Piaget documented after these ages are mainly metaconceptual, but changes at the representational format level in the ability to formulate and evaluate hypotheses occur before these ages. We are now in the same position we have been in twice before. We must decide whether the failures, which we do not doubt, provide evidence that younger children cannot entertain and evaluate hypotheses. I believe that they do not, for the simple reasons that these experiments confound knowledge of particular scientific concepts with scientific reasoning more generally. It is well documented, by Piaget and others (Piaget & Inhelder, 1974; Smith, 1981) that before ages 10 or 11 or so the child has not fully differentiated weight, size, and density and does not have a clear conception of what individuates different kinds of metals (density being an important variable). If these concepts are not completely clear in the child's mind, due to incomplete scientific knowledge, then the child will of course be unable to separate them from each other in hypothesis testing and evaluation. Coming to distinguish two related concepts, such as weight and size, both different kinds of bigness, reflects theory change on the part of the child, just as coming to distinguish heat and temperature reflected theory change among self-conscious, formal operational, adult scientists in the 17th and 18th centuries (McKie & Heathcote, 1935). The Inhelder and Piaget (1958) book on formal operational reasoning repeats this fundamental confounding in every chapter; every study involves scientific concepts not available to the younger of the children tested, and so in each case, general scientific reasoning is not separable from knowledge of particular scientific domains. Similarly, Case's study concerned variables such as weight and kind of material, even in the training procedure. Little wonder that 6-year-olds who were nonconservers of weight and substance failed to benefit from the training procedure.

Of course, in order to rule out developmental changes at the format level in ability to formulate and evaluate hypotheses, positive demonstrations of this ability among still younger children are needed. I return to the this-is-the-only-theory-you've-got argument. How does the child learn the meanings of words such as red and big from uses in contexts except by formulating hypotheses that require the separation of the variables of size and colour for their evaluation? More empirically, it is possible to show that many of the phenomena that typify doing science by adults also typify the behaviour of young children with respect to their hypotheses. This point is elaborated in detail in Carey and Block (1976) and is merely touched on here.

Kuhn (1962), Hanson (1961), Toulmin (1953), Feyerabend (1962), and others have sketched a view of the activity of science according to which hypotheses are generated and evaluated relative to conceptual systems (called "paradigms" by Kuhn). Paradigms determine what questions are asked, what hypotheses entertained, what data are relevant, indeed, even what data are seen. Although contemporary philosophy of science has rejected an extreme interpretation of these claims, according to which paradigms render themselves immune from refutation and cannot contradict each other because they are incommensurable, a less extreme version is widely accepted (see Shapere, 1966 and Suppe, 1974, for summaries of the issues). In support of the core of truth to this position, many historical examples are cited of scientists not seeing phenomena counter to their hypotheses and seeing confirmation of their hypotheses when it is not actually there. For example, Chinese astronomers observed many comets, new stars, and other stellar phenomena that went unnoticed by contemporary pre-Copernican western astronomers committed to the Aristotelian doctrine of the immutability of the heavens. And Galileo claimed to observe that his prediction that the period of a pendulum is independent of its amplitude was born out of his experiments, even though air resistance makes this prediction far from true. Another manifestation of the core of truth to the Kuhnian position is tolerance of anomaly. Here counterevidence to a hypothesis is seen and recognized as counterevidence, but the hypothesis is not abandoned. For example, according to Newtonian mechanics, the difficulty in predicting the perihelion of Mercury was a pesky puzzle of little consequence; according to relativity theory, it was one of the crucial facts that show that Newtonian mechanics were false and relativity theory was true.

This characterization of how adult science makes sense of the world also characterizes the activity of children making sense of their world. Karmiloff-Smith and Inhelder's (1975) classic paper on children's coming to understand some aspects of the determination of balance points provides many examples. An early hypothesis formulated by children is that blocks balance in their spatial middle. Presented with a stimulus such as that in Fig. 6.4, children with this hypothesis repeatedly tried to balance it in the middle, failed, announced that it could not be done, but remained unshaken in the belief that blocks balance in the spatial middle. This massive counterevidence was treated merely as a pesky anomaly. Going even further, children at this point were asked to find the balance point with their eyes closed and could solve the problem by feel, but they rejected the solution when they opened their eyes. The same experience on the part of children who had begun to formulate the concept of a centre of gravity led them to reject their hypothesis. Like adult scientists, they rejected a well-confirmed hypothesis in the light of counterevidence only when the glimmerings of an alternative had been appreciated. Carey (1972) provides many examples of this sort involving children as young as 2.

Two developments during childhood in formulating and evaluating hypotheses are certain. First, the child elaborates conceptual systems that allow more and more sophisticated hypotheses and encompass wider and wider classes of phenomena as evidence of the evaluation of these hypotheses. This is acquisition of particular domains of knowledge. Second, the child can engage in hypotheses formation and evaluation more consciously. This is acquisition of metaconceptual knowledge. But although these developmental processes are important and far from understood, neither constitutes a change at the level of representational format.

It is of course possible that other changes than those discussed so far (Cases 1 and 2) do occur at the level of representational format. A full discussion of this issue would require consideration of every proposal ever made, clearly beyond the scope of this reading. In all the cases I have examined, the same problems as those that appeared here also arise. Basically, other interpretations of the phenomena offered in support of developmental changes in representational format seem preferable. The reinterpretation commonly involves distinguishing a format change from a metaconceptual change, or else it involves specification of particular real-world knowledge the child does not command.

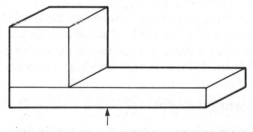

FIG. 6.4.   Stimulus from Karmiloff-Smith and Inhelder's balance task.

METACONCEPTUAL DEVELOPMENT

I have appealed to metaconceptual development several times already in this chapter and do so more in later discussions. I granted that the child does not appreciate class inclusion nor the logic of confirmation metaconceptually, but I argued that nonetheless he or she represents the inclusion relations among natural language concepts and uses inductive reasoning in learning about the world. That there is metaconceptual development during childhood (and adulthood, for that matter) is beyond doubt. The child's conception of thought, language, memory, and learning changes with age. These domains of knowledge certainly cross-cut other domains, so it is possible that we should accept the fundamental-differences proposition on the second interpretation. It remains to be demonstrated, however, just *how* metaconceptual change affects learning in other domains. For example, how does having the concepts *hypothesis, experiment, confirmation* consciously available actually affect inductive reasoning? There are only two ways to answer this question. One is to compare cases of conceptual change among self-consciously experimenting adults and metaconceptually unaware children. Of course there will be differences – the adult will set up experiments and discuss the logic of confirmation. But at the level of theory change itself – the representations of the domains, the use of evidence, the concepts that articulate both the phenomena and explanatory mechanisms, the kinds of explanatory mechanisms – will the two cases differ? I am currently involved (with M. Wiser and C. Smith) in such a comparison – the adult case is the development of the concepts of heat and temperature in the 17th and 18th centuries and the childhood case is the development of the concepts of weight and density. A second way to answer the question is to teach the metaconceptual skills to subjects who lack them and then compare knowledge acquisition in a new domain by subjects so taught and controls subjects. Although such studies have been attempted, the results are by no means in.

Case 3 concerns a tiny aspect of metalinguistic development. I argue that there is metalinguistic change against a background of constancy at the level of representational format. I also argue that the metalinguistic change involves nothing more than domain-specific knowledge acquisition; the domain here is language. Finally, I argue that metalinguistic development of this sort *does* have implications for other domains of learning, although the evidence so far concerns only very closely related domains.

Case 3: The Mental Lexicon

Any theory of the mental representation of language must specify a lexical component. Represented here are the words of the language, including how they are pronounced, what syntactic categories and subcategories they belong to and their meaning. The young child is a word-learning wizard. Miller (1977) estimated that between the ages of 6 and 8 children learn over 20 new words a day, and following him I estimated that between the ages of 18 months and 6 years, children learn approximately 9 new words a day (Carey, 1978). By age 3 (and probably earlier) there is every reason to believe that the child's lexicon is represented as is the adult's. Although the child will not have worked out the exact adult meaning for many of the words in this lexicon, there is no evidence that his or her meanings differ in kind from the adult (see Case 1 and Carey, 1982, for a review). Young children also certainly represent the syntactic categorization and subcategorizations of words, for they use both the open class (nouns, verbs, adjectives, and adverbs) and closed class (prepositions, articles, conjunctions, demonstratives, and so on) productively and syntactically correctly, although again, they have not worked out much of the syntactically complex rules of this language, nor the morphological rules for irregular verbs and nouns. Thus, at the level of representational format, words are not represented differently by 3-year-olds and adults.

However, it is abundantly clear that the 3-year-old, or even the average 5-year-old, does not have the concept of a *word*. Piaget (1929) introduced the phenomenon of nominal realism to psychology, showing that preschool children cannot answer questions such as "Is the word 'needle' sharp?" correctly; they say yes. Another example, "Which word is longer, 'snake' or 'caterpillar?" Answer: "the word 'snake.'" Apparently, the child has difficulty focusing on the word itself, rather than on what is represented by the word. Nominal realism errors are also revealed when the child is asked to say what is and what is not a word. Preschool children deny that "ghost" is a word, because there are no ghosts (Papandropoulou & Sinclair, 1974) and claim that if all the giraffes in the world were destroyed there would no longer be the word "giraffe" (Osherson & Markman, 1975). Problems other than nominal realism are also revealed in this paradigm. When asked to distinguish words from nonwords (e.g., "tiv"), the young child denies that closed class items (e.g., "very," "of," "more,", "this," "and," and "he" are words). This is not a simple matter of concreteness of reference, for abstract content words (e.g., "idea," "go") are granted word status (Egido, 1983). When asked to tap once for each word of a spoken sentence, the child either taps only for content words or taps for every syllable. Thus, there seem to be several aspects of the concept *word* that the 5-year-old does not yet command – the notion of word as representation and several purely linguistic distinctions such as word/syllable or word/ bound morpheme.

Acquiring these concepts is garden-variety domain-specific learning, where the domain in this case is language. The child must be a linguist examining his or her own language (as a representational system) to formulate these notions. I do not mean to say that characterizing the acquisition of metalinguistic knowledge is easy. Rather, I am arguing that it is the same difficult problem as characterizing the acquisition of any domain of knowledge (see the last section of this chapter on domain-specific knowledge).

Not having the metalinguistic concept word has clear implications for learning in some other domains – most notably, learning to read. If one does not know what a word is, it will obviously be difficult to learn what the convention of spaces in text represents. And indeed, these metalinguistic tasks arc part of the reading readiness batteries, and training in concepts such as word and syllable help poor readers learn to read (Liberman, Schankweiler, Fischer, & Carter, 1974). Of course, the converse is also true: Learning to read is one occasion for becoming a little linguist working out the concepts. Osherson and Markman (1975) show that metalinguistic awareness of the type discussed here is a prerequisite for the notion of logical necessity, although there the distinction the child must master is validity/truth rather than word/referent. In sum, learning such basic linguistic notions as word does have implications for other domains of knowledge, albeit ones that also intimately concern linguistic representations – reading and logic.

Other domains of metaconceptual development that do not concern language and logic so directly have also been studied. Most notable is metamemorial development (cf. Flavell, 1977, for a review). The story is familiar: That there is metamemorial development is not in doubt, nor is there doubt that such development contributes to the developmental changes in the capacity for memorizing, especially in the case of relatively unstructured materials. What is yet to be shown is whether, or how, metamemorial development contributes to the most important problem concerning memory – the changes in knowledge structures that constitute our vast store of knowledge (called in the literature our long-term memory).

THE FOUNDATIONAL CONCEPTS INTERPRETATION

Piaget's parallels between childhood and the history of science extended beyond common metaconceptual developments concerning the nature of science. Other putative parallels concern changes in the content of foundational concepts such as *cause*. According to Piaget, the only causal concept available to the young child is intentional causality, in which an object seen as agent is the purposeful initiator of an event that results in an effect. Development consists, among other things, in the differentiation of human, physical causality and physical mechanical causality. As evidence for this claim, Piaget (1929) offered such phenomena as childhood animism and artificialism. Children below age 10 claim that inanimate causal agents such as the sun, the wind, and clouds are alive, do what they do on purpose, and so on (animism). Children of this age also claim that all things that exist were made by people or God (artificialism).

Clearly, a developmental change of this sort would have wide-ranging ramifications for the acquisition of knowledge in all domains where mechanistic causality is at issue and would therefore qualify as a fundamental change in learning.

Piaget claimed that there has been a similar domain-independent change historically in the notion of causality. Kuhn (1977a) disagrees decisively with Piaget's historical claim. I present his argument and suggest that it applies equally to claims concerning development of causal notions in childhood.

Case 4: Causal and explanatory notions

Kuhn (1977a) distinguishes concepts like space, time, motion, and atom, which are the object of scientific inquiry, from concepts like cause, which are not. The former concepts figure in laws, are subject to measurement, and are objects of study; theories get built around them. The latter concept, cause, in contrast, functions entirely differently in scientific theories. All theories provide causes and explanations.

Kuhn (1977a) argues that every theory has its own explanatory concepts, but that at the level of the structure of explanation, there is no historical change. "Studied by themselves, ideas of explanation and cause provide no obvious evidence of that progress of the intellect that is so clearly displayed by the science from which they derive" (p.30).

He describes the phenomena that led Piaget to claim that the concept of cause itself has changed during the history of physics. Kuhn agrees that four stages in the evolution of causal notions in physics can be distinguished. According to Aristotelian thought, which dominated Western science until Galileo, every change, including coming into being, has four causes: material, efficient, formal, and final. The Aristotelian example most often cited in illustrating these is the causal explanation of a new statue:

material cause – the marble
efficient cause – the artist's chiselling and shaping the marble
formal cause – the idealized form that was the sculptor's intention
final cause – the increase in the total number of beautiful objects.

Aristotle's efficient cause is the narrow notion of causality; the other three types are aspects of the broader notion of explanation. In Aristotelian physics proper, only formal causes were considered adequate as explanation. Violent motions, such as thrown balls, had efficent causes but were not in the domain of physics. For example, the explanation of why smoke rises and most objects fall is the respective innate levity or gravity of each object; an object's form can only be completely realized in its natural position, and it seeks that position if unimpeded. In the 17th century, explanations of this sort were seen as defective and subject to derision, as in Moliere's doctor who explained that opium put people to sleep because it had dormitive power. This parody is fair, but not because of the form of the doctor's explanation – this form of explanation becomes a problem only if there begin to be as many powers, or formal causes, as there are things to be explained. Physics in the 17th and 18th centuries stressed mechanical explanation – all change was to be understood as the result of the physical impact of one group of particles on another. This is a species of Aristotle's efficient cause. But in the 19th and 20th centuries, formal explanation again became dominant, as in the case of the orbit of Mars discussed earlier. As types of causes, innate levity and Newton's gravity do not differ. They differ, of course, but only because of the power and precision of the physical theory in which each is embedded. There have been further revolutions in the 20th century, whereby fields replace particles and positions as the basic forms of matter, and whereby individual events such as alpha-particle emission are uncaused, due to Heisenberg's uncertainty principle and the emergence of probabilistic explanation. But although the explanatory principles have changed, the structure of explanation has not.

In sum, Kuhn does not deny that explanatory concepts in physics have changed through history. He does deny that the foundational notions, cause and explanation, have themselves changed. Causal explanation has the same form it did in Aristotle's day. Explanatory concepts are parasitic on the theories from which they derive, so the root of increased explanatory power is theory change. But theory change is domain-specific knowledge acquisition.

Although Kuhn's arguments are directed toward the cause of conceptual change in history, I believe they apply equally to conceptual change in children. It is just as important for developmental psychologists as for historians of science to distinguish between concepts that are the object of scientific enquiry from foundational concepts that are not. In Piaget's study of the former type of concepts – e.g., time, velocity, space, weight, density, he often explicitly considered the theory change in which the conceptual change is embedded. This is perhaps clearest in *The Child's Construction of Quantities* (Piaget & Inhelder, 1974) in which the development of the concepts of size, weight, and density was discussed in terms of the child's construction of a naive atomistic theory of matter. For children, as in the history of science, these concepts become elaborated in the course of knowledge acquisition and the accompanying theory change. Piaget claims that in addition to limitations in domain-specific knowledge, limitations in the young child's causal reasoning constrain his or her achievements in any particular domain. It is possible, of course, that Kuhn is correct in believing that there have been no changes in the structure of causal explanation since Aristotle, that there have been only changes in theories. It is possible too that Piaget is correct that in child development both kinds of changes occur.

Unfortunately, Piaget's experimental demonstrations of immature causal reasoning on the part of the child all involve phenomena in domains where the child does not yet command the relevant domain-specific concepts or principles. For example, in *The Child's Conception of Physical Causality*, Piaget (1972) considered the nature of air, wind, heavenly bodies, the floating of boats, and shadows. Dickenson (1982) has shown that the child under 12 has shaky notions of material kind and cannot sharply distinguish differences in kind (plastic, glass) from differences in phase (ice, water, steam). These confusions are related to the child's problems with the concept of matter – children under 6 are unclear how shadows differ from, say tables – that in turn are related to the child's problems with weight and density. Such profound differences in domain-specific knowledge between children and adults may account for the child's inability to provide adequate causal accounts of phenomena from these domains (e.g., Archimedes' law). Thus, in his work on causal reasoning, just as in his work on formal operational thought, Piaget utterly confounded an aspect of domain independent reasoning with theory change.

There is by now much evidence that when physical mechanisms the child knows about are at issue, the child's causal reasoning (at least from age 4 on) does not differ from the adult's. The young child knows that causes typically precede their effects, and the young child reasons as does an adult about physical mechanisms that consist of chains of simple contact forces acting on successive objects (see Bullock, Gelman & Baillargeon, 1982, for a review). Similarly, Shultz (1982) has shown that children as young as 4 appreciate causal relations among objects that act on each other at a distance (e.g., a fan blowing out a candle, a flashlight shining on a wall) and that they conceive of these events in terms of transmission of some causal power (to call it energy would be misleading, because 4-year-olds do not have anything like the physical concept energy). The main evidence for Shultz's assertion is that properties of the path between the cause and effect dominate the child's causal attribution and explanation.

Bullock et al. point out that although the child's causal attributions and predictions indicate that they appreciate the same principles of causal explanation as does the adult, the 3- and 4-year-old is markedly deficient, compared to children 5 and older, at articulating explanations and justifications that embody those principles. Although the young preschooler's reasoning embodies the same explanatory principles as does the adult's, there is metaconceptual change concerning the concepts of cause and explanation. Also, there is acquisition of knowledge of causes and explanations, this knowledge being domain specific.

The preceding remarks concern the child's reasoning in domains of physical science. Research of my own suggests that acquisition of knowledge specific to a different domain – biology – also plays a role in the phenomena Piaget offered in support of his claims for development changes in causal reasoning. Remember, Piaget (1929) claimed that the child does not distinguish mechanical efficient causes from animate efficient causes. The result is that the child sees as alive those inanimate objects that are active and capable of motion, especially autonomous motion (Piaget, 1929). In this way Piaget explained the overattribution of life to inanimate objects, as when the child says that the sun or fire is alive, in terms of limitations in causal reasoning.

My studies show a major reorganization of biological knowledge between the ages of 4 and 10. For young children (4- to 7-year-olds), biological properties such as eating, breathing, sleeping and having internal organs such as hearts are primarily properties of people and only secondarily properties of animals. This is shown from the analysis of how children generate answers to questions such as "Does a shark breathe?" – namely, by comparing the animal in question to people. The more similar the animal is seen to be to people, the more likely the child is to judge that the animal breathes, sleeps, eats, has a heart, and so on. One consequence of this organization is that properties that are in fact true of all animals, such as the fact that they eat, have the same pattern of attribution as properties of people that are not true of all animals, such as having bones; that is, 4- to 7-year old children are just as likely to say that worms have bones (about 30–40% of the time) as that they eat. And a new property, taught as a property of people, e.g., that people have spleens, is attributed to other animals according to the same similarity metric. Strikingly, the same property taught as a property of dogs is not attributed to any other animals. By age 10 this has all changed. Fundamental biological properties such as eating and breathing are attributed to all animals and differentiated from other properties of people such as having bones. More important, people are now just a mammal among many, so the pattern of attribution of a property taught for dogs is the same as that taught for people. I interpret these changes as reflecting reorganization of knowledge about animal properties; for 4- to 7-year-olds these properties are primarily organized in terms of children's knowledge of human activities. By age 10 they are organized in terms of biological function. Presumably, the main impetus for this reorganization is the acquisition of biological knowledge in school.

What does all this have to do with childhood animism? *Alive* is a theoretical term in biology. If the child knows so little biology that he or she does not even know that all animals must eat, how on earth is he or she to understand what animals and plants have in common? But children do know that both animals and plants are alive; this they have been taught. I am suggesting that the overattribution of life to inanimate objects results from the child's inability to justify the inclusion of animals and plants into a single category, and that this, in turn, results from the child's lack of biological knowledge. A child who does not know enough biology to understand that all animals must eat and breathe is unlikely to be able to understand why animals and plants are alike. This proposal has been put to a simple test: The patterns of generalization when children were taught that people and bees have golgi were compared to the patterns of generalization when children were taught that people and flowers have golgi. In the second case there was substantial attribution of golgi to inanimate objects and virtually none in the former case. In this respect, the pattern of judgements for having golgi, about which children knew nothing more than that people and flowers have golgi scattered through them, was remarkably similar to the pattern of judgments for being alive that characterize childhood animism (Carey, in press).

This research places the phenomenon of childhood animism squarely in the court of knowledge acquisition, and acquisition of domain-specific scientific knowledge, at that. It is difficult to state precisely what structural reorganization of knowledge about biological properties occurs during these years and it is also difficult to understand exactly what occasions it. As Piagetians and historians of science stress, knowledge acquisition is not the mere accretion of facts. Nonetheless, the lesson of this case is clear. A phenomenon taken to reflect developmental changes in the concept of causality, childhood animism, is seen to actually reflect the acquisition of domain-specific knowledge.

Case 5: The Appearance/Reality Distinction

Piaget and others (Braine & Shanks, 1965a; 1965b) claim that before concrete operations the young child cannot distinguish between appearance and reality. This failure is putatively one reason behind nonconservation; the young child is seduced by the perceptually salient changes in length (number conservation) or height (quantity conservation) and cannot distinguish between looking like more and being more. Braine and Shanks attempted to show that distinguishing appearance and reality is a far-reaching conceptual achievement of children around age 5 or 6. They studied various illusions, such as that illustrated in Fig. 6.5. The shaded shape was actually larger than the unshaded shape, could be seen when the figures were superimposed (Fig. 6.5a). Children were shown the shapes in Fig. 6.5a and asked which was bigger, to which they replied the darker. The two shapes were then rearranged as in Fig. 6.5b, where the illusion made the

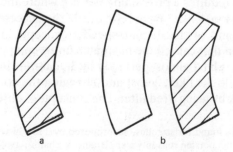

FIG. 6.5.   Stimuli from Braine and Shanks' appearance/reality task.

unshaded one appear larger. If the child now answered that the lighter was bigger, he or she was asked, "Is it really bigger, or does it just look bigger?" Children under 5 were happy to maintain that the darker was really bigger in Fig. 6.5a and the lighter was really bigger in Fig. 6.5b.[4]

The distinction between appearance and reality is an example of what I am calling a foundational distinction. Discovering reality, like finding causal mechanisms, is the goal of all scientific enterprise; it is not the object of domain specific enquiry. Almost every particular scientific advance involves inter alia some distinction between relatively surface appearance and some deeper reality. Each succeeding theory has its own commitments to the nature of reality – e.g., Copernicus demonstrated that the powerful appearance of the sun revolving around the world was misleading and the underlying reality was that the earth turns on its axis while revolving around the sun. Thus, coming to distinguish appearance and reality is not a very promising candidate for an across the board developmental change, for the same reasons as Kuhn outlined in the case of causality.

What then of Braine and Shank's results? Their task requires knowledge and concepts the child under 5 very probably does not have. For adult performance on this task, one must know that appearance when the objects are superimposed is a better measure of relative size than appearance when the objects are side by side. But the concepts of size and measurement are shaky, to say the least, in 5-year-olds, as Piaget has taught us. Also, the child must know that mere spatial rearrangement does not change size, and we all know what a literature there is on that! These are aspects of domain-specific knowledge. Again, we are seeing the confusion of particular scientific advances with general ways of thinking.

Of course, to make this argument convincing, one needs a demonstration of very much younger children succeeding at an appearance/reality distinction with the same structure of Braine and Shanks' task. Flavell, Flavell, and Green (1983) provide an elegant review of studies that show children failing to distinguish appearance and reality and provide three experiments of their own that show that 3-year-olds command the distinction. The success of the 3-year-olds requires a pretraining period, where the locutions "really, really," and "just looks like" were rehearsed. The success also depends on the child's command of the domain-specific concepts in question and of the transformation that caused the mismatch between appearance and reality. Two problems solved almost perfectly by 3-year-olds involved disguising a clown doll so it looks like a ghost and changing the colour of something from white to pink by using a red filter. The concepts of objects and disguises,

---

[4]Similar results were found for size illusions produced by a magnifying lens and for shape illusions produced by immersing rods in water (Braine & Shanks, 1965a; 1965b).

of colours and colour filters, are available to children of this age.[5] De Vries (1969) also showed good command of the appearance/reality distinction with materials involving a disguise (she fitted a cat with a life-like mask of a dog), at least from age 4 up.

Although 3-year-olds are able to distinguish appearance from reality, there is definitely marked improvement in the years between 3 to 5. Flavell et al. suggest there is metaconceptual development concerning this distinction – the child becomes increasingly *aware* that things are not always as they appear, and this awareness helps in these tasks. The other source of improvement on these tasks is likely to be acquisition of domain-specific knowledge that allows the child to tell, in every particular case, the difference. Thus, the conclusions we draw in the case of putative development of the appearance/reality distinction thus exactly parallel those drawn in the case of putative developmental changes in the notion of causality. The evidence suggests that the young child's learning and thinking about the world is not constrained by different causal and explanatory notions from the adult's, nor by the failure to distinguish appearance from reality.

My argument in cases 4 and 5 closely parallels that in cases 1 and 2, which concerned putative changes at the level of representational format. Here, too, there can be no a priori argument that other candidate foundational notions will never be found where young children differ radically from adults. Those other candidates that have come under the same kind of scrutiny as those in cases 3 and 4 have suffered a comparable fate.[6]

In summary, I have argued that the first proposition, that there are fundamental developmental differences in thinking or learning, should be rejected on two of the three interpretations so far discussed – 1 and 3 in Fig. 6.1. Let us turn now to the fourth interpretation.

TOOLS OF WIDE APPLICATION

Causal explanation plays a role in all theories and it is unlikely that one particular moment saw its invention, either historically or ontogenetically. Not so for certain mathematical systems, such as calculus in the 17th century

---

[5]Flavell et al.'s paper goes far beyond the use to which I am putting it here. Three- to five-year-olds still make errors. Flavell et al. attempt to distinguish the conditions under which children make realism errors from the conditions under which children make phenomalism errors.

[6]For example, Piaget claimed that there is a domain general shift from egocentric to nonegocentric thinking during the years of 5 to 7. It is a nontrivial finding that when point of view is at issue the immature response is usually to neglect the other fellow's. However, point of view is at issue in many different domains (e.g., moral reasoning, use of deixis in language, astronomy) and the egocentric errors are overcome at 18 months in some cases and not until adulthood in others (cf. Flavell, 1977, for a review).

or arithmetic in the elementary grades. These achievements are datable and it is likely that the acquisition of such powerful tools affects knowledge acquisition in a diversity of domains.

Case 6: The Concepts of Number and Measurement

It is certainly true that the child does not acquire an abstract concept of number until age 5 or 6. The best known phenomenon that shows this nonconservation – children who agree that two bunches of pebbles each contain the same number will say that they no longer have the same number when one is spatially rearranged. Piaget (1965) argued that the absence of concrete operations prevented younger children from representing the concept of number, that is, he argued that format limitations were responsible for nonconservation of number by children under 5 or 6. Gelman and Gallistel (1978) argue that the 2-year-old's competence with counting requires all the operations Piaget formalized as concrete operations, and indeed, they showed that children as young as 3 conserve number, so long as they know what number it is (i.e., it is within their counting competence). Gelman and Gallistel see the achievement of age 5 or 6 as the abstraction of the concept *number* from particular numbers.

It is also certainly true that facility with measurement develops in the early elementary grades. This achievement, too, has been tied to the development of concrete operations. For example, the use of a measuring device to tell whether two quantities are the same along some dimension requires a transitive inference, putatively beyond preoperational children. The claim that children younger than 6 or 7 cannot make transitive inferences has already been refuted (see Case 1). Bryant (1974) discusses these issues as they relate to measurement.

Although I am denying the account of the acquisition of the abstract concepts of number and of measurement in terms of concrete operation, I am not denying that these tools become available to the child for the first time in the years from 6 to 9 or 10. And it is certainly plausible that the acquisition of such tools affects learning and thinking quite broadly, at least in all domains where quantitative measurement is an issue. But before we simply accept the fundamental-differences proposition on this fourth interpretation, two caveats are in order. First, nobody has yet shown the impact of acquiring these tools on the learning of any particular domain-spe-specific knowledge. As of yet, the argument for developmental changes in learning or thinking on this fourth interpretation is merely one of plausibility. Second, in the history of science it is quite clear that the important aspect of most breakthroughs in measurement have concerned qualitative reasoning rather than the quantitative techniques involved in each breakthrough. Even when new instruments are invented, such as the thermometer, hundreds of years have sometimes intervened before scientists have discovered what they measured (Kuhn, 1977b; see Wiser & Carey, 1983, for a discussion of the earliest systematic work using the thermometer). The bottleneck has not been the concept of measurement but rather the conceptualization of the quantities to be measured. The bottleneck has been domain-specific knowledge. There is every reason to expect this to be so in the case of individual child development as well. Strauss' work on the child's concept of temperature illustrates the same point. Well after the achievements of the abstract concept of number, arithmetic, and the notion of measurement, the child reasons as follows: If you have two cups of water at 200° and you mix them together, you get water at 400° (Strauss, Stavey, & Orpaz, 1981). Sorting this out requires realizing that temperature is an intensive quantity, and this in turn requires a minimal differentiation of the concepts of heat and temperature. We should not be surprised that the 10-year-old has not worked this out; it took over 100 years in the history of science!

In conclusion, although I do not doubt that the child is a fundamentally different kind of learner from the adult on this fourth interpretation, it is likely that in most cases what distinguishes the child from the adult in the use of quantitative reasoning in any given domain is domain-specific knowledge, not the quantitative reasoning skills themselves. An important task for development psychology is to show the limits of my pessimistic generalization, to show the ways in which lack of some tool that cuts across different domains actually does constrain knowledge acquisition in any particular domain.

ACQUISITION AND REORGANIZATION OF DOMAIN-SPECIFIC KNOWLEDGE

Nobody doubts that the 3-year-old knows less than the adult. Indeed, if the lesson drawn in cases 1 and 2 about putative format-level developmental changes (i.e., there are none) is correct, then all the ways in which 3-year-olds differ from adults reduce to their knowing less. Even granting that some domains of knowledge cross-cut others (e.g., metaconceptual knowledge, mathematical knowledge), the acquisition and reorganization of strictly domain-specific knowledge (e.g., of the physical, biological, and social worlds) probably accounts for most of the cognitive difference between 3-year-olds and adults. I have argued that in many cases developmental changes that have been taken to support format-level changes, or changes due to the acquisition of some tool that cross-cut domains, in fact are due to acquisition of domain-specific knowledge. This point was often a comment on methodological artifacts – e.g., one cannot study the schema for controlling variables by using variables the child cannot conceptualize given the nature of his or her naïve physics! In other cases the point was more conceptual. I argued (following Kuhn) that putative changes in concepts that cross-cut different domains (e.g., in causality, or the appearance/reality distinction) are actually entirely parasitic on theory change, i.e., change in domain-specific knowledge.

Let us explicitly dispense with the implicit *mere* in the second proposition, that children differ from adults merely in the accumulation of knowledge. There are hosts of unsolved problems concerning the acquisition of knowledge, and these are where developmental psychologists may fruitfully concentrate their attention to advance explanations of developmental change. One such outstanding problem can serve as illustration: What kinds of reorganization of knowledge occur during development?

I know of two bodies of literature specifically concerned with the acquisition of domain-specific knowledge. Cognitive scientists studying the so-called "novice/expert shift" (cf. Chi, Glaser, & Rees, 1982, for an excellent review) and historians and philosophers of science studying theory change (cf. Suppe, 1974, for a review) both agree that the acquisition of domain-specific knowledge cannot be thought of as the mere accumulation of facts. Both groups emphasize the reorganization that is a crucial part of the process. Chi et al. review two well-studied examples of the novice/expert shift – from novice to expert chess players, and from novice to expert physics (mechanics) problem solvers. Two kinds of restructuring seem to be involved. Most important is the emergence of higher order concepts (e.g., weak pawn position in chess, or problems solvable by application of the principle of conservation of energy in mechanics that organize the expert's view and that are unavailable to the novice). As Chi et al. put it, what is basic level for the novice is subordinate for the expert. Also important is the enrichment of connections (on a semantic network metaphor) among the concepts that articulate the domain, giving the domain stability and inferential power. Notice, on these two views of the restructuring there is nothing *incompatible* between the expert's conceptual system and the novice's; rather, the novice's is merely incomplete in some very crucial ways. The view of restructuring that emerges in literature on theory change is more radical. There is a degree of incompatibility between successive theories; the concepts that articulate successive theories carve the world at different joints that are not merely hierarchically related to each other. Wiser and Carey (1983) provide an example from the historical development of the physics of heat. The earliest practitioners of this science, students of Galileo, worked in Florence during the 17th century. Although they had the thermometer, they did not know what it measured; indeed, they had not distinguished heat and temperature. Their source-recipient model of thermal phenomena allowed them certain successes – the description of the thermal expansion of solids, the description of the contraction and expansion of water during freezing – but it also fundamentally inhibited progress. In their view, heat and cold were necessarily different concepts. Heat (or cold) was emitted from hot (or cold) sources such as fire or the sun (or ice). Passive recipients were affected by the heat (or cold) entering them. The effects the Florentine scientists were interested in were mechanical – the rate and force of expansion and contraction. Wiser and Carey (1983) argue that their source-recipient model was quite incompatible with the modern equilibrium theory of heat exchange in which heat is exchanged between two bodies as a function of temperature differences. In modern theory, the effects of source and recipient are mutual. This incompatibility between the two theoretical frameworks played a role, we argue, in the Florentine experimenters' failure to differentiate heat and temperature. Indeed, this differentiation was not achieved until 100 years later, by Black, who finally laid the foundations for modern theories of thermal phenomena.

Clearly, stating precisely what kinds of restructuring characterize theory change and finding ways for representing them is a major challenge for cognitive scientists. Equally important is to establish whether restructuring in this stronger sense also occurs in at least some cases of the novice/expert shift; that is, do some novice/expert shifts involve theory change, rather than merely the transition from no theory to first theory? Recent work on the physics misconceptions of novice physicists (Caramazza, McCloskey, & Green, 1981; Clement, 1982) and of the differences between novice and expert representations of problems (Larkin, 1983) suggest that the stronger sense of reorganization will be needed in the description of the novice/expert shift. Most important for us here is to carry this question one step further – does knowledge acquisition in the case of the child exhibit the properties of theory change, as I suggested earlier? Much analytic work is required before that question may be answered either yes or no.

CONCLUSIONS

If one is free to use the locution think differently however one pleases, then whether the young child thinks differently from the adult or not is partly a semantic matter. But only partly. I have argued that on two interpretations of think differently (1 and 3 on Table 6.1), considered judgement dictates that young children and sophisticated adults think alike.

Developmental psychologists wish to account for the variance in behaviour among populations of different ages. I have argued that by far the most important source of variance is in domain-specific knowledge. Children know less than adults. Children are novices in almost every domain in which adults are experts. Perhaps, too, children hold theories in some domains actually at variance with the adults'.

If my diagnosis of the problem that developmental psychologists face is correct, then at least we know what we are up against – the fundamental problems of induction, epistemology, and philosophy of science. We ignore the work in these fields at our peril.

ACKNOWLEDGEMENTS

This chapter was prepared while I was a Sloan Fellow at the University of California, Berkeley's, Center for Cognitive Science. My research was supported by NIE-NSF grant number SED 791 3278 (1979–1982).

REFERENCES

Braine, M., & Shanks, B. (1965a). The conservation of shape property and a proposal about the origin of the conservations. *Canadian Journal of Psychology, 19,* 197–207.

Braine, M., & Shanks, B. (1965b). The development of conservation of size, *Journal of Verbal Learning and Verbal Behavior, 4,* 227–242.

Bruner, J. S., Olver, R., & Greenfield, P.M. (1966). *Studies in cognitive growth.* New York: Wiley.

Bryant, P. (1974). *Perception and understanding in young children.* New York: Basic Books.

Bullock, M., Gelman, R., & Baillargeon, R. (1982). The development of causal reasoning. In W. Friedman (Ed.), *The developmental psychology of time* (pp. 209–253). New York: Academic Press.

Caramazza, A., McCloskey, M., & Green, B. (1981). Naive beliefs in "sophisticated" subjects: Misconceptions about trajectories of objects. *Cognition, 9,* 117–123.

Carey, S. (1972). *Are children little scientists with false theories of the world?* Unpublished doctoral dissertation, Harvard University.

Carey, S. (1978). The child as word learner. In J. Bresnan, G. Miller, & M. Halle, (Eds.), *Linguistic theory and psychological reality.* Cambridge, MA.: MIT Press.

Carey, S. (1982). Semantic development, state of the art. In L. Gleitman, & E. Wanner, (Eds.), *Language acquisition, state of the art.* Cambridge, England: Cambridge University Press.

Carey, S. (In press) *Conceptual change in childhood.* Cambridge, MA: Bradford Books, MIT Press

Carey, S., & Block, N. (1976, June). *Conceptual change in children and scientists.* Paper presented to the Piaget Society, Philadelphia.

Case, R. (1974). Structures and strictures: Some functional limitations on the course of cognitive growth. *Cognitive Psychology, 6,* 544–573.

Chi, M., Glaser, R., & Rees, E. (1982). Expertise in problem solving. In R. Sternberg, (Ed.), *Advances in the psychology of human intelligence* (Vol. 1, pp. 7–75). Hillsdale, N.J.: Lawrence Erlbaum Associates Inc.

Clement, J. (1982). Students' preconceptions in introductory mechanics. *American Journal of Physics, 50,* 66–71.

De Vries, R. (1969). Constancy of generic identity in the years three to six. *Monographs of the Society for Research in Child Development, 34*(3, Serial No. 127).

Dickenson, D. (1982). *The development of children's understanding of materials: A study of theory construction and conceptual development.* Unpublished doctoral dissertation, Harvard University.

Egido, C. (1983). *The functional role of closed class vocabulary in children's language processing.* Unpublished doctoral thesis, Massachusetts Institute of Technology.

Feyerabend, P. (1962). Explanation, reduction and empiricism. In H. Feigl, & G. Maxwell, (Eds.), *Minnesota studies in philosophy of science* (Vol. III). Minneapolis: University of Minnesota Press.

Flavell, J.H. (1963). *The developmental psychology of Jean Piaget.* Princeton, N.J.: Van Nostrand.

Flavell, J. (1977). *Cognitive development.* Englewood Cliffs, N.J.: Prentice-Hall, Inc.

Flavell, J., Flavell, E., & Green, F. (1983). Development of the appearance-reality distinction. *Cognitive Psychology, 15*(1), 95–120.

Fodor, J. (1967). How to learn to talk, some simple ways. In F. Smith, & G. Miller (Eds.), *The genesis of language.* Cambridge, MA: MIT Press.

Fodor, J. (1972). Some reflections on L. S. Vygotsky's *Thought and language. Cognition, 1,* 83–95.

Fodor, J. (1975). *The language of thought.* New York: Thomas Y. Crowell.

Gelman, R., & Baillargeon, R. (1983). A review of some Piagetian concepts. In J. H. Flavell & F. M. Markman, (Eds.), *Cognitive development* (Vol. II) of P. H. Musson (Gen. Ed.), *Handbook of child psychology.* New York: Wiley.

Gelman, R., & Gallistel, C. (1987). *The child's understanding of number.* Cambridge, MA: Harvard University Press.

Hanson, N.R. (1961). *Patterns of discovery: An inquiry into the conceptual foundations of science.* Cambridge, England: Cambridge University Press.

Harris, P. (1975). Inferences and semantic development. *Journal of Child Language, 2,* 143–152.

Inhelder, B., & Piaget, J. (1958). *The growth of logical thinking from childhood to adolescence.* New York: Basic Books.

Inhelder, B., & Piaget, J. (1964). *The early growth of logic in the child.* New York: Norton.

Karmiloff-Smith, A., & Inhelder, B. (1975). If you want to get ahead, get a theory. *Cognition, 3*(3), 195–212.

Katz, J. (1972). *Semantic theory.* New York: Harper & Row.

Kuhn, T. S. (1962). *The structure of scientific revolutions.* Chicago: University of Chicago Press.

Kuhn, T. S. (1977a). Concepts of cause. In *The essential tension.* Chicago: University of Chicago Press.

Kuhn, T. S. (1977b). The function of measurement in modern physical science. In *The essential tension.* Chicago: University of Chicago Press.

Larkin, J. H. (1983). The role of problem representation in physics. In D. Gentner & A. Stevens (Eds.), *Mental models.* Hillsdale, N. J.: Lawrence Erlbaum Associates Inc.

Liberman, I., Shankweiler, D., Fischer, F., & Carter, B. (1974). Explicit syllable and phoneme segmentation in the young child. *Journal of Experimental Child Psychology. 5,* 201–212.

Markman, E. M. (1978). Empirical versus logical solutions to part-whole comparison problems concerning classes and collections. *Child Development, 49,* 168–177.

Markman, E. M. (1981). Two different principles of conceptual organization. In M. E. Lamb & A. L. Brown (Eds.), *Advances in developmental psychology* (Vol. 1). Hillsdale, N. J.: Lawrence Erlbaum Associates Inc.

Markman, E., & Callanan, M. (1983). An analysis of hierarchical classification. In R. Sternberg (Ed.), *Advances in the psychology of human intelligence* (Vol. 2). Hillsdale, N. J.: Lawrence Erlbaum Associates Inc.

Markman, E. M., Horton, M. S., & McLanahan, A. G. (1980). Classes and collections: Principles of organization in the learning of hierarchical relations. *Cognition, 8,* 227–241.

McKie, D. & Heathcote, N. (1935). *The discovery of specific and latent heats*. London: Edward Arnold.

Miller, G. (1977). *Spontaneous apprentices: Children and language*. New York: Seabury Press.

Osherson, D. N. (1974). *Organization of length and class concepts: Empirical consequences of a Piagetian formalism*. Potomac, M. D.: Lawrence Erlbaum Associates Inc.

Osherson, D., & Markman, E. (1975). Language and the ability to evaluate contradictions and tautologies. *Cognition, 3*(3), 213–226.

Papandropoulou, I., & Sinclair, H. (1974). What is a word? *Human Development, 17,* 241–258.

Parsons, C. (1960). Inhelder and Piaget's *The growth of logical thinking: A logician's viewpoint*. *British Journal of Psychology, 51,* 75–84.

Piaget, J. (1926). *The language and the thought of the child*. New York: Harcourt, Brace, & World.

Piaget, J. (1929). *The child's conception of the world*. Totowa, N. J.: Littlefield, Adams.

Piaget, J. (1932). *The moral judgment of the child*. New York: Harcourt, Brace & World.

Piaget, J. (1965). *The child's conception of number*. New York: Norton.

Piaget, J. (1972). *The child's conception of physical causality*. Totowa, N. J.: Littlefield, Adams.

Piaget, J., & Inhelder, B. (1967). *The child's conception of space*. New York: Norton.

Piaget, J., & Inhelder, B. (1974). *The child's conception of quantities*. London: Routledge & Kegan Paul.

Pinker, S. (1979). Formal models of language learning. *Cognition, 7*(3), 217–283.

Rosch, E., Mervis, C., Gray, W., Johnson, D., & Boyes-Braem, P. (1976). Basic objects in natural categories. *Cognitive Psychology, 3,* 382–439.

Ross, G. (1980). Categorization in 1- to 2-year-olds. *Developmental Psychology, 16,* 391–396.

Shapere, D. (1966). Meaning and scientific change. In R. Colodny (Ed.), *Mind and cosmos*. Pittsburgh: University of Pittsburgh Press.

Shultz, T. R. (1982). Rules of causal attribution. *Monographs of the Society for Research in Child Development*.

Smith, C. (1979). Children's understanding of natural language hierarchies. *Journal of Experimental Child Psychology, 27,* 437–458.

Smith C. (1981). *A study of the differentiation of the concepts of size and weight*. Paper presented to the Society for Research in Child Development, Boston.

Smith, E. E., & Medin, D. (1981). *Concepts and categories*. Cambridge, MA: Harvard University Press.

Strauss, S., Stavey, R., & Orpaz, N. (1981). *The child's development of the concept of temperature*. Unpublished manuscript, Tel-Aviv University.

Suppe, F. (1974). *The structure of scientific theories*. Urbana, Ill: University of Illinois Press.

Toulmin, S. (1953). *The philosophy of science: An introduction*. London: Hutchinson.

Vygotsky, L. (1962). *Thought and language*. Cambridge, MA: MIT Press.

Winner, E. (1976). New names for old things: The emergence of metaphoric language. *Journal of Child Language, 6,* 469–491.

Wiser, M. & Carey, S. (1983). When heat and temperature were one. In D. Gentner & A. Stevens (Eds.), *Mental models*. Hillsdale, N. J.: Lawrence Erlbaum Associates Inc.

7 Metacognitive Skills

Ann L. Brown and Judy S. DeLoache

This reading consists of two sections from a paper by Brown and DeLoache entitled "Skills, plans and self-regulation". In the first section, "Self-interrogation and self-regulation", the authors discuss the metacognitive skills that may be used in a variety of different tasks. That is, they consider those metacognitive skills that are sufficiently abstract to apply to a range of different situations. They point out that young children may not be aware of these skills, and that even once they have acquired them, they may not always see the opportunities to use them. This point is illustrated more fully in the second extract, "Selected tasks and strategies", where Brown and DeLoache describe the application of metacognitive skills to three different activities. The activities are extracting basic information from texts, visual scanning, and retrieval processes. The authors refer to these activities because they are used in a range of situations, and because they are carried out by both children and adults. The development of metacognitive skills, and their influence on performance over a wide age range, can therefore be considered.

SELF-INTERROGATION AND SELF-REGULATION

The main premise we discuss is that when faced with a new type of problem, anyone is a novice to a certain extent. Novices often fail to perform efficiently, not only because they may lack certain skills but because they are deficient in terms of self-conscious participation and intelligent self-regula-

Source: Donaldson, M. et al. (Eds) (1983). *Early childhood development and education.* Oxford: Blackwell, pp. 280–289.

tion of their actions. The novice tends not to know much about either his capabilities on a new task or the techniques necessary to perform efficiently; he may even have difficulty determining what goals are desirable, let alone what steps are required to get there. Note that this innocence is not necessarily related to age (Chi, 1978) but is more a function of inexperience in a new problem situation. Adults and children display similar confusion when confronted with a new problem. A novice chess player (Chi, 1977) has many of the same problems of metacognition that the very young card player experiences (Markman, 1977). For both, the situation is relatively new and difficult. Barring significant transfer from prior experience, the beginner in any problem-solving situation has not developed the necessary knowledge about how and what to think under the new circumstances.

The point we wish to emphasize is that children find themselves in this situation more often than do adults, and very young children may be neophytes in almost all problem situations. Thus, an explanation of why young children have such generalized metacognitive deficits (Brown, 1978b; Flavell & Wellman, 1977) is that most of our experimental tasks are both new and difficult for them. It is this lack of familiarity with the game at hand that leads to a concomitant lack of self-interrogation about the current state of knowledge and to inadequate selection and monitoring of necessary steps between starting levels and desired goals. The child's initial "passivity" in many memory and problem-solving tasks, his failure to check and monitor his ongoing activities, and his failure to make his own task analysis could be the direct result of gross inexperience on such tasks. This does not mean that young children are incapable of self-regulation, only that they tend not to bring such procedures to bear immediately on new problems. Children are universal novices; it takes experience before they build up the knowledge and confidence that would enable them to adopt routinely the self-interrogation mode of the expert (Bransford, Nitsch & Franks, 1977).

Although absolute novices tend not to incorporate effective metacognitive activities into their initial attempts to solve problems, it is not simply the case that experts do and novices do not engage in effective self-regulation. As Simon and Simon (1978) have pointed out in their study of physics problem solvers, the expert engaged in less observable self-questioning than did the relative novice, for the processes of problem solving in this domain had become relatively automatic for the expert. The relative novice, on the other hand, showed many instances of overt self-questioning and checking. Notice that Simon and Simon's novice had received sufficient background instruction so that the basic rules for solution were known to her. We would characterize her state of knowing as being typical of the learner: acquainted with the rules of the game and beginning to acquire expertise.

We would not be surprised to find that the following pattern is typical. First, the absolute novices show little or no intelligent self-regulation. Then, as the problem solver becomes familiar with the necessary rules and sub-processes, he enters into an increasingly active period of deliberate self-regulation. Finally, the performance of the expert would run smoothly as the necessary sub-processes and their coordination have all been overlearned to the point where they are relatively automatic.

We have as yet little developmental data to suggest that such a pattern is a characteristic feature of growth during problem solving, but we predict that such a progression may be a common feature of learning in many domains. Furthermore, although age and experience are obviously intimately related, we do not believe that the growth pattern is necessarily related to age. Young children may show the same progression of naïveté to competence within simpler task domains. Evidence such as that provided by Chi's (1978) young chess experts is exactly the kind needed to support this conjecture. If we wish to understand how much of the young child's ineptitude is due to lack of expertise, rather than age per se, we must look at behaviour in areas in which the child is competent as well as those in which he is inefficient.

There is one other factor that might contribute to the young child's general metacognitive problem. In addition to being hampered by the novelty of most experimental situations, young children may simply not realize that certain metacognitive operations are useful in practically any situation. These general metacognitive skills are discussed at length in another paper (Brown, 1978b), and we only briefly summarize them here. The basic skills of metacognition include *predicting* the consequences of an action or event, *checking* the results of one's own actions (did it work?), *monitoring* one's ongoing activity (how am I doing?), *reality testing* (does this make sense?), and a variety of other behaviours for *coordinating* and *controlling* deliberate attempts to learn and solve problems. These skills are the basic characteristics of efficient thought, and one of their most important properties is that they are trans-situational. They apply to the whole range of problem-solving activities, from artificially structured experimental settings to what we psychologists defensively refer to as "real world, everyday life" situations. It is important to check the results of an operation against some criterion of acceptability, whether one is memorizing a prose passage, reading a textbook, or following instructions in a laboratory experiment, a classroom, or on the street. A child has to learn these various skills, but perhaps of equal importance, he has to learn that they are almost universally applicable, that whenever he is faced with a new task, it will be to his advantage to apply his general knowledge about how to learn and solve problems.

SELECTED TASKS AND STRATEGIES

(1) Extracting the main idea

Getting the gist of a message, whether it is oral or written, is an essential communicative as well as information-gathering activity. Without this ability, children would never learn a language and would certainly never come to use that language to communicate. The ability to extract the main idea to the exclusion of nonessential detail may be a naturally occurring proclivity given, of course, a reasonable match between the complexity of the message and the receiver's current cognitive status (Brown, 1975).

In a recent series of studies (Brown & Smiley, 1977a, 1977b) we have been considering the situation in which children must extract the main theme of a prose passage, a story. Our subject population has ranged from preschoolers as young as three years of age to college students, and the stories are adapted to suit the different age groups. We find the same pattern across age: with or without conscious intent to do so, subjects extract the main theme of a story and ignore trivia. Older children have more highly developed scripts (Nelson, 1977; Nelson & Brown, 1978) for storytelling, but even very young children apprehend the essential gist of a story plot (Brown, 1976).

Children are misled in their comprehension of stories by the same snares that trap adults (Brown, Smiley, Day, Townsend & Lawton, 1977). Led to believe certain "facts" concerning a main character or the location of an action, facts that never appear in the original story, children disambiguate and elaborate in the same way as adults. They falsely recognize theme-congruent distractors in recognition tests and include their pre-existing knowledge when recalling. In addition, they had difficulty distinguishing between their own elaborations and the actual story content.

If there is such essential similarity across ages in the way children construct a message from prose passages, what then is the interesting developmental trend? Not surprisingly, given the theme of this chapter, we believe that what develops is an increasingly conscious control of the naturally occurring tendency, a control that allows more efficient gathering of information.

As children mature they begin to predict the essential organizing features and crucial elements of texts (Brown & Smiley, 1977a, 1977b). Thanks to this fore-knowledge, they make better use of extended study time. If given an extra period for study (equal to three times their reading rate), children from the seventh grade up improve considerably their recall for important elements of text; recall of less important details does not improve. Children below the seventh grade do not usually show such effective use of additional study time; their recall improves, if at all, evenly across all levels of importance. As a result, older students' recall protocols following study include all the essential elements and little trivia. Younger children's recall, though still favouring important elements, has many important elements missing.

To substantiate our belief that metacognitive control governs this developmental trend, we have observed the study actions of our subjects. In particular, we have examined their physical records that can be scored objectively – notes and underlining of texts. A certain proportion of children from the fifth grade and up spontaneously underline or take notes during study. At all ages, the physical records of spontaneous subjects favoured the important elements, that is, the notes or underlined sections concentrated on elements previously rated as crucial to the theme. Students induced to adopt one of these strategies did not show a similar sensitivity to importance; they took notes or underlined more randomly. Some of the very young children underlined all the text when told to underline. Although the efficiency of physical record keeping in induced subjects did improve with age, it never reached the standard set by spontaneous users of the strategy. Furthermore, the recall scores of spontaneous producers were much superior. Even fifth graders who spontaneously underlined showed an adult-like pattern and used extra study to improve differentially their recall of important elements. When we combined all fifth graders, the efficient pattern of the spontaneous children was masked.

It should be pointed out that we do not believe there is a magical age at which children become able to detect the important elements of a text. This is obviously a case of headfitting (Brown, 1975, 1978b) – that is, the intimate relation of the child's current knowledge to the complexity of the stimulus materials. We have found that children can pick out the main ideas of much simpler texts at much earlier ages. We are currently examining whether, given this foresight, they show a concomitant decrease in the age of onset of simple strategies.

In short, knowledge about texts (or any message source for that matter) must consist of general knowledge about consistent features of all texts and specific knowledge about the particular example at hand, a specific knowledge that must be influenced by idiosyncratic characteristics such as complexity. Similarly, we would expect that strategies for learning from a text would depend on general strategic knowledge about suitable activities, but these would have to be triggered by certain specific features of the text being studied. Quite simply, if the text is so complicated that the reader cannot identify the main points, he can scarcely be expected to select them for extra study, even if he possesses the prerequisite strategic knowledge that this would be a good study ploy. Thus, we would predict that even the sophisticated college student may behave immaturely when studying a difficult text.

This brief summary of some of our ongoing research (for details see Brown & Smiley, 1977b) illustrates what we believe to be a repetitive pattern in cognitive development. What develops is often an increasingly conscious control over an early emerging process. Even young children extract the essential gist of messages if they are not misled by red herrings, such as artifically increased salience of nonessential detail (Brown, 1980). All our subjects have shown this ability to a lesser or greater extent – even preschool children (Brown, 1976), poor readers (Smiley, Oakley, Worthen, Campione & Brown, 1977), and slow learners (Brown and Campione, 1978). What develops with age are strategies and control over these strategies. Using knowledge about elements of texts, knowledge about how to study, and the interface of these two factors, the older student can become much more efficient at processing information presented in texts.

(2) Visual scanning

Our next selection of a naturally occurring ability that shows interesting refinement and increasingly conscious control with age and experience is visual scanning, the process by which one, as Day (1975, p.154) says, "actively, selectively, and sequentially acquires information from the visual environment". Effective and efficient visual scanning requires a high degree of executive control, directing fixations and sequencing eye movements from one point of the visual array to another.

Visual scanning begins in the first hours of life. Even newborn infants scan visual stimuli (Salapatek, 1975) but in a very restricted fashion; the young infant is likely to limit his fixations to only one corner of a simple geometric figure (Salapatek, 1968) or to just one feature of a face (Maurer & Salapatek, 1976). The young infant's attention is drawn, almost compelled, to small areas of high contrast. He seems to have very limited voluntary control over his looking and has been characterized as being "captured" by visual stimuli (Ames & Silfen, 1966; Stechler & Latz, 1966).

This involuntary looking gradually gives way during the first few months to much more voluntary control. By three or four months a baby scans the entire pattern, not just a single feature (Gibson, 1969), and thus becomes capable of extracting more and higher-level information. In addition, active stimulus comparison is performed (Ruff, 1975). When presented with two visual patterns, a baby looked back and forth between the two. The degree of shifting increases with age. The more similar the stimuli, the more looking back and forth the infant does, suggesting that even for infants, deployment of a strategy depends on the difficulty of the task. Thus, in the first few months of life we can see important refinements in visual scanning. The behaviour comes more and more under voluntary control and produces an ever-increasing amount of information.

The later development of visual scanning parallels the changes that occur during infancy. Many aspects of development can be attributed to the expanding role of internal, planful, self-regulation of scanning and the concomitant decreasing importance of external variables. Although the young infant gradually stops being "captured" by simple stimuli, we see repeated examples of this same problem in older children attempting to cope with more complex tasks. The exact manifestation varies according to the situation. For example, when studying an unfamiliar irregular shape, three-year-old subjects made fewer eye movements than did six-year-olds (Zinchenko, Chzhtitsin & Tarakanov, 1963). Furthermore, the younger children fixated primarily in the centre of the figure, whereas the older children's fixations covered its more informative contours.

Although six-year-olds in the Zinchenko et al. study showed relatively mature scanning, if a more complex stimulus had been presented, they might have displayed immature scanning. Mackworth and Bruner (1970) showed to adults and six-year-old children sharply focused photographs containing much detailed information. The six-year-olds often became "so hooked by the details" that they failed to scan broadly over the rest of the stimulus. "Having arrived at a 'good place' on which to rest their gaze, they seem to feel 'disinclined' to leap into the unknown areas of the sharp pictures" (p. 165). Mackworth and Bruner concluded that adults possess an effective visual search programme that enables them to *coordinate* central and peripheral vision together but that children do not. Children can extract detailed information centrally, and they can detect peripheral stimuli. However, they cannot execute the two operations *simultaneously*. Thus, the main problem is one of coordination and control, not the presence or absence of specific skills.

Increased cognitive control is also reflected in other important developmental changes in visual scanning. For example, children's scanning gradually becomes more systematic, indicating the presence of higher-order organization. Vurpillot (1968) filmed the eye movements of four- to nine-year-old children as they were deciding if two houses were identical. Unlike the older subjects, the youngest children rarely made the systematic paired comparisons of comparably located windows that are necessary for successful performance. Furthermore, the young children's scanning was less exhaustive. When two identical houses were shown, they often failed to look at all the windows before pronouncing the houses the same.

Another important developmental change is in focusing on the more informative areas of a visual stimulus. The older the child, the more likely he is to fixate those distinctive features that give him the greatest amount of relevant information for the task at hand (Mackworth & Bruner, 1970; Olson, 1970; Zinchenko et al., 1963). Conversely, young children find it more difficult to ignore irrelevant information. Just as in incidental memory studies and in prose-studying experiments, the younger the child, the more attention he is likely to devote to stimuli that are irrelevant to the task he is performing (Pushkina, 1971).

Although by adulthood scanning has usually developed into quite an efficient, individualized process (Noton & Stark, 1971), adults are by no means immune to the metacognitive problems children experience so frequently. If required to perform a difficult scanning task, such as inspecting chest x-rays for signs of pathology (Thomas, 1968), adults (relative novices) often suffer some of the same deficiencies seen in children (e.g. failing to scan as exhaustively as necessary or failing to focus on the most informative areas).

Scanning tasks thus reveal the same general pattern illustrated by the gist-recall procedure. Scanning a visual array, like extracting the main idea, is a naturally occurring response necessary for a wide variety of tasks and for survival. As the child matures, he develops the ability to control and coordinate scanning, to make scanning a strategic action tailored to changing task demands.

(3) Retrieval processes

For our third example we have selected retrieval, considered broadly to encompass finding objects hidden in the external environment as well as retrieving information temporarily lost in memory. In both cases the subject often must use some other information to help him track down the desired object or thought. Although children use external cues to search the environment before they use internal cues to search their own memories, many of the same strategies are relevant to both activities. Furthermore, in both activities the child is increasingly able to direct and control his search procedures, that is, he achieves increasing metacognitive control, including planning ahead to facilitate later retrieval and executing a search according to a logical plan. Our discussion here will draw heavily on the work of John Flavell and his colleagues, for they have been by far the most active and creative investigators in this area.

Retrieval activities occur naturally at an early age and continue to develop over a long period of time. Even infants are capable of organizing a sequence of behaviours into a search, but their initial efforts are very limited. The earliest information we have about the development of retrieval comes from object-permanence tasks. When six- or seven-month-old infants first start searching for hidden objects, they often do something very interesting from the point of view of self-regulation. A child may initiate what appears to be an attempt to remove the cloth concealing a desired object, only to become distracted by the cloth itself. We can characterize this as a failure to maintain executive control. In the midst of conducting a search, the child appears to forget the goal and subsequently ceases those behaviours originally directed towards achieving it. A minimal requirement for the coordination and control of retrieval efforts is the ability to keep the goal in mind for a sufficient period of time and in the face of distractions.

Another interesting aspect of early retrieval activities is that even toddlers employ rudimentary search strategies, as revealed by the regular errors they make in object-permanence tasks (the Stage IV error).[1] Beginning at about eight months, an infant who has previously found an object hidden at one place (A) is likely to search for it again at A, even though he has just witnessed the object being hidden at a second location (B). We would say with Harris (1973) that the infant seems to employ a strategy of looking for an object in the place where he found it before. Although this strategy has obvious limitations and often causes the infant to fail in object-permanence tasks, it seems reasonable that looking for an object where he found it before would serve the child relatively well in his everyday environment. Interestingly, children as old as two years have been found to rely on this same strategy (Loughlin & Dachler, 1973; Webb, Masur & Nadolny, 1972).

We have characterized the toddler's search as strategic because it suggests the systematic execution of a plan. The degree of self-conscious participation involved however, is probably minimal. As with the other areas we have reviewed, children's retrieval processes become increasingly sophisticated as conscious, voluntary control over them intensifies. In the case of retrieval, this sophistication is clearly reflected in at least two characteristics of performance. Children become more likely to do something deliberate *at the time of storage* to facilitate later retrieval, and their attempts at retrieval become more *systematic* and efficient.

Even very young children engage in relatively simple behaviours whose sole function is to help them remember. Children as young as three years, informed that they will later have to recall the location of an object (Wellman, Ritter & Flavell, 1975) or an event (Acredolo, Pick & Olsen, 1975), show better memory than children not so informed. Thus, the children must do something to help them remember during the delay. Wellman et al. (1975) observed their subjects and reported that while they waited, the children in the instructed memory condition looked at and touched the location they were supposed to remember. Preschool children are also able to use a specific cue provided for them. When an external cue marking the location of an object is made available, they can use it to help retrieve the object (Ritter, Kaprove, Fitch & Flavell, 1973). In addition, they are sometimes capable of arranging a cue themselves to aid their later retrieval (Ryan, Hegion & Flavell, 1970).

Not surprisingly, the tendency to use such cues improves with age. However, even when they think to use a retrieval cue, younger children may fail to use it as effectively as older children. In a study by Kobasigawa (1974), first graders who spontaneously used an available category cue still

---

[1]Piaget (1955) distinguishes six stages in the development of the object concept. At Stage IV, children make the error of looking for an object where they previously found it even when they have seen it being moved elsewhere.

recalled fewer items per category than did third graders. In other words, even when they thought to use the retrieval cues, the younger children failed to conduct an exhaustive search for the items associated with each cue. Istomina (1975) also noted the tendency of younger children not to execute an exhaustive search of their memories. Although some of her four- and five-year-old subjects actively attempted to recall a list of items, they did not try to retrieve items not immediately recalled. Older children, however, often showed signs of conducting an active internal search (Istomina, 1975, p.31): "In some cases the child recalled what he had forgotten only with long pauses, during which he would try not to look at those around him, i.e. he would direct his gaze downward, to the side or screw up his eyes". The non-exhaustive search could result from several possible factors. The child may not check his output against a criterion of acceptability, or, alternatively, he may have a different criterion from that of the experimenter's (Kobasigawa, 1974). Or his monitoring of his own memory may be inadequate to inform him that there are items yet to be recalled. In any case, these all represent metacognition problems of one sort or another. The essential similarity of non-exhaustiveness in both visual scanning and retrieval is obvious.

We have argued that there are some essential similarities between the retrieval of objects from the environment and the retrieval of information from memory and that many of the same strategies are relevant in both cases – for example, conducting an exhaustive search. However, it is clear that external retrieval is an easier task than memory scanning. Object retrieval studies show evidence of intentional efforts to remember and the use of strategies in children as young as three years, a much younger age than that at which Istomina's (1975) children could deliberately adopt the goal of remembering and recalling a list of words. In object-retrieval situations the cues available to aid memory are external and physically present; all the child must do is think to use them or orient to them. Thus, the problem is much simpler than one in which the child must initiate and maintain a purely internal, cognitive orientation to information in memory. The latter requires a greater degree of metacognitive control. The child must use internal processes, cognitions, to control other internal processes.

REFERENCES

Acredolo, L. P., Pick, H. L., & Olsen, M. G. (1975). Environmental differentiation and familiarity as determinants of children's memory for spatial location. *Developmental Psychology, 11*, 495–501.

Ames, E. W. & Silfen, C. K. (1966). *Methodological issues in the study of age differences in infants' attention to stimuli varying in movement and complexity.* Paper presented at the meeting of the Society for Research in Child Development, Minneapolis, March.

Bransford, J. D., Nitsch, K. W., & Franks, J. J. (1977). Schooling and the facilitation of knowing. In R. C. Anderson, R. J. Spiro, and W. E. Montague (Eds), *Schooling and the acquisition of knowledge*. Hillsdale, N. J.: Lawrence Erlbaum Associates Inc.

Brown, A. L. (1975). The development of memory; knowing, knowing about knowing, and knowing how to know. In H. W. Reese (Ed.), *Advances in child development and behaviour*, Vol. 10. New York: Academic Press.

Brown, A. L. (1976). The construction of temporal succession by preoperational children. In A. D. Pick (Ed.), *Minnesota Symposia on Child Psychology, Vol. 10*. Minneapolis: University of Minnesota.

Brown, A. L. (1978b). Knowing when, where, and how to remember: a problem of metacognition. In R. Glaser (Ed.), *Advances in instructional psychology*. Hillsdale, N. J.: Lawrence Erlbaum Associates Inc.

Brown, A. L. & Campione, J. C. (1978). Memory strategies in learning: training children to study strategically. In H. Pick, H. Leibowitz, J. Singer, A. Steinschneider, and H. Stevenson (Eds), *Application of basic research in psychology*. New York: Plenum Press.

Brown, A. L. & Smiley, S. S. (1977a). Rating the importance of structural units of prose passages: a problem of metacognitive development. *Child Development. 48*, 1–8.

Brown, A. L. & Smiley, S. S. (1977b). *The development of strategies for studying prose passages*. Unpublished manuscript, University of Illinois.

Brown, A. L., Smiley, S. S., Day, J. D., Townsend, M. A. R., & Lawton, S. C. (1977). Intrusion of a thematic idea in children's comprehension and retention of stories. *Child Development. 48*, 1454–1466.

Chi, M. T. H. (1977). *Metamemory and chess skill*. Unpublished manuscript, University of Pittsburgh.

Chi, M. T. H. (1978). Knowledge, structures and memory development. In R. S. Siegler (Ed.), *Children's thinking: What develops?* Hillsdale, N. J.: Lawrence Erlbaum Associates Inc.

Day, M. C. (1975). Development trends in visual scanning. In H. W. Reese (Ed.), *Advances in child development and behaviour, Vol. 10*. New York: Academic Press.

Flavell, J. H. & Wellman, H. M. (1977). Metamemory. In R. V. Kail, Jr. & J. W. Hagen (Eds), *Perspectives on the development of memory and cognition*. Hillsdale, N. J.: Lawrence Erlbaum Associates Inc.

Gibson, E. J. (1969). *Principles of perceptual learning and development*. New York: Appleton-Century-Crofts.

Harris, P. L. (1973). Perseverative errors in search by young infants. *Child Development, 44*, 28–33.

Istomina, Z. M. (1975). The development of voluntary memory in preschool-age children. *Soviet Psychology, 13*, 5–64.

Kobasigawa, A. (1974). Towards an ethnography of black American speech behaviour. In N. E. Whitten and J. Szwed (Eds). *Afro-American anthropology*. New York: Free Press, pp. 145–162

Loughlin, K. A. & Dachler, M. A. (1973). The effects of distraction and added perceptual cues on the delayed reaction of very young children. *Child Development, 44*, 384–388.

Mackworth, N. H. & Bruner, J. S. (1970). How adults and children search and recognize pictures. *Human Development, 13*, 149–177.

Markman, E. M. (1977). Realizing that you don't understand: A preliminary investigation. *Child Development, 48*, 986–992.

Maurer, D. & Salapatek, P. (1976). Developmental changes in the scanning of faces by young infants. *Child Development, 47*, 523–527.

Nelson, K. (1977). Cognitive development and the acquisition of concepts. In R. C. Anderson, R. J. Spiro & W. E. Montague (Eds), *Schooling and the acquisition of knowledge*. Hillsdale, N. J.: Lawrence Erlbaum Associates Inc.

Nelson K. & Brown, A. L. (1978). The semantic-episodic distinction in memory development. In P. Ornstein (Ed.), *Memory development*. Hillsdale, N. J.: Lawrence Erlbaum Associates Inc.

Noton, D. & Stark, L. (1971). Eye movements and visual perception. *Scientific American*, *224*, 34–43.

Olson, D. R. (1970). *Cognitive development: The child's acquisition of diagonality*. New York: Academic Press.

Pushkina, A. G. (1971). Mechanisms of transposition of relations in preschool-age children. *Soviet Psychology, 9*, 213–234.

Ritter, K., Kaprove, B. H., Fitch, J. P., & Flavell, J. H. (1973). The development of retrieval strategies in young children. *Cognitive Psychology, 5*, 310–321.

Ruff, H. A. (1975). The function of shifting fixations in the visual perception of infants. *Child Development, 46*, 857–865.

Ryan, S. M., Hegion, A. G., & Flavell, J. H. (1970). Nonverbal mnemonic mediation in preschool children. *Child Development, 41*, 539–550.

Salapatek, P. (1968). Visual scanning of geometric figures by the human newborn. *Journal of Comparative and Physiological Psychology, 66*, 247–258.

Salapatek, P. (1975). Pattern perception in early infancy. In L. B. Cohen & P. Salapatek (Eds), *Infant perception. Vol. 1*. New York: Academic Press.

Simon, D. P. & Simon, H. A. (1978). Individual differences in solving physics problems. In R. S. Siegler (Ed.), *Children's thinking: What develops?* Hillsdale, N. J.: Lawrence Erlbaum Associates Inc.

Smiley, S. S., Oakley, D. D., Worthen, D., Campione, J. C., & Brown, A. L. (1977). Recall of thematically relevant material by adolescent good and poor readers as a function of written versus oral presentation. *Educational Psychology, 69*, 381–387.

Stetchler, G. & Latz, E. (1966). Some observations on attention and arousal in the human infant. *Journal of the American Academy of Child Psychiatry, 5*, 517–525.

Thomas, E. L. (1968). Movements of the eye. *Scientific American, 219*, 88–95.

Vurpillot, E. (1968). The development of scanning strategies and their relation to visual differentiation. *Journal of Experimental Child Psychology, 6*, 632–650.

Webb, R. A., Masur, B. & Nadolny, T. (1972). Information and strategy in the young child's search for hidden objects. *Child Development, 43*, 91–104.

Wellman, H. M., Ritter, K. & Flavell, J. H. (1975). Deliberate memory behaviour in the delayed reactions of very young children. *Developmental Psychology, 11*, 780–787.

Zinchenko, V. F., Chzhi-tsin, B., & Tarakanov, V. V. (1963). The formation and development of perceptual activity. *Soviet Psychology and Psychiatry, 2*, 3–12.

III THE DEVELOPMENT OF KNOWLEDGE AND PROCESSES

8 Order of Acquisition of Subordinate-, Basic-, and Superordinate-Level Categories

Carolyn B. Mervis and Maria A. Crisafi

The present research was concerned with the order of acquisition of the ability to categorize at different hierarchical levels. The first experiment was designed to test the hypothesis that categorization ability is acquired in the following order: basic, superordinate, subordinate. Children aged 2–6, 4, and 5–6 were asked to indicate which, of 2 nonsense stimuli, was the same kind of thing as a standard for sets at each hierarchical level. The results supported our hypothesis. The second and third experiments considered 1 hypothesis concerning the basis for the obtained order: the greater the differentiation of categories at a given hierarchical level, the earlier categorization at that level should be acquired. To determine degree of differentiation, subjects made pairwise similarity judgments for stimuli used in the first experiment or for members of 2 natural-category hierarchies. Because of the complexity of the task, adults rather than children participated. Order of degree of differentiation paralleled acquisition order. Therefore, degree of differentiation is a possible determinant of acquisition order.

Psychologists who study the categorization of natural objects usually consider three levels of abstraction: subordinate, basic, and superordinate. For example a rocking chair (subordinate) is a type of chair (basic) which is a type of furniture (superordinate). In the present research, we used artificial stimuli which could be categorized at each level of abstraction to investigate the order in which young children acquire the ability to form categories at

Source: *Child Development* (1982). *53*, pp.258–266.

different levels of abstraction. In addition, we examined one possible basis for this order of acquisition.

Rosch, Mervis, Gray, Johnson, and Boyes-Braem (1976) have argued that one level of abstraction, the basic level, is more fundamental than the other levels. According to Rosch et al. (1976) the basic level is most fundamental because it is the most cognitively efficient level. This level is the most general level at which category members have similar over-all shapes and the most general one at which a person uses similar motor actions for interacting with category members. While categories at all levels are based on correlated attribute clusters, the correlations are most apparent for basic-level categories. The basic level is, accordingly, the level at which the similarity of members of the same category is maximized relative to the similarity of items from different categories. Thus, basic-level categories are the categories which are most differentiated from one another. On the basis of these findings, Rosch et al. have predicted that children will be able to categorize at the basic level before learning to categorize at other levels of abstraction.

Two studies which have used objects from natural categories have provided support for the developmental primacy of the basic level of categorization over the superordinate level. (The subordinate level has not been considered.) Rosch et al. (1976) found that the performance of 3-year-olds was much more accurate when sorting objects at the basic level compared with performance when sorting at the superordinate level. Daehler, Lonardo, and Bukatko (1979) reported that the performance of 2-year-olds was better when matching related objects at the basic level than at the superordinate level. These results indicate that very young children appreciate relationships among objects that share both functional and perceptual attributes (basic level) before appreciating relationships which rely on more abstract conceptualizations (superordinate level).

There is also linguistic evidence in support of the primacy of the basic level. According to Brown (1958, 1976), the name chosen to refer to an object should be applicable to all objects to which the child behaves in a similar way. Brown has argued that, because basic-level terms (or in his 1958 terminology, terms at the "level of usual utility") best meet this requirement, they are almost always used by parents when naming objects for young children. It has also been argued that children acquire basic-level names before names at other hierarchical levels (Anglin 1977; Rosch et al. 1976). Finally, there is indirect evidence, based on analyses of Brown's (Note 1) transcripts for Sarah and on Rinsland's (1945) lists of words used by first graders, that not only are basic level words acquired first but also that superordinate-level words are acquired before subordinate-level ones.

The purpose of the first experiment was to examine the development of the ability to categorize at different hierarchical levels. We hypothesized that ability to categorize at the basic level would be acquired first, and that ability to categorize at the superordinate level would precede ability to categorize at the subordinate level. Our hypothesis was confirmed by the results of the first study. We therefore performed two additional experiments, using a similarity-rating format, in order to test the hypothesis that the degree of differentiation of categories from one another is greatest for basic-level categories, next largest for superordinate-level categories, and smallest for subordinate-level categories. (Measures of degree of differentiation are based on the relationship between within-category similarity and between-category similarity for categories at a particular hierarchical level.) If our prediction is correct, then degree of differentiation would provide a reasonable basis for the obtained order of acquisition of the ability to categorize at different hierarchical levels.

EXPERIMENT 1

The present study provided a more stringent test of the ability to categorize at a particular level of abstraction than previous studies had, in two ways. First, in this study accurate sorting of category members was possible only by attending to cues specific to that level. For example, if we were interested in the category "dog", we might ask the child which two of the following three pictures were the same kind of thing: beagle, cocker spaniel, Siamese cat. This problem can be correctly solved only by attending to basic-level ("dog") cues; attention to superordinate-level ("animal") cues will lead to an incorrect response two-thirds of the time. Thus, consistently correct solutions indicate that the child knows something about the category dog. In previous studies, however, sorting cues were available from both the target level and all levels above the target one because of the nature of the distractors used. Thus, for example, for the category dog, the following three pictures might have been used: beagle, cocker spaniel, airplane. The problem would now be solvable by attending to either basic-level or superordinate-level cues. Correct solution therefore does not necessarily indicate anything about the child's knowledge of the category dog. Second, in the present study, nonsense forms which were never named were used as stimuli. Therefore, our data were not influenced by prior linguistic knowledge. In previous studies, familiar items were used as stimuli. Therefore, one could argue that ability to correctly name a category was the primary determinant of correct sorting.

Method

Subjects. Subjects included children from three age groups: 2–6-year-olds (mean: 2–8; range: 2–6 to 2–11), 4-year-olds (mean: 4–3; range: 4–0 to 4–5), and 5–6-year-olds (mean: 5–8; range: 5–6 to 5–11). There were five girls and five boys in each group. All of the last group attended kindergarten; the younger children were all enrolled in preschool programs.

Stimuli.   Stimuli were 24 different unfamiliar "nonsense" pictures. They were designed to form two superordinate categories, each with 12 members. Each superordinate category could be divided into two basic categories, each with six members. Each basic category could be divided into two subordinates, each with three members. The attribute structure of the categories was designed to correspond to the attribute structure of natural categories, as analyzed by Rosch et al. (1976). Therefore, members of a superordinate category shared a very general abstract attribute ("angular" for one superordinate; "curved" for the other). Members of a basic-level category had very similar overall shapes and had three additional attributes in common that were not shared by members of the other basic categories. The two subordinate categories subsumed under the same basic category differed slightly in outside contour and in the placement of detail. Thus, each subordinate category included two modifications of attributes present in the basic-level category. The three exemplars of a subordinate category differed from each other only in minor changes in the placement of detail. Thus, as for natural categories (Rosch et al. 1976), the present basic categories were the categories most differentiated from one another. Superordinate-category members shared only one very general attribute. Subordinate-category members shared more attributes than members of basic-level categories, but there was a large overlap in attributes shared between the two subordinates of one basic category, making the two subordinates quite similar.

In Fig. 8.1, we have shown line drawings of one member of each subordinate category and have indicated the hierarchical relationships among these categories. In order to explicate the general attribute description provided in the previous paragraph, we will delineate the attribute relationships for the two quasi-rectangular subordinate categories. Members of both these categories share the attribute, angular. This attribute is also shared by the two quasi-triangular subordinate categories; thus, it is a superordinate-level attribute. In addition, members of the two quasi-rectangular categories share four other attributes which are not shared by the

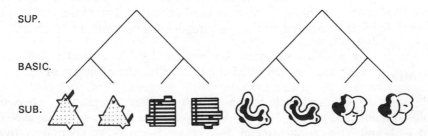

FIG. 8.1.   Representative stimuli used in the study.

quasi-triangular categories: overall shape (quasi-rectangular), presence of a thick vertical bar, several evenly spaced thin horizontal stripes, and an internal diamond. Thus, these are basic-level attributes. Members of one quasi-rectangular subordinate category have protrusions on the left and on top of the form; members of the other have protrusions on the right and on the bottom. Members of the first category have their diamond located in the upper left of the form, while members of the second category have their diamond located in the lower right. Thus, these two attributes (location of protrusions, which modifies the overall shape; and the position of diamond, which is a change in the placement of detail) are subordinate-level attributes. The three members of each subordinate category differed in the exact locations of the protrusions and the diamond, subject to the constraints imposed by the subordinate-level attributes.

The stimuli were drawn in full color on pale yellow paper. Each was mounted on 3 × 3-inch white cardboard and covered with clear contact paper. The stimulus filled most of the 3 × 3-inch space available. The colors of the stimuli varied randomly; color did not provide any clues to taxonomic sortings at any hierarchical level.

Three copies of each stimulus were used in the study. The stimuli were divided into 24 sets: eight testing subordinate, eight testing basic, and eight testing superordinate categories. Each set consisted of three pictures. Since the purpose of the study was to determine the order of development of the ability to sort taxonomically at the three different levels of abstraction, it was essential that correct sorting of a given set be possible only if the child were attending to cues specific to the target level. Therefore, all subordinate sets included two different members of one subordinate and one member of the other subordinate of the same basic category. All basic sets included one member of each of the two subordinates of one basic category and one member of the other basic category subsumed under the same superordinate. All superordinate sets included one member of each of the two basic categories subsumed under the same superordinate category and one member of the other superordinate category.

Before we began the actual study, it was important to be certain that the stimuli would provide an appropriate test of our hypotheses. Therefore, two requirements had to be met. First, the stimulus structure had to correspond to natural-category stimulus structure. This was accomplished by designing the attribute structure to correspond to the attribute structure of natural categories, as described above. Second, the members of the two subordinate categories subsumed under the same basic category had to be discriminable from one another for the youngest children who were to participate in the experiment. In order to ensure that these categories were discriminable, five additional 2–6-year-olds were tested. Photocopies of the stimuli were used, so that the stimuli were black and white rather than colored. The children were given a standard stimulus and were asked to choose which of two other stimuli were "just like" the standard. One of the choices was identical with the standard; the other choice was a member of the other subordinate of the same basic-level category. (For each basic-level category, nine different triads were available.) On each trial, feedback was provided. If an error was made, the child was shown the correct choice. The left-right positions of the two choices were then reversed, and the child asked to indicate the correct choice. Feedback was again provided. After the child had correctly responded to a given triad twice in a row, the three stimuli were removed, and another triad from the same basic category was presented. The procedure was repeated until the child made four consecutive correct responses to the initial presentation of a triad. None of the children made errors after the second triad. Triads from each of the three remaining basic categories were then presented, one category at a time, until the same criterion as that for the first category was reached. The mean total number of errors for triads from these three categories was 0.6 (range: 0–2). These results indicate that the attributes necessary to differentiate subordinate-level categories are discriminable for 2–6-year-olds. The stimuli were therefore accepted for use in the experiment.

Procedure. The child was told that he or she was going to play a game, the object of which was to determine "which pictures are the same kind of thing, which ones go together". The first set was then arranged in front of the child, with one card (the standard) centred above the remaining two. The experimenter pointed to the standard and said to the child, "Do you see this one? Can you show me the one that is the same kind of thing as this one, the one that goes with it?" The 24 sets were presented in a different random order for each subject. When given a subordinate set, children at all age levels frequently indicated that both the available choices were correct. When this happened, the child was asked which one was "better" the same kind of thing, which one went "better" with the standard. The question was repeated until the child indicated only one of the two possible cards; this choice was considered to be his response. In addition, a few of the 2–6-year-olds indicated that neither of the choices was the same kind of thing as the standard for some of the superordinate sets. When this happened, the procedure just described for children who indicated that both choices were correct was followed. No feedback concerning correctness of responses was provided. When children asked whether a response was correct, or seemed anxious, they were assured that they were doing well. Since two of the three cards in each set (the two from the same target-level category) could potentially serve as the standard, each one was used with half of the children from each group.

In order to encourage the 2–6-year-olds to participate, the study was introduced to them as a game in which the children would teach Randy (a raccoon puppet) "which pictures are the same kind of thing, which ones go together." These children were given practice trials (with correction) using trios of photographs of real objects (two virtually identical objects and one very dissimilar one) until they sorted two consecutive sets correctly. Every child reached criterion by the end of the third trial. The experimental sets were then presented as described above.

Results

In order to establish a basis for determining that performance for a given set of stimuli was significantly above chance, the binomial distribution was used. According to this distribution, seven or eight correct responses (out of eight possible) indicate performance significantly above chance level. For the basic level triads, all the children performed significantly more accurately than would be expected by chance. For the superordinate-level triads, one of the 2–6-year-olds, nine of the 4-year-olds, and all of the 5–6-year-olds performed significantly more accurately than chance. For the subordinate-level triads, none of the 2–6-year-olds or 4-year-olds performed significantly more accurately than chance, while all of the 5–6-year-olds did. Thus, the 2–6-year-olds performed significantly better than chance for only the basic level sets. The 4-year-olds performed significantly better than chance for both basic and superordinate-level sets. Finally, the 5–6-year-olds performed significantly better than chance for all three sets.

In order to determine whether some types of sets were more difficult than others for a given age group, Wilcoxon tests (using the adjusted significance-levels method) were performed, with number of correct responses for a given level as the dependent variable. Results indicated that 2–6 year-olds sorted basic-level sets more accurately than either superordinate- or subordinate-level sets ($T = 0$, $N = 10$, $p < 0.01$, in each case). They also sorted the superordinate sets more accurately than the subordinate sets ($T = 0$, $N = 8$, $p < 0.01$). For the 4-year-olds, there was no significant difference between performance on basic- and superordinate-level sets. However, performance on both these sets was significantly better than performance on subordinate-level sets ($T = 0$, $N = 10$, $p < 0.01$, in each case). For the 5–6-year-olds, there were no differences in accuracy of sorting at the three hierarchical levels. The mean numbers of correct responses, arranged according to age group and category level, are listed in Table 8.1.

Finally, in order to determine whether there were significant differences between age groups in accuracy of sorting at the different levels, Mann-Whitney U tests were performed (using the adjusted significance-levels method),

TABLE 8.1
M N Correct Responses[a]

| | CATEGORY LEVEL | | |
AGE[b]	Basic	Super-ordinate	Sub-ordinate
2–6	7.9	5.3	3.9
4	7.9	7.4	4.6
5–6	8.0	8.0	7.7

[a]Out of a possible eight.
[b]In years and months.

with number of correct responses for a given level as the dependent variable. Results indicated no significant differences in accuracy of sorting for basic-level sets. For the superordinate sets, the 5–6-year-olds sorted more accurately than the 2–6-year-olds ($U = 0$, $N = 10$, $p < 0.01$), as did the 4-year-olds ($U = 8.5$, $N = 10$, $p < 0.01$). For the subordinate sets, the 5–6-year-olds sorted more accurately than either the 2–6-year-olds or the 4-year-olds ($U = 0$, $N = 10$, $p < 0.01$, in each case). The performance of the 4-year-olds was not significantly different from the performance of the 2–6-year-olds on these sets.

Thus, our hypothesis concerning the order of acquisition of the ability to categorize at the three hierarchical levels was confirmed. Two additional experiments were therefore performed in order to examine a possible basis for the obtained order of acquisition.

EXPERIMENT 2

One possible explanation for the obtained order of acquisition is that the order is based on the degree of differentiation of the categories at a given hierarchical level. The possible schemes for categorizing a given set of stimuli vary in terms of the degree of differentiation of the categories in that scheme. The more differentiated the categories in a given scheme are, the more obvious (transparent) that categorization scheme is. Obvious schemes should be easier to learn than less obvious ones. The purpose of the present experiment was to determine whether the degree of differentiation of categories at the subordinate, basic, and superordinate levels could be used to predict the order of acquisition of the ability to categorize at those levels. In both this experiment and experiment 3, adults were asked to serve as subjects, since the complexity and length of the task made it impossible for young children to participate.

Method

Subjects.   Subjects were 12 University of Illinois at Urbana-Champaign students (six males and six females), who received course credit for participation in the study.

Stimuli.   The 24 forms used in the first experiment were also used in the present experiment.

Procedure.   The stimuli were arranged in front of the subject in three rows. The position of each stimulus was predetermined randomly. Stimuli in the top row were numbered 1–8; in the middle row, 9–16; in the bottom row, 17–24. Subjects were given a stack of 3 × 5-inch cards. Each card included the numbers of two stimuli, plus a number from 1 to 96 (corresponding to a space on the answer sheet). Subjects were asked to judge the similarity of the two stimuli whose numbers appeared on the card, using a one (not at all similar) to nine (extremely similar) scale. They then entered their judgment in the correct space on the answer sheet. The cards were shuffled between subjects, so that each subject made judgments in a different random order.

Altogether, subjects rated the similarity of 96 pairs of stimuli. Equal numbers of four different types of pairs were included. The first type, subordinate, was composed of two different members of the same subordinate category. The second type, basic (between-subordinate), was composed of two members of the same basic, but different subordinate, category. The third type, superordinate (between-basic), was composed of two members of the same superordinate, but different basic, category. The fourth type, between-superordinate, was composed of one member from each of the two superordinate categories. Within each type of pair, items were counterbalanced so that each of the 24 stimuli appeared equally often.

Results

As predicted, basic-level categories are more differentiated from one another than are categories at other hierarchical levels, while superordinate-level categories are more differentiated from one another than are subordinate-level categories. The statistical support for this statement is presented below.

In order to determine the differentiation scores for categories at each of the three levels, it was first necessary to calculate the mean similarity scores for each of the four types of pairs which subjects had considered. The means were: subordinate, 7.73; basic (between-subordinate), 6:91; superordinate (between-basic), 2.85; between-superordinate, 1.38. Adjacent means were all significantly different from one another: for subordinate versus basic, $t(23) = 4.82$, $p < 0.001$; for basic versus superordinate, $t(23)$ $= 36.91$, $p < 0.001$; for superordinate versus between-superordinate, $t(23)$ $= 21.0$, $p < 0.001$.

Differentiation scores were calculated according to the following formula: within-category similarity at a given level minus between-category similarity at that level. For example, the differentiation score for subordinate categories was found by subtracting the between-subordinate (basic) similarity score from the subordinate similarity score. The differentiation scores were: subordinate level, 0.82; basic level, 4.06; superordinate level, 1.47. If these scores are arranged from highest to lowest, the order is identical with the order of acquisition found in the first study. These data provide correlational support for our hypothesis that order of acquisition is determined by order of degree of differentiation.

EXPERIMENT 3

The results of experiment 2 indicated that the order of degree of differentiation of categories at various hierarchical levels was the same as the order of acquisition of these categories found in experiment 1. In both experiments, artificial stimuli structured to correspond to natural stimuli were used. In the present experiment, the order of degree of differentiation of natural categories at three hierarchical levels was determined to confirm that the order of differentiation obtained in experiment 2 was not restricted to the particular artificial stimuli used.

Method

Subjects.   Subjects were 10 University of Illinois at Urbana-Champaign students (all female) who volunteered to participate in the study.

Stimuli.   Two of the hierarchies included in the Rosch et al. (1976) study of the attribute structure of natural categories were used in the present study. As in the Rosch et al. study, the furniture hierarchy included the following categories: furniture (superordinate); table, lamp, chair (basic); kitchen table, dining room table, floor lamp, desk lamp, kitchen chair, living room chair (subordinate). The clothing hierarchy included the following categories: clothing (superordinate); pants, socks, shirt (basic); Levi's, double knit pants, knee socks, ankle socks, dress shirt, knit shirt (subordinate). The 24 photographs used included two typical exemplars of each of the 12 subordinate categories.

Procedure.   The procedure was identical to that used in experiment 2, except that subjects were asked to rate the similarity of 48 pairs of photographs, evenly divided among the four types described for experiment 2, rather than 96 pairs.

Results

The results of the present experiment also support the predicted order of differentiation. Mean similarity scores for each of the four types of pairs were as follows: subordinate, 7.70; basic (between-subordinate), 6.91; superordinate (between-basic), 3.27; between-superordinate, 1.18. Adjacent means were all significantly different from one another: for subordinate versus basic, $t(11) = 3.76$, $p < 0.01$; for basic versus superordinate, $t(11) = 16.55$, $p < 0.001$; for superordinate versus between-superordinate, $t(11) = 13.93$, $p < 0.001$. The differentiation scores for the three types of categories were: subordinate level, 0.79; basic level, 3.65; superordinate level, 2.09. As in experiment 2, the obtained order of differentiation is identical with the order of acquisition found in the first study. These data provide further correlational support for our hypothesis that order of acquisition is determined by order of degree of differentiation.

GENERAL DISCUSSION

In the present section, we consider how the differentiation hypothesis might explain the obtained order of acquisition of the ability to categorize at different hierarchical levels. The primary claim of the differentiation hypothesis is that the order of availability (and therefore the order of acquisition) of different categorization schemes for a given set of stimuli is determined by the relative degree of differentiation of each of these categorization schemes. The most differentiated categorization schemes should be acquired first. It is important to note that this is not a claim about the importance solely of degree of within-category similarity or, alternatively, about the importance solely of degree of between-category similarity. Rather, it is a claim about the importance of the relationship between within-category similarity and between-category similarity.

According to the differentiation hypothesis, children should be able to categorize first at the basic level, second at the superordinate level, and last at the subordinate level. The basis for this prediction is as follows: the within-category similarity of basic-level categories is high, while the between-category similarity is low, resulting in the highest differentiation score. The high within-category value indicates that category members look very similar to one another, while the low between-category value indicates that members of different categories look very different from one another. Thus, the basic-level categorization scheme should be obvious. The differentiations score is next highest for the superordinate-level categories. Superordinate categories have relatively low within-category similarity. However, this is partially compensated for by the extremely low similarity of members of different superordinate categories. Members of a superordinate category do not look very similar, on the other hand, members of different superordinate categories look extremely dissimilar. Thus, the categorization scheme should be somewhat obvious but not as obvious as the scheme for basic-level categories. The differentiation score is lowest for subordinate-level categories. These categories have a significantly higher within-category similarity value than do basic-level categories. However, subordinate categories also have a very high between-category similarity value. The result is a very low differentiation score. These values indicate that members of the same subordinate category look extremely similar, but that members of different subordinate categories also look very similar. This leads to the nonobviousness of the subordinate categorization scheme as reflected in the low differentiation score.

This nonobviousness was also reflected in the performance of the children for the subordinate-level triads. At this level, the stimuli could not be divided into categories based on overall attribute structure; such a division results in basic-level categories. Instead, assignment had to be based on differences in particular attributes. The younger children consistently based their judgments on overall structure rather than on a particular component attribute. This was demonstrated by their continued insistence that both choices were the same kind of thing as the standard even after being told to choose which one was "better" the same kind of thing. Only the oldest children were willing to use information about specific attributes as a basis for category assignment, and even these children frequently had to be prompted with an explicit request to choose which one was "better" the same kind of thing. Note that our findings refer to children's spontaneous categorization. It is likely that even 2-6-year-olds could be trained to correctly sort particular subordinate categories.

The special difficulty young children encounter in categorizing at the subordinate level is related to findings reported by Smith and Kemler (1977; 1978; Kemler & Smith 1979) for tasks assessing classification of stimuli which varied on separable dimensions. Smith and Kemler found that 5-year-olds (the youngest children tested) preferred to classify by overall similarity rather than on the basis of possession of the same value on a particular dimension. If young children prefer to attend to a stimulus as a whole, then one would expect them to have particular difficulty in forming subordinate categories since subordinate classification requires that a stimulus not be treated as an integral whole; at least some of the component dimensions must be treated separably.

In the present study, the stimuli did not have any "functions". Thus, the preceding discussion has been concerned with form attributes. Had the stimuli been given functions, the same differentiation argument, taking function into account, would be appropriate. As Rosch and Mervis (1975) have pointed out, the correlation between form attributes and function attributes is very high since the two are closely interrelated.

Recently, Horton and Markman (1980) considered the effects of explicit instruction on the acquisition of artificial basic- and superordinate-level categories. The authors found that, overall, acquisition was greater for basic-level categories than for superordinate-level categories . In addition, explicit instruction concerning the attributes of category members resulted in improved acquisition only for superordinate categories. This finding is congruent with the differentiation relationships we have found for basic- and superordinate-level categories. Because basic-level categories have a very high differentiation score, based on high within-category similarity and low between-category similarity, the relevant attributes for categorization are extremely obvious and need not be pointed out to the children. Superordinate categories also have a relatively high differentiation score. However, because the within-category similarity of superordinate categories is low, the attribute basis for the categorization scheme is not apparent. Therefore, (as Horton and Markman have also suggested) it should be helpful to children if these attributes were pointed out. Once the attributes are known, categorization should be easy, since between-category similarity is extremely low. Our predictions can also be extended to subordinate-level categorization. This type of categorization should be more difficult, even with instruction, than superordinate categorization. When instructing children concerning superordinate categorization, one need point out only the shared attributes. However, when instructing children concerning subordinate categorization, one must teach them both to concentrate on the few attributes that differentiate the categories and to ignore the numerous attributes which are common across the subordinate categories.

The stimuli used in this study were designed to be new to the children and thus free from their previous experience. In addition, the stimuli were never labelled. If natural categories had been used as stimuli, our finding – that young children are able to categorize first at the basic level, second at the superordinate level, and last at the subordinate level – could be accounted for not only by a perceptual-cognitive explanation such as the differentiation hypothesis but also by various linguistic explanations (e.g., basic-level names are the ones children have heard most frequently, etc.). However, since we have obtained the predicted results by using artificial stimuli which were never named, it appears that a perceptual-cognitive explanation, independent of any linguistic explanation, provides a sufficient basis for the order of acquisition (see also Mervis & Crisafi, Note 2; Murphy & Smith, Note 3).

We have argued that the order of acquisition of the ability to categorize at various levels can be explained by the degree of differentiation of the categories at a given hierarchical level: the more differentiated categories at a given level are, the earlier categorization at that level will be acquired.

For the vast majority of natural-category hierarchies, basic-level categories are most differentiated, followed by superordinate, and finally subordinate, categories. Thus, we have argued that in the general case, the order of acquisition should be: basic, superordinate, and subordinate. However, in the hypothetical case of a hierarchy for which subordinate categories were more differentiated than superordinate ones, we would predict that these particular subordinate categories would be acquired before the relevant superordinate categories. Thus, we are claiming that degree of differentiation takes precedence over hierarchical level. Therefore, the differentiation hypothesis can also be used to predict ease of acquisition when it is difficult or impossible to apply one of the three hierarchical labels to a particular categorization scheme.

ACKNOWLEDGEMENTS

We are grateful to John Pani for his help in designing the stimuli used in this study. Doug Medin suggested the formula used to operationalize the differentiation measure in experiments 2 and 3. Experiment 3 was suggested by an anonymous reviewer; Cindy Mervis assisted us with it. Ann Brown, Doug Medin, Elissa Newport, Emilie Roth, and Linda Smith provided thoughtful criticisms of previous drafts of this manuscript. We would like to thank the children and staff of the Toddler Program, Child Development Laboratory, University of Illinois at Urbana-Champaign, of the First Methodist Church Nursery School, Champaign, and of Pleasant Acres Elementary School, Rantoul, Illinois, for their cooperation and participation in experiment 1. The research reported here was supported by grant BNS79—15120 from the National Science Foundation.

REFERENCE NOTES

1. Brown, R. *Transcripts of Sarah's early speech.* Unpublished manuscript, Harvard University. Department of Psychology and Social Relations, n.d.
2. Mervis, C. B., & Crisafi, M. A. (1981). *The perceptual-cognitive primacy of basic level categories.* Unpublished manuscript, University of Illinois at Urbana-Champaign, Department of Psychology.
3. Murphy, G., & Smith, E. E. (1981). *Levels of categorization and object identification.* Unpublished manuscript, Stanford University, Department of Psychology.

REFERENCES

Anglin, J. M. (1977). *Word, object, and conceptual development.* New York: Norton.
Brown, R. (1958). How shall a thing be called? *Psychological Review, 65,* 14–21.
Brown, R. (1976). Reference: in memorial tribute to Eric Lenneberg. *Cognition, 4,* 125–153.
Daehler, M. W., Lonardo, R., & Bukatko, D. (1979). Matching and equivalence judgments in very young children. *Child Development, 50,* 170–179.
Horton, M. S. & Markman, E. M. (1980). Developmental differences in the acquisition of basic and superordinate categories. *Child Development, 51,* 708–719.

Kemler, D. G. & Smith, L. B. (1979). Assessing similarity and dimensional relations: effects of integrality and separability on the discovery of complex concepts. *Journal of Experimental Psychology: General, 108*, 133–150.

Rinsland, H. D. (1945). *A basic vocabulary of elementary school children.* New York: Macmillan.

Rosch, E. & Mervis, C. B. (1975). Family resemblances: studies in the internal structure of categories. *Cognitive Psychology, 7*, 573–605.

Rosch, E., Mervis, C. B., Gray, W. D., Johnson, D. M., & Boyes-Braem, P. (1976). Basic objects in natural categories. *Cognitive Psychology, 8*, 382–439.

Smith, L. B. & Kemler, D. G. (1977). Developmental trends in free classification: evidence for a new conceptualization of perceptual development. *Journal of Experimental Child Psychology, 24*, 279–298.

Smith, L. B. & Kemler, D. G. (1978). Levels of experienced dimensionality in children and adults. *Cognitive Psychology, 10*, 502–532.

9 The Development of Children's Reasoning Ability: Information-Processing Approaches

Jane Oakhill

INTRODUCTION

The information-processing approach to cognitive development can be seen as an alternative to, or an extension of, Piaget's theory (see Reading 1 this volume). In the information-processing approach the child's mind is conceived of as a complex system that is able to encode, process, store and manipulate information in a variety of ways. The objectives of the information-processing approach are to give a precise account of what happens in the cognitive system when a child performs a particular task, and of how developmental changes can be accounted for in terms of changes in the cognitive system, thus providing a detailed account of *why* changes occur. The ultimate aim of this approach is to produce a model of cognitive processing that is so detailed and precise that it could be implemented as a computer program. Not all developmental psychologists who adhere to the information-processing approach use computer modelling, but all have the goal of producing explicit, testable models of cognitive functioning.

Research in the information-processing paradigm also differs from Piaget's in terms of the *methods* used to study children. In the Piagetian approach, theories are based on observations of children in real-world situations and on children's explanations of what they are doing. The interactive nature of the Piagetian approach is captured in a quote from Smedslund (1977, p.1):

Source: Oakhill, J. (1987). – specially commissioned for this Reader.

My first encounter with Piagetian psychology occurred . . . . in the autumn of 1957. I still remember vividly the excitement of being free to *converse* with my subjects and particularly being free to ask for their *explanations*. As a well trained experimental psychologist I had up to that time been mainly confined to marks on sheets of paper as my data.

Whilst such procedures might be praised for being more "naturalistic", they are also criticised as lacking in experimental control. In many cases, success on Piagetian tasks has been shown to rely on language concepts that children may not use in the same way as adults (Donaldson, 1978). Work in the information-processing tradition has focused on the use of controlled experiments to explore cognitive development.

In summary, the research that will be considered in this chapter differs from Piaget's in two main ways. First, it attempts to describe cognitive development by using information-processing models rather than models based on symbolic logic. Second, the method of investigation is by controlled experiments rather than by interview and observational techniques. The emphasis is on a fine-grained analysis of tasks, and on attempts to infer what the cognitive system is doing at each stage of the task execution. Siegler (1983) provides a comprehensive account of the background to and methods of the information-processing approach, and discusses its applications to a wider range of developmental domains than will be discussed here.

This reading is in two parts. In the first I will outline two theories of cognitive development in the information-processing tradition, to give the flavour of this work. In the second part I will be concerned with the development of children's performance on verbal reasoning problems (deductive inferences) and will consider how developmental progression on such tasks can be modelled within the information-processing framework.

INFORMATION-PROCESSING THEORIES OF COGNITIVE DEVELOPMENT

There has been much recent work in the information-processing tradition. Some researchers ("neoPiagetians") have tried to modify and supplement Piagetian theory to take account of information-processing considerations (e.g. Pascual-Leone, 1970; Case, 1978, 1985). Others have re-investigated some of Piaget's findings, using concepts and methods from the information-processing approach.

Siegler's (1976, 1978) *rule-assessment approach* is an example of the latter type. It will be outlined as an example of how performance on Piagetian tasks can be studied from an information-processing perspective, and described in information-processing terms. Siegler sees cognitive development as the acquisition of increasingly sophisticated problem-solving strategies. His hypotheses about the strategies that children use at different ages are derived, at least in part, from Piaget's findings. For instance, Siegler has explored children's performance on the balance-beam problem (Inhelder and Piaget, 1958). In this task, the child is shown a balance beam with equally-spaced pegs on either side of the fulcrum. One or more equal weights can be placed on the pegs, and the child has to predict which side of the beam will go down when a lever holding it in place is released. Siegler identified four rules that children might use (see Fig. 9.1). He employed a variety of balance problems so that he could deduce from the pattern of responses which, if any, rule a particular child was using. A summary of the types of problem and predictions of the four rules is given in Fig. 9.2. Children using the most elementary rule took account of only the total weight on each side, and ignored distance from the fulcrum. Those using Rule II also predicted on the basis of weight, except when the weights were equal, in which case they also took distance into account. Children using Rule III tried to use both weight and distance to make their assessment. If one was equal and the other not, then they based their decision on the unequal dimension. If both dimensions were unequal children could only solve the task if both weight and distance favoured descent of the same side, otherwise they guessed. They had no way of combining weight and distance information that were in conflict. Rule IV children proceeded as for Rule III when a single dimension gave a determinate answer. When weight and distance information were in conflict, they calculated the torques on each side (weight × distance) and compared them. Siegler showed that most (90%) of the children tested (who varied in age from 5–17 years) could be classed as using one of these rules, although very few used Rule IV: the only one that consistently produces the correct answer. Most 5-year-olds used Rule I, 9-year-olds Rule II, and 13–17-year-olds, Rule III.

Siegler (1978) has applied this rule-assessment approach to a range of Piagetian domains, with similar patterns of results (i.e. a set of strategies that increase in complexity). Siegler's strategies can be classified in terms of the number of decisions each requires. The more complex ones demand the interrelation of a greater number of pieces of information. Developmental progression occurs as the child becomes more adept at encoding information relevant to the task. This improved encoding contributes to enhancing the ability to learn which, in turn, contributes to an improved level of existing knowledge (see Siegler, 1978, p.144).

The idea that cognitive development is restricted by processing limitations is central to many current theories. It is well established that the total attentional resources of humans are severely limited. Hitch and Baddeley (1976) argue that temporary storage and processing tasks compete for a memory of limited capacity, a system which they term "working memory". Hence, there will be constraints on the amount of information that can be stored and/or processed at any one time. It is quite possible,

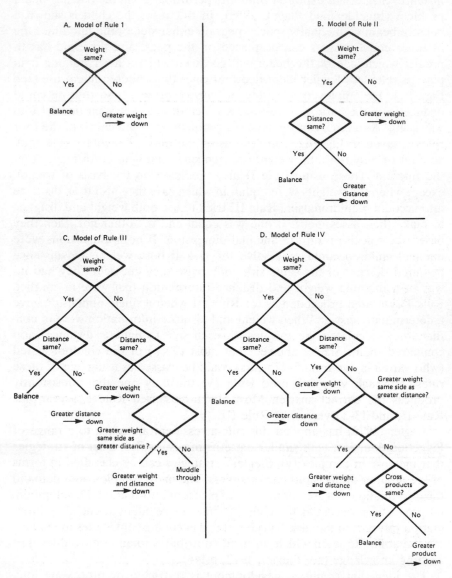

FIG. 9.1. Models of rules for performing the balance-scale task.

From: R. S. Siegler (1983). Information processing approaches to cognitive development. In W. Kessen (Ed.), *Handbook of Child Psychology* (Vol. 1). New York: Wiley, p.160.

Problem—type	Rule			
	I	II	III	IV
Balance 	100	100	100	100
Weight 	100	100	100	100
Distance 	0 (Should say "Balance")	100	100	100
Conflict— weight 	100	100	33 (Chance responding)	100
Conflict— Distance 	0 (Should say "Right Down")	0 (Should say "Right Down")	33 (Chance responding)	100
Conflict— Balance 	0 (Should say "Right Down")	0 (Should say "Right Down")	33 (Chance responding)	100

FIG. 9.2.   Problems used to assess understanding of the balance scale.

From: R. S. Siegler (1983) Information processing approaches to cognitive development. In W. Kessen (Ed.), *Handbook of Child Psychology* (Vol. 1). New York: Wiley, p.160.

therefore, that the demands of a task will exceed the available processing capacity. Information-processing theorists argue that, as processing resources gradually increase with age, so more complex and sophisticated forms of reasoning and problem solving can be achieved. Thus, below a certain age, children may find it difficult or impossible to solve problems or acquire concepts beyond a certain level of complexity, because their working memories are not sufficiently developed to enable them to attend to and interrelate all the relevant information. Growth in working memory could occur either through an *increase* in the total processing space, or through a *decrease* in the proportion of the space that must be devoted to basic operations, so that the *available* resources increase even if the total capacity remains constant. Both speed and automaticity of basic processes could contribute to such an increase in resources. There is evidence to support the idea that an increase in functional capacity can be achieved by an increase in processing speed. People's memory span increases in direct proportion to the speed with which they can identify (name) the items to be remembered. Those who can process faster have greater "operational efficiency" (Case, Kurland and Goldberg, 1982). Speed of processing might be increased by practice and experience, and Hulme, Thompson, Muir and Lawrence (1984) have shown that speech rate is also an important factor.

The importance of knowledge in memory development, and in cognitive development more generally, has been stressed by some researchers. Chi (1978) provides evidence to show that adults do not have *structurally* larger working memories than children. She argues that increased knowledge of a domain (i.e. "expertise") can greatly increase memory capacity when dealing with a problem in that domain. In fact, a young child may be *better* at memory tasks than an adult in an area where the child has acquired some expertise. Chi showed that 10-year-olds who were knowledgeable about chess showed much better immediate recall of a chess board than did adults who were not chess players, presumably because the more experienced players could hold a configuration of pieces in memory as a single unit. The children's immediate memory, as measured by digit span was, however, worse than that of the adults. These data suggest that the size of working memory does not increase with age, but that older (more experienced) subjects' greater knowledge may aid them in the meaningful chunking of items. If differences between younger and older children are due, at least in part, to quantitative differences in knowledge, then Piaget's description of development in terms of "stages" that are qualitatively different seems misleading. It is doubtful, however, that cognitive development can be accounted for entirely in terms of the acquisition of knowledge in various domains, in the absence of *conceptual* reorganisations (see Flavell, 1985, pp.91–92, for a discussion of this issue, and Carey, 1985, who explores the relation between conceptual change and the development of knowledge systems).

Although Piaget's concept of stages has been heavily criticised in recent years, and is still controversial, it could be reconciled with an information-processing approach. For instance, Pascual-Leone (1970) has brought together the idea of growing attentional resources (M-space) and Piaget's stage theory of development, and argues that an increase in attentional capacity is a prerequisite for transition to a higher stage of development. Case (e.g. 1978, 1984), who builds on the ideas of Pascual-Leone, also takes a stage approach – he views development as the acquisition of increasingly complex cognitive structures that are constant across many content domains. Case is interested in how the child's cognitive functioning should be characterised at different stages, and how the transition between stages comes about. Like Siegler, Case proposes that cognitive development proceeds via the acquisition of more complex strategies (*executive control structures*) and that the acquisition of more-sophisticated strategies is limited by the child's experience and working memory capacity. Case's view is that development depends on the interaction of age-invariant activities, such as exploration and problem solving, that are evident from a very early age, and general factors that are *not* invariant in development, such as available memory capacity. These latter factors limit the effectiveness of the former. Thus, the child's ability to use his experience of a task to develop appropriate problem solving procedures will be constrained by age-dependent limitations in working memory. Case distinguishes between two components of working memory which he terms "operating space" and "short-term storage space", and argues from his own data (Case, Kurland and Goldberg, 1982; Case, 1985, Chapter 16) that growth in working memory occurs not through a change in the size of the total processing space but through a decrease in the proportion of this space that must be devoted to basic operations (operating space). As basic operations become more automatic, and demands on operating space are fewer, so more space is freed for additional operations and/or storage.

Case's theory provides an explanation of why similar experiences with a problem will result in one strategy in a 4-year-old, but a different one at 6 years (the 6-year-old has more available working memory to integrate his experiences). It also explains why, although the child's experiences of different domains may vary widely, parallel "integrations" occur in the same period, and the child seems to perform at much the same level across a wide variety of domains.

As an example of the way in which working memory limits the child's problem-solving strategies, Case (1978) cites a study by Noetling (1975), in which children have to decide which of two mixtures will taste more strongly of orange juice, given that a certain number of cups of orange and water have been tipped into each. He identifies four strategies for solving such problems (shown in Fig. 9.3), and shows how increased sophistication goes hand in hand with an increase in the number of reasoning steps and

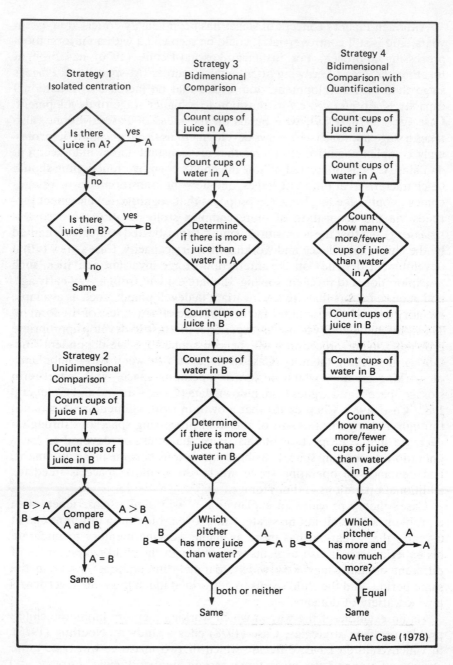

FIG. 9.3. Four strategies for solving juice mixture problems.

From: R. E. Mayor (1983). *Thinking, problem solving, cognition.* NewYork: Freeman, p.285.

the number of items that need to be held in working memory simultaneously, to a maximum of seven steps and four items. As with Siegler's balance beam problems, the particular strategy that is required to solve a particular problem depends on that problem's complexity. Example problems, together with appropriate strategies and their memory demands are shown in Fig. 9.4 (further details can be found in Case, 1978). One obvious difficulty with Case's theory is that there is no independent means of assessing the memory demands of a particular task (see Flavell, 1978). However, as Flavell also notes, Case's theory is one of the most ambitious and wide-ranging of recent theories of development.

INFORMATION-PROCESSING APPROACHES TO THE DEVELOPMENT OF DEDUCTIVE REASONING

In the field of deductive reasoning, the two opposing theoretical stands correspond roughly to the Piagetian and information-processing approaches. The distinction between them has been neatly summed up by Gellatly (in press) as "whether logic is descriptive of thinking processes or merely prescriptive of what is considered sound reasoning". Although the first approach admits the influence of processing limitations, it holds that there are rules of inference in the mind that closely resemble formal inference rules (e.g. Braine, 1978; Braine and Rumain, 1983; Rips, in press).

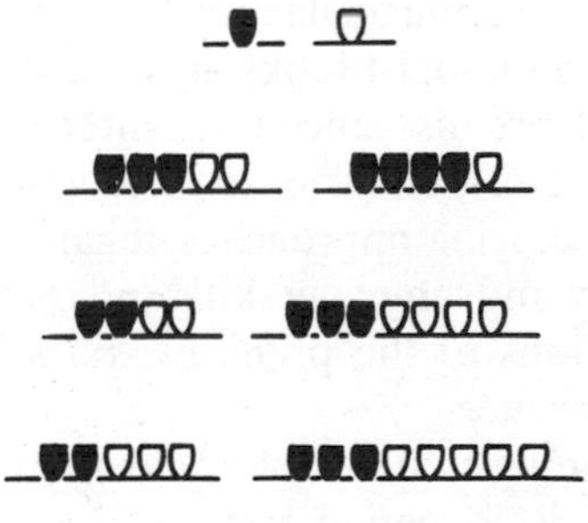

Problem type	Example	Strategy name	Number of steps in strategy	Memory demand for strategy
1	_🔴_ _⬜_	1. Isolated centration	2	1
2	_🔴🔴🔴⬜⬜_ _🔴🔴🔴⬜_	2. Unidimensional comparison	3	2
3	_🔴🔴⬜⬜_ _🔴🔴🔴⬜⬜⬜⬜_	3. Bidimensional comparison	7	3
4	_🔴🔴⬜⬜⬜_ _🔴🔴🔴🔴⬜⬜⬜⬜⬜_	4. Bidimensional comparison with quantification	7	4

After Case (1978)

From : R. E Mayer (1983) *Thinking, Problem Solving, Cognition.* New York : Freeman. p 283

FIG. 9.4. Four types of juice mixture problems.

From: R. E. Mayor (1983). *Thinking, problem solving, cognition.* New York: Freeman, p.285.

Piaget espoused an extreme version of the mental logic (descriptive) approach. He saw the development of reasoning ability as the acquisition of a series of increasingly complex logics, culminating at the formal operations stage in the propositional calculus: ". . . reasoning is nothing more than the propositional calculus itself" (Inhelder & Piaget, 1958, p.305). The second view holds that, rather than requiring the acquisition of a set of rules of logic, reasoning is mediated by an information-processing system in much the same way as other forms of cognition. The main proponent of this approach is Johnson-Laird (e.g. 1983), who has identified a number of problems with the idea of a mental logic.

Although information processing accounts of performance on deductive problems have not been worked out in as much detail as for the particular tasks illustrated above (the most detailed is perhaps Trabasso's, 1977, account), it is easy to see how certain principles of the information-processing approach might apply. Deductive inference can be conceptualised as a series of operations, each of which takes up some working memory capacity. The concept of working memory plays an important role in recent theories of adult reasoning, and research to be discussed later suggests that it also imposes limitations on children's reasoning. Information-processing theorists regard cognitive development as a continuous process, and view adult thinking as qualitatively similar to that of the child. Development is seen as *quantitative* in that it depends on an expansion of knowledge structures and an increase in the efficiency with which processes can be executed. (This contrasts with the Piagetian approach, in which adults are assumed to think in an essentially different way from children – development is seen as discontinuous, with a series of *qualitatively* different stages each of which is characterised by a particular set of cognitive structures). The information-processing psychologist looks at the task demands (in the case of deductive inferences: premise encoding, interpretation in working memory, question encoding, etc.), and tries to infer *how* the problem is solved. Thus, information-processing approaches regard reasoning ability as being dependent on memory and language skills and on the ability to form and manipulate representations of the premises, rather than on the possession of formal rules of inference.

The most frequently studied reasoning skill in children is their ability to make transitive inferences. The classic Piagetian task involves transitive inferences about length. To make a transitive inference of this sort is to conclude, for example, that A is longer than C, given that A is longer than B, and B is longer than C. According to Piaget, children cannot make such inferences until they reach the concrete operational stage at about 7–8 years. Before this age they cannot understand that "larger" and "smaller" are relative terms, and that the same object can be both larger and smaller in different situations. Once they reach the concrete operational stage, they can understand that B is both relatively large and relatively small, and can assess the relative lengths of A and C with reference to B. The precise age at which transitivity is "acquired" varies according to the task demands and content of the problem. Children generally understand transitivity of length by 7–8 years, but performance on verbal problems that do not involve perceptible objects, lags about two years behind.

Many studies have been carried out to evaluate Piaget's theory of transitive inference. One of the first challenges to Piaget's claim about the age at which children can draw transitive inferences came from Bryant and Trabasso (1971). They deliberately adapted the standard Piagetian task, adopting a more experimental approach, and used very different criteria for transitivity: judgement not justification. As we will see later, this approach lays them open to criticism from Piagetians. Bryant and Trabasso used a *five* stick problem in an attempt to preclude solution by one non-inferential strategy: that of "labelling". A child using this strategy is said to recall what was said about the A and C sticks in the original comparisons, label them "long" and "short" and then get the A/C comparison correct on the basis of these labels, without making an inference. When five sticks are used, the middle three sticks are equally often referred to as "longer" and "shorter".

In the training phase of Bryant and Trabasso's procedure, subjects are presented with pairs of coloured sticks, whose actual length is obscured. The relations among the five sticks can be described using four premises (A>B, B>C, C>D, D>E). On presentation of each pair of sticks, the child is asked which is longer or shorter, and is then told (and in some conditions also shown) the correct answer. Training on the premise pairs continues until a pre-determined memory criterion has been reached. In the test session, the child is presented with all 10 possible pairs of the sticks and has to say which is longer in each case. The crucial comparison is that between the B and D sticks, whose relative lengths can only be judged with reference to the C stick. Bryant and Trabasso showed that, providing they received sufficient training on the original pairs, even 4-year-olds were able to get the answer right. Bryant and Trabasso argue that children's problems arise not because they are incapable of making transitive inferences, but because they cannot remember the relations on which the inference should be based. Subsequent work has investigated the manner in which the premises are represented in working memory, and suggests that both children and adults solve such problems by constructing a visuo-spatial representation of the full array and "reading off" individual comparisons from it. However, research by Kallio (1982) showed that 4-year-olds' performance was much poorer on such tasks when the premise pairs were systematically disordered during the training phase, than when they were presented in serial order. In a further experiment, he showed improvement with disordered premises between 4 and 18 years of age. Kallio argued that serial order of premise presentation leads to nominal coding in younger children, and only later is contrastive coding used to construct an internal linear order at presentation.

Bryant and Trabasso's work has been criticised from a number of perspectives. It has been argued that five-term problems can also be solved by non-inferential strategies. De Boysson-Bardies and O'Regan (1973) have produced a labelling model, and Breslow (1981) a sequential contiguity model. Breslow argues that young children form a linear order during training, but not by making transitive inferences. Instead, they generate a set of contiguity relations in terms of which sticks "go with" others, and can derive linear order information in a sequential fashion on the basis of these contiguity relations by working from the end sticks – the only ones which are permanently labelled "long" and "short". In addition, Piagetians deny that operationalised experimental procedures, such as those used by Bryant and Trabasso, can be used to measure the ability that Piaget was describing. They argue that the child's verbal justifications are essential to deciding whether or not a concept has been acquired. The obvious problem with this criterion is that children are not necessarily able to express verbally their understanding of a concept. Thus, since their investigations derive from different theoretical assumptions about cognitive development, Piagetians and information-processing psychologists are asking different types of question. Piagetians focus on whether a particular child has or has not acquired the concept of transitive inference, whereas information-processing psychologists are more interested in asking about the cognitive processes and strategies underlying the ability to give correct answers in tasks designed to assess transitive inference (these correspond to what Flavell terms "assessment" and "conceptualisation" questions, respectively see Flavell, 1985, p.273). Perhaps the important question is not which is the "right" approach, but which is more likely to give us interesting insights into development. Piagetian theorists have not attempted any detailed study of the cognitive processes underlying transitivity, but such work seems essential if a full description and explanation of cognitive development is to be attained.

In this context, it is of note that Jager Adams (1978) was able to show that children only make transitive inferences when they cannot utilise other cues to solve the task. Following Piaget and Inhelder (1973, p30), she regarded the test of whether a child could insert a new stick into a series as the crucial test of whether that child really understood transitivity. Jager Adams showed that, when sticks differ markedly in length (2″ as in the Bryant and Trabasso study), children as young as 5 years are just as good at answering questions about non-adjacent sticks as they are when the sticks vary by a barely-perceptible amount. However, only the children who were shown the sticks that varied very little in length (Low Saliency group) were able to incorporate an unseen novel stick into the series by inference. Jager Adams argues that, although both the High Saliency (large difference) and the Low Saliency groups encoded the sticks into a transitive series, the High Saliency group did so on the basis of absolute length, but the Low Saliency group were forced to use transitive inference, and so only they could perform the insertion task. The important implication of her results is that 5-year-olds are capable of seriation and transitive inference under conditions when other strategies are precluded (though see Breslow, 1981, who argues that these results, too, can be explained by his sequential contiguity model). Thayer and Collyer (1978) provide a thorough review of the work in this area, and try to account for the disagreement between Piagetian and information-processing researchers in relation to differences in the methods they employ. They suggest that the Piagetians, who claim that transitivity is not attained until about 8 years, may have identified the age at which the principle can be actively and spontaneously applied in most situations:

> . . . Piagetian methods of diagnosis exclude those younger children for whom transitivity is evocable, given appropriate environmental conditions, but not yet spontaneously utilised in the absence of special conditions. . . . Transitive inference may become available to the young child by age 4 or 5 under optimal conditions of training, feedback, and so forth; however, there is some reason to judge that the principle is not fully developed until age 8 or 9 when it can function reliably with minimal environmental support across many varied situations.

Indeed, Mills and Funnell (1983) present evidence to show that even 2- and 3-year-olds can make deductive inferences when the problem is set within the child's own experience.

A more fundamental and problematic question about Bryant and Trabasso's research is whether children truly understand the logic of the task. Recent debate has centered round the question of whether, even though children get the right answer, they understand its "logical necessity". Breslow (1981) stresses that, for the child to "have" transitivity, he or she must demonstrate an understanding of the necessity and reversibility that underlie the concept, i.e., appreciation of the truth or falsity of the conclusion regardless of the truth or falsity of the premises, and understanding that A>B implies B<A. The questions of non-transitive strategies and logical necessity have been discussed extensively elsewhere and will not be discussed further here (see Breslow, 1981, for a discussion of non-inferential strategies, and Gellatly, 1987 for a discussion of the development of the concept of logical necessity).

Returning to the role of memory in transitive inference, it is of interest to note that the strong form of Bryant and Trabasso's "memory failure hypothesis" was incompatible with data already in existence. Studies by

Smedslund (cited by Russell, 1981) had demonstrated that children may make incorrect inferences even though they can recall the premises correctly. Russell (1981) showed that many young children who make incorrect inferences often justify their conclusions by citing correct premises. Even when the premise information can be recalled, children have difficulty making some sorts of deductions (though see Trabasso, 1977, who points out that a distinction should be drawn between rote learning of the premises and understanding them. He made sure that children in his experiments were *not* simply recalling the premises – training on premises in both directions, i.e. A›B and B‹A ensured that they *understood* the contrastive relation).

There is another aspect of memory that might affect performance on transitive inference tasks: the "working memory" needed to maintain and manipulate information from the premises in order to formulate a conclusion. As we saw above, the effective capacity of working memory depends on how quickly and automatically basic processes, such as encoding, can be carried out. The extent to which reasoning is restricted by working memory may depend on particular characteristics of the problem. Direct evidence that children's reasoning is limited by their working memory comes from experiments on another transitive task – verbal seriation (three-term series) problems. An example of such a problem is:

Ann is better than Betty.

Betty is better than Carol.

Who is best?

Piaget (1928) claimed that concrete operational children are unable to solve verbal seriation problems. These problems are difficult because they often necessitate the conversion of relations, and thus require the ability to perform what Piaget terms formal operations (i.e. the ability to carry out such operations not on concrete objects, but on abstract propositions). However, Walker (1982) was able to show a substantial improvement from 7–9 years on such problems, with almost all of the oldest children passing the task.

Some recent research by the present author (Oakhill, 1984) has addressed the question of why children have difficulty with such problems. Although there is no consensus on how adults solve these three-term series problems (see Sternberg, 1980, for a review), most information processing theories would agree on a number of processes:

1. Perception and encoding of the premises.
2. Transfer of the premise information to working memory.
3. Combination of the premise representations in memory to form an integrated representation.
4. Encoding a question, if there is one, and scanning the representation of the premises to answer a question or to formulate a conclusion.

If one of these processes is difficult, then this difficulty may affect other aspects of the deduction. As we saw above, if the processing components of a task are attention-consuming, then the storage capacity of working memory may be reduced. Such a reduction would make it more difficult to retain the representation of the premise or premises already stored and to execute other processes such as integrating the separate representations, scanning the integrated model, and encoding the question. The extent to which reasoning is restricted by working memory may depend on the particular characteristics of the problem. One variable that would be expected to affect the ease with which a conclusion can be derived is the linguistic form of the premises, which will determine how difficult it is to encode and to construct a mental representation of them. Clark (1969) has demonstrated that problems containing *unmarked* adjectives, such as "good", take significantly less time to solve than those with *marked* adjectives, such as "bad" (marked adjectives presuppose one end of a continuum, e.g. *A is not as bad as B* implies that they are both bad, whereas an equivalent expression with *good* does not carry the presupposition that A and B are both at the good end of the continuum). In similar manner, linguistically more complex premises, such as negatives, will also make encoding more difficult, and will increase the chances of at least part of the representation being lost from memory. Hence, it should be easier to solve the problem illustrated above, where the premises are affirmative and unmarked, than one with negative premises containing marked adjectives, such as:

Ann is not as bad as Betty.
Betty is not as bad as Carol.
Who is best?

Oakhill's (1984) study of 8–9 year-olds showed that both these factors affected performance – problems with negative or marked premises resulted in more errors. Moreover, the children's performance improved significantly when they were given an aid to help them externalise the information in the premises, and thus reduce the load on working memory. Residual errors in the memory aid condition seemed to arise because the children still had difficulty understanding and representing the linguistically more complex premises. There was no evidence from their error patterns that the children were using a labelling strategy, and their high level of performance in the memory aid condition, and on the linguistically simpler problems overall, suggests that they could make transitive deductions providing that the demands on working memory were not too great.

Children's reasoning on another sort of deductive problem – syllogisms – can also be accounted for, at least in part, in terms of memory limitations. Syllogisms – deductions from quantified assertions – such as:

All artists are beekeepers.
All beekeepers are chemists.
Therefore, all artists are chemists.

have recently been extensively investigated, and there are a number of theories of how they are solved (see Evans, 1982; Johnson-Laird, 1983, for recent critical accounts). Johnson-Laird's information-processing account of syllogistic reasoning incorporates his idea of mental models (details of the theory as it applies to syllogistic reasoning have been published elsewhere, Johnson-Laird & Bara, 1984). The theory based on mental models makes detailed predictions about the relative difficulty of syllogisms, and about the sorts of error responses that will occur, whereas a theory based on mental logic does not make such detailed predictions.

The theory assumes that a successful deduction takes place in three main stages. First, the reasoner builds a representation (model) of the information in the premises. Second, he tries to formulate an informative conclusion from that model. In the third stage, he must test the validity of the putative conclusion by considering whether there are alternative models of the premises in which the initial conclusion fails to hold and, if so, whether there is an alternative conclusion that is compatible with all possible models of the premises. Johnson-Laird, Oakhill and Bull (1986) argue that the development of reasoning ability may depend on the acquisition of procedures for constructing and testing models, and not on the development of formal rules of logic.

Every syllogism requires either one, two or three distinct models and, as the number of models increases, so does the memory load involved in producing a conclusion. Another factor that has been shown to affect reasoning with syllogisms is the *figure* of the premises – i.e. the order in which the terms are presented. There are four possible figures:

A−B	B−A	A−B	B−A
B−C	C−D	C−D	D−C

Both the form of the conclusion and the ease with which it can be derived will be affected by the figural arrangement of the premises (for further details see Johnson-Laird & Bara, 1984; Johnson-Laird, Oakhill & Bull, 1986). The number of models and figural difficulty of the premises make increasing demands on working memory, and a trend in difficulty across each of the factors has consistently been shown in experiments with adults (see Johnson-Laird & Bara, 1984).

Although most studies of syllogistic reasoning have been conducted with adults, the study by Johnson-Laird, Oakhill and Bull (1986) looked at performance in two groups of children (9–10 and 11–12 year-olds). The children's performance, although worse overall than that of adults, was affected in a similar manner by both figure and number of models, the more models required to make an inference, the harder the children found the task, thus confirming the predictions about the relative difficulty of syllogisms.

However, neither the mental models theory nor other information-processing theories of transitive inference have much to say about *how* children develop the various information-processing skills needed to encode and manipulate models of the premises. As we have seen from the work of Case and Siegler, the idea that children's cognitive development is related to a corresponding development in working memory has proved a fruitful one, and the research so far conducted on children's deductive reasoning suggests that it would be profitable to look at its development in similar terms, and at the level of detail employed for other tasks.

In sum, it would seem that the information-processing approach can make a useful contribution to our understanding of the development of reasoning skills in children. As Sternberg (1984) points out, the two fundamental questions in developmental psychology are about the psychological *states* that the child passes through, and the *mechanisms* by which development occurs. However, very little work has been done to address this second question, and it is likely that theoretical progress has been hindered by the lack of understanding of the mechanisms by which children's thinking develops (see, too, Siegler, 1983, p.200). Recent research (see, for example, several papers in Sternberg, 1984) suggests that the information-processing approach may hold the key to a better understanding of such mechanisms.

EDUCATIONAL IMPLICATIONS OF THE INFORMATION-PROCESSING APPROACH

Finally, I will consider briefly the educational implications of the information-processing approach, and how they compare with those from a Piagetian perspective. The implications from both perspectives have some features in common – both recognise the need to begin at the child's current level of development, and the need to promote the development of high-level cognitive operations. They also agree that, in order to make progress, the child must be *actively* engaged in appropriate tasks. They differ, however, in what they see as the nature of the higher level operations that are to be attained, and the processes by which they develop. The Piagetian perspective would point to a child-centred approach, with an emphasis not on direct instruction, but a broadening of the child's experience through exposure to tasks relevant to the stage. Thus, the emphasis is on discovery, *not* teaching. It is assumed that development is a prerequisite for learning, and that if the child's mental functions are not sufficiently mature to enable him to grasp a particular concept, then instruction will not be of any use. The information-processing approach, by contrast, views children's intellectual operations as increasingly complex strategies, and sees coaching and instruction as appropriate means of fostering development. The particular skills taught would be based on an analysis of the relevant structures at child and adult level, with the aim of reducing the difference between them. This conception of fostering development is closely related to what Vygotsky termed the *Zone of Proximal Development* (Vygotsky, 1978, Chapter 6). As Vygotsky points out, although learning should be matched in some sense to the child's developmental level, the child has to be helped to progress beyond that level. In order to provide such help, Vygotsky argued, one must not only know the current intellectual level the child has attained, but also the child's *potential* level of performance when given some hints or guidance to help with the problem in hand. The Zone of Proximal Development is the difference between these two levels. Vygotsky defined it as (1978, p.86):

> . . . the distance between the actual developmental level as determined by independent problem solving and the level of potential development as determined through problem solving under adult guidance or in collaboration with more capable peers.

Some measure of the Zone of Proximal Development can, thus, be seen as an index of the child's current potential for improvement over current performance levels.

It is also worth mentioning Case's theory, since its educational implications have been worked out and tested in some detail (see Case, 1985, Chapter 18). Like Piaget, Case views the child as a problem solver, but presents his theory of *how* the child goes about solving problems in information-processing terms. Briefly, his idea is that the educator should first establish a hierarchy of executive control structures for the task in question and the stage that the child has attained in that hierarchy. He should then enable the child to engage in tasks appropriate to his current level of development and, through a suitable instructional programme, make subroutines automatic, thus freeing some working memory to enable the child to develop more complex control structures. Case has shown that instructional programmes based on his principles are successful not only in improving performance on the classic problems in developmental research, but also on problems from the school curriculum, providing that they are amenable to an executive hierarchy analysis.

ACKNOWLEDGEMENTS

I should like to thank Alan Garnham, Angus Gellatly, Phil Johnson-Laird, Josef Perner and Nicola Yuill for many helpful comments on an earlier version of this reading, and Roger Goodwin for a discussion which helped me to formulate a preliminary framework for the reading, and for providing many useful references.

REFERENCES

Braine, M. D. S. (1978). On the relation between the natural logic of reasoning and standard logic. *Psychological Review, 85*, 1–21.

Braine, M. D. S. & Rumain, B. (1983). Logical reasoning. In J. H. Flavell & E. M. Markman, (Eds.), *Handbook of child psychology*, (Vol. III). Chichester: Wiley.

Breslow, L. (1981). Reevaluation of the literature on the development of transitive inferences. *Psychological Bulletin, 89*, 325–351.

Bryant, P. E. & Trabasso, T. (1971). Transitive inferences and memory in young children. *Nature, 232*, 456–458.

Carey, S. (1985). *Conceptual change in childhood*. Cambridge, Mass.: MIT Press.

Case, R. (1978). Intellectual development from birth to adulthood: A neo-Piagetian interpretation. In R. W. Siegler, (Ed.), *Children's thinking: What develops?* Hillsdale, N. J.: Lawrence Erlbaum Associates Inc.

Case, R. (1984). The process of stage transition: A neo-Piagetian view. In R. J. Sternberg, (Ed.), *Mechanisms of cognitive development*. New York: Freeman.

Case, R. (1985). *Intellectual development: A systematic reinterpretation*. New York: Academic Press.

Case, R, Kurland, D. M., & Goldberg, J. (1982). Operational efficiency and the growth of short-term memory span. *Journal of Experimental Child Psychology, 33*, 386–404.

Chi, M. T. H. (1987). Knowledge structures and memory development. In R. S. Siegler, (Ed.), *Children's thinking: What develops?* Hillsdale, N. J.: Lawrence Erlbaum Associates Inc.

Clark, H. H. (1969). Linguistic processes in deductive reasoning. *Psychological Review, 76*, 387–404.

De Boysson-Bardies, B. & O'Regan, K. (1973). What children do in spite of adults' hypotheses. *Nature, 246*, 531–534.

Donaldson, M. (1978). *Children's Minds*. London: Fontana.

Evans, J. St. B. T. (1982). *The psychology of deductive reasoning*. London: Routledge & Kegan Paul.

Flavell, J. H. (1978). Comments. In R. S. Siegler, (Ed.), *Children's thinking: What develops?* Hillsdale, N. J.: Lawrence Erlbaum Associates Inc.

Flavell, J. H. (1985). *Cognitive development* (2nd. Ed.) Englewood Cliffs, N. J.: Prentice Hall Inc.

Gellatly, A. R. H. (1987). The acquisition of a concept of logical necessity. *Human Development, 30*, 32–47.

Gellatly, A. R. H. (In press). Human inference. In K. Gilhooly, (Ed.), *Human and machine problem solving*. London: Plenum.

Hitch, G. J. & Baddeley, A. D. (1976). Verbal reasoning and working memory. *Quarterly Journal of Experimental Psychology, 28*, 603–621.

Hulme, C., Thompson, N., Muir, C., & Lawrence, A. (1984). Speech rate and the development of short term memory span. *Journal of Experimental Child Psychology, 38*, 241–251.

Inhelder, B. & Piaget, J. (1958). *The growth of logical thinking from childhood to adolescence*. London: Routledge & Kegan Paul.

Jager Adams, M. (1978). Logical competence and transitive inference in young children. *Journal of Experimental Child Psychology, 25*, 477–489.

Johnson-Laird, P. N. (1983). *Mental models: Towards a cognitive science of language, inference, and consciousness*. Cambridge: Cambridge University Press.

Johnson-Laird, P. N., Oakhill, J. V., & Bull, D. (1986). Children's syllogistic reasoning. *Quarterly Journal of Experimental Psychology, 38A*, 35–58.

Johnson-Laird, P. N. & Bara, B. (1984). Syllogistic inference. *Cognition, 16*, 1–61.

Kallio, K. D. (1982). Developmental change on a five-term transitive inference. *Journal of Experimental Child Psychology, 33*, 142–164.

Mills, M. & Funnell, E. (1983). Experience and cognitive processing. In S. Meadows, (Ed.), *Developing thinking*. London: Methuen.

Noetling, G. (1975). Stages and mechanisms in the development of proportionality in the child and adolescent. In G. I. Lubin, J. F. Magery, & M. K. Poulsen, (Eds.), *Piagetian theory and the helping professions* (Vol. 5). Los Angeles: USC press.

Oakhill, J. V. (1984). Why children have difficulty reasoning with three-term series problems. *British Journal of Developmental Psychology, 2*, 223–230.

Pascual-Leone, J. (1970). A mathematical model for the transition rule in Piaget's developmental stages. *Acta Psychologica, 32*, 301–345.

Piaget, J. (1928). *Judgement and reasoning in the child*. London: Routledge & Kegan Paul.

Piaget, J. & Inhelder, B. (1973). *Memory and intelligence*. New York: Basic Books.

Rips, L. J. (In press). Mental muddles. In M. Brand and M. Harnsih, (Eds.), *Problems in the representation of knowledge and belief*. Tucson, Arizona: University of Arizona Press.

Russell, J. (1981). Children's memory for the premises in a transitive measurement task assessed by elicited and spontaneous justifications. *Journal of Experimental Child Psychology, 31*, 300–309.

Siegler, R. S. (1976). Three aspects of cognitive development. *Cognitive Psychology, 8*, 481–520.

Siegler, R. S. (1978). The origins of scientific reasoning. In R. S. Siegler, (Ed.), *Children's thinking: What develops?* Hillsdale, N. J.: Lawrence Erlbaum Associates Inc.

Siegler, R. S. (1983). Information processing approaches to development. In P. H. Mussen, (Ed.), *Handbook of child psychology*, (Vol. 1), 4th edition. Chichester: Wiley.

Smedslund, J. (1977). Piaget's psychology in practice. *British Journal of Educational Psychology, 47*, 1–6.

Sternberg, R. J. (1980). The development of linear syllogistic reasoning. *Journal of Experimental Child Psychology, 29*, 340–356.

Sternberg, R. J. (Ed.). (1984). *Mechanisms of cognitive development*. New York: Freeman.

Thayer, E. S. & Collyer, C. E. (1978). The development of transitive inference: a review of recent approaches. *Psychological Bulletin, 85*, 1327–1343.

Trabasso, T. (1977). The role of memory as a system in making transitive inferences. In R. V. Kail and J. W. Hagen, (Eds.), *Perspectives on the development of memory and cognition*. Hillsdale, N.J.: Lawrence Erlbaum Associates Inc.

Vygotsky, L. S. (1978). *Mind in society*. Cambridge, Mass: Harvard University Press.

Walker, L. J. (1982). Verbal seriation: Children's solution strategies and stage of cognitive development. *Canadian Journal of Behavioral Science, 14*, 175–189.

10 Children's Reasoning

Margaret Donaldson

Can young children reason deductively? That is, from a given set of premises, can they draw the conclusion that these premises warrant? In experimental tests of this question, the answer has frequently been in the negative. And yet, as Donaldson points out in the present reading, evidence that children as young as four years old can reason deductively may be obtained in observations of their spontaneous reasoning, particularly as they listen to stories. The fact is, it is difficult to devise experimental procedures which allow the reasoning abilities of young children to be revealed. However, as the present reading also makes clear, while difficult, the task is not impossible.

Piaget has not been alone in claiming that young children are incapable of inferences which, to an adult, seem elementary. From a type of psychological theory utterly opposed to his own, precisely the same conclusion has been drawn. One of the most eminent of the associationist – or behaviourist – psychologists, Clark Hull, claimed that the essence of reasoning lies in the putting together of two "behaviour segments" in some novel way, never actually performed before, so as to reach a goal. Serious objections can be raised to this way of defining reasoning but let us accept it for the moment and look at what happens if we study children's thinking in a way guided by the Hullian conception.

When Hull spoke of the joining of two "behaviour segments" he spoke against a background of studies of rats learning to run mazes – studies of

Source: Donaldson, M. et al. (Eds.) (1983). *Early childhood development and education*, Oxford: Blackwell.

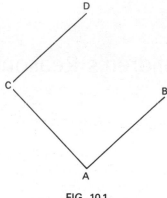

FIG. 10.1.

a kind so popular with the behaviourists. A "behaviour segment" was then exemplified by the running from one point in the maze to another.

The claim was as follows: suppose you arrange the maze as in the diagram above. Now suppose that a rat learns to run from A to B to get a small reward; and from A to C to get an equally small reward; and from C to D to get a much bigger reward (all of these bits of learning taking place on separate occasions). If you then place him at point A and he chooses the path A → C → D, instead of the path A → B, he must be *reasoning* that you can get to D that way, for he has never actually *been* from A to D that way before.

Of course, there is a 50/50 chance of taking that road randomly, with no reasoning at all. But if a large number of rats were all to take it, that would be evidence of rodent reasoning.

In fact this evidence has not been obtained. Rats don't, apparently, figure things out in this way.

More strangely, evidence has been obtained which makes it look as if children under the age of seven don't either.

Two followers of Clark Hull, Howard and Tracy Kendler (1967) devised a test for children that was explicitly based on Hullian principles. However, it did not involve running a maze. Instead the children were given the task of learning to operate a machine so as to get a toy. In order to succeed they had to go through a two-stage sequence corresponding to the segments of the maze. The children were trained on each stage separately. The stages consisted merely of pressing the correct one of two buttons to get a marble; and inserting a marble into a small hole to release the toy.

The Kendlers found that the children could learn the separate bits readily enough. Given the task of getting a marble by pressing the button they could get the marble; given the task of getting a toy when the marble was handed to them, they could use the marble. (All they had to do was put it in a hole.) But they did not for the most part "integrate", to use the

Kendlers' terminology. They did not press the button to get the marble and then proceed without further help to use the marble to get the toy. So the Kendlers concluded that they were incapable, like the rats, of deductive reasoning. This work was done in the 1960s. No wonder Chomsky could so readily convince people of the need to postulate a highly specific device for the acquisition of language.

On the other hand, the Kendlers' results are bound to seem deeply puzzling to anyone who has watched children playing in a nursery or listened to their conversation, and who really brings the two kinds of data together in his mind.

Here is a striking example of the kind of reasoning of which children seem to be capable if one observes their spontaneous behaviour, by contrast with their behaviour when they are being tested.

This exchange happened to be tape-recorded, so it can be quoted very accurately. It took place shortly after the death of Donald Campbell when he was trying to break the world water speed record, and some months after a visit by a research worker called Robin Campbell to the school where the conversation took place. The speakers were a little girl of five and another research worker.

Child: "Is that Mr Campbell who came here – dead?"
(Dramatic stress on the word "dead".)
Research worker: "No, I'm quite sure he isn't dead."
(Much surprised.)
Child: "Well, there must be two Mr Campbells then, because Mr Campbell's dead, under the water."

This child has put together, if not two "behaviour segments", two quite distinct pieces of information: Mr Campbell who came here is not dead and Mr Campbell is dead, and has drawn a valid conclusion, which she states as a necessary consequence: ". . . there must be two Mr Campbells then . . ." Her reasoning involves the understanding that the existence of a living person is incompatible with the death of that same person. So if Mr Campbell is dead and Mr Campbell is alive, there simply must be two of them!

How can it be that children of five are capable of reasoning like this, yet can fail to "integrate" two very simple bits of separately learned behaviour in a task such as the Kendlers used?

The mystery at first appears to deepen when we learn, from Michael Cole and his colleagues (Cole, Gay, Glick & Sharp, 1971) that adults in an African culture apparently cannot do the Kendlers' task either. But it lessens, on the other hand, when we learn that a task was devised which was strictly analogous to the Kendlers' one but much easier for the African adults to handle.
CDA—G*

Instead of the button-pressing machine, Cole used a locked box and two differently coloured match-boxes, one of which contained a key that would open the box. Notice that there are still two behaviour segments ("open the right match-box to get the key" and "use the key to open the box") so the task seems formally to be the same. But psychologically it is quite different. Now the subject is dealing not with a strange machine but with familiar meaningful objects; and it is clear to him what he is meant to do. It then turns out that the difficulty of "integration" is greatly reduced.

Recent work by Simon Hewson (1978) is of great interest here for it shows that, for young children too, the difficulty lies not in the inferential processes which the task demands, but in certain perplexing features of the apparatus and the procedure. When these are changed in ways which do not at all affect the inferential nature of the problem, then five-year-old children solve the problem as well as college students did in the Kendlers' own experiments.

Hewson made two crucial changes. First, he replaced the button-pressing mechanism in the side panels by drawers in these panels which the child could open and shut. This took away the mystery from the first stage of training. Then he helped the child to understand that there was no "magic" about the specific marble which, during the second stage of training, the experimenter handed to him so that he could pop it in the hole and get the reward. A child understands nothing, after all, about how a marble put into a hole can open a little door. How is he to know that any other marble of similar size will do just as well? Yet he must assume this if he is to solve the problem. Hewson made the functional equivalence of different marbles clear by playing a "swapping game" with the children.

These two modifications together produced a jump in success rates from 30 per cent to 90 per cent for five-year-olds and from 35 per cent to 72.5 per cent for four-year-olds. For three-year-olds, for reasons that are still in need of clarification, no improvement – rather a slight drop in performance – resulted from the change.

We may conclude, then, that children experience very real difficulty when faced with the Kendler apparatus; but this difficulty cannot be taken as proof that they are incapable of deductive reasoning.

With this conclusion in mind, let us see now how children behave in a very different type of situation.

It is highly informative to listen to the comments children make and the questions they ask when they listen to stories. In this situation a rich harvest of evidence of reasoning may be reaped.

Here are a few examples:

"What a lot of things he's taking! He wouldn't have . . . he's only got two hands and he wouldn't have space for his two hands to carry all these things."

(*Premises:* (1) Peter has more to carry than two hands can carry; (2) Peter has only two hands. *Conclusion:* It is not possible for Peter to carry all that he is represented as carrying. Implied criticism of the story.)

"She must have eaten all her food on the other day."
(*Premises:* (1) Houses normally have food in them; (2) This house has no food. *Conclusion:* The food must have been all eaten up.)

"But how can it be [that they are getting married]? You have to have a man too." (The book contains an illustration of a wedding in which the man looks rather like a woman. The child thinks it is a picture of two women.)
(*Premises:* (1) You need a man for a wedding; (2) There is no man in the picture. *Conclusion:* It can't be a wedding.)

"I think you have missed a page. You didn't say that he cut out the leather."
(*Premises:* (1) There is a page on which the story tells of cutting out leather; (2) No reference has been made to cutting out leather. *Conclusion:* A page has been missed.)

Child: "You're not looking."
Teacher: "Pardon?"
Child: "Why are you not reading it?"
Teacher: "Because I know it."
(*Premises:* (1) When you read a book you look at it: (2) The teacher is not looking at the book. *Conclusion:* She is not reading the book.)

It is impossible to take account of this evidence and at the same time to maintain that children under the age of six or seven are incapable of reasoning deductively. So if sometimes – as in certain experimental situations – they do not appear to reason deductively, we must look more closely at what is happening. If we cannot get children to reason when we contrive experiments, whereas we can observe them reasoning spontaneously, then we must ask why.

It turns out, however, that in spite of the findings of Piaget and the Kendlers and some others, it is not impossible to get children to reason in the contrived circumstances of an experiment. It is harder but it is not impossible.

Barbara Wallington (1974) conducted a series of experiments where the task was to find a toy in one – or more than one – of a set of boxes which might or might not have stars on the lids. She designed her studies with great care and a desire to give children every chance to grasp what it was that she wanted of them. The results were revealing.

The children were given information which they could use to guide their search. For instance, they might be told: "If there is a star on the box, then there is a wee animal in the box", or, "If there is no star, then there is a wee animal in the box". After hearing a statement of this kind, they were asked to predict which boxes would contain a toy and to check whether they were right.

The pattern of the children's choices and the nature of their answers when they were asked why they had made the choices showed very clearly that many of them were engaging in processes of strict reasoning in the sense that they were using the experimenter's statement as a basis from which to deduce conclusions. They very rarely drew all the conclusions which would be judged correct by the canons of traditional formal logic – but neither did a group of adults to whom the same task was given. The older children (and "older" in this case means between four years, three months and four years, eleven months) frequently responded in just the same way as the adults, taking "if there is a star . . ." to mean "*if and only if* there is a star . . ." and reasoning accordingly. Some of the children were also able to give explanations very like those of the adults, using such expressions as: *it must be, it has to be.* Here are two examples, by way of illustration: "When there's no star, there's supposed to be a wee animal in the box". "It must be in there [box with no star] if it's not in there [starred box]." In this last case the given statement had been: "If there is a star, then there is no wee animal".

Notice that these justifications were made after the children had indicated which boxes they were choosing but before they had been allowed to open them.

From children under four years, such responses as these were relatively uncommon. But even the youngest children did not behave randomly. They tended to have systematic search strategies, even if these were as primitive and unrelated to the experimenter's words as starting with a box at one end and working along the row.

Further evidence that, even in experimental situations, children can sometimes give proof of their ability to reason is now being obtained. Peter Bryant and Paul Harris have each independently looked at the child's ability to engage in the kind of inference which is concerned with transitive relations such as "equal to" or "greater than". (This is yet another form of inference which Piaget regards as criterial for operational thought and which, therefore, according to his theory, is not normally to be found in children under age seven.)

Harris and his colleagues (personal communication) showed four-year-old children two strips of paper placed about three feet apart. The strips differed in length by about a quarter of an inch – too small a difference to be perceptible. Thus when the children were asked which strip was longer approximately half their judgements were correct, this being, of course, the result that would be expected by chance alone. Then a third strip of paper, equal in length to one of the other two, was produced; and it was briefly placed alongside each of the others in turn. The question was then repeated. And now most of the children gave the correct answer. This seems to show clearly that they were capable of understanding measurement, which is to say that they were able to make inferences of the form: if A equals B and if B is longer than C, then A must be longer than C.

Bryant and Kopytynska (1976) have reached conclusions similar to those of Harris about the ability of young children to make measurements.

Let us take stock. From the evidence we have been considering, it emerges that children are not so limited in ability to reason deductively as Piaget – and others – have claimed. This ability shows itself most markedly in some aspects of their spontaneous behaviour – and we have seen that it reveals itself with great clarity in the comments they make while listening to stories. But it can be demonstrated also in the contrived situation of an experiment from about the age of four, if not sooner, even though many experiments have failed to elicit it.

REFERENCES

Bryant, P. E. & Kopytynska, H. (1976). Spontaneous measurement by young children. *Nature, 260*, 772.

Cole, M., Gay, J., Glick, J. A., & Sharp, D. W. (1971). *The cultural context of learning and thinking*. London: Methuen.

Hewson, S. (1978). Inferential problem solving in young children. *Developmental Psychology, 14*, 93–98.

Kerndler, T. S. and Kendler, H. H. (1967). Experimental analysis of inferential behaviour in children. In L. P. Lipsitt and C. C. Spiker (Eds). *Advances in child development and behaviour. Vol. 3*. New York: Academic Press.

Wallington, B. A. (1974). *Some aspects of the development of reasoning in preschool children*. Unpublished doctoral dissertation, University of Edinburgh.

IV SOCIAL FOUNDATIONS OF COGNITIVE DEVELOPMENT

11 On the Social Development of the Intellect

Willem Doise

Why and how do children of the human species become intelligent, at least generally, during the first years of their existence? In the first part of this paper, we would like to show how the response to this question has been formulated in terms of social psychology, but without applying social psychological investigative methods to explicate the response. As it were, the social role in cognitive development is frequently accepted as a postulate. In the second part of this chapter, we would like to show that psychological experimentation permits illustrating, if not verifying, some characteristics of the manner in which social factors intervene in cognitive development.

THE SOCIAL POSTULATE

Most theories on the development of intelligence, phylogenetic as well as ontogenetic, support the postulate that adaptation to the physical environment is the principal function of the elaboration of the cognitive instruments. But is this adaptation developed with respect to that environment? When the development of knowledge is studied in primates, the prototypical environment is often comprised of a bit of food that is unreachable by the subject with a stick, or even with two sticks that fit together, that the individual, becoming intelligent, will use to seize the food. Different theories on cognitive development and on human learning, even those elaborated in Geneva, often assume that the human environment is com-

Source: Shulman, V. L., Restaino–Baumann, L. C. R, & Butler, L. (Eds.) (1985). *The future of Piagetian theory: The neo-Piagetians*, New York: Plenum Press, pp. 99–121.

prised exclusively of objects, particularly at the level of constructing experimental paradigms.

Fortunately, at the theoretical level, such limitations seem to be outdated. First, we will present the perspective of an ethologist. Humphrey (1976) observed that members of the anthropoid species, and some human tribes, rarely use all of their cognitive capacities to solve problems concerning biological survival in their natural habitat (1976, p.307):

> We are thus faced with a conundrum. It has been repeatedly demonstrated in the artificial situations of the psychological laboratory that anthropoid apes possess impressive powers of creative reasoning, yet these feats of intelligence seem simply not to have any parallels in the behavior of the same animals in their natural environment. I have yet to hear of an example from the field in which a chimpanzee (or for that matter a Bushman) uses his full capacity for inferential reasoning in the solution of a biologically relevant practical problem.

Why, then, are higher primates intelligent and, in any case, much more intelligent than other species? Because they are obliged to acquire factual knowledge that they use within the context of the social community, and the principal role of creative intelligence is then to adapt to the social life. In the course of his presentation, Humphrey argued effectively that the more complex cognitive demands made on higher primates are of social origin. It would then be through their adaptation to their social environment, which from the cognitive perspective is much more complex, that higher primates and humans are adapted to their physical environment.

It should be noted that some of Humphrey's points of reasoning are not very different from arguments advanced by a psychologist who has argued in favour of a more social approach to studying cognitive development in children. In effect, Smedslund (1966; p.161) also regrets that, in this domain, "actual research uniformly considers cognitive development as an interaction between the child and his non-human environment". Nevertheless (p.162):

> it is well known that the child's interests (and consequently the majority of his experiences) are concentrated on the principal aspects of the social life, notably rules (roles), values, and symbols. Even when the child plays alone, his play causes roles, symbols, and social products to intervene. For this reason, one must admit that social interaction must be a major factor in cognitive development.

Then again, "the logico-mathematical tests seem to have relatively little intrinsic interest for children, and in an instance where interest intervenes, it seems to reflect a novelty effect of short duration" (p.161). Nevertheless, when such problems are embedded in a social context, and more precisely, when they give way to communication conflicts between individuals having different concentrations, cognitive progress can be verified in the form of intellectual decentration.

Hypotheses on the social role in cognitive development advanced by an ethologist and a psychologist can seem to be reasonable. That precisely poses the problem: too many of these researchers are content to affirm social importance without being concerned with empirically verifying their hypotheses. In that regard we cite Mead and Piaget.

We know that for Mead (1934), social interaction or, more precisely, "gestural communication" occurs at the beginning of cognitive development. "Conversation of gestures" assumes a reciprocal adaptation:

> Just as in fencing the parry is an interpretation of the thrust, so, in the social act, the adjustive response of one organism to the gesture of another is the interpretation of that gesture by that organism – it is the meaning of that gesture. (p. 78)
>
> "Conversations through gestures" are also based upon the use of vocal gestures, which are interiorized: the gestures thus internalized are significant symbols because they have the same meanings for all individual members of the given society or social group, i.e., they respectively arouse the same attitudes in the individuals making them that they arouse in the individuals responding to them; otherwise the individual could not internalize them. (p. 47)

But where in Mead does one find evidence permitting verification of this thesis?

For Piaget (1967), the epistemologist, there was no doubt that "human intelligence is developed in the individual as a function of social interactions that are, in general, greatly neglected" (p. 269). Elsewhere (Doise, 1978), we have had the opportunity to show how a certain fluctuation characterizes Piagetian reflections on this problem. The explicative approach adopted in the book *The Moral Judgment of the Child*, published in 1932, arises from social psychology; the passage from heteronomy to the autonomy of childlike moral conceptions, the passage from an objective interpretation of the responsibility is explained by the multiple interactions of the cooperation between equals, in which the children participate in their societies. It is not only moral development but also knowledge in general that is thus explained (Piaget, 1932, p. 324):

> Social life is necessary to permit the individual to become aware of the functioning of the spirit and to transform it in their own norms, the simple functional equilibrium immanent in each mental or even vital activity.

Again, the social is involved as an explicative factor but without being demonstrated in the proper sense.

In *Sociological Studies* (1965), Piaget reexamined "the question, as often debated, of the social or the individual nature of logic" (p. 143). The question is posed with great precision: Can the individual alone attain an operatory idea, this organization of actions that are interiorized, composable, and reversible? Before responding, Piaget first illustrated that there is correspondence between the child's development of cognitive activities and certain forms of social cooperation. The simultaneous changes in the two domains constitute the point of departure of Piagetian reflection (1965, p. 157):

> To the period properly called the stage of operations (7–11/12 years) corresponds . . . a very clear progress in socialization; the child becomes capable of cooperation, that is to say that he no longer thinks in function only of himself but of the actual or possible coordination of points of view.

The theme is concisely formulated in *Moral Judgment* (1932, p. 75): "The social life and the individual life are one".

It is, then, shown how, in the case of equilibrium, the relations of intellectual exchange, as well as the exchange of values, manifest a logic identical to what also becomes actualized in individual operations (Piaget, 1965):

> social relations equilibrated in cooperation will then constitute the "groupings" of the operations, exactly the same as all logical operations exercised by the individual on the external world, and the grouping laws define the form of the ideal equilibrium common to the first as to the second. (p. 159).
>
> . . . between individual operations and cooperation, in the final account, will be fundamental identity, from the perspective of the laws of equilibrium which govern the two. (p. 162)

Can one be truly content with a verification by a correlation, seeing an identity between structures that intervene in physical reality and those that intervene in social interactions, and that no longer pose the problem of eventual social influence?

Evidently, this is not the opinion of authors such as Leontiev, who base their work on dialectical materialism. If that author forcefully called for psychological study as such and combatted the falsely interdisciplinary attitude of psychologists who address others with their request "Come into psychology and rule over us," he has nevertheless constantly reverted to the need of studying the human psychysm in its social context, affirming that such a study must (1976, p. 5) "put in evidence the category of psychological awareness, and that means understanding the actual passages which connect the concrete individual psychism and social awareness and different forms of the latter".

How did he proceed to attain this objective? We know of his celebrated experiments that illustrate how certain sensory thresholds can be considerably lowered when the sensation becomes more relevant, especially when it is embedded in a system of actions. As human activities are essentially social, we understand that such experiments can illustrate the passages that link individual psychysms to the social group. Other experiments reported by Leontiev (1970–1971) directly studied the effects that different types of social interventions exert on the regulations of cognitive nature. Nevertheless, historical reconstruction seems to be Leontiev's preferred approach to link the psychysm to the social. This approach reflects the thesis of Marx and of Engels, according to which work is the origin of development in human history. Now (Leontiev, 1976, p. 67):

> work carried out under conditions of common collective activity, such that man is at once within this process, not only with nature, but with other men, members of a given society. It is only through this relationship with other men that man finds himself in relation with nature.

Leontiev (1976, p. 71s) developed the example of "beating up the game" (the big game hunt), a wild-game stalk and kill in which one group of individuals stalks a wild animal that will be chased into an open area, where it will be captured by another group. Apparently for the individual beater (hunter), this is an activity that lacks sense; it acquires meaning only in making a correspondence with the other hunter's activity. In addition, manufacturing a tool, which is specifically a human activity, is basically a social activity. Thus, the tool is a social object, the product of a social practice, a social work experience. Consequently, the generalized reflection of the work object's objective properties are crystallized and also become the product of an individual practice. As a result, the most simple human knowledge is directly carried out in a concrete action of work by a tool. It is not limited to the individual's personal experience; it is carried out on the basis of acquiring the experience of a social praxis (1976, p. 76).

The actual development of intelligence in our children is embedded in social history in the same way through a "process of appropriation from the accumulated experience of humanity throughout social history" (Leontiev, 1976, p. 312). If the child is surrounded by an objective world created by humans, which incorporates the history of their social history, the child does not adopt this heritage by himself alone. For example, this would be an abstract supposition, a Robinson Crusoe story, as in thinking that a child adapts himself to a spoon. In reality, the situation is that the mother feeds the child with a spoon (1976, p. 314): "The mother helps the child, intervenes in his actions, and in the common action that results, the child develops a skill in using a spoon. Thereafter, he knows how to use the spoon as a *human* object".

Tran Duc Thao (1973) also cited dialectical materialism in order to explain the historical development and the ontogenesis of human intelligence. In a daring manner, he traced a parallel between the steps of the historical and the ontogenetic development of human intelligence, trying to fill our knowledge gaps in each of these developments with what we know, or believe we know, from the other. The pointing gesture would constitute the essential element of intellectual development. It is a social act, an appeal to intervention, as with the child who shows a container of jam to his mother. With the aid of this gesture, Tran Duc Thao reconstructed "the origins of the representational sign in prehuman development", reverting in his way to the story of the hunt, at the point where the hunters have already developed the habit of pointing toward the hunt.

In the child, the adaptation of the sign would be accomplished in an analogous manner (Tran Duc Thao, 1973, p. 124):

> The appearance of this new structure of the sign has *without doubt* been prepared by the child's social experience, who must have seen on diverse occasions people who point a finger at him to indicate an object behind a screen which he can not see.

It is necessary that we again stress how social intervention is accepted as a postulate. If that is, perhaps, an indispensable step to the level of prehistoric reconstruction, one would think that this is not the case when one studies child development, where experimentation provides useful support to a thesis as important as the one described herein.

The six authors mentioned here are evidently not the only ones who have adhered to the social postulate. One could, for example, add Berry and Dasen (1974), who attempted to illustrate how different ecological contexts moderate the individual's cognitive functioning, with the intermediary of cultural systems and different systems of socialization. However, in their research, ecological contexts were the ones that were studied. But seeing the limits of this account, it is now time to relate how we have tried to study experimentally the links between social interaction and cognitive development.

EXPERIMENTAL ILLUSTRATION

Research that indicates that a certain correspondence exists between cognitive development and the development of the modalities of participation in social interactions is not lacking. Here, we are content to cite the research completed in Geneva by Piaget (1932), Nielsen (1951), Moessinger (1975), and Dami (1975), as well as other research by Flavell and his collaborators

(1968), Feffer (1970), Waller (1971, 1973), and Mikula (1972). Naturally, this enumeration is not exhaustive. Its only objective is to recall how much research already exists that effectively shows that the development of social skills and competence ranks with cognitive development. However, this body of research also has in common not dealing with the problem of causality. Thus, the objective for our own research in this domain was mainly to illustrate how – at least, at certain phases of genetic development – social interactions can foster the emergence of certain cognitive operations. Contrary to the research cited, we explicitly introduce the modalities of social interaction as independent variables at the level of the experimental paradigm in order to study the effect on certain aspects of cognitive development.

To defend the thesis that social interaction plays a causal role in cognitive development is not so much to adhere to the conceptions that would imply that the individual is passively fashioned by the regulations imposed from the outside. Our conception is interactionist and constructionist; in ques tioning the surrounding environment, the individual elaborates systems of organization from his action on reality. In the majority of cases, it is not only a question of reality; it is precisely in coordinating his own actions with those of others that he elaborates the systems of coordinations of his actions and consequently arrives at reproducing them all alone. The causality that we attribute to social interaction is not unidirectional; it is circular and progresses in a spiral. Interaction permits the individual to master certain coordinations, which then permit him to participate in more elaborate social interactions, which, in their turn, become the source of cognitive development for the individual.

The intention of my co-workers, G. Mugny and A. N. Perret-Clermont, as well as my own, is to undertake the empirical examination of this very question, a domain that has been dropped by the Genevan school. Our basic hypothesis is that social interaction exercises a causal effect on cognitive development. We follow Piaget in considering cognition the coordination of actions, interiorized and reversible. However, we think that these individual coordinations are first made possible by coordination *between* individuals. Interindividual coordinations precede and promote intraindividual coordinations.

Of course, this is a very general thesis that, therefore, is unlikely to be proved in one experiment. In fact, our team has now compiled some 20 experiments (see Doise & Mugny, 1981) on different phenomena, illustrating varied aspects of this general thesis. First, we tried to show that, indeed, interindividual coordinations appear to be earlier developmentally than individual coordinations. More specifically, we tried to show that, at certain ages, children collectively perform more advanced coordinations than they do alone. Second, we are examining the subsequent effects of this participation on the individual in making more advanced coordinations. These experiments illustrate a sentence of Vygotsky (1965): "What children can do together today, they can do alone tomorrow". Third, we are studying one important mechanism of social interaction: sociocognitive conflict. In a paper dealing with the social origin of decentration, Smedslund (1966) developed the idea that children can progress when confronted with the centrations of others, even when these centrations are in error. Centrations are here to be understood in the Piagetian sense, as more elementary cognitive schemes that have to be coordinated in more complex cognitive structures in order to give rise to operational thinking. As the rationale of our thesis, we place the role of the sociocognitive conflict at its very core: if a child, all by himself, approaches reality with successive and different centrations, these differences are made explicit when two individuals are engaged at the same time in the same problem with opposing centrations. Such simultaneity unveils the more urgent necessity of coordinating those insufficient centrations. Of course, this coordination can be enhanced by some other factors, for instance, by submitting the child to a systematic questioning, by assigning him a given responsibility in a social interaction, or by facilitating the initial capacity that he is endowed with in approaching the social interaction. The role of these factors has been examined in various studies, references to which can be found in the appended reference section.

More recently, our research group has begun a fourth series of studies concerned with the correspondence between social relations and cognitive coordinations. When such correspondences materialize in situations of sociocognitive conflict, they are thought to facilitate cognitive coordinations.

In the same broad sense, these studies introduce one new perspective into the classical research on group performance: generally, these studies try to find out which modalities of interaction improve the group efficiency in specific tasks. Our aim, on the other hand, is to examine the effect that those interactions exert on bringing about more elaborated cognitive processes in the individual participating in social interaction. More specifically, when our research deals with an effect of social facilitation, it is not in the sense as Zajonc (1965), who examined primarily the activation of cognitive processes that are already there; specifically, our research goes after the very construction of new cognitive capacities in a given social interaction.

Let us now describe some of our main research paradigms, together with the results that they have provided.

This game consists of a motor coordination task. Three activities can be carried out on pulleys attached by strings to a lead pencil target: pulling, releasing, or blocking. A response on one pulley must be coordinated with responses on either one or two other pulleys in order to move the target along a predetermined route; in this sense, the task involves cognitive

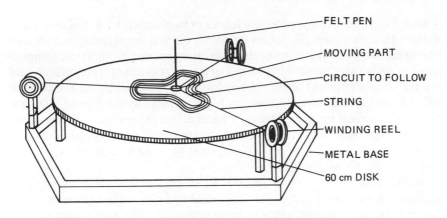

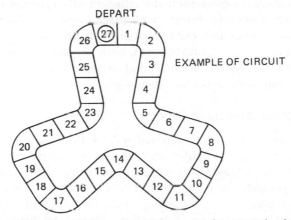

FIG. 11.1.   The cooperative game: the instrument and an example of the tracing circuit.

skills. The scores are obtained by summing across the number of segments in which the target remains correctly in the middle of the "road", and by then subtracting the number of segments where the target leaves the road (errors). (See Fig.11.1.)

In the first experiments, we (Doise, 1978; Doise & Mugny, 1975) compared the individual performances of younger children (ages 7–8) and older children (ages 9–10), each manipulating pulleys, with the collective performances of pairs in which each member handled only one pulley. As predicted, the younger children performed better in the collective condition. There were no such differences for the older children. Furthermore, developmentally more complex coordinations were observed in interindividual interactions before they were found in individuals acting alone. Similar patterns of findings were obtained when situations were "individualized", either by appointing a leader or by eliminating verbal communication. In both cases, the group performance was contingent to a greater extent on the individual's respective abilities and not on their coordinated efforts. As before, these differences between experimental conditions held for the younger but not for the older children. These results are reminiscent of findings from studies of group problem-solving, where logical tasks are better performed by hierarchical or centralized groups and creative tasks by more homogeneous groups. In our experiment, the older children performed a task that, to them, had acquired logical characteristics, as they mastered the necessary coordinations.

In the fourth experiment (Doise & Mugny, 1981), children of three different ages carried out either individual tasks or collective tasks, interposed between a pretest and a posttest criterion. The same apparatus was used in both conditions. The experimental question was concerned with improvement in the performance on the criterion as a function of performance on the intervening task. For the younger children, only the collective condition had effect, whereas for the older children (who already had some mastery over the necessary coordinations), both conditions had an effect. Thus, again, from the developmental point of view, it was the collective experience that took precedence in efficiency.

The Conservation-of-Liquid Task

These particular experiments were devised by A. N. Perret-Clermont (1979) to study the effects of a social interaction setting on the individual, using the well-known Piagetian tasks as described by Inhelder, Sinclair, and Bovet (1974). On the pretest, the children were categorized as nonconservers, intermediates, or conservers. According to the original and now-famous investigations, the non-conserver is one who, although admitting that two identical glasses equally filled contain the same amount of liquid, judges these amounts to be different when one is transferred to a tall, slender glass and the other to a short and wide glass. On the other hand, the conserver maintains that the two quantities remain the same. To support this inference, conservers usually offer at least one of the following arguments: (a) nothing has been added to or taken from either glass (the identity argument); (b) if the two quantities were poured back into the original glasses, the latter would be found to be equally full again (the reversibility argument); and (c) the liquid is higher in one glass but wider in the other, so that width compensates for height (the compensation argument).

There were two conditions in the present experiment: a control condition with a pretest and a posttest and an experimental condition with an intervening social interaction. A child already defined as nonconserving (or intermediate) was required to serve the same amount of fruit juice to each of two conserving children, where one possessed a tall, slender glass and the other a short and wide one. The would-be donor also had a short and wide glass. The nonconserver was allowed to drink only if the other two children agreed that they had received the same amount of juice. As the two recipients were selected on the basis of being conservers, the nonconserving donor was to some extent forced to act out the role of conservation. Often, the nonconservers were brought to use their own short or wide glass to measure juice for the tall and slender glass. On the posttest, 65% of the subjects in the experimental condition progressed on this task, compared with only about 18% of the control subjects. The authenticity of this progress was marked by the fact that out of the 23 subjects who had progressed, 13 were able, during the posttest, to offer at least one of the three arguments for conservation that had not specifically been voiced during the intervening social interaction. Furthermore, in a replication of this experiment, the subjects who had progressed on the conservation of liquid improved in generalizing as they showed progress on other conservation tasks.

Conservation-of-Length Task

In our research, the role of sociocognitive conflict was first studied in the context of the conservation-of-length task. In all of our experiments on length, we used subjects who were nonconservers, on the conservation of both equality and inequality of length. Conservation of length can be assessed as follows. Two rulers of equal length are laid side by side so that their ends perceptually coincide. They will, of course, be judged to be of equal length. However, if one ruler is displaced to the left or to the right, so that the ends of the two rulers no longer coincide, the nonconserving child fails to compensate for the shift and says that one ruler is now longer than the other. For the conservation of inequality, two wires or chains of different length are first presented in parallel, stretched out. When the longer wire is folded so that its extremities coincide with those of the shorter one, the nonconserving child now says that the two wires are of equal length. When the extremities of the longer wire are brought still closer together, the nonconserving child may actually now consider the shorter wire the longer one. Three conditions were used in our first experiment (Doise, Mugny, & Perret-Clermont, 1976).

Control condition.   Each time, starting with the two rulers in line, four different configurations were obtained by alternatively displacing each ruler in the two opposite directions. After each of these four displacements, the subject was asked whether the rulers were of the same length or not. This was a condition of individual conflict.

Condition of incorrect model.   Starting with the two rulers in the line and after recognition of their equal length, one ruler was displaced. When the subject claimed that the displaced ruler was longer than the other one, the assistant experimenter pointed to the opposite end of the other ruler and said, "I think this ruler is longer; you see, it goes further there." This judgment was, of course, as incorrect as the subject's own, but it was based on a symmetrical concentration. If the subject complied with the assistant, the experimenter reminded him of his previous answer. This was a condition of individual sociocognitive conflict.

Condition of correct model.   This condition was the same as the previous condition, but the adult assistant performed a correct judgment: "I think both rulers are equal in length; you see, this one goes further here and that one goes further there, so both are the same length." In Piagetian terms the argument given by the assistant was that of compensation.

The results showed that not only the correct-model condition but also the opposed-centration condition led to progress, in about 50% of the subjects, in terms of the generalization of conservation. A second posttest 10 days later, in a double-blind condition with a new experimenter, showed that this progress remained quite stable. These results have been replicated with nonconserving children contradicting each other on the same task (Doise, Giroud, & Mugny, 1978–1979).

A conservation-of-unequal-length task was also used to initiate our studies on the correspondence between social and cognitive relations (Doise, Dionnet, & Mugny, 1979). Two steel chains of unequal length were shown to nonconserving children with the instruction that they could be used as bracelets to wrap around two cylinders of unequal diameter. The longer chain was designed to fit the larger cylinder and the shorter chain to fit the smaller one. There were four presentations of the two chains, and the experimenter systematically folded the extremities of the longer chain until they came closer and closer together, while the subject watched. After each presentation, half the subjects were required to match the bracelets to the cylinders. The subjects often made an error in judging the length or in choosing the bracelet for a cylinder, at which point the experimenter made explicit the conflict between the subject's choice and the preceding judgment or choice. The procedure was similar for the other half of the children, but instead of cylinders, the experimenter's wrist and the child's wrist were used. Of the 17 subjects, 2 progressed in the cylinder condition, and 11 out of 18 progressed in the wrist condition. Again, the stability of this progress was checked by using a new experimenter in a second post-test one week later, as well as by demonstrating generalization in the conservation-of-equal-length task.

The Spatial Transformation Task

Two tables were placed together in such a way that their surfaces formed an angle of 90 degrees. On one, the experimenter formed a village of three differently coloured houses, bearing a spatial relation to a fixed marker (e.g., a mountain or a lake) in the upper-left-hand corner. The subject's task was to construct the same village on the other table in such a way that someone coming from the lake or the mountain would find the individual houses in their respective orientations. This is not a difficult task for children 5–6 years of age when the marker on the model table is in the same position on the copy table, relative to the position of the subject (e.g., in the upper-left-hand corner in both cases). The child merely transposes all elements by a body turn of 90 degrees, what is on the left on the model table is also on the left on the copy table, and so on. (See Fig.11.2.) But when, for example, the marker is in the near right corner of the model table and in the far left corner of the copy table, the perceptual relations present a far more difficult task for the child. In the individual condition of the first experiment, children working alone were required to copy a task of that level of difficulty, twice, each time using three houses. On the average, they placed only 1.3 out of 6 houses in the correct place. On easy items, they placed 4.75 houses correctly. In a collective situation, children working together performed significantly better, placing an average of 3.3 houses in the correct place on difficult items (Doise, 1978).

Three strategies emerged in the task: no compensation, partial compensation, and total compensation. In the first, the children located the houses

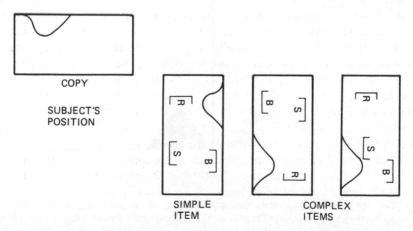

FIG. 11.2.   Examples of one simple and two complex items in the spatial transformation task.

on the copy table by a 90-degree body shift, regardless of the position of the marker. In the second, the children located the houses correctly on one dimension (e.g., near and far), but not on the other (e.g., left and right). In the third, total compensation yielded the correct solution.

In a second experiment (Mugny & Doise, 1978), we required children of different cognitive levels to work together. One important result was that when partially compensating children worked with noncompensating children, both progressed. In other words, the partially compensating children did not need the presence of a correctly responding model in order to improve their performance. The noncompensating children, it must be added, did not improve much when interacting with another noncompensat-

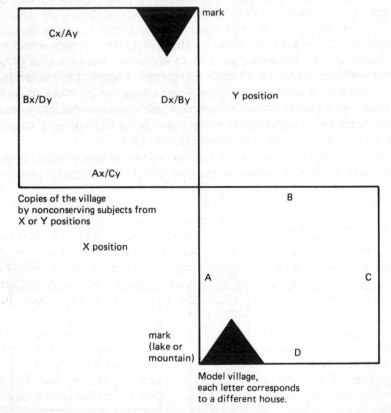

FIG. 11.3.   An example of an interaction situation and of the conflicting performances of two nonconserving subjects in different positions. In the interindividual situation, two children, one in the X position and one in the Y position, constructed the copy together; in the intraindividual condition, the child constructed his copy alone in the X or Y position before moving to the other position in order to check his copy.

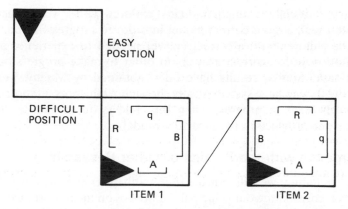

FIG. 11.4. Examples of spatial transformation tasks with a difficult and an easy position.

ing child, but then again, the same was true when the interaction was with a totally compensating child. In the latter condition, the advanced subject tended to solve the problem alone. In so doing, he ignored the suggestions of the noncompensating child, and no opportunity was provided to coordinate approaches. In the case of two noncompensating subjects, they tended to agree in their errors from the beginning and therefore to show no improvement.

Nevertheless, there is a way of relating two noncompensating children to each other so that their interaction leads to progress. Consider the layout in Fig.11.3. When one noncompensating subject was in Position X and the other in Y, they gave, by definition, contradictory solutions. In such a situation, 13 out of 21 subjects progressed. This result can be compared with that of an individual condition where the same subject moved from X to Y in order to evaluate his responses from both positions. In this condition, only 6 out of 19 subjects progressed. If we take the results for partially compensating children into account also, it was shown that interindividual conflict leads to significantly more progress than mere intraindividual conflict (Doise & Mugny, 1979).

In another experiment (Carugati & Mugny, 1979), a noncompensating subject was placed in a position from which the situation was viewed as easy and was confronted with another subject from whose position the tasks appeared difficult (see Fig.11.4). In such a condition, the child for whom the task was easy was not much perturbed by the difficulties encountered by the other. Later, the first child did not show progress (2 out of 12 progressed) on a posttest. However, when the subject was confronted with *two* others in the difficult position, the sociocognitive conflict was increased, and progress was then shown for 5 out of 7 subjects on a subsequent difficult task.

Usually, in social learning paradigms, children with a wrong answer are confronted with a more correct model in order to progress. In our experiment, the children with a correct answer needed to experience a strong confrontation with incorrect answers in order to make progress on a subsequent task. Similar results have been obtained by Mugny, Levy, and Doise (1978), who have systematically shown how the presentation of incorrect models leads to progress when the child is questioned by an adult about his performance in the incorrect model.

Convergence with the Results of Other Research

Before concluding, we will indicate that many other authors have obtained results that corroborate our principal hypothesis on the importance of social interaction in cognitive development. F. B. Murray (1972) published an article reporting that children who had responded by means of consensus to different problems of conservation progressed individually. Silverman and Stone (1972) likewise verified significant progress after an interaction on a test of the conservation of space; Silverman and Geiringer (1973) verified that the social interaction carried on on a given test can give rise to progress on other tests as well. Maitland and Goldman (1974) also obtained improvement at the time of the interaction on problems of moral judgment, and Miller and Brownell (1975) reported on the domain of the conservation of length and weight. Our first experiments, having been initiated without our having known of these research data, thus carried an independent validation.

Many other researchers (Kuhn, 1972; J. P. Murray, 1974; Rosenthal & Zimmerman, 1972; Zimmerman & Lanaro, 1974) have likewise observed progress in the domain of conservation after only observing models. Does that finding mean that an explanation of cognitive development based on the idea of sociocognitive conflict becomes insufficient? We do not think so, because the effect of the model can very well be realized by the conflict that is induced. Kuhn (1972, p. 843) wrote:

> Thus, the observation of a model performing a task in a manner discrepant from (but not inferior to) the child's own conceptualization of the task may be sufficient to induce in the child an awareness of alternative conceptualizations and will perhaps lead to disequilibrium and reorganization.

We are in agreement, providing, however, that the restriction within the parentheses be omitted.

A domain in which our research will soon be developed is the elaboration of formal thought. Laughlin and Jaccard (1975) have likewise shown that, at this stage of cognitive development, the group prevails over the individual. With a different task, but also causing hypothetico-deductive thinking to intervene, Stalder (1975) verified that the variables modifying social interaction in groups likewise modify the cognitive strategies of their members during this interaction. It is necessary to examine whether or not it results in effects after the interaction. A vast area still remains to be explored.

CONCLUSION

A problem with which one can find fault at the end of this account is the apparent lag between the broad span of theoretical considerations reported in the first part of this chapter and the limits of the conclusions that can be drawn from experiments as specific as those described in the second part of the chapter. To be sure, we have seen authors who do not hesitate to open very broad historical perspectives when they are nevertheless reduced to describing imaginary situations of specific interactions within the framework of prehistoric reconstructions or in frameworks that are more familiar in the development of the child. Why, then, not study experimentally the concrete interactions that are accessible to us?

However, there is another domain of history as well where there are some other indications that often serve as a daring basis of reconstructions. It is the domain of the "sociocultural handicap" with regard to the institution of the school. It is certainly not our intention to deny the existence of this handicap, nor to argue that there is no difference between life and the social interactions of the dominated and the dominant groups of our society, and that these differences could eventually be reflected in behaviour of a cognitive nature in school. We would only like to show how certain indications suggest that perhaps the experimentation is useful in advancing this debate.

This evidence, obtained by A. N. Perret-Clermont (1979) and also by Mugny, Perret-Clermont, and Doise (1981), is as follows: when they reanalyzed the results of the tests on the conservation of liquids and the conservation of number, taking into account the socioeconomic origin of the subjects, they observed that the differences between the children of different backgrounds that existed before the social interaction no longer existed after this interaction. This finding is merely an indication, which must be corroborated by research carried out elsewhere. But if these results are found again, the fact that the interaction between children coming from the same underprivileged environment could be brought up to the same level as the performance of children from a more privileged environment, we would substantiate that the handicap does not bear on cognitive operations. For how can it be considered a serious handicap if it is a difference that the interaction of a few moments is sufficient to erase?

On the other hand, our research seems already to have implied a result that could be of concern in educational practice. It provides a new basic theory to the innovations in this domain that have led teachers to create educational situations in which children are invited to teach each other (Gartner, Kohler, & Riessman, 1971). If these proposed tasks are well chosen, according to our hypotheses, both more advanced and less advanced children must profit equally from these interactions. Thus, Allen and Feldman (1973) verified that, in response to such experiences of mutual education, the children "teachers" progress considerably in relation to other children who work alone. Certainly, motivational factors intervene in situations such as these and can promote or impede the processes of cognitive order. However, these situations do provide the opportunity for cognitive dynamics to develop according to processes that can be studied experimentally.

REFERENCES

Allen, V. L. & Feldman, R. S. (1973). Learning through tutoring: Low achieving children as tutors. *The Journal of Experimental Education, 42,* 1–5.

Berry, J. W. & Dasen, P. R. (1974). *Culture and cognition.* London: Methuen,

Carugati, F. & Mugny, G. (1979). Psicologia sociale dello sviluppo cognitivo. *Italian Journal of Psychology, 5,* 323–352.

Dami, C. (1975). Stratégies cognitives dans les jeux competitifs à deux. *Archives de Psychologie.*

Doise, W. (1978). *Groups and individuals: Explanations in social psychology.* Cambridge, England: Cambridge University Press.

Doise, W. & Mugny, G. (1975). Recherches socio-genétiques sur la coordination d'actions interdépendantes. *Revue Suisse de Pyschologie, 34,* 160–174.

Doise, W. & Mugny, G. (1979). Individual and collective conflicts of concentrations in cognitive development. *European Journal of Social Psychology, 9,* 105–106.

Doise, W. & Mugny, G. (1981). *Le développement social de l'intelligence.* Paris: Intereditions.

Doise, W., Mugny, G., & Perret-Clermont, A. N. (1976). Social interaction and cognitive development: Further evidence. *European Journal of Social Psychology, 6,* 245–247.

Doise, W., Giroud, J. Ch., & Mugny, G. (1978–9). Conflit de centrations et progrès cognitif. II: Nouvelles confirmations expérimentales. *Bulletin de Psychologie.*

Doise, W., Dionnet, S., & Mugny, G. (1979). Conflit socio-cognitif, marguage social et développement cognitif. *Cahiers de Psychologie Cognitif.*

Feffer, M. (1970). Developmental analysis of interpersonal behavior. *Psychological Review, 77,* 197–214.

Flavell, J. H., Botvin, P. T., Fry, C. L., Wright, J. W., & Jarvis, P. E. (1968). *The development of role-taking and communication skills in children.* New York: Wiley.

Gartner, A., Kohler, M. C., & Riessman, F. (1971). *Children teach children: Learning by teaching.* New York: Harper & Row.

Humphrey, N. K. (1976). The social function of intellect. In P. P. G. Bateson, & R. A. Hinde, (Eds.), *Growing points in ethology.* Cambridge, England: Cambridge University Press.

Inhelder, B., Sinclair, H., & Bovet, M. (1974). *Learning and development of cognition.* London: Routledge and Kegan Paul.

Kuhn, D. (1972). Mechanisms of change in the development of cognitive structures. *Child Development. 43*, 833–844.

Laughlin, P. R. & Jaccard, J. J. (1975). Social facilitation and observational learning of individuals and cooperative pairs. *Journal of Personality and Social Psychology, 32*, 873–879.

Leontiev, A. (1970–71). Le mécanisme de la coordination des fonctions motrices interdépendantes réparties entre divers sujets. *Bulletin de Psychologie, 24*, 693–696.

Leontiev, A. (1976). *Le développement du psychisme*. Paris: Éditions Sociales.

Maitland, K. A. & Goldman, J. R. (1974). Moral judgment as a function of peer group interaction. *Journal of Personality and Social Psychology, 30*, 699–704.

Mead, G. H. (1934). *Mind, self and society*. Chicago: University of Chicago Press.

Mikula, G. (1972). Die Entwicklung des Gewinnaufteilungsverhaltens bei Kindern und Jugendlichen. *Zeitschrift für Entwicklungspsychologie und pädagogische Psychologie, 4*, 151–164.

Miller, S. A. & Brownell, C. A. (1975). Peers, persuasion and Piaget; Dyadic interaction between conservers and nonconservers. *Child Development, 46*, 992–997.

Moessinger, P. (1975). Developmental study of fair division and property. *European Journal of Social Psychology*.

Mugny, G. & Doise, W. (1978). Socio-cognitive conflict and structure of individual and collective performances. *European Journal of Social psychology, 8*, 181–192.

Mugny, G., Levy, M., & Doise, W. (1978). Conflit socio-cognitif et développement cognitif. *Revue Suisse de Psychologie, 37*, 22–43.

Mugny, G., Perret-Clermont, A. W., & Doise, W. (1981). Interpersonal coordinations and social differences in the construction of the intellect. In G. M. Stephenson & J. M. Davis (Eds.), *Progress in applied psychology* (Vol. 1). New York: Wiley.

Murray, F. B. (1972). Acquisition of conservation through social interaction. *Developmental Psychology, 6*, 1–6.

Murray, J. P. (1974). Social learning and cognitive development: Modeling effects on children's understanding of conservation. *British Journal of Psychology, 65*, 151–160.

Nielsen, R. (1951). *Le développement de la sociabilité chez l'enfant*. Neuchâtel: Delachaux et Niestlé.

Perret-Clermont, A. N. (1979). *Social interaction and cognitive development in children*. London: Academic Press.

Piaget, J. (1932). *Le jugement moral chez l'enfant*. Paris: Presses Universitaires de France.

Piaget, J. (1965). *Études sociologiques*. Geneva: Droz.

Piaget, J. (1967). *Biologie et connaissance*. Paris: Gallimard.

Rosenthal, T. L. & Zimmerman, B. J. (1972). Modeling by exemplification and instruction in training conservation. *Developmental Psychology, 6*, 392–401.

Silverman, I. W. & Geiringer, E. (1973). Dyadic interaction and conservation induction: A test of Piaget's equilibrium model. *Child Development, 44*, 815–820.

Silverman, I. W. & Stone, J. M. (1972). Modifying cognitive functioning through participation in a problem-solving group. *Journal of Educational Psychology, 63*, 603–608.

Smedslund, J. (1966). Les origines sociales da la décentration. In *Psychologie et épistémologie génétique, thèmes Piagétiens*. Paris: Dunod.

Stalder, J. (1975). *Lernen in kleinen Gruppen* (Inaugural dissertation der Philosophisch-Historischen Fakultät Bern). Bern: Kopierservice.

Tran DucThao. (1973). *Recherches sur l'origine du langage et de la conscience*. Paris: Éditions Sociales.

Vygotsky, L. S. (1965). *Thought and language*. Cambridge, Mass.: MIT Press.

Waller, M. (1971). Die Enwicklung der Rollenwahrnehmung: Ihre Beziehung zur allgemeinen kognitiven Entwicklung und sozialstrukturellen Variabelen. *Zeitschift für Sozial psychologie, 2*, 343–357.

Waller, M. (1973). Die Stereotypität vs. Personorientiertheit der Verhaltenserwartungen von Kindern in Abhängigkeit von deren Alter und der untersuchten Verhaltensdimension. *Zeitschrift für Entwicklungspsychologie und pädagogische Psychologie, 5,* 1–15.

Zajonc, R. B. (1965). Social facilitation. *Science, 149,* 269–274.

Zimmerman, B. J. & Lanaro, P. (1974). Acquiring and retaining conservation of length through modeling and reversibility cues. *Merrill-Palmer Quarterly of Behavior and Development, 20,* 145–161.

12 Context, Conservation, and Conversation

Paul Light

INTRODUCTION

Our view of cognitive development in early childhood has been subject to two quite clear shifts in the last ten years or so. One of these has to do with precocity: much recent work seems to show that young children, especially three- to six-year-olds, are much more intellectually capable than we had previously supposed. The other pronounced shift has been in our awareness of the significance of the social context of children's cognitive functioning. The two issues are of course closely related; exploration of the effects of varying the social context in which cognitive tasks are presented has been a major source of evidence for high levels of cognitive competence in the pre-school child. As I shall argue, however, it is unclear whether the role of social context can be properly understood simply in terms of "masking" or "revealing" the child's true levels of cognitive competence. An alternative conception seems to be emerging in which "the social context" moves to centre stage, as a fundamental and constitutive element in cognitive development.

In the English-speaking world the study of cognitive development has for the last quarter of a century been dominated by Piaget, so much so that the label "cognitive developmental" is synonymous with Piagetian or neo-Piagetian approaches. Earlier theoretical positions which attempted to ground an account of cognitive development in the child's social experiences (e.g., Mead, 1934; Vygotsky, 1962) were almost totally eclipsed by

Source: Richards, M. and Light, P. (Eds.) (1986). *Children of social worlds*. Cambridge: Polity, pp. 170–190.

Piaget's essentially individualistic account of cognitive development. Even with the more recent rise of "social cognition" as a research topic, the dependence of social development upon cognitive development has been stressed while the role of social experience in cognitive development has received scant attention (Light, 1983).

Nevertheless, the hegemony of the cognitive over the social has been challenged, and is increasingly being challenged in contemporary work. In this chapter I shall examine just one aspect of such work, that concerning Piagetian tests of operational thinking. Detailed evaluation will be restricted to one key element in the Piagetian scheme, namely conservation. I hope, however, that even within such a narrow compass it will be possible to illustrate some of the arguments for a radically social reconstruction of the still prevailing Piagetian account.

The tests which Piaget and his co-workers devised to distinguish the pre-operational from the operational thinker (Piaget, 1952, 1955; Piaget & Inhelder, 1956, 1969) achieved very wide currency in the 1960s and 1970s, and Piaget's findings were broadly replicated in countless studies. But increasingly in the last decade other studies with different methodologies have generated conflicting data, indicative of a whole range of seemingly precocious logical abilities. As well as in conservation, this can be seen for classification, number concepts, arithmetic and measurement (Donaldson, Grieve & Pratt, 1983). In all these areas it is claimed that "pre-operational" children's abilities have been underestimated in previous (Piagetian) research.

Should this issue be seen as merely a matter of methodology, with improved methods offering more sensitive indices of the young child's abilities? Or is there more to be learned from these disparities? I shall argue the latter case, and suggest that a more fundamentally *social* approach both illuminates the sources of the apparent disparities in performance and hints at the need for a very different account of the process and nature of cognitive development itself. At the outset, however, a rather more detailed sketch of some aspects of the Piagetian account of the development of operational thinking will be necessary.

PIAGET: STRUCTURES AND STAGES

At the heart of Piaget's theory is the idea of structure. Cognitive development, and in particular the emergence of operational thought, is characterized in terms of the emergence of new logical or logicomathematical structures. While Piaget's theory has a functional aspect, concerned with intelligence as adaptation, with assimilation, accommodation and equilibration, his main contribution and influence lay in his structural account of cognition.

Logic was used extensively to model cognitive structures – to the extent that the two were sometimes identified one with the other. Thus, for example, Inhelder and Piaget claimed that "reasoning is nothing more than the propositional calculus itself" (1958, p. 305). Further, the structures were posited as real, "actually present" (1958, p. 307). They were not merely heuristic devices whereby psychologists could better conceptualize some aspect of the child's behaviour – the structures directly reflected "actual psychological activities" (Piaget, 1957, p. 7) going on in the child's head.

The role of specific types of experience in the elaboration of cognitive structures was left largely unexplored by Piaget. His starting point was very much the individual thinking subject. Moreover, he placed heavy emphasis on the individual's structuring of his or her own experience. The focus on the isolated individual, and on assimilation as a condition for experience, means that experience is in large measure an individual construct. Ultimately, this conception makes genuine interaction with the environment impossible, and stages reduce to the unfolding of a pre-ordained programme (Broughton, 1981; Moore, 1985). Certainly the stages outlined by Piaget in respect of the achievement of operational thought would seem to have more to do with the constraints of endogenous organization than with the exigencies of the external environment.

Children's thought was to be interpreted in terms of their "possession of" or "lack of" certain operational competences. The local, historical, particular aspects of a child's situation and behaviour were treated by Piaget as merely obscuring the emerging competence, defined in terms of logicomathematical structures. The image was of a clear-cut underlying "form" beneath the untidy surface of actual day to day behaviour (Light, 1983; Russell, 1978). Since everyday behaviour offered only occasional and unreliable glimpses of this underlying order, relatively formal investigatory procedures were needed, and Piaget and his co-workers consequently devised a wide range of procedures designed to demonstrate the presence or absence of particular hypothesized logical competences.

During the 1960s and 1970s Piaget's tests of operational competences became very much part of the "stock in trade" of developmental psychologists and educators. Perhaps the best known and most widely used of these "litmus tests" of cognitive development were the various conservation tests, their popularity probably owing as much to their apparent elegance and simplicity as to the central significance which Piaget (e.g., 1952) attached to conservation in the development of logical thought. It is to these conservation tests that we now turn.

CONSERVATION

Perhaps the best known of Piaget's procedures for assessing conservation is the equivalence test for liquid quantities, so that this provides a suitable vehicle for outlining the basic three-stage procedure. First, the equality of two quantities is established. In this case, for example, juice might be poured into two identical beakers to the same level. The child is asked to judge the equality of amount. Next, one of the two entities is transformed – in this case the juice from one beaker might be poured into another beaker of a different shape. Finally the child is asked whether the equality of amount still obtains.

Piaget observed that children below about seven years of age typically have no difficulty correctly judging the *initial* equality of the two quantities, but erroneously suppose that the post-transformation quantities are no longer equal. They may judge that the juice in the "new" beaker is more, or less, basing their answers on single salient perceptual dimensions ("it's taller", or "it's fatter", etc.) rather than on any logical inferences. Older children correctly judge that the quantities remain the same after the transformation, and can support their answers using "logical" justifications, linking the pre and post-transformation states (e.g. reversibility) or linking the several dimensions of difference in the post-transformation array (compensation).

These judgements and justifications are evidence, according to Piaget, of the emergence of a new logical competence in the child, marked by a "decentred" consideration of the interplay of multiple co-varying elements within a logical grouping. Up until this stage the pre-operational, egocentric, child is the creature of his own perceptions. Appearance and reality are not distinguished; the child does not recognize that changes in shape are reversible, or that changes in different dimensions can compensate for one another.

Just as young children fail to recognize that liquid quantity is unchanged by pouring, so they fail to recognize that weight is unchanged by alterations of shape, or that number is unchanged by spatial rearrangement of the elements. All of these quantitative concepts, so important in an educational context, depend crucially upon mastery of conservation.

Mastery of conservation is thus a critical element in the emergence of operational thought – Piaget sometimes refers to it as *the* psychological criterion of operational structures (e.g., Piaget, 1968, p. 121). Any experimental findings which point to the need for a radical reappraisal of the development of conservation may thus offer a significant challenge to the Piagetian account of cognitive development. In fact there have been a number of such findings over a considerable period (e.g., Braine, 1959; Mehler & Bever, 1967), but the resulting skirmishes have been more or less inconclusive. Recently, however, a distinctive strand of research focusing on the social context of cognitive testing has begun to offer an important new dimension to this debate.

"NAUGHTY TEDDY" AND AFTER

A landmark in the study of contextual factors in conservation testing was the publication of a paper entitled *Conservation Accidents* (McGarrigle & Donaldson, 1975). Four- and five-year-old children's judgements on number and length conservation problems were studied under two conditions, which differed only in how the transformation of the materials was handled. In the standard condition, following Piaget, the rearrangement of the materials after the child's judgement of equality was made quite deliberately and openly by the experimenter. In the modified condition the same rearrangement was achieved, but this time by agency of a "naughty" teddy bear. The toy bear (manipulated by the experimenter) "escaped" from his box and rushed about causing mayhem until "captured". The rearrangement of materials was thus represented as accidental. Only 16 per cent of the children gave consistently conserving judgements after the standard transformation, whereas 63 per cent did so after the modified, "naughty teddy" transformation.

In a partial replication, Light, Buckingham and Robbins (1979) conducted conservation of length tests with five year olds, comparing standard Piagetian and "naughty teddy" transformation conditions. The overall frequencies of conserving judgements were lower than McGarrigle and Donaldson had found in both conditions, but their finding of a significantly higher success rate in the accidental condition was confirmed. Other studies using similar procedures have found similar results, though the differences have not always been statistically reliable (e.g., Hargreaves, Molloy & Pratt, 1982; Miller, 1982; Neilson, Dockrell & McKechnie, 1983a).

McGarrigle and Donaldson's interpretation of their results is essentially that young children's failure to conserve in Piaget's tests arises, at least in part, from misleading features of the procedure. The experimenter, in drawing the child's attention to his own actions in rearranging the materials, is giving implicit cues to the child as to what to expect next. Thus if the experimenter lengthens or shortens one row of counters relative to another the child may interpret the ensuing question as having to do with length, whereas in fact it has only to do with the number of counters. The experimenter's actions seem to refer to one dimension while his words refer to another, and the child's incorrect response may simply reflect a confusion between these two. The child's non-conserving responses thus reflect not so much a misunderstanding of the effects of the transformation as a misunderstanding of the experimenter's intentions. Having the transformation effected by an errant teddy bear goes a long way towards removing the confusion.

McGarrigle and Donaldson conclude that their results (1975, p. 347): "give clear indications that traditional procedures for assessing conservation seriously underestimate the child's knowledge". They regard their modified procedure as giving a truer, more sensitive indication of the young child's logical competence. The competence in question is at least implicitly accepted as that described by Piaget. As Hughes puts it (1983, p. 207) "It seems that some children may fail on the standard conservation task yet still have a good understanding of . . . conservation".

McGarrigle and Donaldson do not address themselves to the origins of this precocious logical competence, though others (e.g., Gelman, 1982) have suggested that it may be innate. Gelman describes the pre-school child's competence as fragile, visible only in restricted settings, revealed only under "appropriate circumstances" (1982, p. 218). Donaldson, in her influential book *Children's Minds* (1978) has offered a broader characterization of such "appropriate circumstances" with her concept of *human sense*.

The child's true cognitive abilities will only be revealed, Donaldson argues, in situations which make human sense to the child, i.e. when the cognitive task is set within a context which is fully intelligible to the child as a social interchange. To take a well-known example from another domain of cognitive development, Hughes and Donaldson (1979) have shown that perspective-taking tasks involving a boy doll hiding from one or more toy policemen are much easier for pre-schoolers than Piaget & Inhelder's (1956) classic "three mountains" task. Why are the new tasks easier? "We believe it is because the policemen tasks make human sense in a way that the mountains task does not. The motives and intention of the characters are entirely comprehensible" (Hughes & Donaldson, 1983, p. 253). In much the same way McGarrigle and Donaldson's modifications to the conservation task can be seen as reshaping a socially unintelligible or even paradoxical procedure so as to give the sequence of events some degree of human sense.

In the case of the modified perspective-taking tasks, it could be argued that the relatively familiar nature of the materials and events is an important aspect of their intelligibility. But in fact with conservation it appears that using natural and familiar transformations, such as boats floating apart or children moving around, does *not* produce precocious successes (Miller, 1982). The vital ingredient of "human sense" would seem to lie in the intelligibility of the social exchange between the experimenter and the child, rather than in the familiarity of the materials or events per se. Setting the transformation within a socially intelligible action sequence makes it possible for the child to express his latent grasp of the invariance of quantity, number, or whatever.

Using the perspective-taking example again, however, it is arguable that a more important difference between the modified procedure and Piaget and Inhelder's original lies in the relatively elementary level of the inferences required for success (Light, in press). In a similar vein it has been held that success on the "naughty teddy" task may actually be achieved on the basis of less than "operational" abilities. Indeed it has been suggested by some that apparent success on this task may be no more than an artefact, having little or nothing to do with an understanding of conservation.

One source of doubt about the status of young children's judgements on the "naughty teddy" task has come from the examination of the justifications they offer for their judgements. McGarrigle and Donaldson did not seek justifications from the children, but examination of justifications has led authors of some subsequent studies to view the precociously correct judgements as only partially "operational" (Parrat-Dayan & Bovet, 1982) or even as essentially spurious (Neilson, Dockrell & McKechnie, 1983b).

Neilson, Dockrell and McKechnie replicated the "naughty teddy" study successfully, with more than twice as many four to six year olds offering conserving judgements in the "naughty teddy" as in the standard condition. However, when it came to offering justifications for their conserving judgements only about a quarter of those asked in either condition were able to offer any "logical" justification. On the basis of a detailed appraisal of the justifications given in the modified condition, the authors concluded that many of the children saw the teddy bear as simply having made a mess of things. This being so, they ignored the post-transformation array altogether and responded to the conservation question in terms of how things were before they were messed up. The apparent successes, therefore, have little to do with genuine conservation.

Neilson, Dockrell and McKechnie's quantitative analysis of their data on justifications is ambiguous, however, as Donaldson (1983) has pointed out. What they do show clearly is that most children in *both* conditions are unable to provide logical justifications for their judgements. But, as Donaldson (1983) also notes, the status of justifications as criteria for the genuineness of conservation, or any other logical operation is itself questionable (Brainerd, 1973; Brown & Desforges, 1979). Children may not be able to articulate, or may not even be aware of, the factors which influence their responding.

Thus the issue of the "operational status" of young children's successful judgements on the "naughty teddy" task remains unresolved at this point. In order to provide a broader base from which to discuss the issue further, I want for the moment, to leave the argument about the "naughty teddy" effect and to turn to a group of studies which have explored other ways of manipulating the context of the conservation task.

INCIDENTAL TRANSFORMATIONS

While the children in the "naughty teddy" studies were clearly willing to play along with the experimenter in attributing agency to the teddy bear, they clearly also knew that the experimenter was responsible for both introducing and manipulating it. We have expressed the matter thus (Light et al., 1979, p. 307): "The extent to which the child holds separate the intentions of the tester and those of the teddy must remain in doubt. As any parent knows, children at this age have an unnerving tendency to "step outside" role-playing situations of this kind just when the adult has been drawn in most deeply".

In an attempt to create a less ambiguous situation, we designed a conservation test in which the transformation of materials would appear to be merely *incidental* to some other activity. Five and six year olds were tested in pairs. In the standard condition children watched as two identical beakers were filled to the same level with pasta shells. When the children had both judged the quantities equal, the experimenter introduced a further, larger container, into which he tipped the contents of one of the beakers. The children were then asked (in turn) to judge whether or not the amounts of shells were still the same.

In the "incidental" condition the pairs of children were first shown grids into which the pasta shells could be inserted, one per cell, and it was explained to them that they would be playing a game in which the first child to get all his or her shells into the grid would be the winner. So when, in this condition, the shells were initially put into the two identical beakers, the children understood this to be preparatory to the competitive game. When the children had judged that the two beakers contained the same amount (i.e., that the game was fair) one of the beakers was given to one of the children. But just as the other was about to be handed over to the other child, the experimenter "noticed" that the rim was chipped to a razor sharp edge. With suitable non-verbal accompaniments (signifying surprise and alarm, followed by perplexed pause, followed by "ah") the experimenter "found" another container and tipped the shells from the chipped beaker into it. The usual conservation question followed.

Since social influence within the pairs might amplify any differences, we looked at just the first child questioned in each pair. We found 5 per cent of children offered conserving judgements in the standard condition, while 70 per cent offered conserving judgements in the "incidental" condition. The effect of the change of conditions was thus a fairly massive one.

Miller (1982) has replicated this "chipped beaker" study, as have Bovet, Parrat-Dayan and Deshusses-Addor (1981), though in this case without a standard comparison condition. In both studies the level of conserving judgements obtained from five year olds in the incidental condition was around 80 per cent. Miller (1982) also showed significant facilitation of conservation judgements in a quantity conservation task in which the experimenter "accidentally" knocked over one of the beakers. In yet another version Miller (1982) got the child at the end of a session to help him to spread out two rows of counters equally. He then "remembered" that only one of the rows was supposed to be spread out for the next child, and so changed it. Here again the idea was to render the transformation incidental to the main course of events, and in this case over 90 per cent of the five year olds asserted that the two rows still contained the same number of counters.

Rates of conserving judgements approaching 90 per cent have also been obtained from five year olds by Hargreaves, Molloy and Pratt (1982). In their procedure two equal rows of counters in 1:1 correspondence were set up and initial judgements of equality obtained. Then a second adult, ostensibly testing other children in the next room, came in to "borrow" some of the counters, taking them from the table. The experimenter protested that the counters were needed, and they were returned. Naturally, in the course of this they became disarranged. Here again the transformation has been successfully embedded within a socially intelligible sequence of actions and events. And here again children who fail on a "standard" version of the conservation tests, involving the same rearrangement of materials, offer what appear to be conserving judgements.

The authors of these "incidental transformation" studies have for the most part been fairly equivocal as to the status of the correct conservation judgements obtained. The Genevan view is that they simply reflect distraction of the child's attention from the task in hand (Bovet et al., 1981). But before entering into the issue of interpretation in any detail, I want to draw upon one further group of empirical studies.

CONSERVATION AND CONVERSATION

We have thus far been considering the effects of changing the way in which the transformation of materials is handled within the conservation task. As far back as 1974, Rose and Blank published a paper concerned with the effects of changing quite a different aspect of the procedure. The conservation procedure basically consists of two questions, separated by a transformation. The two questions are the same (e.g., "are there more smarties in this row, or more in this row, or do the two rows have the same number of smarties?"). Normally, almost all children will answer the question correctly at the first time of asking, since the materials are arranged so as to make the equality obvious. When the question is put again, after the transformation, young children characteristically (and erroneously) change their answer. Rose and Blank speculated that the repetition of the question itself may have a significant role in generating this error. Repetition of the question by the adult may lead the child to suppose that his first answer was wrong. Alternatively, repetition of the question after the transformation may lead the child to suppose that the transformation *must* be relevant to the question, whereas, of course, it is not.

Rose and Blank (1974) tested this idea in a study of number conservation carried out with six year olds. They compared the standard, two-question procedure with a modification in which the initial question was simply left out. They found significantly higher levels of correct post-transformation judgement in the modified, one-question condition. While attempts to replicate this study have not always succeeded (Miller, 1977) it has been successfully replicated not only for number, but for several other quantity conservation tasks (Samuel & Bryant, 1984). The one-question task has been found to be easier compared not only to the standard task but also to a control condition in which the child only saw the post-transformation array.

Perner, Leekam and Wimmer (1984) have recently extended this work in a slightly different direction. They have sought to alter the impact of question repetition not by omitting one of the questions but by having the two questions asked by different people. In the context of a task involving a horse and a cow who were to be given equal drinks, the children (four to six year olds) had to fill two identical buckets to equal levels. They were asked at this point whether the two amounts were equal. They then poured the "drinks" into the animals' drinking troughs, which were of different shapes. For some of the children the experimenter then once again asked for a judgement as to the equality of the two amounts. For others, though, the experimenter suddenly said that he had to leave, and asked another adult from the next room to take over. In this condition, therefore, the post-transformation question was asked by someone who had not asked a similar question previously, and who had not seen the pre-transformation array. Substantially more children offered correct conserving judgements in this condition.

There is a problem with this study, in that the post-transformation question actually used was "did you give them the same?" This might well have been taken to refer to the pre- rather than to the post-transformation array, and such a "retrospective" question would seem especially natural in the modified condition. While this consideration perhaps weakens the force of their evidence, the authors' analysis of their own and others' studies is of interest.

Answering a question "correctly", they suggest, involves the respondent in discerning why the question was asked in the first place. Taken as a straightforward request for information the crucial question in the conservation test is anomalous, since the respondent has no privileged information inaccessible to the questioner. If the child knows the answer, so too must the adult. Why then is he asking the question? The reality is, of course, that this question is what Searle (1969) termed an "examination question", rather than a straightforward request for information. If the child does not realize this, he or she will be in difficulty.

Perner, Leekam and Wimmer suggest that young children may be unable to grasp such second-order questions (not "I want to know X", but "I want to know whether *you* know X"). Failing to comprehend this second-order intention the child falls back upon an interpretation of the question simply as a request for comment on what is happening – in this case perhaps a comment on whether the amounts now look the same, which typically they do not.

Extending this analysis to the case of Rose and Blank's one-question task, described earlier in this section, they suggest that asking the first question establishes mutual appreciation of equal quantity beyond dispute, while omitting it leaves open the possibility that the experimenter might not have noticed or remembered the equality. This possibility allows the child to treat the post-transformation question as a sincere request for information about amount, and thus to answer it correctly.

Similarly, the "accidental" and "incidental" transformation studies described in earlier sections could be interpreted not so much in terms of the distraction of the child (cf. Bovet et al., 1981), as in terms of the putative distraction of the experimenter. The apparently unforeseen events (interruptions, etc.) associated with the transformation allow of the possibility that the experimenter is unsure about the actual state of affairs when the critical question is asked, so once again the question can be understood by the child as being "in good faith".

Such an interpretation clearly rests on the assumption that young children do in fact have an understanding of conservation. In effect the source of difficulty in the conservation task is relocated from conservation per se to the complexities of second-order questions. The difficulties are still conceived in terms of the individual child's cognitive capacities and limitations, and the modified formats are seen as giving a better indication of the child's underlying competence. In my own work I have adopted a more sceptical view, but one which, I shall argue, points toward a more radical revision of the Piagetian account.

ACQUIESCENCE AND ACQUISITION

At this point I want to return to the question of the interpretation of the accidental and incidental transformation studies, and in particular to our own interpretation of the "chipped beaker" study (Light et al., 1979).

Although the context manipulation used in this study produced a very large effect, we were doubtful about the kind of interpretation which had been offered by McGarrigle and Donaldson (1975) for such effects. As indicated earlier, they saw their "naughty teddy" manipulation as a way of circumventing an artefact in the standard assessment procedure, and thus as offering a better estimate of the child's true logical ability. We suggested a rather different interpretation of the success of the accidental or incidental transformation conditions in promoting correct conservation judgements.

We agreed with McGarrigle and Donaldson that in the case of the standard Piagetian procedure, failures may arise as a consequence of the implicit message "take note of this transformation – it is relevant", contained in the experimenter's actions. However, by extension of the same argument we further suggested that in the "incidental" conditions of testing successes may arise from the converse message; "this transformation makes no difference – ignore it", implicit in the experimenter's actions.

For example, in our own "chipped beaker" condition the experimenter was apparently faced with an unexpected problem – a hitch that threatened to interfere with the flow of the game. The experimenter "solved" this problem by pouring the contents from the chipped beaker into another, larger beaker. In asking the children afterwards whether the amounts were equal (i.e., whether it was still fair), the experimenter could be seen as simply asking the children to endorse his "solution". Seen in this light, their apparently conserving judgements represent little more than acquiescence.

Thus, the same kinds of social-interactional processes which militate against conserving judgements in the standard condition of testing may militate in favour of them in the modified condition. Indeed, once this Pandora's box is opened, it becomes hard to see how any testing situation could ever be neutral. The very human sense or social intelligibility deemed so necessary for a valid test of the child's ability will surely almost inevitably introduce such subtle social cues and biases. Our conclusion was that "we seem to be further from, rather than nearer, an unbiased assessment of the child's logical abilities" (Light et al., 1979, p. 310).

This scepticism about the claim that the modified conservation tasks revealed a true logical grasp of conservation led us to a further study (Light & Gilmour, 1983). Here we sought to demonstrate that the same factors which lead children to "success" on a conservation task can lead children into error in a situation where the properties in question are not in fact conserved. In all the studies we have examined this far, the precocious conserving judgements elicited by the modified formats have been correct, the difficulty being to know whether the children are right for the right reasons. In this study we sought to establish whether conserving judgements could be facilitated by the modified formats even when they were *in*correct.

The task chosen involved transformations of area within a fixed perimeter. Two square fields, each made up of eight 10 cm fence sections (i.e., 20 × 20 cm fields), were assembled on a large green board, and the children selected animals to put in these fields. The children (five and six year olds) were then asked whether the animals in the two fields had the same amount of grass to eat. All agreed that they did. In the standard condition the experimenter then rearranged one of the fields by pulling it out from a 20 × 20 cm square to a 30 × 10 cm rectangle, without disconnecting the fence sections from one another. The children were then once again asked whether the animals in the two fields had the same amount to eat. Only about 20 per cent of the children judged that they had.

In the modified condition the only difference was in the provision of a plausible reason for transforming one of the fields into a rectangle. After the initial equality of the fields had been established, the experimenter produced a model farmhouse and went as if to put this on the board next to the fields. The farmhouse was the wrong shape for the space. After a suitable "pause for thought" the experimenter put the farmhouse down beside the board while transforming the field as if to make a suitable space for it. The question about the equality of "amounts to eat" was then asked, before the farmhouse was positioned. In this condition some 60 per cent of the children judged the fields still to be equal.

Since the areas of the fields were in fact substantially different after transformation, the modified format could hardly be said in this case to be revealing a latent grasp of conservation. Rather it seemed to us that the children were simply tending to comply with what they saw as the exerimenter's request for support and confirmation. The implicit request may be glossed as: "Oh dear, the farmhouse doesn't fit, so I've got a problem. Ah, but I can solve it just by rearranging this field. There, that's OK isn't it?" The implication being that the transformation does not prejudice the fairness of the situation – in this case the equality of the amounts of grass. The child is in effect being given a strong hint that the transformation is irrelevant, or at least that the experimenter wishes to regard it as such.

The issue of the *relevance* of the transformation is the central one, as Donaldson (1982) has acknowledged. What distinguishes the task we have used here from bona fide conservation tasks is not that the transformation lacks reversibility, nor that it lacks co-variation of different dimensions – the rectangular field is after all longer but thinner than the square one. It is simply that this kind of fixed perimeter transformation does, as a matter of fact, lead to changes in area.

Shultz, Dover and Amsel (1979, p. 120) have an important point when they argue that the real mystery about conservation acquisition is how children come to distinguish those transformations which alter a quantity from those which do not. Shultz and colleagues suggest that the child comes to appreciate what transformations are relevant to what as much through a process of empirical discovery as through deduction from some internal logical structure. There is no suggestion, however, of a social dimension to this process of "discovery".

What the context-manipulation studies may be showing us is that the child does not have to sort these things out on his or her own. The embedding of quantity terms within socially intelligible contexts of transformation, and the overdetermination of the child's correct responses by cues in the intra and extra-linguistic context, may play an important part in the process of acquisition.

Light and Gilmour focused on a quirky instance of non-conservation where even adults make mistakes. Older children and adults who wrongly suppose that area is conserved in such cases justify their judgements in just the same terms that they use to justify a "genuine" conservation judgement (Gold, undated; Russell, 1976), which perhaps casts further doubt upon the "logical" status of such justifications. One factor responsible for this over-generalization of conservation may have to do with ecological validity. Problems concerning area will most frequently be encountered, both by adults and by children, in the context of fixed surfaces of land, for example, or of paper, or of fabric. In these practical, everyday contexts fixed perimeter transformations just do not arise. Transformations typically take the form of rearrangements – cutting up, sticking together, and so on. Area is an abstract concept catching precisely at what is conserved across such rearrangements.

Likewise, the other quantity terms which are involved in conservation tasks can be seen as *embodying* conservation. What earthly use would a concept of number be for example if it did not refer to a property of a group of objects which was independent of their spatial arrangement? The irrelevance of certain transformations is part of what we mean when we talk about a number or amount, volume, etc., and it is implicit in the way we talk about them. Moreover, at least outside the testing situation, we can reasonably assume that when adults talk to children they intend the children to understand what they mean. The adult's apparent intentions are therefore a good guide to what his or her words actually mean. The child can typically rely on contextual guidance to support an appropriate interpretation of what it is that he or she is being asked or told.

To the extent that this is true, children's contextual sensitivity does not simply leave them exposed to arbitrary and extraneous influences. On the contrary, it offers an access to meanings and may often enable children to make correct judgements in respect of concepts they apprehend only dimly. While such judgements may for some purposes be regarded simply as "false positives", the contextual support which produces them may have an important part to play in securing proper reference for terms such as amount and number, in which conservation across certain kinds of transformation is intended to be implicit.

It may be, therefore, that we should concern ourselves rather less with the issue of whether the child's precocious but context-specific judgements are "genuine" or not, and rather more with the part played by contextual sensitivity in the acquisition of understanding. This issue will be taken up within the broader discussion which follows, which relates not only to conservation, but to "operational thought" in general. Much the same story told here for conservation could be repeated with respect to class inclusion (e.g., McGarrigle, Grieve & Hughes, 1978) and other "operational competences". A number of theorists have begun to use this body of evidence to argue the need for a radical revision of the Piagetian approach to the study of children's thinking.

CONTEXT AND COMPETENCE

Donaldson (1978) has graphically portrayed the young child's logical competence as context bound, dependent for its expression upon suitable "embedding" in familiar, intelligible social contexts. The pre-school child's problem, as Gelman and Gallistel (1978) put it, is typically not in any lack of competence but in the failure of performance. It is not that the child lacks the reasoning principles required, but rather that he or she may fail to *use* them appropriately in many contexts.

It can be seen that while context is important in such a view, a distinction between competence and performance is maintained, and competences continue to be treated, in Piagetian fashion, as substantive entities of some kind, "possessed" by the child. For the young child, as Donaldson sees it, context limits the expression of competence whereas in the older child, thinking has become relatively "disembedded" or context-free.

This approach, and especially the treatment within it of the notion of competence, has come under increasing criticism. Stone and Day (1980) have argued cogently against granting a competence model psychological reality. They use as one analogy the case of web-spinning spiders, where, fairly clearly, formal descriptions of the patterns of the webs need to be sharply distinguished from the operation of the functional systems that are responsible for web construction. They argue that the attempt to treat psychological (or logical) competence models as "properties" of the child generates theoretical confusion (1980, p.337) "and in the case of students of cognitive development, has led to a form of "negative rationalism" rampant in current attempts to explain the cognitive activity of children".

Rommetveit (1974, 1978), who himself coined the term "negative rationalism" to characterize attempts to account for the child's cognitive stage in terms of deviations from some idealized logical structure, has attempted to refocus attention firmly at the level of shared social under-standings. He is dubious about the search for context free and formally defined structures of thought even for adults, and argues that progress in understanding the development of thinking is most likely to be made by studying how people achieve intersubjective reference. Words, statements, questions, all are largely uninterpretable except within the context of the intersubjectively established "here and now" of acts of speech. The process of learning is an inherently social process in which (1974, p.95): "What is initially unknown to the listener is made known to him in terms of a progressive expansion and modification of an actual or intersubjectively presupposed shared social world".

We see here the beginnings of a shift in which the social context moves from having the status of a performance variable, simply limiting the expres-sion of the child's competence, towards a more central and constitutive role. In the UK, Walkerdine has done much to develop this standpoint, criticizing Donaldson's work as an attempt to "weld context onto the Piage-tian edifice" (1982, p.129). The problem, as she puts it, is that cognition remains "inside", influenced by a context which is "outside".

This inside/outside distinction finds an echo in the simple primacy given in the Piagetian account to the signified over the signifier – to the concept over the word, or to knowledge over language. Walkerdine argues that this relationship is in fact a complex and dynamic one, in which meanings are created and negotiated. Social contexts, social practices and discourses are, within this account, granted a key role in the elaboration of the child's conceptual knowledge.

Moreover, the role of context is not a passing phenomenon, overtaken with development by a progressive decontextualization of thought. Even explicitly formal or logical reasoning is a practice, supported and maintained as an activity between people (Walkerdine, 1982). Rommetveit makes the same point. Piaget treats logic as the very stuff of intellectual development, while treating language simply as a conventional system of signs. Rommet-veit (1978) observes that a formal logical system is also a ready-made system of signs and moreover one which was developed for particular purposes and with carefully considered gains and costs. Formal, logical or abstract forms of thought may be considered to be just as closely linked to particular "contexts of appropriateness" as any other. New contexts, and perhaps particularly the forms of discourse associated with schooling and literacy (Olson & Torrance, 1983; Walkerdine, 1982), educe new forms of thought. Intellectual development, viewed from this standpoint, is more a matter of recontextualization than of decontextualization.

The focus of attention is thus shifted away from the abstract "epistemic subject" of Piaget's structuralist approach, towards the real child's experi-ence in specific social contexts. Paradoxically, the achievement of abstract thought is seen as context dependent, and context driven. The classroom is clearly an important setting, and the tacit ground rules of the teacher-child interchange are increasingly coming to be seen as critical features of the effective context (Mercer & Edwards, 1981).

The examination of these ground rules promises to generate an intriguing social psychology of cognitive development. As we have seen in relation to the conservation task, the role of questioning by an adult is of particular interest. The prominent place such questioning has in teacher-child discourse, has often been noted, and is discussed by Wood (1986). The typical "teacher's question" is one to which the teacher already knows the answer. Moreover "even when the form of the question is one which seems to invite a variety of answers, there is often only *one* that is really acceptable to the teacher" (Wells, 1983, p.140).

All such questions are second-order questions in the sense discussed earlier in this reading, and Perner, Leekam and Wimmer have suggested that as such they may be too cognitively complex for pre-school children to grasp. However, these questions are by no means the exclusive prerogative of the school, and at least in some circumstances they would seem to be both familiar and well understood by pre-schoolers (Elbers, 1984; Wood, 1986). For the most part, whether at home or at school, such questions are asked in the context of providing help and support for the child working on some task. However, Elbers (1984) distinguishes between the assumptions and presuppositions involved in this "instructional metacontract" and those which are involved in the "metacontract of testing". Here the relationship of question and context is very different, and questioning is being used not in a supportive and constructive way but rather as a means of examination. It is this form of questioning which characterizes the cognitive testing situation and it is this, Elbers suggests, which will be unfamiliar to children lacking much experience of formal educational practices.

The attempt to refine such distinctions and to characterize what is taken for granted in particular contexts of discourse is clearly a contemporary growth point. Recent studies of children's responses to bizarre and nonsensical questions (Finn, 1982; Hughes & Grieve, 1983) provides an interesting sidelight on this, while Walkerdine's (1982, 1984) detailed observational work on classroom teaching of number concepts more directly illuminates some of the presuppositions and expectations characteristic of particular discourses. I want to return, however, to take a final look at conservation in the light of the theoretical concerns expressed above. If conservation is not to be thought of as a fundamental logical competence signalling the beginning of the operational period, how is it to be thought of?

Cowan (1981) has pointed out that most of the conservations with which we are concerned are in fact rather more matters of rough approximations than of exact truth. In the liquids conservation task described at the outset of this chapter, for example, we conveniently forget differential evaporation, and the residue left in the first container. Cowan observes that (1981, p.7): "if the psychologist was a physics student the physical scientist might regard him as being in need of remedial teaching". Conservation in this case is not exact, but it is nonetheless good enough for most practical purposes.

The practical purposes which the conservations serve seem, however, to have been given little attention. A pragmatic approach to understanding and problem-solving conceived in terms of "tricks of the trade" (Goodnow, 1972) or "rules of thumb" which allow us to work on the world predictably (Simon and Newell cited in Goodnow, 1972), may actually have as much to offer in this area as the universalistic cognitive-developmental account.

The child is apprenticed to a language and a culture which are grounded in practical human purposes. The concepts of amount and number, of area, volume, weight and so on, embodying as they do the various conservations, are a part of that language and culture. Their historical origins can again be assumed to be rooted in particular practical contexts of action. While direct evidence will necessarily be difficult to come by in this area, it may not be wholly inaccessible. The work of Damerow (1984) on the number concepts of early Mesopotamian civilizations offers one example of an attempt to trace such origins and to relate the evolution of concepts to the demands of changing social practices. More work of this kind could be immensely valuable.

Our argument, then, is that conservation concepts can and should be thought of not as transcendent logical entities but as the historically determined products of specific human purposes and practices (cf. Russell, 1978). The child's task, seen in this light, is to gain access to these culturally elaborated abstractions. This is no easy task, given that amount, number, etc. are not pointable-at properties of the materials concerned. However, the child's sensitivity to the subtleties of discourse, of which we have seen much evidence in this chapter, may have a vital part to play in successfully achieving shared reference with these concepts.

Such a formulation is undoubtedly partial and oversimplified. Our ignorance of the processes involved is pitiful, but at least the space within which useful work could be done is becoming clearer. Vygotsky, writing in the 1930s, referred to the then current views of intellectual development as "one-sided and erroneous primarily because they are unable to see facts as facts of historical development, [they] regard them as *natural* processes and formations . . . fail to differentiate the organic from the cultural, the natural from the historical, the biological from the social . . . in a word, these views of the nature of the phenomena in question are fundamentally incorrect" (Vygotsky, 1966, p.12). Nothing is new then, but if ever the time was ripe for building on these criticisms and working constructively towards a new understanding of cognitive development, it is surely now.

REFERENCES

Bovet, M., Parrat-Dayan, S., & Deshusses-Addor, D. (1981). Peut-on parler de précocité et de régression dans la conservation? I Précocité. *Archives de Psychologie, 49,* 289–303.

Braine, M. (1959). The ontogeny of certain logical operations: Piaget's formulations examined by non-verbal methods. *Psychological Monographs, 73,* no. 5.

Brainerd, C. (1973). Judgements and explanations as criteria for cognitive structures. *Psychological Bulletin, 79,* 172–9.

Broughton, J. (1981). Piaget's structural developmental psychology III. Function and the problem of knowledge. *Human Development, 24,* 257–85.

Brown, G. & Desforges, C. (1979). *Piaget's Theory: a psychological critique.* London: Routledge & Kegan Paul.

Cowan, R. (1981, February). *On what must be – more than just associations?* (paper presented at 11th Annual Interdisciplinary Conference on "Piaget and the Helping Professions", Los Angeles).

Damerow, M. (1984, Oct). *Individual development and cultural evolution in arithmetical thinking* (paper presented at second Tel-Aviv Workshop on Human Development, "Ontogeny and Historical Development", Tel-Aviv University).

Donaldson, M. (1978). *Children's minds.* London: Fontana.

Donaldson, M. (1982). Conservation: What is the question? *British Journal of Psychology, 73,* 199–207.

Donaldson, M. (1983). Justifying conservation: Comment on Neilson et al. *Cognition, 15,* 293–295.

Donaldson, M., Grieve, R., & Pratt, C. (1983). *Early childhood development and education.* Oxford: Basil Blackwell.

Elbers, E. (1984, September). *The social psychology of the conservation task* (paper presented at BPS Developmental Section Conference, "Future Trends in Developmental Psychology", Lancaster).

Finn, G. (1982). *Children's experimental episodes, or 'Ask a silly question but get a serious answer'* (unpublished paper, Department of Psychology, Jordanhill College of Education).

Gelman R. (1982). Accessing one-to-one correspondence. *British Journal of Psychology, 73,* 209–220.

Gelman, R. & Gallistel, C. (1978). *The child's understanding of number.* Cambridge, Mass.: Harvard University Press.

Gold, R. (Undated). *Inappropriate conservation judgements in the concrete operations period* (unpublished paper, Department of Psychology, University of Melbourne).

Goodnow, J. (1972). Rules and repertoires, rituals and tricks of the trade. In S. Farnham-Diggory (Ed.), *Information Processing in Children.* New York and London: Academic Press.

Hargreaves, D., Molloy, C., & Pratt, A. (1982). Social factors in conservation. *British Journal of Psychology, 73,* 231–234.

Hughes, M. (1983). What is difficult about learning arithmetic? In M. Donaldson, R. Grieve & C. Pratt (Eds.), *Early childhood development and education.* Oxford: Basil Blackwell.

Hughes, M. & Donaldson, M. (1979). The use of hiding games for studying the coordination of viewpoints. *Educational Review, 31,* 133–140.

Hughes, M. & Donaldson, M. (1983). The use of hiding games for studying coordination of viewpoints. In M. Donaldson, R. Grieve & C. Pratt (Eds.) *Early childhood development and education,* Oxford: Basil Blackwell.

Hughes, M. & Grieve, R. (1983). On asking children bizarre questions. In M. Donaldson, R. Grieve & C. Pratt (Eds.), *Early childhood development and education.* Oxford: Basil Blackwell.

Inhelder, B. & Piaget, J. (1958). *The growth of logical thinking from childhood to adolescence.* London: Routledge & Kegan Paul.

Light, P. (1983). Social interaction and cognitive development: a review of post-Piagetian research. In S. Meadows (Ed.), *Developing thinking.* London: Methuen.

Light, P. (In press). Taking roles. In H. Weinreich-Haste & J. Bruner (Eds.), *Making sense: The child's construction of the world.* London: Methuen.

Light, P., Buckingham, N., & Robbins, A. H. (1979). The conservation task as an interactional setting. *British Journal of Educational Psychology, 49,* 304–310.

Light, P., & Gilmour, A. (1983). Conservation or conversation? Contextual facilitation of inappropriate conservation judgements. *Journal of Experimental Child Psychology, 36,* 356–363.

McGarrigle, J. & Donaldson, M. (1975). Conservation accidents. *Cognition, 3,* 341–50.

McGarrigle, J., Grieve, R., & Hughes, M. (1978). Interpreting inclusion: A contribution to the study of the child's cognitive and linguistic development. *Journal of Experimental Child Psychology, 26,* 528–550.

Mead, G. H. (1934). *Mind, self and society.* Chicago: University of Chicago Press.

Mehler, J. & Bever, T. (1967). Cognitive capacity of very young children. *Science, 158,* 140–142.

Mercer, N. & Edwards, D. (1981). Ground-rules for mutual understanding. In N. Mercer (Ed.), *Language in School and Community,* London: Edward Arnold.

Miller, S. (1977). A disconfirmation of the quantitative identity-quantitative equivalence sequence. *Journal of Experimental Child Psychology, 24,* 180–189.

Miller, S. (1982). On the generalisability of conservation. *British Journal of Psychology, 73,* 221–230.

Moore, C. (1985). *The effect of context on the child's understanding of number and quantity.* (Unpublished Ph. D. thesis, University of Cambridge).

Neilson, I., Dockrell, J., & McKechnie, J. (1983a). Does repetition of the question influence children's performance in conservation tasks? *British Journal of Developmental Psychology, 1,* 163–174.

Neilson, I., Dockrell, J., & McKechnie, J. (1983b). Justifying conservation: A reply to McGarrigle & Donaldson. *Cognition, 15,* 277–291.

Olson, D. & Torrance, N. (1983). Literacy and cognitive development. In S. Meadows (Ed.), *Developing thinking.* London: Methuen.

Parrat-Dayan, S. & Bovet, M. (1982). Peut on parler de précocité et de régression dans la conservation? II. *Archives de Psychologie, 50,* 237–249.

Perner, J., Leekam, S., & Wimmer, H. (1984). The *insincerity of conservation questions.* (Paper presented to BPS Developmental Section Conference "Future Trends in Developmental Psychology", Lancaster).

Piaget, J. (1952). *The child's conception of number.* London: Routledge & Kegan Paul.

Piaget, J. (1955). *The construction of reality in the child.* London: Routledge & Kegan Paul.

Piaget, J. (1957). *Logic and psychology.* New York: Basic Books.

Piaget, J. (1968). *Six psychological studies.* London: University of London Press.

Piaget, J. & Inhelder, B. (1956). *The child's conception of space,* London: Routledge & Kegan Paul.

Piaget, J. & Inhelder, B. (1969). *The psychology of the child*. London: Routledge & Kegan Paul.

Rommetveit, R. (1974). *On message structure*. London: John Wiley.

Rommetveit, R. (1978). On Piagetian cognitive operations, semantic competence, and message structure in adult-child communication. In I. Markova (Ed.), *The social context of language*. Chichester: John Wiley.

Rose, S. & Blank, M. (1974). The potency of context in children's cognition. *Child Development, 45,* 499–502.

Russell, J. (1976). Nonconservation of area; do children succeed where adults fail? *Developmental Psychology, 12,* 367–368.

Russell, J. (1978). *The acquisition of knowledge*. London: Macmillan.

Samuel, J. & Bryant, P. (1984). Asking only one question in the conservation experiment. *Journal of Child Psychology and Psychiatry, 25,* 315–318.

Searle, J. (1969). *Speech acts*. Cambridge: Cambridge University Press.

Shultz, T., Dover, A., & Amsel, E. (1979). The logical and empirical bases of conservation judgements. *Cognition, 7,* 99–123.

Stone, C. & Day, M. (1980). Competence and performance models and the characterisation of formal operational skills. *Human Development. 23,* 323–53.

Vygotsky, L. (1962). *Thought and language*. Cambridge, Mass.: MIT Press.

Vygotsky, L. (1966). Development of the higher mental functions. In A. Leontyev, A. Luria, & A. Smirnov (Eds.), *Psychological Research in the USSR*. Vol. 1. Moscow: Progress Publishers.

Walkerdine, V. (1982). From context to text: A psychosemiotic approach to abstract thought. In M. Beveridge (Ed.), *Children thinking through language*. London: Edward Arnold.

Walkerdine, V. (1984). Developmental psychology and the child centred pedagogy. In J. Henriques, W. Holloway, C. Urwin, C. Venn, & V. Walkerdine (Eds.), *Changing the subject*, London: Methuen.

Wells, G. (1983). Talking with children: The complementary roles of parents and teachers. In M. Donaldson, R. Grieve, & C. Pratt (Eds.), *Early childhood development and education*. Oxford: Basil Blackwell.

Wood, D. (1986). Aspects of teaching and learning. In M. Richards & P. Light (Eds.), *Children of Social Worlds*, Polity: Harvard.

V EDUCATIONAL IMPLICATIONS

13

Piaget and Education: The Contributions and Limits of Genetic Epistemology

Herbert P. Ginsburg,

Piaget's theory of genetic epistemology has been extended beyond its intended domain to deal with problems of education. At first many of these applications involved the *direct teaching* of Piagetian concepts like conservation. An example is provided by Kohlberg and Mayer (1972) who believe that the very aim of education is the promotion of the Piagetian stages and that therefore the curriculum should focus on them. Subsequently, other applications have taken a different form, involving the use of general principles derived from Piaget's theory to guide educational practice. As Sinclair (1976, p.1) puts it:

> I'm not sure that much can be done with applications of Piaget's theory in a detailed way by the Piagetian psychologist . . . As you know there are absolutely no practical applications in the work of Piaget with respect to education. All one can do is to talk about some general principles, some hints and some cautions . . . Piaget has very little to say with respect to specific problems such as how to teach reading and writing, and various other educational techniques.

Hence, it is necessary to limit oneself to a consideration of general principles derived from Piaget.

In all attempts at applying a theory to practical concerns and at extending its principles from one domain to another, there may arise problems of

Source: Sigel, I. E., Brodzinsky, D. M. and Golinkoff, R. M. (Eds.) (1981). *New directions in Piagetian theory and practice*. Hillsdale, N. J.: Lawrence Erlbaum Associates Inc., pp.315–330.

legitimacy and validity. Can the principles discovered in one area be used to provide a valid explanation of phenomena in another? Is the application a legitimate one? With respect to the extension of Piaget's theory to education, issues of this sort need to be examined most closely for several reasons. One is that the applications have concrete effects on the lives of many children; we need to be sure that the interventions are helpful. Another is that the Piagetian approach to education has become something of a faddish movement; clear analysis of the issues is especially warranted so as to avoid dogmatism. Piaget himself has taken a cautious attitude towards educational applications of his theory.

The aim of this chapter is therefore to achieve a clearer understanding of the relations between Piaget's theory and educational practice. The goals are to describe the theory's contributions and limits, to identify misapplications of the theory, and to outline important educational issues which remain to be solved. I shall argue that the literal approach to applying Piaget – e.g., the direct teaching of Piagetian concepts – is a mistake. A more reasonable strategy involves a focus on Piagetian principles which can furnish overall guidance for educational practice. But this approach also has it limits: the Piagetian principles are of a general nature, can be misapplied, and are not easily extrapolated to the classroom context. And there is a more serious difficulty: the very nature of Piaget's theory sets strong limits on its potential contribution to education. In particular, the theory has little to say about cultural knowledge, individual differences, the social context of education, and certain modes of learning prevalent in the classroom. This of course is no criticism of Piaget's theory itself. Although it already deals with an incredibly wide range of phenomena, the theory cannot be expected to concern itself with everything. Given the limits of the theory, a truly Piagetian approach to education requires innovative research going beyond Piaget's particular focus on genetic epistemology.

To develop these arguments, we shall review a number of commonly held propositions concerning the applications of Piaget's theory to educational practice. These propositions are grouped into several categories. First, we consider two relatively literal applications of Piaget's theory: Curriculum development, and Testing. Next we consider somewhat broader applications in the areas of: Learning and Limits and Opportunities. Finally we consider areas where the theory has fundamental limitations with respect to education, namely Individual differences and Academic knowledge.

CURRICULA

One major approach involves the derivation of curricula from Piagetian theory. Kohlberg and Mayer (1972) propose essentially that school curricula can be derived directly from the Piagetian stages. According to Kohlberg and Mayer, the aim of education is to promote the kind of development described by Piaget. What better way to do this than to teach the Piagetian stages? Taking this approach, Kamii (who has subsequently changed her position) has developed a "program of preschool intervention related to each of the chapter headings of Piaget's books: space, time, causality, number . . . [p.488]".

This approach is misguided for several reasons. First, in the vast majority of children, at least in Western cultures, the preoperational and concrete-operational stages develop in a spontaneous fashion, and therefore, do not need to be taught. There is some debate about whether this is true of formal operational thought as well. Our view is that there is no clear evidence indicating the lack of spontaneous development of formal operations in Western adolescents (Ginsburg & Koslowski, 1976; see also Piaget, 1972). Whatever may be true of adolescents, it seems clear that for Western elementary school children, instruction in Piagetian subject matter is likely to be unnecessary. Second, it makes little sense to provide instruction in a topic like conservation since it is intended only as an index for tapping deeper thought structures. The training programs may inculcate only the surface manifestations and not the underlying structure. As Sinclair (1971, p.1) puts it: "Piaget's tasks are like the core samples a geologist takes from a fertile area and from which he can infer the general structure of a fertile soil; but it is absurd to hope that transplanting these samples to a field of nonfertile soil will make the whole area fertile". Third, the aims of education should not be limited to – and perhaps should not at all include – the promotion of the Piagetian thought structures. Surely education must stress the transmission of the cultural wisdom and basic social values. It is not at all clear that Piaget himself would endorse Kohlberg and Mayer's "Piagetian" model.

It is therefore necessary to take a more modest approach in which one attempts to adjust particular curricular materials in line with the child's understanding as described by Piaget. Thus, if a physics curriculum is to be introduced, it behoves the curriculum developer to take into account the child's informal knowledge of physics and his related thought processes. Although rare, work of this type, as for example conducted by Shayer (1972), has great potential for education. A curriculum at least partially based on the psychology of the child is apt to be more effective than one which is not. On the other hand, there is some danger in this approach as well. One must not allow the Piagetian conception of thought in a given area fully to determine one's approach to it. For example, Piaget's view of scientific reasoning in adolescence places heavy stress on the hypothetico-deductive method. Although useful, that is not all there is to science. A curriculum based entirely on such an approach would ignore a good deal that characterizes the essence of scientific activity, for example, exploration, the formation of hypotheses by analogy and intuition, the role of luck and serendipity. Obviously, future research should concentrate on expanding our knowledge of the child's spontaneous understanding of the various subject matter areas – science, mathematics, etc. The more we know about the child's informal reasoning in these areas, the better are we able to design effective curricula in them. We shall return to this topic later when we consider *academic knowledge*.

In brief, an attempt to base education on the teaching of the Piagetian stages is an unfortunate misapplication of the theory. A more useful approach is the modification of the curriculum in line with knowledge of the Piagetian stages, without, however, placing undue emphasis on them and without allowing them to circumscribe one's approach. More research is needed on the nature of the child's informal knowledge of the various subject matter areas.

TESTING

There seem to have been two major approaches to applying Piaget's theory to the question of testing. One approach is to standardize the various Piagetian tests in order to be able to administer them to large numbers of children. The purpose of this is of course not to measure academic accomplishment – the achievement tests are intended for that – but to obtain a psychometrically reliable portrait of the child's cognitive structures, in Piagetian terms. This approach is misguided for two reasons. One is that it is not clear that knowledge of the Piagetian thought structures helps us a great deal in understanding the child's academic work. If one is going to test children in the schools, it would seem more relevant to find out how they go about doing addition than whether they conserve number. A second reason is that, even if one has an interest in measuring the Piagetian thought structures, standardized testing is an inferior method for assessing them. Piaget's clinical method is deliberately unstandardized since that is a superior way to explore the subtleties of the child's cognitive structure. The rationale for the clinical method (for an early account see Piaget, 1929) is straightforward and sensible. Tapping the child's competence requires subtle and sensitive procedures, tailored to the peculiarities of each individual child. Pursuing the idiosyncracies of the child's solution processes requires flexibility in approach. The clinical method, used properly, accomplishes these purposes well; standardizing the procedure only serves to vitiate its power. Perhaps the major gain for standardization is a false sense of scientific respectability.

A second application of Piaget to testing involves retaining both the clinical method and the Piagetian content as well. Sometimes teachers are encouraged to use the clinical method as applied to problems like the conservation of number. Such demonstrations may make an important impression on teachers, showing them that the child's thought can be distinctive. At the same time, the contribution of orthodox clinical interviewing is limited because of its failure to go beyond the Piagetian content, and to address itself directly to the teachers' concerns.

In brief, the standardization of Piagetian tests is not beneficial as it focuses too narrowly on Piagetian phenomena and because it deliberately abandons the strengths of the clinical method. The demonstration of Piagetian phenomena via the clinical method may be of some utility to teachers in illustrating the distinctiveness of the child's thought, but it does not speak directly to their needs. In education, we do not need more standard tests, nor even clinical interviews concerning Piagetian subject matter. Instead we need to exploit the great advantages of the clinical method in order to engage in the direct exploration of children's academic knowledge. It may be helpful for teachers to appreciate children's distinctive reasoning on the conservation tasks. But it would be even more useful for them to observe, via the richness of the clinical method, the unusual patterns of reasoning displayed by young children as they grapple with ordinary school arithmetic. Future work on testing needs to explore the uses of the clinical interview procedure with respect to uncovering the structure of academic knowledge.

LEARNING

One can derive from Piaget's theory several principles concerning children's learning and understanding.

Learning and Understanding as Active Processes

According to Piaget, learning is not simply imposed by environmental forces. Learning is not shaping. The child takes an active role in his own learning. He assimilates environmental events into his own cognitive structures. The result is an active system of knowing. Knowledge is constructed by the child: "to understand is to invent".

These psychological principles have been extended to the educational setting. Piaget's theory provides a general rationale for active approaches which have existed for many years, stemming from Rousseau, Pestalozzi, and Froebel. The logic is simply that to know something in depth requires that one rediscover the matter for oneself. The teacher may guide the student in the direction of rediscovery, but the active learning involved in the rediscovery is itself crucial. If knowledge is active reconstruction, then active methods of education are required. We see then that in this case Piaget's contribution is to provide a psychological rationale for an already existing educational approach which is certainly a useful alternative to traditional education, with its heavy stress on passive learning.

At the same time, the educator must recognize that the Piagetian rationale is a general exhortation, itself solving no educational problems. It needs to be supplemented by specific techniques deriving from the art of the teacher. Further, there are possibilities for mischief in the application of the Piagetian ideas. One involves the misinterpretation of Piaget's notion of active learning. For example, some writers place undue stress on the role of concrete activity. Ginsburg and Opper (1969, p. 221) maintain that: "Children, especially young ones . . . learn best from concrete activities". Further, "The teacher should not teach, but should encourage the child to learn by manipulating things". These undoubtedly well-meaning authors exaggerate. The important Piagetian idea is activity, not necessarily physical, concrete activity. Important for learning are active engagement and commitment, not necessarily actions on things. As Piaget (1970, p.68) puts it: ". . . it has finally been understood that an active school is not necessarily a school of manual labor . . .. The most authentic research activity may take place in the spheres of reflection, of the most advanced abstraction, and of verbal manipulations (provided they are spontaneous and not imposed on the child . . .)".

More important than simply misinterpretation is a limitation in Piaget's theory. It fails to provide an adequate account of receptive learning. We should not forget that education has a *legitimate* receptive side as well. Indeed Piaget (1970, pp.137–138) feels that: "Memory, passive obedience, imitation of the adult, and the receptive factors in general are all as natural to the child as spontaneous activity". One of the many legitimate aims of education is to promote receptive learning. By necessity, students must engage in some "rote learning", such as learning the names of the states, memorizing addition facts, learning the chemical elements, acquiring foreign vocabulary, etc. All this is not the only aim of education, or even the most important one, but receptive learning cannot be avoided. Further, Piaget points out that for learning of this type, the teaching machine and various forms of programmed instruction may be extremely efficient and useful. Yet, while receptive learning or "learning in the narrow sense" is a basic part of education, Piaget has no good theory of it. He simply has not been interested in this type of learning, so that if you wish to understand the teaching of vocabulary or some other aspect of receptive learning you must go to other theorists.[1]

In brief, Piaget's theory provides the theoretical underpinnings for an active approach to education. But it suggests no specific techniques, is

---

[1]The irony is that modern experimental psychology views receptive learning as very much an active process. For example, memory of nonsense syllables involves active organizational strategies. Even rote learning is no longer seen as the stamping in of associations onto a passive learner.

liable to misinterpretation, and does not provide much understanding of receptive learning which is basic for education.

Cognitive Conflict and Equilibration

Another proposition derived from Piaget's theory is that cognitive development is promoted when there is a moderate degree of discrepancy between the child's cognitive structure and some new event which he encounters. This notion has been expressed in various forms within Piagetian theory. Piaget's early work on infancy proposed that moderate novelty tends to attract the infant's interest and hence promotes learning. In later work, Piaget has stressed cognitive conflict as promoting the equilibration process. Certainly Piaget's notion of the role of cognitive conflict gives a different perspective from behaviourists' approaches to learning. The strategy of deliberately jarring the student's cognitive structure and thereby enhancing active learning is an important idea for education.

At the same time, there may be a number of difficulties with the notions of cognitive conflict and equilibration as applied to education. First, the Genevans would be the first to admit that equilibration theory is itself not yet fully developed. It has only been in the past decade that Genevan research has extensively focused on problems of cognitive conflict and equilibration. Equilibration theory itself requires further elaboration.

Second, the proper applications of equilibration theory to school learning are unclear. No doubt, the informed pursuit of cognitive conflict is at least on some occasions a useful model for education. But we do not really know for which circumstances this model is most appropriate and for which circumstances other models are required. Does all school learning involve cognitive conflict? Is equilibration theory a useful approach to reading, for example, which involves some memorization of whole words, and some abstraction of orthographic rules? In other words, while the notion of equilibration may be informative with respect to the development of those cognitive structures of concern to Piaget, it is not clear to which aspects of school learning the notion of cognitive conflict might apply.

Third, and even more fundamentally, whereas the notion of cognitive conflict may be a key notion for educators in many areas, identification of the precise nature of educational conflicts is hardly guaranteed by knowledge of the Piagetian structures. Thus, a student's cognitive conflict in the area of history, for example, may in no way involve the concrete operations of any other Piagetian cognitive structure. If this is so, identification of the precise nature of the conflict requires a theory of the cognitive structures which in fact are involved in school learning. Unfortunately, as we shall see later, such a theory is almost entirely lacking, and Piaget's theory of cognitive structures is not an adequate substitute for such a theory.

In brief, Piaget's principle of cognitive conflict offers a useful educational alternative to receptive teaching procedures. But the theory of equilibration is only in its formative stages; the areas of application of the model to academic knowledge are unknown; and identification of the precise nature of educational conflict is not guaranteed by knowledge of Piagetian structures.

Self-directed Learning

Piaget's theory proposes that sensorimotor and cognitive structures develop in a spontaneous, and self-directed fashion. The child takes a major role in directing the course of cognitive development: the latter does not depend on instruction. No doubt, self-directed learning is a real phenomenon. As Piaget has demonstrated most convincingly in the case of infancy, children *can* learn on their own. The coordination of schemes, for example, is not taught; it is learned spontaneously and parents are often quite oblivious of it.

Piaget's theory of spontaneous, self-directed development of cognitive structures has often been generalized to education in the form of an exhortation to allow children to engage in extensive self-directed learning. For example, Ginsburg and Opper (1969, p.224) state that children ". . . should be allowed considerable freedom for their own learning". They state further that (p.225), "If left to himself the normal child does not remain immobile; he is eager to learn. Consequently it is quite safe to permit the child to structure his own learning". In arguing against adult controlled teaching, writers sometimes point out an analogy with speech. Without instruction, children in all cultures learn to speak. If such natural learning were replaced by formal instruction in school, there would no doubt be disastrous results. Arguments of this sort have been used to justify some long-standing practices of progressive education. Thus Piagetians often support the "open classroom" approach, popularized in the British infant school, in which children are assumed to control a good deal of their own learning.

Although Piaget's theory demonstrates that self-directed learning *can* take place in the natural environment – and indeed in that setting may be the prevalent mode of learning – there is once again a problem of goodness of fit when the psychological principle is applied to the educational setting. The model of self-directed learning was originally designed to explain such phenomena as the development of cognitive structures or sensorimotor schemes. We cannot know a priori whether self-directed learning does indeed characterize some or all academic situations. This is an empirical matter. Unfortunately, little evidence exists concerning the issue. Informal observation of open classrooms suggests that under some circumstances self-directed learning can take place in school and indeed can predominate there. At the same time, it is also obvious that self-directed learning does not always occur and that other forms of learning appear to be successful in some situations. For example, some forms of receptive learning may have to be imposed on children and it may be that only after such an imposition takes place self-directed learning is possible. Music teachers often report that young children have to be *forced* to play an instrument before they can spontaneously appreciate it. Another example involves minority education. In the 1960s, it was reported that some poor black inner-city children who failed miserably in ordinary public schools achieved a high degree of success when they attended extremely structured and indeed militaristic, authoritarian schools run by Black Muslim groups. Presumably these children benefited from the discipline and structure.[2]

All this is to say that the freedom to learn principle may be effective in some cases and may even be an ideal to which education should aspire. Yet, common experience teaches us that the principle does not apply under all circumstances. And Piagetian theory does not concern itself with the nature of these circumstances. The theory does not attempt to disentangle the social, ecological, and political factors which seem to play a major role in determining whether self-directed learning is possible in a given school situation. Those who attempt to apply Piagetian theory must become aware of the realities of the schools; but to learn about these realities, they must look beyond Piaget's theory.

Factors Influencing Development.

Piaget proposes that several factors influence development: maturation, physical experience, logicomathematical experience, social experience, and equilibration. We have already dealt with equilibration, and there is nothing much to say about the role of physical maturation, except that it is important but poorly understood. Now we consider the other factors, physical experience, logicomathematical experience, and social experience.

In the case of *physical experience,* Piaget points out that individuals sometimes obtain knowledge of the world through direct perceptual experience with external objects and the consequent abstraction of properties from them. This is usually classified as perceptual learning, as in the theory of J. J. Gibson (1966). Piaget (1971, p.266) further points out that physical experience involves "a vast category of knowledge".Surely, in schools, physical experience may be very important in some areas. In the case of science, for example, it is often important for children to "mess around" with objects (to use David Hawkins', 1974, phrase) in order to obtain

---

[2]Perhaps an open school environment could work for these children under very special circumstances with very special teachers (for example, Herbert Kohl who had enormous success with his *36 children*[1967]).

through physical cxpcricncc – through perceptual learning – a "feel" for objects' properties. In mathematics, it is important for children to observe the behaviour of numbers. Yet, while perceptual experience is both extensive and important for education, Piaget's theory has tended to slight it. His theory focuses on thought, not perception, and has been unsuccessful in offering an explanation of the means by which individuals manage to abstract knowledge directly from the real world. As a rcsult, Piagct's thcory has virtually nothing to say about this aspect of education, just as it has little to offer concerning the mechanisms of receptive learning.

The notion of *logicomathematical experience* is a unique, and I think very valuable notion in Piaget's theory. The idea that the individual learns from reflecting on his own actions on the world gives a new perspective to learning. In the case of mathematics, for example, the child may, after considerable activity, learn something about *his own actions* with respect to number, and this may be an important acquisition. The perspective afforded by the notion of logicomathematical experience seems to be an extremely useful one for teachers. The only problem with it is that it is so unique that we have little insight concerning the aspects of educational activity to which it applies.

Social experience can have several senses in Piaget's theory. It may refer to the role of language, to the effect of peers, and to that of adults. Consider each in turn.

For Piaget, *language* generally plays a secondary role to thought. Because the child's thought is distinctive, his language therefore bears distinctive meaning. Such an emphasis is extremely useful for education, since it prods teachers to listen with the "third ear" to what children say, and to go beyond teaching by mere verbalisms, in accordance with the mistaken belief that children simply learn by listening.

From his early work in the 1920s and 1930s on egocentrism and moral judgment, Piaget has stressed the facilitating effect of *peer interaction* on cognitive development. In general, the view is that the conflict of opinions generated through peer interaction is instrumental in promoting decentration, and hence development in general. The recent experimental work of Murray (1972) supports this view, showing that peer disagreements seem to promote developments in reasoning concerning conservation.

In general, the Piagetian view on peer interaction seems to have some value. Surely it is wasteful for children to spend a good portion of their time in school observing a vow of silence. Surely debate, the exchange of ideas, and intellectual conflict is all to the good in many classroom situations. At the same time, we must recognize the obvious fact that peer interaction has many dimensions, and does not always promote intellectual growth. Peers interact with one another in many ways, and sometimes this interaction involves the transmission of values which are antithetical both to genuine intellectual activity and to school learning (the two do not always coincide!). On some occasions, the promotion of learning among teenagers may require less peer interaction and more contact with appropriate adult models. All this is to say that in the context of education the social psychology of peer interaction must obviously go far beyond the Piagetian analysis.

With respect to *adult influence*. Piaget feels that it has an important role in the promotion of intellectual development. The adult can help to structure a situation so that the child is able to assimilate it effectively. The adult can intervene in the course of events so as to produce a moderate degree of intellectual conflict within the child. Piaget's position is similar to that of John Dewey who felt that the adult has a distinctive responsibility in the education process, mainly to devise situations in which the child can engage in active learning. In this regard, Piaget (1970) reports a visit he paid to an open school run by Susan Isaacs. Piaget found the school interesting but somewhat undisciplined and felt that the adults should have taken a more active role in structuring the situation for the children.

The principle of adult influence is a most useful emphasis for the teacher. Yet Piaget does not go beyond a very general and well-meaning position. Piaget has nothing further to say on the role of the teacher; he has no theory of instruction. Indeed in Piaget's enormous corpus of writing on child development, one can find virtually no mention of the role of the adult. One exception to this is in the case of moral judgment, where Piaget reports, somewhat plaintively, that as a parent he was unable despite his best efforts to advance his daughter beyond a primitive stage of moral judgment. Because Piaget's almost exclusive emphasis has been on the child, he has virtually nothing to say about teaching.

In brief, a number of factors influence development, among them physical experience, logicomathematical experience, and social experience, although Piaget acknowledges the importance of physical experience, this theory has little to say concerning the perceptual learning it entails and hence can contribute little to the understanding of vast areas of education. The notion of logicomathematical experience is promising, but its sphere of application is uncertain. In the area of social experience, Piaget's view of language encourages in teachers a sensitivity to the unique meanings of children's speech; his conception of the beneficial effects of peer interaction is useful but limited; because of his almost exclusive concentration on children, Piaget has little to say concerning teaching.

LIMITS ON LEARNING AND OPPORTUNITIES

To some extent Piaget's theory has a pessimistic side with respect to education. One principle states that because of the nature of his current stage of intellectual development, the child is limited in what he can learn. Thus, in the stage of concrete operations, he may not be able to engage in certain forms of scientific reasoning. Or, in the preoperational stage, he may not be able to understand certain basic mathematical concepts. In general, this must be true. Everyone knows that you cannot teach a baby to speak or a young child to do the calculus. It is certainly useful for the teacher to be alert to aspects of the child's thought processes which might make it difficult for him to assimilate a certain body of material.

Yet there is a serious danger in the Piagetian position. Some Piagetians have adopted too zealous a view of the child's limitations. It is a common belief, for example, that the preoperational child cannot engage in "abstract thought" or that he cannot perform any useful scientific activity. These are misconceptions. The young child is capable of mental representation from the age of about 18 months, and indeed sometimes thinks *too* abstractly, as when he overgeneralizes the meaning of words. Piaget himself is careful to point out intellectual strengths in the preoperational child, as in the case of the early understanding of functional relations. Similarly, there is a good deal that the young child can do with respect to science, whose scope should not be limited to the kind of hypothetical reasoning Piaget attributes to adolescents. It is even more incorrect to suppose that the preoperational child or even the concrete operational child is not yet "ready" for reading since his thought structures are so primitive. Obviously 3 and 4 year old children can learn to read – this is a common observation – and it is by no means clear that the structures of preoperational or concrete operational thought set any kinds of limits on basic reading. In brief, there is some validity to the Piagetian principle that the nature of the young child's thought limits his learning. But this principle has been applied indiscriminately, with the unfortunate effect of restricting the range of educational experiences for the young child.

Piagetian theory displays an optimistic side as well. According to Piaget, the spontaneously developed thought structures existing at various stages make it possible for the child to assimilate various aspects of school material. These thought structures form the cognitive basis for academic knowledge. Because the child approaches many areas of academic study with spontaneously developed and relatively powerful "intuitions", the task for education is to make connections among the child's intuitions and the formalizations which are taught in school. As Piaget (1970, p.47) puts it; "The pedagogic problem . . . still subsists in its entirety: that of finding the most adequate methods for bridging the transition between these natural but nonreflective structures [that is, the child's spontaneously developed but unaware intuitions] to conscious reflection upon such structures and to a theoretical formulation of them". There is thus a particularly Piagetian form of consciousness raising: in presenting formalizations, the teacher must make an effort to exploit the child's intuitions. As Freud put it in a somewhat different context, "Where id was there ego shall be".

Pursuing this analysis, Piaget claims that children should not have as much difficulty as they do with school mathematics, since it is more or less an elaboration of what they already know. As Piaget (1970, p.44) puts it: ". . . it is difficult to conceive how students who are well-endowed when it comes to elaboration and utilization of the spontaneous logicomathematical structures of intelligence can find themselves handicapped in the comprehension of a branch of teaching that bears exclusively upon what is to be derived from such structures".

The notion of drawing on the child's spontaneous intuitions and relating them to what is taught in school is a key idea for education.[3] Piaget makes an important contribution in stressing that a basic strategy for education should consist in bridging the gap betwen spontaneous and cultural knowledge. Yet the Piagetian analysis cannot carry us very far in this direction because the theory pays scant attention to two areas which we shall consider next, namely *individual differences* and *academic knowledge*.

INDIVIDUAL DIFFERENCES

In many of his works, Piaget takes pains to point out that there exist individual differences in children's rate of attainment of the various cognitive structures. In the Piagetian scheme such individual differences may result from variations in any of the factors promoting development – maturation, physical experience, etc. Such differences may also appear in the rates of development displayed by entire cultures.

Although the theory acknowledges the existence of individual differences – how could it not? – Piaget has little interest in them. His concern is with the "general human mind" of Wundt, with the development of common structures of knowledge. Hence Genevan theory and research have paid scant attention to individual differences in rate of attainment of the various stages. Moreover, the theory has virtually ignored other individual differences. The theory does not concern itself with such variables as impulsiveness, intellectual conscientiousness, persistence, commitment, creativity. These are all individual difference characteristics at the heart of intellectual activity. To observe that Piaget's theory fails to deal with them is no criticism, merely a statement of fact. The theory cannot be expected to solve all psychological problems.

At the same time, this gap in Piaget's theory limits its relevance for the classroom. Individual differences are at the heart of education. To a large degree, education is or should be concerned with developing meaningful forms of learning for individuals who differ in important ways. To some extent, these important characteristics may include individual differences in rates of attainment of the Piagetian stages. Perhaps some topics in

---

[3]Of course, the idea is not completely unique to Piaget. For example. Vygotsky (1962) made a similar distinction between spontaneous and scientific knowledge.

mathematics will come easier to the 7 year old who is in the period of concrete operations than to one who is preoperational. But it is likely that other individual differences – those not discussed by Piaget – are at least equally important for education, and may well be more important than rate of attainment of the Piagetian stages. For real children in classrooms, what matters is creativity, intelligence, cognitive style, and intellectual motivation. A deep understanding of these factors is vital for the effective conduct of everyday education. Yet these are factors concerning which Piaget's theory has virtually nothing to say.

PIAGETIAN THOUGHT STRUCTURES AND SCHOOL KNOWLEDGE

It is usually assumed that educators should be sensitive to the child's intellectual status as described in terms of Piagetian thought structures. There is some validity to this notion. A teacher should be aware of the concrete operational child's one-to-one correspondence or of the formal operational child's capacity for hypothetico-deductive reasoning. To some extent, the structures described by Piaget are informal intuitions which can serve as a foundation for formal instruction and hence the teacher can profit from knowledge of them. The open question, however, is this: in what ways do the Piagetian structures *account for* the nature of academic cognition? To what extent can the concrete operations *explain in detail* the child's performance in algebra or in reading?

It is becoming evident that the explanatory power of the Piagetian structures with respect to academic knowledge is weak. For example, in the case of adolescent science, as we have pointed out below, the Piagetian theory deals with the details of hypothetico-deductive reasoning. Yet this is only one part of the scientific enterprise. Similarly in the case of mathematics, Piagetian theory deals with some fundamental notions of one-to-one correspondence and equivalence, but does not have a great deal to say about the child's uses of counting or the details of his problem solving techniques in algebra. In particular, Piaget's theory does not deal with knowledge which is symbolized and codified. Thus, it does not seem very productive to use Piagetian notions in developing models for reading, either at the level of "decoding" (the technical aspect of reading), or at the level of comprehension. In brief, although Piaget's theory may explicate some fundamental structures of thought, it does not concern itself with, and therefore cannot be directly applied to, basic aspects of academic knowledge in particular, and culturally derived thought in general. Whereas the theory gives insight into such informal "intuitions" as one-to-one correspondence, it does not deal explicitly with the cultural elaborations of these intuitions. Hence the effort to bridge the gap between intuition and formalization is hindered.

Why does Piaget's theory not pay more attention to cultural forms of knowledge? Piaget (1970, p.137) sees education as a dialectic process involving interaction between child and society: "To educate is to adapt the child to an adult social environment, in other words, to change the individual's psycho-biological constitution in terms of the totality of collective realities to which the community consciously attributes a certain value". The culture attempts to transmit to the child its wisdom, its modes of thought, knowledge, and values. On his part, the child attempts to assimilate the cultural wisdom and eventually to contribute to it, to modify it. In the case of mathematics, for example, over the course of centuries the culture has developed codified, written procedures and explicit, symbolized principles, a cumulative legacy which the educational system attempts to inculcate in the child. This accumulated wisdom is powerful and can serve the child well once it is assimilated into his cognitive structures. This having been done, the child is then in a position to make original contributions to the culturally derived body of knowledge.

Although apparently recognizing the central role of the "collective realities" – the cultural wisdom – Piaget's theory does not contribute a great deal to understanding them. As a genetic epistemologist, Piaget has been concerned mainly with the development of fundamental but noncultural forms of knowledge. Thus he is interested in the notion of one-to-one correspondence, not with written algebra. Piaget focuses on ideas and modes of thought operating outside the school context, not within it. Another way of putting it is to say that Piaget is interested in biologically based forms of knowledge, not socially based forms. Piaget (1971, p.268) maintains that:

We are omitting [from consideration] the modes of metaphysical and ideological knowledge because they are not kinds of knowledge in the strict sense but forms of wisdom or value coordinations, so that they represent a reflection of social life and cultural super-structures rather than any extension of biological adaptation. By this we do not mean to dispute their human importance; it simply means that the problems are quite different and are no longer the direct province of biological epistemology.

Thus, Piaget's theory has focused on "biological epistemology", on the basic Kantian categories of thought, and has slighted social knowledge.

If education is in good measure concerned with acculturation – the transmission of the accumulated wisdom of a culture – then Piaget's theory is limited in its explanatory power with respect to academic knowledge. At the very least we can say that it is not clear that there is a strong relation between the Piagetian structures and the kinds of thought processes involved in school learning. To a large extent the question is an empirical one, since we have very little knowledge concerning the thought processes actually employed in academic learning. A productive approach, I think, is for those with a Piagetian orientation to undertake direct investigations of academic cognition in order to determine whether the Piagetian notions are indeed useful, or whether new accounts need to be developed. For education, knowledge of the Piagetian thought structures is only a preliminary first step.

CONCLUSIONS

Piaget's theory yields several principles providing both deep understanding of children and general guidance for the educational enterprise. The principles serve as a basis for a progressive approach to education. At the same time, we must recognize that the theory may be misinterpreted: sometimes this results in too literal and rigid an application of Piaget's views. Much more importantly, we must also understand that Piaget's is a specialized theory, failing to consider many issues crucial for education. In particular, because Piaget is a genetic epistemologist, whose theory focuses on the development of what he considers to be the basic categories of the general human mind – on biologically based, Kantian categories – he has little to say about the acquisition and nature of culturally-based forms of knowledge, the forms inculcated by schooling.

Considering these limitations in Piaget's theory, it seems fair to say that we sometimes rely too much on Piaget, and the result is detrimental to the understanding and practice of education. Too often, we say to teachers that Piaget wants us to look at the child, but then all we show them is what Piaget has seen. We demonstrate the child's distinctiveness through his inability to conserve, but we cannot describe his unique approach to addition. While preaching a child-centred view, Piagetians too often assume a Piaget-centred view.

An effective contribution to education requires utilizing the Piagetian framework to go beyond Piaget. Such an approach requires, among other things, attempts to understand self-directed learning within the social context of the classroom and the ecological setting of the school in the larger society. It requires a direct focus on the structures of academic knowledge in particular and cultural knowledge in general. It requires the use of flexible methods to investigate cognitive structures of direct relevance to education. In these ways can we begin to understand the education of the child.

ACKNOWLEDGEMENT

The writer wishes to thank the following colleagues for their helpful comments on the paper: Kathy Hebbeler, Jane Knitzer, Leon Levy, Barbara Means, Ellin Scholnick, Marilyn Wang.

REFERENCES

Gibson, J. J. (1966). *The senses considered as perceptual systems*. Boston: Houghton Mifflin.

Ginsburg. H. & Koslowski, B. (1976). Cognitive development. *Annual Review of Psychology*, *27*, 29–61.

Ginsburg, H. & Opper, S. (1969). *Piaget's theory of intellectual development: an introduction*. Englewood Cliffs, N.J.: Prentice-Hall.

Hawkins, D.(1974). *The informed vision*. N.Y.: Agathon Press.

Kohl, H. (1967). *36 children*. New York: New American Library.

Kohlberg, L. & Mayer, R. (1972). Development as the aim of education. *Harvard Educational Review, 42*, 449–496.

Murray, F. B. (1972). Acquisition of conservation through social interaction. *Developmental Psychology, 6*, 1–6.

Piaget, J. (1929). *The child's conception of the world*. London: Routledge & Kegan Paul.

Piaget, J. (1970). *The science of education and the psychology of the child*. N.Y.: Orion Press.

Piaget, J. (1971). *Biology and knowledge*. Chicago: University of Chicago Press.

Piaget, J. (1972). Intellectual evolution from adolescence to adulthood. *Human Development, 15*, 1–12.

Shayer, M. (1972). Conceptual demands in the Nuffield O-level physics course. *School Science Review, 186*, 26–34.

Sinclair, H. (1971). Piaget's theory of development: The main stages. In M. F. Rosskopf, L. P. Steffe, & S. Taback (Eds), *Piagetian cognitive-developmental research and mathematical education*, Washington, D.C.: National Council of Teachers of Mathematics.

Sinclair, H. (1976). In T. C. O'Brien (Ed.), *Implications of Piagetian research for education: Interview with E. M. Hitchfield*. St. Louis: Teacher's Center.

Vygotsky. L. S. (1962). *Thought and language*. Cambridge, Mass.: MIT Press.

14 On Teaching Thinking: An Afterthought

Jerome Bruner

[. . .]

DEVELOPMENTAL IMPLICATIONS

In reflecting upon the developmental implications of the theoretical and practical work I shall group my remarks under three questions. These are: (1) What, if anything, must an information-processing model pre-suppose about development?; (2) What is the role of general or metacognitive skills in development?; (3) What is the role of social interaction and cultural milieu in the development of cognitive processes, particularly as seen in the perspective of information processing?

Developmental Models

We have just come through a period in developmental psychology dominated by a Stage Specific Model of the kind referred to by Carey (1985, Ch.6, this volume) as Option 1: development in stages, each with its own format for problem representation, its own logic, its own set of concepts. This, of course, was the legacy of Piaget, and it has yielded great riches. By choosing a limited set of tasks or problems for study, the Genevan psychologists have given us a rare insight into how children deal with issues such as invariance of quantity across transformations, causality, probability, and classification.

Source: Chipman, S. F., Segal, J. W., and Glaser, R. (Eds.) (1985) *Thinking and learning skills,* Vol. 2, Research and open questions. Hillsdale, N. J.: Lawrence Erlbaum Associates Inc., pp. 597–608.

But as Carey noted, the evidence does not support the view that there is qualitative discontinuity between stages. One has to choose one's experimental tasks with care to maintain the illusion of logically self-contained stages. Perhaps it is just as well that development did not, on close inspection, conform to her Option 1. For in fact, none of the extant theories has much by way of a mechanism to account for the child's progress from one self-contained stage to the next. The conditions that alter the equilibration between accommodation and assimilation, and thus permit or evoke change are left discreetly unmentioned by Piaget. Vygotsky (1962) did a bit better in describing the processes whereby the growing child is helped across the Zone of Proximal Development but then it is doubtful whether he was in any proper sense a stage theorist. In those ancient years of the mid-1960s when I was a stage theorist – a bogus one really – I tried to deal with the shift from one stage to the next by introducing a notion of conflict in representations with resulting cognitive incompatibility. But to have conflict, the child must in some way be able to represent problems in different ways at any stage. So that made mine a rather half-baked stage theory, at that.

But whether the account of development as a series of unique, autonomous stages held up to scrutiny or not, the fact of the matter is that the search for stage theories *has* taught us some important things about cognitive growth. There may not be Great Big Stages, each with its own unique structure, but growth *is* characterized by *structural* changes. There are *paradigm* shifts in children's developing theories of the world, and although these may not be reducible to massive stage changes in basic axioms, neither are they matters of the simple accretion of information.

There are two things that convinced me that a stage theory could not be an appropriate account of development, and I want to mention them here for they help specify what an information-processing theory must take into account about development. The first was my own and others' data on development in early infancy. Whatever stages you may postulate, you can devise situations for testing young infants, once you get clever at it, that can easily bring the infants to a level way beyond where they are supposed to be developmentally. It is no great trick. If you make the testing task one that demands actions that they easily control, so that they have some surplus processing capacity to spend, you can bring off wonders.

Ilze Kalnins and I (1973), for example, were interested in the extent to which the 6-week-old infant could manage instrumental tasks involving a flexible or combinatorial deployment of means to achieve arbitrary or non-natural ends. Well, the 6-week-old does not have a large repertory. He can, we know, suck; he can look or avert his gaze – both quite expertly. He sucks for self-comforting and for nutriment, both quite naturally, quite expertly, and indeed even cannily (see Hillman & Bruner, 1972). It also happens to be the case, at that age, that infants prefer clearly focused pictures to blurred ones. Could we teach the infants in question to suck on a pacifier to produce a clearer focus in pictures they are viewing? The answer was a plain yes, and a trivial yes at that. Indeed, without additional prompting or training, the infants knew enough to keep their gaze averted until after they had sucked awhile and removed the blur from the displays. If sucking was made to produce blur, the same infants cannot suppress sucking entirely, however aversive its blurry outcome. But now they keep looking at the picture during the early phase of blurring, hanging on till the last aversive moment, when they finally look away.

It is hard not to conclude from this experiment, and many like it, that so long as you can get the problem translated into the child's processing space by honouring his limited attention span and leave some left over for combinatorial activity, then the child can solve problems "way over his head". What this means, I think, is that given the right support – you can call it tutorial support – the child will do much as Vygotsky suggested he would, given proper nurturing of his "zone of proximal development". The literature on infancy is rich in such demonstrations. They do not encourage much faith in a hard-line stage theory!

The same phenomenon occurs later in childhood, at school age. Children, given mathematical problems couched in the right embodiment and presented in a happy sequence, can also solve problems that are way over their heads and beyond their stage. Page (1960), using "box" notation, could produce surprisingly good intuitive algebraists among children not at all into the Piagetian stage of formal operations. Again, it is a question of providing familiar instantiation of principles that are within the child's span and leaving some spare capacity over (see Shatz, 1978).

But this sounds, you will say, as if paradigm shifts are *not* involved in development at all. Indeed, *no* shift is needed, only an externalization of some sort of implicit, native knowledge, very much indeed like that evoked in the young slave "learning" geometry from Socrates in the *Meno*. Is it that Socrates is "merely" providing manageable representations for knowledge the slave already "possesses" in some way?

I suppose one could say that the first big paradigm shift consists of a representation or an instantiation for what was before only a mute and implicit intuition. After that, one encounters paradigm shifts to what might be called conceptually higher ground of the kind Carey (1985, Ch.6, this volume) reports. There are also more gradual changes that are not so much paradigmatic as procedural, and these may be more like skill learning. We know from work on hypothesis development in children's problem solving that children come rather gradually to be more systematic in the application of such routines as "win-stay-lose-shift," that, bit by bit, they come to use feedback from attempted solutions to guide their decisions about whether to keep or jettison an hypothesis, etc. It is not that they start as nonproblem solvers and one day manage to get over the wall into problem solving. They are problem solvers from the start. What they are developing are workable strategies and modes for representing knowledge in some explicit, externalized way, for correcting that knowledge, and eventually for monitoring the whole process as it unfolds.

I agree with Gelman's (1985) account of cognitive development: the older child tends to be more explicit, has a better grasp of how to access and manipulate structures and routines in order to get a job done or a problem solved. His recognition routines in looking for means are not only more explicit but tend to be driven increasingly by criteria of consistency and congruency. Markman (1985) comments on the same matter: the younger child does not know explicitly enough what he knows, to be able to tell whether he is being consistent or not in organizing information. It may well be that the child deals successively with small chunks, until these become sufficiently routinized (or environmentally supported) for him to combine them into larger information structures. Then, and only then, can he be aware of consistency or even be able to know clearly what it is that he knows. It is at this point that metacognition begins to pay off – whether it is self-induced or evoked by a Socrates.

I think we can now begin to close in on the things that an information-processing theory must presuppose, and can safely presuppose, about development. It must presuppose that organisms are natural problem solvers who deploy means to achieve ends and use feedback increasingly well to control their deployment of means, etc. I think the evidence strongly supports this presupposition. The child from the start recognizes the means-end structure of problems and represents them in terms of such structures. He learns to use feedback and to develop greater regularity in his tryout of hypotheses, etc. The instantiations or "props" that he learns from the stored knowledge of the culture permit him not only to cope better with the problems he undertakes, but also to communicate with others in a common language so that he may learn more by vicarious means.

Metacognition and Development

I think that there is now sufficient evidence from work done by Brown and her colleagues (1985), and others in this volume, to make it plain that children can assess their own performances and improve their procedures for remembering, for solving problems, and so on. It is not too far off the mark to say that this reflecting on one's own performance increases with age. We do not know for certain whether guided practice increases the likelihood of more appropriate and unprovoked reflection in the future, although the extant evidence suggests that this is the case, at least for memory strategies.

Work on the self-monitoring of speech (or on "linguistic awareness", as it is called) suggests that even the very young child has the capacity to reflect on his or her own speech flow and to correct it in the interest of being understood. Kasermann and Foppa (1981) have shown that such repairs are systematic even at 18 months. The literature has been reviewed recently by Eve Clark (1978) and it is simply not clear to what extent linguistic awareness is an accompaniment of or a factor in language acquisition. One study (Sinclair, 1981) suggests that, as far at least as "speech acts" are concerned, linguistic awareness is evoked not by errors in utterance form, but by errors in the behaviour produced by the incorrect speech act form; that is to say, we become aware of what we are saying principally when we see through others' actions that our message has failed to convey its intended meaning.

I would like to raise a question now about children's play as a form of metacognition, possibly *the* form of early metacognition. I take metacognition to be reflection upon or monitoring of those acts that have to do with achieving, storing and retrieving, or using information. Its principal hallmark is its reflexivity. Play is not usually reflexive in this sense, but it represents nonetheless a form of activity from which the operator is more detached, better able to improvise. It is closer to a simulation than to a real thing. What is most characteristic of play is the manner in which it loosens the coupling between means and ends and allows for exploration of combinatorial possibilities among alternative means.

There is evidence that by getting children to play with materials that they must later use in a problem-solving task, one gets superior performance from them in comparison with those children who spend time familiarizing themselves with the materials in various other ways. The principal differences between the "players" and the other children may tell us something about the metacognitive function of play. For one thing, the players generate more hypotheses, and for another they reject wrong ones more quickly. Finally, they seem to become frustrated less and fixated less. They are going for feedback, one might say, rather than for self-esteem (Sylva, Bruner, & Genova, 1976). The playfulness fostered in the initial contact with the task seems to carry over into the problem-solving phase. Indeed, when you consider the matter, it should not be surprising. For play has the unique character of dissociating means and ends to permit exploration of their relation to each other. In "work", what one typically does is to hold an end or objective invariant while varying the means until one achieves it. In play, we uncouple the two in a different, more symmetrical way. We may hold the means constant while varying the end – the baby's typical routine of taking a block, for example, and achieving all possible outcomes with it: banging it, mouthing it, dropping it to the floor, etc. Or one holds the end invariant and varies the means, not with the object of achieving success but of exploring how many different routes one can use to get there. The infant bangs his or her cup, bangs a block, bangs any detachable object within reach. It may be a bit of an exaggeration, but may it not be the case that what we speak of as unprompted metacognition or monitoring, or reflection could be an internalized form of play? After all, the commonsense way of referring to a metacognitive approach to a problem is to say that we are "playing around" with it a little.

One small aside before developing this point. There has been a good deal of analogizing in our discussions about how development is like going from being a novice to being an expert. Now that we have touched on play, I can tell you why I doubt it. Play is *the* business of childhood. Interestingly enough, when we try to impose the novice-to-expert regimen on children – which is principally what school is about – it very often produces a massive turning off of cognitive activity. Let me be very plain about it. I have (as I shall relate in a moment) studied hundreds of hours of play behaviour. I have never, in all that time, seen a child glaze over or drop out or otherwise turn off while engaged in play. I wish I could say the same for the children I have observed in classrooms and even in one-to-one tutorials. This leads me to wonder whether play is not quite different from work, by which I mean the classical model of problem solving with the goal held constant and the means varied. Let me return to the main argument.

I want to pursue a problematic course. My colleagues and I have been engaged in an extended study designed to find out what conditions improve the "quality" of children's play (Bruner, 1981; Sylva, Roy, & Painter, 1981). Perhaps that can tell us something about how to improve their metacognitive activity as well. Let me not bore you with the details of how we compute quality or richness of play. Roughly, it consists of measuring the number of contingent steps within a play sequence, their elaboration, the recruitment of objects or props in support of the play, and, finally, the sheer length of the play sequence which, of course, is highly correlated with its richness. In any case, in intensive observational studies of children aged 3–5 in playgroups, nursery schools, and kindergartens, we found four conditions that strikingly increase the richness and length of play. I want to describe the four conditions first and then to consider what they might tell us about the metacognitive side of play.

In no particular order, they are the following. First is the presence of *one* other child as a playmate: not two or none, but one. Two children in a shielded situation in which they can exchange and negotiate meanings, rules, etc. are the stuff of long and elaborated bouts of interactive play. The loner rarely plays long at one thing. As one would expect, two children will spend a great deal of time in deciding upon the procedures they will follow and how they may be instantiated. A second condition promoting long bouts of play is material that (a) has a clear-cut variable means-end structure, (b) has some constraints on the nature of the material that can be deployed, and (c) yields feedback that a child can interpret on his own without having to depend on authorities – i.e., direct rather than indirect feedback. Puzzles, building blocks, miniaturized versions of life activities, etc. all provoke longer and richer play bouts than the traditional quartet of water, sand, clay, and fingerpaint. These are the materials that provoke combinatorial exploration.

The third condition reminds one of *Lord of the Flies*. Play bouts are longer and richer among young children when there is an adult nearby who is buffering the situation, keeping it from getting out of hand, providing occasional comfort and response (Like: "See this airplane?" "Hm, what a nice plane.") The adult is not *in* the action, but a source of stability in the situation. The fourth and final condition is best called modelling. Those children who attended play-groups or nursery schools that spent some time each day in joint and compulsory high-level activity (e.g., school readiness games, so-called) were more likely to play longer and more elaboratedly than others when they were on their own.

In a world, then, negotiation, structure, stability, and a model of what is possible produces the richest play. I want to juxtapose with these findings one other observation, this time from Erik Erikson. He told me that, upon going back over the adult records from the California Growth Study, he had found that the most creative people were the ones with least separation in daily life between work and play. Now this could be an effect rather than a cause, and it doesn't matter much. That is to say, being creative and therefore not separating work and play may not be all that different from not separating work and play and therefore being creative. Like the Chinese and the structural linguists, I am not all that keen about establishing a temporal order for cause and effect. In linguistics, a verb phrase that follows in some sense causes the noun phrase that precedes it – or at least makes it possible for it to be a noun phrase. What I am saying, in effect, is that play at its best may be an early prototype, an *external* prototype of internal metacognitive activity in the more mature.

It is a hard case to establish, and I am not so much trying to establish it as to enter it into the lists for discussion. The argument is that all forms of external negotiation of meaning, all external prods to reflection have the effect of *stimulating* internal negotiation, reflection, metacognition. Let me give some instances from the literature on the matter. In a recent study, for example, Tizard et al. (1980) show that the children who ask the most searching and deictically imbedded questions are the ones whose parents are most likely to give them full, intelligent, and elaborated answers to any questions they may ask. They become accustomed to negotiating interpretations and seeing alternative meanings. In a quite similar vein, Dunn and Beveridge (1981) have shown that children of mothers who concentrate during the second year on communicative intent, trying to explain to children what they and their siblings *intend* to express, regardless of what they *actually* say, show more sophisticated speech than the children of parents who do not. This is not strong evidence that earlier encouragement to go to higher ground produces greater likelihood of occupying higher ground when solving problems, but at least it is a start. Playful, negotiatory, flexible, mindful interaction early on may become a model later for what you do when you encounter problems. Having played around in fact, and with good effect, you may now feel encouraged to play around in your own head.

Culture and Cognitive Development

This brings me to my last topic: the impact of culture on cognitive growth. Let me begin with the Cultural Practice Model of Mike Cole and Warren Simmons, and I refer you to Simmons (1985). He gives a striking example of cultural micropractice that fits the point I want to make. You recall the difference between the interpretation of a tutor's corrections made by a low-income, low-status kid and that made by his more privileged peer. The former takes the correction as punishment, the latter as feedback. There is an old finding from a study by Sroufe and Wunsch (1972) that I cite as often as I can, so important is it. They reported that those things most likely to make a young child laugh when done by a parent or familiar were the things most likely to make the child cry when done by a stranger. The tutored poor child is seeing his tutor as a stranger, as an adversary. But he, the child, has not *invented* the adversarial role of the tutor. It is a role established by a system in which poor children are defeated. An enormous amount of subtle rearranging of the social system is needed to bring the tutee into a position where he sees the tutor as a friend who gives him tips on how he is proceeding. I would add to this as well Virginia Shipman's finding. Those children in her study who early on are managed by a rationale rather than by physical coercive means do better in cognitive performance; that is to say, parents are not automatically in the category of allies whose response can be treated as feedback rather than punishment.

I have used the word "micropractices" to describe what a culture generates that affects the likelihood of particular kinds of cognitive activities developing in its members. It would be a mistake, however, to think of these as some sort of *list* of disparate elements. For the micropractices that shape cognitive growth, whether generated by parents, teachers, or adults in general, are highly patterned. They resemble what in linguistics is called a register (Snow & Ferguson, 1977): a patterned way of responding to another person's speech. As we know from the work of Cross (1977), these registers matter greatly for growth – even in language acquisition, where the received wisdom holds that everybody eventually learns to handle the language equally well. The cognitive register, so to say, is of a simple kind, I think. It consists of treating another as if they were of a certain kind or category of person. A good way of producing a dumbbell is to treat the person as a dumbbell. It is not surefire in its results, but it is a good beginning. It helps to get everybody else in that child's environment to treat him as a dumbbell too. If *you* didn't convince him, then perhaps a consensus will.

Rather than talking about how children can be shaped cognitively by the cultural micropractices of an environment, I will take older, indeed, aged subjects, and I refer to the experiments of Ellen Langer (Langer & Rodin, 1976). If old people in a nursing home are treated as if they are incapable of remembering and planning, they rapidly begin to perform accordingly. If now you introduce interventions so that old people are treated as if you expect them to be able to plan and to remember events as needed, then indeed there is a dramatic improvement in planning activity and in actual memory performance. One can wonder whether there may be something of this order operating in the Rosenthal effect as well.

Let me conclude by noting that the hidden agenda for middle-class children of well-educated parents is precisely to *expect* them to be reflective and metacognitively astute. And when their parents send them off to schools, the schools they go to are likely to expect just that of them. In a paper I wrote some years ago reviewing the literature of poverty and child-hood (1975), I came to the conclusion that there was as discernible a pattern to be found among the fortunate as there was among those who were exploited by the society. Often, we signal our expectations about the use of mind subtly or not so subtly – whether we expect a person to be "stupid" or "impulsive" or "childish".

Bertrand de Jouvenal, the French philosopher, once tried to convince me that there was one sociological law that surpassed all others: "People do what you expect of them". I think he was not far off the track. I would end with one simple point, an extension of this. If you expect people to examine their thoughts, to be mindful about their use of mind, all of the evidence points to the fact that they can and will do so. If they have learned to play, perhaps, they can do it more readily, for they may be doing what comes naturally. But it would take a fair amount of rearranging of a society to assure that everybody has the opportunity to play richly. And it takes even more rearranging to see to it that we expect of each human being the best cognitive performance, the best and most mindful metacognitive per-formance of which he or she is capable, and that we make it worthwhile by rewarding him or her with the power and responsibility that their efforts deserve. That is what the challenge is about.

[. . .]

REFERENCES

Brown (1985). In S. F. Chapman, J. W. Segal, & R. Glaser (Eds.), *Thinking and Learning Skills, Vol 2, Research and Open Questions*, Hillsdale, N.J.: Lawrence Erlbaum Associates, Inc.

Bruner, J. S. (1975). Poverty and childhood. *Oxford Review of Education, 1,* 31–56.

Bruner, J. S. (1981). *Under five in Britain*. Ypsilanti, MI. High Scope Press.

Carey (1985). In S. F. Chipman, J. W. Segal, & R. Glaser (Eds.), *Thinking and Learning Skills, Vol 2, Research and Open Questions*, Hillsdale, N.J.: Lawrence Erlbaum Associates Inc.

Clark, E. (1978). Awareness of language: Some evidence from what children say and do. In A. Sinclair, R. J. Jarvella, & W. J. Levelt (Eds.), *The child's conception of language*. Berlin: Springer-Verlag.

Cross, T. (1977). Mothers' speech adjustments: The contribution of selected child-listener variables. In C. E. Snow & C. A. Ferguson (Eds.), *Talking to children: Language input and acquisition*. Cambridge: Cambridge University Press.

Dunn, J. & Beveridge, M. (1981, September). *The effect of a sibling on mother-infant communication*. Paper delivered to Developmental Section British Psychological Society, Edinburgh, Scotland.

Gelman (1985). In S. F. Chipman, J. W. Segal, & R. Glaser (Eds.), *Thinking and Learning Skills, Vol 2, Research and Open Questions*, Hillsdale, N.J.: Lawrence Erlbaum Associates Inc.

Hillman, D. & Bruner, J. S. (1972). Infant sucking response to variations in schedules of feeding. *Journal of Experimental Child Psychology, 13,* 240–247.

Kalnins, I. & Bruner, J. S. (1973). The coordination of visual observation and instrumental behavior in early infancy. *Perception, 2,* 307–314.

Kasermann, M. L. & Foppa, L. (1981). Self-repairs in early speech. In W. Deutsch (Ed.), *The child's construction of language*. New York & London: Academic Press.

Langer, E. J. & Rodin, J. (1976). The effects of choice and enhanced personal responsibility for the aged: A field experiment in an instructional setting. *Journal of Personality and Social Psychology, 34,* 191–198.

Markmann (1985). In S. F. Chipman, J. W. Segal, & R. Glaser (Eds.), *Thinking and Learning Skills, Vol 2, Research and Open Questions*, Hillsdale, N.J.: Lawrence Erlbaum Associates Inc.

Page, D. (1960). Reported in J. S. Bruner. *The process of education*. Cambridge, MA: Harvard University Press.

Shatz, M. (1978). The relationship between cognitive processes and the development of communication skills. In C. B. Keasey (Ed.), *Nebraska symposium on motivation*. Lincoln: University of Nebraska Press.

Simmons, W. (1985). In S. F. Chipman, J. W. Segal, & R. Glaser (Eds.), *Thinking and Learning Skills, Vol 2, Research and Open Questions*, Hillsdale, N.J.: Lawrence Erlbaum Associates Inc.

Sinclair, A. (1981). Speech act development. In W. Deutsch (Ed.), *The child's construction of language*. New York & London: Academic Press.

Snow, C. E. & Ferguson, C. A. (1977). *Talking to children: Language input and acquisition*. Cambridge: Cambridge University Press.

Sroufe, A. & Wunsch, J. P. (1972). The development of laughter in the first year of life. *Child Development, 43*(3–4), 1326–1344.

Sylva, K., Roy. C., & Painter, M. (1981). *Child watching at playgroup and nursery school*. Ypslanti, MI: High Scope Press.

Sylva, K., Bruner, J., & Genova, P. (1976). The role of play in the problem solving of children 3–5 years old. In J. S. Bruner, A. Jolly, & K. Sylva (Eds), *Play: Its role in development and evolution*. Harmondsworth: Penguin Books.

Tizard, B., Hughes, M., Carmichal, H., & Pinkerton, G. (1980). Children's questions and adults' answers. *Journal of Child*, 269–281.

Vygotsky. L. (1962). *Thought and language*. Cambridge, MA. MIT Press.

15

Learning Processes in Social and Instructional Interactions

A. N. Perret-Clermont and N. Bell

Any instructional interaction is necessarily a social interaction and therefore the analysis of the process of learning implies the understanding of social discourse and communication. Research aimed at studying these processes has often used a three-step paradigm comprising (1) a pretest where the child's existing knowledge is assessed by asking him to display a performance to the adult, (2) an instructional intervention where the adult provides the child with an opportunity for learning, and (3) a post-test where the child is asked to re-display a performance. The object of study in phase 1 is the child's response (i.e., what the child manages to say to the adult [experimenter or teacher] who tests him). In phase 2, the object of focus is centered on the communication directed to the child by the adult. In phase 3, it is again the child's discourse (communication directed toward the adult) which is the object of study. In studies using this three-step paradigm, it is the difference between the phase 1 and 3 performances which is supposed to reveal "learning". We have conducted research in this perspective and have discussed elsewhere (Perret-Clermont 1980; Perret-Clermont & Brossard, in press; Perret-Clermont & Schubauer-Leoni, 1981). its interest for the educational field.

However, a certain number of questions concerning these studies remain unanswered. For example: What is learned? How is it learned? What was not known? Will it be remembered? When will it be remembered? Is the knowledge learned transferable to other situations? At times, what is learned may not necessarily be what the adult intended to teach. The child's

Source: *Proceedings of the First European conference on Learning and Instruction.* Leuven, June 1985. Now published in De Corte, E., Lodewijks, H., Parmentier, R., & Span, P. (Eds.) (1987). *Learning and instruction.* Oxford: Pergamon Press and Leuven University Press. Reprinted with permission from A.N. Perrot-Clermont, Copyright 1987, Pergamon Books Ltd.See also p. 321 (Appendix) for further information.

learning seems to depend on the context and the type of task. It is clear that the child's perception and his interpretation of the situation in which he finds himself will determine his behaviour and hence his performance which will in turn be interpreted by the adult as evidence of learning (or lack thereof).

In convening this symposium we wanted to foster an opportunity to explore these questions through different methodological and theoretical approaches and we will try to outline here the present state of understanding of learning processes as it emerges from these studies.

METHODOLOGICAL CONCERNS

Patry and Oser (1985) examine a number of methodological problems concerning research on learning which has used this three-step paradigm; particularly concerning the generalizability of results. A question often arises in this type of instructional situation: is the researcher eliciting cognitive development or is he really just indoctrinating his subject? These authors also draw attention to other important problems, e.g. often these studies approach the learning situation as a sort of tabula rasa, ignoring the past experience and acquired knowledge of pupils as well as teachers. How can the existing competence of the partners in the didactic situation be fully exploited?

In their respective research, Delamont (1985) and Woods (1985) draw attention to the methodological problems inherent in the three-step paradigm by their use of alternative investigative methods using participant observation, interviews and discussions with the actors in the scholastic situation. These methods have enabled a fuller understanding of the meaning and interpretation of behaviours of participants in the learning situation and of their interpretations of what is at stake in school contexts.

Concerning our own research using this three-step paradigm, we have shown that, in certain circumstances, peer interaction is likely to be more efficient for cognitive development than certain other methods of learning based on the usual child-adult discourse; and this holds true at times when the interaction partners both have erroneous opinions of the object of the interaction. The instruction given to the child by the adult (corresponding to phase 2 of the paradigm presented above) is therefore not the only model of interaction and communication which is liable to result in learning. However, the process of learning is complex and these findings admittedly do not fully account for it.

THE SOCIAL AND SYMBOLIC FRAMEWORKS OF LEARNING

In many studies, the generalization of learning, whether it be a result of direct instruction or informal social interaction, is never as large as expected and continues to pose problems for researchers and teachers. Bell, Grossen

& Perret-Clermont (1985) are currently undertaking detailed analyses of children's perceptions and behaviour in testing and interaction situations which have called attention to the fact that the child's performance does not occur in a social vacuum, but rather in a framework of symbolic interactions with the child's environment. This perspective addresses issues that are also illuminated by ethnographic analysis of learning and instructional situations.

In situations where an adult experimenter or teacher communicates not only with one child but with a group of children, communicative exchanges are not only directed from the adult to the child but also from the child to the adult as well as between children. Pontecorvo (1985) has delineated the variety of strategies used by teachers to modulate the cognitive conflicts occurring in these situations and to deal with the alternative modalities of thinking which appear during discussion and the existing cultural differences between pupils or between the teacher and pupils. She has also shown that the class-group plays an important role for the child's actualization of knowledge through sharing of effort, sustaining the emotional level and reducing anxiety.

THE ACTIVE ROLE OF THE CHILD

The adult usually has a specific vision of the task in instructional situations that is influenced by his professional training, cultural background, and personal experience. The adult can never render a task entirely explicit to his interlocutors. Children therefore have access to a task only through the manner in which it is presented by the adult. In order to approach the adult's vision of the task, the child must attempt to re-construct it by going beyond the adult's presentation. The child must therefore learn to focus his thinking in such a way as to adjust it to the vision of the adult. This adjustment is accomplished by direct exchanges concerning the task as well as indirect processes of regulation.

Sirota (1985) has observed a variety of children's strategies of adaptation and survival in the classroom. It seems that these strategies differ in function of the social distance existing between the child and the school culture.

Bennett (1985) points out that the pupil is a mediator in his own learning. Other authors (e.g., Flammer, 1980) have illustrated the active role of the learner who intervenes in the process of instruction by his questions, demands, requests for information, etc. Pontecorvo (1985) describes the epistemic operations underlying these interventions (providing information and data, drawing analogies and metaphors, producing metacognitive and methodological reflexions ["How do you know?"]). In their research, Patry & Oser (1985) also refer to these processes of metareflexion in the developing child.

Each partner comes to the didactic situation with a particular conceptual referential framework reflecting his thoughts and pre-occupations. In effect, when teachers and pupils are confronted with "scholastic matters", they do not only consider the defined task in cognitive terms but also take into consideration the relational structure of the situation. There exists a social and moral order in the classroom which is apprehended differently by teachers and pupils. Delamont (1985) has pointed out that in the everyday life of the classroom pupils are often confronted with a type of culture clash between their cultures and that of the school. Woods (1985) has evidenced the existence of pupil sub-cultures which are not without influence on pupils' attitudes regarding school subjects such as science, sex education, etc. Gilly (1985) calls attention to misunderstandings in the teacher-pupil relation which, for pupils, are often situated on an emotional level. It seems that pupils value aspects of the relation which are not at the center of teachers' representations of the same relation. Gilly maintains that teachers' representations are marked by the obligation to adequately fulfil their role as it is institutionally defined (in order to be a "good teacher", one needs "good pupils"). In trying to understand the dynamics of teaching and learning situations, it is necessary to analyse how each actor pursues his own interests even when they are seemingly incompatible with the situation (Perret-Clermont, 1983, 1984a).

Looking at the dynamics of didactic situations, one can see that the didactic contract between teachers and pupils establishes in some sense the social order in the classroom. Within the didactic relation between teacher and pupil, the teacher is supposed to transmit an object of knowledge. This object is embedded in the referential universe of the teacher and is linked to his academic life history (teaching experiences, training, etc.). The pupil's comprehension of the transmitted object is likewise influenced by experiential factors. The consideration of these differing conceptual frameworks demands a re-examination of assumptions about content in the learning process: what is really being taught? What is learnt? Where does this object of knowledge come from? What is the pupil's goal in this pedagogical situation? Is it always the understanding of the material presented? Or does formal qualification sometimes take precedence?

THE TRANSFORMATION OF KNOWLEDGE

The transmission of knowledge implies the process of de-contextualization and re-contextualization. Taking the mathematical notion of "sets" as an example, one can illustrate the process by which this object of knowledge is transformed (Perret-Clermont et al., 1981). Set theory as elaborated by mathematicians becomes in the hands of curriculum experts (who are influenced by politicians and other subject experts) the notion of "sets" as an object of the scholastic curriculum. This decontextualized object is in turn transformed by teacher trainers (with the influence of educational psychologists, school authorities, etc.) into the notion of "sets" as an object to be taught. This version of "sets" then becomes the object of a lesson or exercise as it is transformed by teachers in the classroom. This transformed (deformed?) object finally reaches the child who in turn re-contextualizes the notion of "sets" as an object to be learnt.

Thus, at the end of this process the (naive) psychologist discovers that there is little in common between the notion of "set" as initially elaborated by mathematicians and the notion of "set" as learnt by pupils. However, this description of the transmission of knowledge as a descending process constitutes an uni-directional model of the progressive "degradation" of "pure" knowledge to "deformed" scholastic material. One could reverse the process by starting with the child's activity on sets and collections in interaction with the teacher and thereby evidence other mechanisms of de-contextualization and re-contextualization. The teacher's interference (instrumenting) with the child's cognitive activity serves as feedback on his professional knowledge and skills transmitted to him by teacher training whose curriculum is, in turn, ameliorated in function of both practice and scientific research. This reversal of the process of de-contextualization and re-contextualization presents a more dynamic perspective of the transmission of knowledge while, at the same time, it calls into question the meaning of knowledge learned at school. For example, it is assumed that the notion of "sets" has a meaning in theoretical mathematics. Can it also have meaning to the child? To what extent and under which circumstances?

In pursuing research on learning and teaching, we are invited to remember that the object of knowledge is not uniquely the property of the teacher-student relation, as other actors also have a vested interest in its transmission (parents, for example). This object can take on different symbolic meanings for the different actors concerned. These symbolic differences could result in a kind of culture clash for the child who is caught in the middle (as it were) of different referential universes (Perret-Clermont 1984b).

ACKNOWLEDGEMENT

Preparation of this reading was made possible by a grant from the Swiss National Science Foundation (Project No. 1.738.083).

REFERENCES

Bell, N., Grossen, M., & Perret-Clermont, A. N. (1985). Socio-cognitive conflict and intellectual growth. In M. Berkowitz (Ed.), *Peer conflict and psychological growth*. New York: Jossey-Bass.

Bennett, S. N. (1985, June). *Recent research on teaching-learning processes in classroom settings.* Paper presented at the First European Conference for Research on Learning and Instruction, Leuven, Belgium.

Delamont, S. (1985, June). *Understanding social relations in classrooms: the British and American ethnographic traditions compared.* Paper presented at the First European Conference for Research on Learning and Instruction, Leuven, Belgium.

Flammer, A. (1980). Towards a theory of question asking. *Research Bulletin of the University of Fribourg, No. 22.*

Gilly, M. (1985, June). *Institutional roles, representations of the partner and expectations of attitudes in educative interactions.* Paper presented at the First European Conference for Research on Learning and Instruction, Leuven, Belgium.

Patry, J. L. & Oser, F. (1985, June). *Intervention studies for socio-cognitive competencies: some examples and theoretical reflexions.* Paper presented at the First European Conference for Research on Learning and Instruction, Leuven, Belgium.

Perret-Clermont, A. N. (1980). *Social Interaction and Cognitive Development in Children.* London: Academic Press.

Perret-Clermont, A. N. (1983). Des conditions psychosociales d'émergence des connissances scientifiques (du chercheur adult à l'élève). In A. Giordan & J. L. Martinand (Eds.), *Actes des cinquièmes journées d'education scientifique à chamonix.* Paris: UER Didactique des Disciplines.

Perret-Clermont, A. N. (1984a). Quel est l'enjeu des situations didactiques? In A. Giordan & J. L. Martinand (Eds.), *Actes de sixièmes journées d'education scientifique à chamonix.* Paris: UER Didactique des Disciplines.

Perret-Clermont, A. N. (1984b). Psychologie social de l'apprentissage et migration culturelle. *Revue Belge de Psychologie et de Pédagogie, 46,* 188, 123–127.

Perret-Clermont, A. N. & Brossard, A. (In press). On the interdigitation of social and cognitive processes. In R. Hinde, A. N. Perret-Clermont & J. Stephanson-Hinde (Eds.), *Relationships in cognitive development.* London: Clarendon Press.

Perret-Clermont, A. N., Brun, J., Conne, F., & Schubauer-Leoni, M. L. (1981). Decontextualisation et recontextualisation du savoir dans l'enseignement des mathématiques de jeunes élèves. *Interactions didactiques,* No.1. Universities of Geneva and Neuchâtel.

Perret-Clermont, A. N. & Schubauer-Leoni, M. L. (1981). Conflict and cooperation as opportunities for learning. In W. P. Robinson (Ed.), *Communication in development.* London: Academic Press.

Pontecorvo, C. (1985, June). *Discussing for reasoning: The role of argument in knowledge construction.* Paper presented at the First European Conference for Research on Learning and Instruction, Leuven, Belgium.

Sirota, R. (1985, June). *Practices, strategies and interactions.* Paper presented at the First European Conference for Research on Learning and Instruction, Leuven, Belgium.

Woods, P. (1985, June). *Social interaction in the classroom: The pupil's perspective.* Paper presented at the First European Conference for Research on Learning and Instruction, Leuven, Belgium.

16 What is Difficult About Learning Arithmetic?

Martin Hughes

"Maths is like learning a foreign language, Marcie. No matter what you say, it's going to be wrong anyway."

Peanuts

In a paper by Gelman and Gallistel (1983) it was shown that preschool children have more knowledge of the principles of number and counting operations than was previously supposed. Why then do some children find it so difficult to master arithmetic when they enter school? In the present reading, Hughes discusses the arithmetic system and describes some novel studies on the child's understanding and use of arithmetic symbols, statements, and operations. Part of the power of the arithmetic system is that it is highly abstract, and not tied to particular contexts. But as Hughes shows, it may be so abstract that young children may fail to realize that arithmetic symbols have anything to do with particular contexts. Thus they fail to appreciate that arithmetic symbols can be used to represent objects, and arithmetic symbols and statements can be used to represent operations carried out on objects. Children's difficulties with what Hughes calls "the formal code of arithmetic" are well illustrated in the original studies that are described in this reading.

As our society becomes more and more dependent on high levels of computer-based technology, it becomes increasingly important that children should grow up with a basic competence and familiarity with numbers, and

Source: Donaldson, M., Grieve, R., and Pratt, C. (Eds.) (1983). *Early childhood development and education*, Oxford: Blackwell, pp. 204–221.

Note: The ideas put forward in this chapter are developed more extensively in Hughes, M. (1986). *Children and number*. Oxford: Basil Blackwell.

that they should feel at home in the world of calculation and computation. Of course, there are many children who easily develop a facility with numbers. Yet there are also many children who share the sentiments of the Peanuts character above, and who approach numerical problems with a mixture of confusion and helplessness. Some of these children manage to scrape by in school, by picking up a collection of techniques, tricks and rules of thumb. These may suffice to get them through the exams, but they may be only hazily understood. Other children do not even manage this, and remain almost totally at sea.

Why do children find arithmetic so difficult? Why does it seem like a foreign language to so many of them? For some years now one of the standard responses from educationalists to such questions is that formal arithmetic has been imposed on children long before they were conceptually ready for such learning. This position has often been justified by appealing to the work of Jean Piaget and his colleagues in Geneva.

THE PIAGETIAN EXPLANATION

Piaget's explanation of young children's difficulties with number can be found in various books and articles published over a period of some thirty years. However, one particularly influential article of his appeared in *Scientific American* in 1953. The first two paragraphs of this article are worth quoting in full:

> It is a great mistake to suppose that a child acquires the notion of number and other mathematical concepts just from teaching. On the contrary, to a remarkable degree he develops them himself, independently and spontaneously. When adults try to impose mathematical concepts on a child prematurely, his learning is merely verbal; true understanding of them comes only with his mental growth.

> This can easily be shown by a simple experiment. A child of five or six may readily be taught by his parents to name the numbers from one to ten. If ten stones are laid in a row, he can count them correctly. But if the stones are rearranged in a more complex pattern or piled up, he no longer can count them with consistent accuracy. Although the child knows the names of the numbers, he has not yet grasped the essential idea of number: namely, that the number of objects in a group remains the same, is 'conserved', no matter how they are shuffled or arranged.

These paragraphs contain several characteristically Piagetian ideas. We find here, for example, the belief that teaching children before they are conceptually "ready" is likely to produce only superficial learning, that true learning comes only with the child's mental growth, and that mathematical concepts cannot be taught. There is also the underlying implication that learning mathematics is not essentially difficult, for it is something which children can for the most part acquire "independently and spontaneously".

At the centre of Piaget's argument, however, is the idea of conservation. Piaget maintains that if children cannot conserve number – that is, if they appear not to understand that the number of objects in a group remains the same however the objects are arranged – then they are not yet ready to start on school arithmetic. Indeed, Piaget suggests that teachers should mistrust any apparent ability – such as counting – that young children bring with them to school. If the children cannot conserve then this apparent knowledge is likely to be "merely verbal" parrot-style learning.

Many of these ideas have now become widely accepted within early mathematics education. For example, the idea that mathematical concepts are acquired through the child's mental growth – and in particular through activities involving concrete objects – is taken as virtually axiomatic by most nursery and infant school teachers. The majority of infant school mathematics schemes start off with very concrete activities, such as matching objects on a one-to-one basis, or sorting them into sets. These activities are intended to develop the young child's general concept of number, as measured by a Piagetian conservation test. It is only when children seem to have grasped the idea of number conservation that they are considered ready to start on addition and subtraction.

NEW EVIDENCE ON THE ABILITIES OF THE PRESCHOOL CHILD

If children arrive at school as limited in their concept of number as Piaget suggests, then it is clearly undesirable to proceed as if they were more advanced. However, while Piaget's ideas have become increasingly influential within early childhood education, they have been attracting increasing amounts of criticism within developmental psychology (Donaldson, 1978; Gelman and Gallistel, 1978). In particular, there is now a considerable amount of evidence that children starting school are by no means as limited in their number concepts as Piagetian theory maintains.

Much of this evidence is concerned with Piaget's claim that children starting school do not, on the whole, understand the idea that number is conserved when a collection of objects is displaced or rearranged. In order to understand these criticisms, we need to consider the nature of the conservation task itself. In what is generally regarded as the "standard" number conservation procedure, a young child is confronted with two identical rows of objects placed in one-to-one correspondence (Piaget, 1952). Virtually all children will agree at this stage that the two rows contain the same number of objects. The critical part of the task comes next. The adult displaces one of the rows so that it is now longer (or shorter) than the other, and asks the child if the two rows still contain the same number of objects. Piaget found that children younger than six or seven years will not, as a rule, conserve their judgements, but will incorrectly say that one row now contains more objects than the other. It is only when children reach the age of six or seven years that they will regularly conserve; that is, they will reply that the rows still contain the same number of objects

There is widespread agreement that young children do in fact respond to the standard number conservation task in the way Piaget describes. However, it is increasingly being questioned whether this standard procedure is really testing what it claims to test. Several studies have now compared the standard procedure – in which the adult displaces one of the rows in a deliberate manner – with alternative procedures in which the displacement is either "accidental" or "incidental" (McGarrigle & Donaldson, 1974; Light et al., 1979; Neilson and Dockrell, 1981). In each of these studies, significantly more children gave the right answer with the alternative procedure than with the standard procedure. It seems that some children may fail on the standard conservation task yet still have a good understanding of number conservation.

More direct evidence that young children have coherent number concepts comes from the work of Rachel Gelman and her associates in America (Gelman, 1972; Gelman and Gallistel, 1978; Gelman and Tucker, 1975). Much of Gelman's evidence comes from studies using an ingenious "magic" game. In this game, children develop an expectancy that a particular array will contain, for example, three objects. The array is then surreptitiously altered in one of two ways. In one condition objects are added to or taken from the array, while in the second condition the objects are simply rearranged. In both cases, the reaction of the children to the change in the array is carefully noted.

On the basis of her magic studies, Gelman claims that children as young as three years understand the *invariance* of small number arrays (three objects or less). That is, they seem to understand that displacing the objects in an array does not affect its numerosity in the way that adding or subtracting objects does. While this is not quite the same thing as Piaget's idea of conservation (see Silverman et al., 1979 for further discussion of this point), it does seem that Piagetian theory cannot easily account for Gelman's findings.

Gelman also claims that many three- and four-year-old children understand the idea of addition and subtraction. In the course of a "magic" game children who notice that objects have been removed from an array can usually say that more objects must be added if the game is to be "fixed" (i.e. restored to its original condition), and they can often say how many objects need to be added to do this. Again such a claim does not fit easily with Piaget's own belief that children below six or seven years do not really understand addition or subtraction (Piaget, 1952, p. 190).

Gelman's claim that preschool children understand addition and subtraction is based on somewhat indirect evidence: her children were not actually asked to carry out additions or subtractions. More direct evidence comes from a study I have recently carried out in Edinburgh (Hughes, 1981). In this study, 60 children aged between three and five years were given simple addition and subtraction problems in a variety of different forms. In one task the children watched as bricks were added to or taken from a box, and they were then asked how many bricks were now in the box. For example, they might know there were three bricks in the box to begin with, and might see two bricks being taken out but not see what was left. Their task was to work out that only one brick remained. Like Gelman, I found that if the numbers involved were small (one, two, three or zero) then the children performed surprisingly well (83 per cent correct). The children also performed well (62 per cent correct) when simple additions and subtractions were presented in a hypothetical form (e.g. "If there were three children in a sweetshop and two went out, how many children would be left in the shop?"). Just over a quarter of the children could also carry out similar additions and subractions when the numbers involved were slightly larger (five, six, seven and eight).

Such findings give strong support to Gelman's claim that preschool children have "a coherent set of principles for reasoning about number", particularly if the numbers involved are small. Most children who are approaching school age, it would seem, understand the invariance of number, and can carry out simple additions and subtractions, when the numbers involved are small. Moreover, a sizeable proportion of children have similar competence with slightly larger numbers. While the abilities involved are obviously not as sophisticated as those possessed by older children or adults, they still reveal a striking degree of competence in very young children.

THE NATURE OF SCHOOL ARITHMETIC

If these conclusions are correct, then we need to think again about why young children may find difficulty with school arithmetic. The Piagetian explanation is that children are being introduced to formal arithmetic too early, at an age when they lack a coherent concept of number. It now seems that children starting school are not so incompetent with number as Piaget has made out. But if this is so, there is even more of a puzzle: if children are more competent at the outset, why do so many still have difficulty learning school arithmetic?

Some clues to this problem come from the study of addition and subtraction mentioned above (Hughes, 1981). As well as the tasks already described – involving bricks in boxes and children in sweetshops – the children were also asked "school arithmetic" questions such as "What does one and two make?" Most children found these questions extremely difficult: overall, only about 10 per cent of such questions were answered correctly. Similar difficulties arose when the questions were phrased slightly differently – e.g. "How many is one and two?", or "What is one and two more?" It seems, in other words, that while most children approaching school age know that one brick added to two bricks makes three bricks, very few can answer questions involving "one and two".

At first sight this result does not seem too surprising. Questions involving "one and two" do feel intuitively harder than those involving "one brick and two bricks". But what exactly does this "hardness" consist of?

The first point to make is that questions like "What does one and two make?" are totally unfamiliar to most preschool children. According to Corran and Walkerdine (1981), such a use of language occurs very rarely in conversations between four-year-olds and their mothers at home. When number words such as "one" and "two" do occur, they almost invariably refer to objects: "one cup", "two spoons", and so on. Corran and Walkerdine argue that questions like "What does one and two make?" are part of a very restricted form of discourse – which I will call the *formal code of arithmetic*. Unlike ordinary language, this formal code will not be acquired simply through the child's participation in everyday conversations, but will have to be learned in the more formal setting of school. Rather surprisingly, some preschool children seem to be aware of this fact. One four-year-old in the study who was asked what one and two made replied that she could not answer questions like that because she "didn't go to school yet".

The second point to make about the formal code of arithmetic is that statements in the code are *context-free*. They make no reference to any particular objects or entities, they are not about anything specific. Yet this property is precisely what makes arithmetic such a powerful tool for thinking and problem-solving. The formal code of arithmetic is essentially a representational device in which words such as "one" and "two" can represent, or stand for, a whole range of objects: one brick, two houses, and so on. The quantity is what matters, the nature of the objects is irrelevant. Statements like "one and two makes three" get their power from this very great generality. They are not about anything in particular, yet they are relevant to just about everything.

It seems, however, that the context-free nature of arithmetic statements is the source of much of children's difficulty with them. In the following dialogue, Ram (four years, seven months) makes his puzzlement quite explicit:

Adult: What's three and one more? How many is three and one more?
Child: Three and what? One what? Letter – I mean number?
(We had earlier been playing a game with magnetic numbers and Ram is presumably referring to them here.)

Adult: How many is three and one more?
Child: One more what?
Adult: Just one more, you know?
Child: I *don't* know (disgruntled).

These observations provide a new perspective on the difficulties facing young children when they first encounter formal arithmetic. The problem is not that young children are completely lacking in their number concepts, for we have already seen that this is not so. Rather the problem is that they are encountering a novel code, or representation system, which may well be like a foreign language to them. Pursuing this analogy further, what they need are procedures for *translating* between this new language and the modes of representation which they already have. In other words, the problem is one of creating links between the novel, formal language of arithmetic and their existing number knowledge.

One question of obvious importance is whether young children can create these links for themselves, or whether they need to be helped. The study described earlier (Hughes, 1981) suggests that most preschool children do not spontaneously translate formal code questions, such as "What does one and two make?", into a more concrete form. When asked these questions "out of the blue", they usually replied by naming a number, such as "six", which bore no obvious relationship to the question being asked. Very few children appeared to be reasoning along the following lines: "Well I don't know what one and two makes, but I do know that one brick and two bricks makes three bricks, so maybe the answer's three." Naturally, one would not expect preschool children to verbalize the problem in exactly this way, but their thinking might have proceeded along such lines.

At first sight this might seem to be an unlikely thing for a young child to do. However a group of young children did something very similar in a study carried out by Bob Grieve and myself (Hughes and Grieve, 1980). In this study children aged five and seven years were asked questions like "Is red bigger than yellow?" We wanted to see how young children would react when asked questions which, to us, seemed quite bizarre. To our surprise, we found that virtually all the children treated these questions seriously and constructed sensible meanings for them. One tactic they often used was to translate the questions into a specific context. For example, one child looked round the room and then replied that yellow was bigger than red "because that red cushion there is smaller than that yellow curtain there".

If children spontaneously translate unusual questions involving colour into specific contexts, then it is reasonable to suppose that they might be encouraged to do the same with unusual questions involving number. In an attempt to facilitate this process I presented preschool children with formal code questions either immediately before or immediately after questions about particular objects. Even with this procedure, though, the children rarely translated between the two types of question. The following dialogue with Amanda (three years, eleven months) was typical of this approach:

> *Adult:* How many is two and one?
> *Child:* (long pause: no response).
> *Adult:* Well, how many bricks is two bricks and one brick?
> *Child:* Three.
> *Adult:* OK . . . so how many's two and one?
> *Child:* (pause) Four? (hesitantly).
> *Adult:* How many is one brick and one more brick?
> *Child:* Two bricks.
> *Adult:* So how many is one and one?
> *Child:* One, maybe.

Amanda clearly sees no connection between the formal code questions and the questions concerned with bricks. Indeed, she seems to be using a strategy of giving a *different* response to the formal code questions. It is as if she is thinking "Well I don't understand this question but I know it's not the same as the previous one, so I'll try a different answer".

I have also tried another approach which emphasizes what is common to a whole series of addition questions about specific objects. This approach, however, was equally unsuccessful. The child in the following example is Patrick (four years, one month).

> *Adult:* How many is two and one more?
> *Child:* Four.
> *Adult:* Well, how many is two *lollypops* and one more?
> *Child:* Three.
> *Adult:* How many is two *elephants* and one more?
> *Child:* Three.
> *Adult:* How many is two *giraffes* and one more?
> *Child:* Three.
> *Adult:* So how many is *two* and one more?
> *Child:* (looks adult straight in the eye) Six.

It is interesting that children find questions involving colour words easier to translate into specific contexts than those involving number words. This may reflect some universal property of number as an abstract system, or it may be a particular property of our own number words, such as "one" and "two". There are some cultures, for example, where the connection between the number words and the number being represented is made more directly. Menninger (1969) describes an early Indian system in which the word for "one" was the same as the word for "moon"; the word for "two" the same as that for "eyes", that for "four" the same as that for "brother" (in Indian mythology Rama has three brothers); the word for "seven" the same as that for "head" (the head has seven openings) and so on. It is possible that young children would find it much easier to learn formal arithmetic if our own number system contained similar links between number words and concrete objects.

WRITTEN ARITHMETICAL SYMBOLISM

So far we have been concerned with formal arithmetic in its spoken form, that is, when it is expressed in verbal statements like "one and two makes three" or "three take away two makes one". But these same statements can of course be represented in written form, such as:

$$1 + 2 = 3$$
or
$$3 - 2 = 1$$

The age at which children are introduced to this kind of written symbolism varies from country to country and from school to school. The children whose work is shown in Fig.16.1 below attended a socially-mixed school in Edinburgh, run by the local authority. Towards the end of their first year in school (age five to six years) the children are introduced to simple additions like those shown in Fig.16.1A. By the end of their second year in school (age six to seven years), they can produce the more complex additions and subtractions shown in Fig.16.1B.

Our interest in what the children were doing in their workbooks grew out of a study of their spontaneous written representations of simple number concepts. In this study, carried out by Miranda Jones and myself, we wanted to know how children would represent on paper, without any prompting from us, basic arithmetical concepts such as cardinal number (the number of objects in a group), addition and subtraction. In particular, we wanted to see whether they would use the conventional symbolism (1,2,3, +, −, =, etc.) which they had been taught and which they used in their workbooks, or whether they would use their own more idiosyncratic methods.

A group of 72 children between five and seven years of age were given three tasks in random order. In the *cardinal number* task, a group of bricks numbering between one and six was placed on a table. The child was given paper and pencil and asked to show how many bricks were on the table. In this task the children were also asked to represent zero: i.e., to show there were no bricks on the table. In the other two tasks, the *complete operations* and the *transformation* tasks, the children were asked to produce

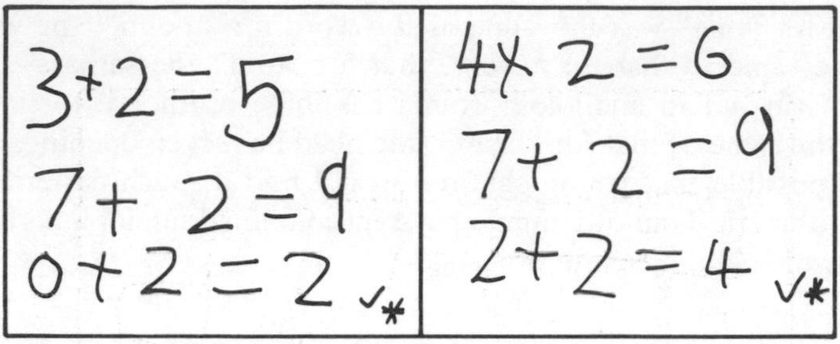

3+2=5   4ⅹ 2 =6
7+ 2=9   7+ 2 = 9
0+2 = 2 ✓*   2+2 = 4 ✓*

Class 1 (five to six years)

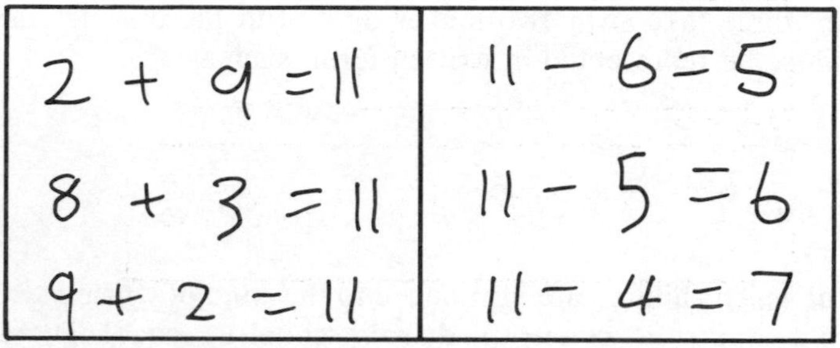

2 + 9 =11   11 – 6=5
8 + 3 = 11   11 – 5 =6
9 + 2 = 11   11 – 4 = 7

Class 2 (six to seven years)

FIG. 16.1.   Pages from children's workbooks

paper and pencil representations of simple additions and subtractions. In the *complete operations* task, the child was asked to show, for example, that there were originally three bricks on the table, that one brick was then taken away, and that two bricks were left. In the *transformation* task, the child was asked to show that a specified number of bricks had been added to or taken away from a large pile of bricks of unknown number.

The children's responses were extremely interesting. On the whole the *cardinal number* task provided few difficulties, with almost all the children providing an accurate representation of the number of bricks on the table. The most frequent response (45 per cent overall) was simply to draw the required number of bricks, with the next most frequent (38 per cent) being to write conventional numerals (1, 2, 3 . . .). Several children drew single vertical strokes or tallies for each brick, while others drew vague blob-like shapes. Some children, interestingly enough, drew the appropriate number of some different object – like one girl who said "I'll draw houses" and drew three houses to represent three bricks (see Fig.16.2 for examples of these responses).

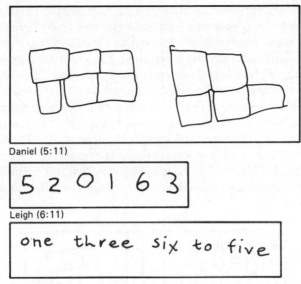

Daniel (5:11)

5 2 0 1 6 3

Leigh (6:11)

one three six to five

Kashif (7:4)

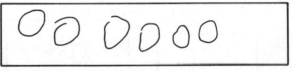

Emma (5:2)

Pamela (5:1)

FIG. 16.2.   Responses to cardinal number task

The two tasks which involved representing addition and subtraction proved very much harder. In the *complete operations* task, no child in any age group was able to produce an adequate representation of any of the operations, with the commonest response (69 per cent) being simply to represent the final number of bricks on the table. We had expected this task might be difficult because it required the child to represent three different quantities (the initial amount, the transformation and the final amount). For this reason we had also included the *transformation* task, in which the child was only required to represent a single transformation – what had been done to the pile. Surprisingly enough, the *transformation* task proved just as difficult as the *complete operations* task. Most of the children (69 per cent of all responses) correctly represented the number of bricks which were added or subtracted, but very few represented whether an addition or subtraction had taken place. Only 11 children managed to

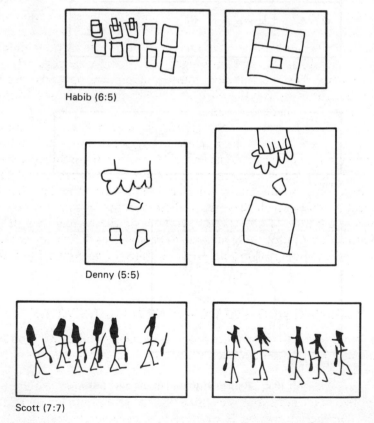

Habib (6:5)

Denny (5:5)

Scott (7:7)

FIG. 16.3.   Attempts to discriminate between addition and subtraction

differentiate between addition and subtraction in their responses, and only four of these did so in a way which might have been understood by anyone else. One seven-year-old wrote "took 1 away" or "add 3", while a six-year-old drew the added bricks superimposed on the pile and the subtracted bricks inside the box (see Fig.16.3). A five-year-old drew a hand adding bricks to the pile, while subtracted bricks were drawn being put into the box (see Fig.16.3). Finally, another five-year-old drew the bricks which were added but drew dashes to show those which had been removed.

Some children went to ingenious lengths in their attempts to represent addition and subtractions. For example, one seven-year-old represented bricks that were added with the appropriate number of British soldiers marching from left to right, while bricks that were subtracted were represented by Japanese soldiers marching from right to left (see Fig.16.3). Other children attempted to represent movement by drawing arrows or hands (see Fig.16.4) but these attempts almost invariably failed to convey what had happened.

The most surprising finding from the two addition and subtraction tasks however, was that *not a single child used the conventional operator signs* + *and* − *to represent additions or subtraction*. We know from the children's workbooks, (Fig.16.1) that operator signs were being used regularly – in some cases daily – by the children from age five years upwards, yet not one child thought of solving the difficult problem of representing addition and subtraction by using these signs.

This total reluctance to use operator signs, together with the similar, but less extreme reluctance to use numerals, suggests that what the children are doing in their school workbooks may be a wholly self-contained activity, which few of them see as being relevant to the tasks they are being asked to perform. In other words, many children do not seem to realize that the arithmetical symbols which they use in their workbooks can also be used to represent quantities of objects or operations on these quantities. If this conclusion is correct, then there appears to be a serious deficiency in many children's understanding of the nature and utility of written arithmetical symbolism.

LEARNING ARITHMETIC – A NEW FRAMEWORK

It seems that if we are to make much progress in understanding why children have difficulty with arithmetic then we need a framework something like that shown in Fig. 16.5.

This figure illustrates schematically the fact that a simple arithmetical statement like "one and two makes three" can be represented in two different forms. On the left hand side we have various concrete realizations of this addition, involving physical objects such as bricks, children in a sweet-

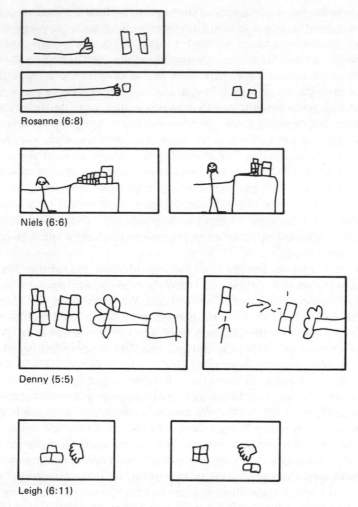

FIG. 16.4. Attempts to show movement in representing addition and subtraction

shop and so on. On the right hand side we have the same addition expressed in the formal code, both in its spoken form: "one and two makes three", and in its written form: $1 + 2 = 3$. Linking the two forms of representation are what I have called *translation procedures*. These are perhaps the most important part of the picture.

Now being competent at arithmetic has two important components. At the most obvious level, it means being able to operate solely within the formal code, to carry out arithmetical calculations and computations free from any concrete realizations. This aspect of arithmetical competence was emphasised most strongly by traditional teaching methods, and is what people nowadays have in mind when they talk of going "back to basics". But there is more to arithmetical competence than that. As the progressivists quite rightly pointed out, we do not want children simply to churn out arithmetical statements by rote, we want them to *understand* what they are doing, what the arithmetical statements mean. Unfortunately, many progressivists, taking their lead from Piaget, have taken this to mean an overemphasis on concrete experience, and a corresponding devaluation of operating with the formal code. In other words, the traditionalists have emphasized the right hand side of Fig.16.5 at the expense of the left, while the progressivists have emphasised the left at the expense of the right.

The framework presented here suggests the beginnings of a way out of the "progressivist versus traditionalist" dilemma. This framework not only puts a more equal emphasis on *both* modes of representation, but also gives particular importance to the links between them. These links are important in learning the formal code, but they are also used in solving arithmetic problems long after the code has been acquired. Many problems, for example, come in concrete form and have to be translated into their appropriate formal representation before they can be solved. At the same time, we often have to translate formal problems into concrete realizations in order to understand them fully, or to check that a particular solution is reasonable. A truly competent user of arithmetic should not only be able to operate within the formal code of arithmetic, but should also be able to make fluent translations between formal and concrete representations of the same problem.

On this analysis, the ability to translate between different modes of representation is of central importance in arithmetical competence. Yet much of the work described earlier suggests that this is precisely what children find difficult. We have seen that few preschool children will spontaneously translate questions asked in the formal code into concrete situations which they can understand – even when, like Amanda and Patrick, these formal questions are asked immediately before or after questions referring to concrete situations. Clearly, translation involving numbers does not come easily to very young children. But neither does it seem to have

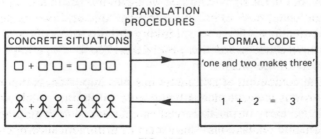

FIG. 16.5.

been grasped by older children in primary school. Despite being able to cover page after page of their workbooks with addition and subtraction sums, many children were still reluctant to represent concrete events by arithmetical symbols. Being able to manipulate the formal code does not, it would seem, guarantee that the user understands the kind of code that it is.

HOW CAN WE HELP?

An important implication of this argument is that learning arithmetic is by no means a natural and effortless process. On the contrary, in asking young children to master a novel context-free code we are requiring them to do something which runs very much counter to their "natural" mode of thinking. Not only that, we are asking them to move in two directions at once. On the one hand, we are trying to free their thinking from the concrete, to introduce them to the power and usefulness of a context-free mode of thought. But at the same time we want to avoid doing this in a way that severs all links with the concrete, for these links are essential for understanding the representational nature of the formal code.

We must accept, then, that in introducing young children to formal arithmetic we are demanding a great deal of them. But how can the task be made easier? What principles and techniques can we offer which might make the process more successful?

Some procedures that might assist children are emerging from a study I have recently carried out. The aim of this study was to introduce arithmetical symbols to four-year-old preschool children, through the use of simple games. My purpose in doing this was two-fold. I wanted to see whether such an enterprise was possible, whether very young children could grasp the idea of using symbols at all. But I was also concerned about how the symbols were introduced. I wanted to find a way of introducing them which was not only enjoyable to the child but which provided a clear rationale as to why the symbols were being used, and why they might be helpful to the child.

This point may become clearer when I describe the games. The basic set-up involves a number of identical tins containing different numbers of "sweets" (in fact, bricks wrapped up in silver paper). The child is shown that one tin contains one sweet, another contains two sweets, and so on. The lids are put back on and the tins shuffled round. The child is asked to guess which tin has one sweet in, and so on. After a few turns of guessing in this way, the adult introduces a set of plastic numerals, with magnets on the back, and suggests the child sticks them on the tins to help distinguish between them. Most of the children I have worked with respond readily to this suggestion. Some children respond in the way an adult might, by sticking the number 1 on the tin with one sweet in, the number 2 on the tin with two in, and so on. Other children, interestingly enough, often use the magnetic numbers in one-to-one correspondence with the sweets: they stick one number – it doesn't matter which – on the tin containing one sweet, two numbers on the tin containing two sweets and so on. Whatever form of response they use, almost all the children seem to appreciate that this helps them distinguish the tins. As Craig (four years, three months) put it: "It's easy now, 'cos we put the numbers on!"

Once children can use the magnetic numbers to represent the number of sweets, the game can be extended to introduce operator signs + and −. In one version, for example, the child shuts his eyes while the adult puts some more "sweets" in one of the tins. However, the adult leaves behind a message on the lid of the tin to show what he has done. For example, he might put on + 1 to show he has added one more sweet.

The following dialogue comes from a game with Thomas (four years, no months). We started with the number 1 on the tin and one sweet inside. I explained that if I then put one more sweet in the tin I would leave the signs + and 1 on the lid; if I put in two more sweets, I would leave + 2 and so on. While Thomas's eyes were shut I put one more sweet in the tin and added the signs + 1. The tin now had 1 + 1 on the lid.

Child: (guesses with eyes shut) Three!
Adult: Open your eyes.
Child: (notices 1 + 1 on tin) I said three! (he seems to realize his guess was wrong).
Adult: How many sweets have I put in?
Child: Two . . . (pause) . . . one to begin with (points to 1 on left hand side) and then you put in two (points to 1 on right hand side).
Adult: No I didn't.
Child: You put in one more.
Adult: I put in one more.
Child: Which makes two!
(Thomas replaces the 1 + 1 with 2 and hides his eyes again. I put in two more sweets and put + 2 on the tin. The tin now has 2 + 2 on the lid).
Adult: Open your eyes. How many have I put in this time?
Child: (looks at 2 + 2 on tin) That means three . . . 'cos you started with two and then you put in one . . . two (puzzles over + 2).
Adult: I put in two more, didn't I?
Child: You put in two more, so it makes four!

While Thomas is not totally fluent at reading and interpreting the message on the tins, he seems to have grasped some of the ideas involved. He appears to understand that a message left behind in this way can tell us about events that have happened in the past. He is also on the verge, it seems, of mastering the convention that such messages are conventionally read from left to right. It is also interesting to note how he is detaching himself from thinking about the sweets and is instead thinking in terms of numbers. In the dialogue above, Thomas does not once refer to "sweets", but instead uses terms like "you started with two", "you put in two more" and "so it makes four".

Thomas is clearly a long way from being competent at arithmetic. Nevertheless, games like these are important in demonstrating two points. First, they show that even before they go to school, children can begin to grasp the beginnings of arithmetical symbolism, provided we are careful to introduce the symbols in appropriate ways. But more importantly perhaps, the games are showing young children the usefulness of arithmetical symbols. They are demonstrating that there are situations where numbers – and operator signs – do indeed make life easier, where there is a rationale for using them, and where there is a purpose for making translations between symbols on the one hand and concrete objects and events on the other. If we can continue to keep this principle at the forefront of our teaching throughout school, then we may be able to make learning arithmetic a much easier process.

17

Reading

Sara Meadows

Frith (1980) calls reading and spelling "complex and astonishing accomplishments", a description which is obviously correct. We do not yet have a full account of what people do when they read. Researchers agree that very many linguistic, perceptual, attentional, memory and cognitive skills are involved, but they vary considerably in which they emphasize. Research in experimental cognitive psychology often concentrates on "bottom-up" analyses (see, for example, Crowder, 1982) and emphasizes the reader's use of, for example, eye movements or pattern recognition processes. Other investigators may assert that the reader's knowledge of what is likely to be the meaning of a word or piece of text may be crucial in whether it can be read, and emphasize "top-down" models (e.g. Smith, 1978). In some cases there has been a regrettable tendency to make the "top-down" or "bottom-up" emphases too strong, so that some accounts of reading as a matter of comprehension have taken the perceptual components as uninteresting and mechanical, and some accounts of reading as a matter of decoding visual information into a verbal form have excluded anything more "cognitive" than word recognition. "Top-down" and "bottom-up" have to be co-ordinated in theories as they are in ordinary reading, where most of the time processes at all levels are used. Recently theories which integrate different levels have appeared. Morton's "logogen" system (Morton, 1969, 1980) and Rumelhart's model (Ellis, 1984; Rumelhart, 1977) are important examples. It is clear that "reading" includes many different activities at different perceptual, linguistic and cognitive levels, which no doubt interact in changing ways as the reader becomes more skilled, or

Source: Meadows, S. (1986). *Understanding child development*. London:Hutchinson, pp. 77–84.

when the reader is faced with different sorts of reading task or text. The "reading" involved in recognizing "cereals" in a supermarket is probably not quite the same as the "reading" involved in understanding the same word in a newspaper article on the government's farming policy, and the "reading" might well be different again when "cereals" appears in a scientific article or a poem. Similarly, children learning to read may use different processes to make sense of the written message, varying according to, for example, familiarity, the availability of context, and the child's own preferences such as willingness to guess (Francis, 1982).

Development in Reading Processes

Although we cannot yet specify the developmental course of interacting reading processes, it does seem likely that it is the basic perceptual processes which change least. Visual discriminations between symbols like b and d, for example, can be shown even in infants (Banks & Salapatek 1983). There is, on the other hand, obvious and enormous development in the child's knowledge of language, of the world, and of reading and literature. Variations here are predictive of success or failure in learning to read. I shall have more to say about these "top-down" constituents of reading than about the perceptual basics, but I would not wish to imply either that the latter are unimportant or that they remain unchanged throughout the development of reading.

Children as they begin to learn to read probably have, then, most of the perceptual capacities – eye movements, pattern recognition and discrimination, attention – which they need. They are also very well used to dealing with the language that they hear. They have had much practice in extracting meaning from it. They have also probably analysed it into segments at the levels of phrases, words and morphemes (McShane, personal communication). In reading, they have to do rather similar things to language which they see rather than hear. There has been much debate over whether writing is decoded into imagined speech which is then processed as if it were really heard, or whether reading goes straight from symbol to meaning. The possible relationships between speech and reading are complex, and the evidence is so too (Crowder, 1982; ch.9; Ellis, 1984). The debate may perhaps be resolving into an agreement that the skilled reader, at least, may use imagined sound or may go direct from written word to meaning. What is done depends on the reader's skills, the novelty or familiarity of words, the difficulty of the text and the purpose of reading, among other variables.

Sound-letter correspondences. Children learning to read often have problems over the relationship between sound and letter. In English there are many complexities in the correspondence between phoneme and grapheme – consider for example "a" in "cat", "fate" and "arm", and "c" in "cat", "ceiling" and "chuckle". There may be more regularities in combinations of graphemes. As Stubbs (1980) points out, Bernard Shaw overstated his case for spelling reform when he suggested a pronunciation for "ghoti" which followed precedents in other words ("gh" as in "cough", "o" as in "women", "ti" as in "station", hence "ghoti" is pronounced "fish"), as "gh" is always pronounced as a hard "g" when it appears at the beginning of words ("ghost", "ghastly", "ghetto"). There are however many irregularities even in common words. The letter string "ough" has a different pronunciation each time it appears in the words "bough", "cough", "dough", "lough", "nought", "rough" and "through". Further , Liberman et al. (1977) show that it is unlikely that speech sound is experienced as ready-segmented phonemes or that phonemes blend obviously into words. Young children and illiterate adults find it relatively easy to segment words into syllables and almost impossible to segment into phonemes. Symbol-sound correspondences are somewhat easier to learn in regularized alphabets such as the Initial Teaching Alphabet (i.t.a.) (Downing, 1979) but such alphabets do not allow for regional pronunciation differences, nor do they preserve the lexical and syntactic information which irregular spelling carries (for example the semantic relationship between "bomb" and "bombardment"). Stubbs (1980) argues that the English spelling system works extremely well for a native speaker who knows its phonological and morphological rules, that is it is better suited to adult fluent readers than to children (or foreigners) learning to read English. Awareness of language would thus appear to be a most important component of learning to read. Awareness of sounds is a predictor of speed of becoming a reader, teaching about sounds ("phonics") seems to be a useful part of teaching reading (Bryant & Bradley, 1985). Phonemic analysis is quite hard to learn but becoming able to do it is an important breakthrough in the early stages of reading. "Sounding out" words, if successful, reduces dependence on recognizing their visual pattern and supplements the child's knowledge of likely meaning and vocabulary. Experience of reading increases both the child's general knowledge and his or her knowledge of the underlying rules of written language so that gradually correspondences between letter and sound become less crucial to understanding what is being read. Adult fluent readers may only use sound deliberately in their reading when they are having problems with understanding or remembering what they read.

Language awareness in learning to read.   Various studies have now picked up linguistic awareness and experience as an important predictor of learning to read, perhaps even a prerequisite for it. Wells (1981a, b) found significant positive correlations between parents' and children's interest in literacy, particularly the frequency with which stories were read to the child, and the child's progress in learning to read, for his representative sample of 120 children. Francis (1982), in a sensitive case study of ten children, found that understanding the task of reading and writing was crucial both for doing it successfully and for appreciating why it was worth doing. Children who learn to read early and easily (Clark, 1976) tend to have acquired such an understanding before beginning school. How much the child is read to, how much he or she sees other people reading, how much and how explicitly written material is used in daily activities like shopping, knowledge of concepts like "sound", "word" and "sentence", are related to rate and efficiency of learning to read. These activities seem to contribute to achieving insight into the links between written symbol and word meaning, they also serve to establish that reading is or can be useful and entertaining.

Children who lack these experiences tend to be slower in learning to read. For some, lack of reading-related experiences may be due to a home background which also does not provide experience related to other school activities. Children from such homes may not know, when they first enter school, what is required of them. Classroom tasks may be relatively strange and incomprehensible. It is harder to learn to do something which makes no sense in itself and which you cannot link to your other experience than something part familiar whose purpose you appreciate, and when the "something" is as complex and artificial as learning to read, it may be the best you can do to do it slowly, weakly and by rote, as some of the children described in Francis (1982) did. Only when the children achieved an insight into the general relation between reading and writing on the one hand and spoken language on the other, only when reading and writing became meaningful activities, did they make much progress.

Reading stages and strategies.   The problem is certainly not a simple one of deficient home background, and it is not so much one of inadequacies of language or of concentration on the part of the child as of inexperience in reflecting on language and how it is used. In other words, it is often essentially a metacognitive and metalinguistic problem, interacting with the social problem of adjustment to school life. Children solve the problem of learning to read in different ways. Ellis (1984) sketches a common developmental course. The 5-year-old beginning to learn to read recognizes and uses a spoken vocabulary of several hundred words, and speaks grammatically. The first step made in learning to read is often to "glance-and-guess": a few words are recognized by shape, otherwise an unfamiliar word is guessed using the context as a guide, its graphemic or phonemic characteristics being rather unimportant in the guess. Unfamiliar words without context cannot be read at all. Errors tend to preserve meaning but look and sound different from the correct word. Later, in the second step of "sophisticated guessing", the vocabulary recognized by sight is larger, and unfamiliar words met in or out of context are guessed in terms of their visual similarity with familiar words, with contextual cues used where possible. Visual cues from the beginnings of words are probably more easily used than those from the middle or end of words: words in context are easier than words isolated in word lists (an instance of the usefulness of top-down cues). Poor readers incidentally may tend to rely on pictures for cues, or even believe that the story is contained in the pictures rather than in the text (Francis, 1982; Yule & Rutter, 1985).

Francis (1982) also reports that even her quicker readers rarely used phonic cues until they had a fair grasp of visual and contextual cues. They then used sounding out unfamiliar words largely to supplement a not-quite-adequate visual and contextual analysis. Realizing, or being taught, that there is some consistency between words in how letters or groups of letters are pronounced, increases the child's chance of decoding written word into meaning. It may be particularly useful to do left-to-right sounding-out on words which are phonemically regular but visually nondescript, such as "bun"; words which are phonemically irregular but visually distinctive, such as "light", may be more easily recognized by their shape than by sounding -out. Bryant and Bradley (1980, 1985) report that some young children have separate reading and spelling strategies, and hence can read some words (such as "light") which they cannot spell, and spell others (such as "bun"), which they cannot read, a phenomenon found also among Francis' sample.

Insight into analysing words into phonemes, phoneme-grapheme correspondences and the integration of phonic strategies, visual memory and use of context, with of course further vocabulary growth and increasing knowledge of the worlds which reading conjures up, combine to form the basic achievement of reading. Top-down and bottom-up strategies can now be used interdependently. They become, no doubt, more fluent with practice just as any other skills would, and the balance adopted between different reading strategies probably becomes more flexible and more efficient. There is considerable development, in other words, in the uses to which reading is put. Chall (1983) provides a table (Table 17.1) to illustrate this point: reading is an instrument for knowing, heavily influenced in its development by the demands of the ecosystem, and both an object and a result of practice in "study skills" (Chall, 1983, pp.85–7).

Children and Stories

There is a history several centuries old of producing special story books for children, and behind that a longer tradition of folk tales and rhymes and other narratives which took children for their audience. Most children hear stories and tell them themselves, many read them or write them. In

TABLE 17.1
Stages of Reading Development: An Outline of the Major Qualitative Characteristics and How They are Acquired

1 Stage designation	2 Grade range (age)	3 Major qualitative characteristics and masteries by end of age	4 How acquired	5 Relationship of reading to listening
Stage 0: Prereading, 'pseudo-reading'	Preschool ages 6 months–6 years	Child 'pretends' to read, retells story when looking at pages of book previously read to him/her; names letters of alphabet; recognizes some signs; prints own name; plays with books, pencils, and paper.	Being read to by an adult (or older child) who responds to and warmly appreciates the child's interest in books and reading; being provided with books, paper, pencils, blocks, and letters.	Most can understand the children's picture books and stories read to them. They understand thousands of words they hear by age 6 but can read few if any of them.
Stage 1: Initial reading and decoding	Grade 1 & beginning Grade 2 (ages 6 & 7)	Child learns relation between letters and sounds and between printed and spoken words; child is able to read simple text containing high frequency words and phonically regular words; uses skill and insight to 'sound out' new one-syllable words.	Direct instruction in letter-sound relations (phonics) and practice in their use. Reading of simple stories using words with phonic elements taught and words of high frequency. Being read to on a level above what child can read independently to develop more advanced language patterns, knowledge of new words, and ideas.	The level of difficulty of language read by the child is much below the language understood when heard. At the end of stage 1, most children can understand up to 4000 or more words when heard but can read only about 600.

1	2	3	4	5
Stage designation	Grade range (age)	Major qualitative characteristics and masteries by end of age	How acquired	Relationship of reading to listening
Stage 2: Confirmation and fluency	Grades 2 & 3 (ages 7 & 8)	Child reads simple, familiar stories and selections with increasing fluency. This is done by consolidating the basic decoding elements, sight vocabulary, and meaning context in the reading of familiar stories and selections.	Direct instruction in advanced decoding skills; wide reading (with instruction and independently) of familiar, interesting materials which help promote fluent reading. Being read to at levels above their own independent reading level to develop language, vocabulary, and concepts.	At the end of stage 2, about 3000 words can be read and understood and about 9000 are known when heard. Listening is still more effective than reading.
Stage 3: Reading for learning the new	Grades 4–8 (ages 9 –13)	Reading is used to learn new ideas, to gain new knowledge, to experience new feelings, to learn new attitudes; generally from one viewpoint.	Reading and study of text-books, reference works, trade books, newspapers, and magazines that contain new ideas and values, unfamiliar vocabulary and syntax: systematic study of words and reacting to the text through discussion, answering questions, writing, etc. Reading of increasingly more complex fiction, biography, nonfiction, and the like.	At beginning of stage 3, listening comprehension of the same material is still more effective than reading comprehension. By the end of stage 3, reading and listening are about equal; for those who read very well, reading may be more efficient.
Phase A	Inter-mediate, 4–6			
Phase B	Junior high school, 7–9			

1	2	3	4	5
Stage designation	Grade range (age)	Major qualitative characteristics and masteries by end of age	How acquired	Relationship of reading to listening
Stage 4: Multiple viewpoints	High school grades 10–12 (ages 15–17)	Reading widely from a broad range of complex materials, both expository and narrative, with a variety of viewpoints.	Wide reading and study of the physical, biological, and social sciences and the humanities; high quality and popular literature; newspapers and magazines; systematic study of words and word parts.	Reading comprehension is better than listening comprehension of material of difficult content and readability. For poorer readers, listening comprehension may be equal to reading comprehension.
Stage 5: Construction and reconstruction	College and beyond (age 18+)	Reading is used for one's own needs and purposes (professional and personal); reading serves to integrate one's knowledge with that of others, to synthesize it and to create new knowledge. It is rapid and efficient.	Wide reading of ever more difficult materials, reading beyond one's immediate needs; writing of papers, tests, essays, and other forms that call for integration of varied knowledge and points of view.	Reading is more efficient than listening.

this country, at least (see Schieffelin & Cochran-Smith, 1984 for notes on two other cultures), there is a positive correlation between being read stories during the pre-school years, on the one hand, and both metalinguistic competence and prospects of learning to read and write easily, on the other. Children learn a great deal about written language and about the structure of stories from being read to (e.g., Clark, 1976; Clay, 1979; Wells, 1985). They also take part in a shared activity with the older person reading to them (and indirectly with the author). Where this is enjoyable for both parties, it doubtless provides motivation for further reading. Involving parents in hearing their older children read to them has proved a most effective way of improving children's reading skills (e.g. Tizard, Schofield, & Hewison 1981).

Being read to can involve children in several different ways of "taking from text" (Teale, 1984). Sometimes the child is required to be a passive audience. Sometimes adults encourage a great deal of active participation from the child, requesting identification of objects in pictures, comments on the action, and predictions about what will happen next. Sometimes analogies will be drawn between the events of the story and the child's own experience. If such elaborations of the reading and listening activity are sensitively used, children become adept at relating stories to a wider context and dealing with their implications more deeply, skills useful in the classroom (Hayward, 1980; Heath, 1982, 1983; Mills & Funnell, 1983). Stories are a constant part of classroom social life, and a delight in many children's home lives.

Stories socialize children in other ways besides the interaction which is required of a reader or listener. They can convey the culture to the child and socialize him or her into culturally approved patterns of attitudes and values. They can do this both overtly and covertly, and can carry both admirable and deplorable messages. Hilaire Belloc's *Cautionary Tales for Children*, for example, has overt morals such as "don't tell lies", "don't slam doors" and "don't play with loaded guns", which are, however, less memorable, and less enjoyed by children, than his gleeful callousness. Louisa May Alcott's *Little Women* proposes that girls should be quiet, ladylike, self-sacrificing and dominated by men, a mode of existence which was impossible and destructive for Alcott herself (Saxton, 1978).

This sort of socialization is hard to quantify. Its existence has however been a source of anxiety to many adults who wish to censor the "unsuitable" out of their children's reading (and indeed out of other adults' too), and often have wished to substitute more "suitable" reading. There are a number of discussions of the socializing effects of traditional fairy-tales, for example (Steedman, 1982; Tucker, 1981; Zipes, 1983). We do not know whether women were more self-effacing and long-suffering as a result of being told the story of Patient Griselda, the archetypal victimized wife whose patience wins her back the affections of her dreadful husband, or whether there was more adultery between wives and servants after the publication of *Lady Chatterley's Lover*. Many of us may remember being (less strongly!) influenced by a story we have read. In so far as stories reflect the entire culture, and so are reinforced by other experiences, they may have a powerful effect. There is little clear evidence.

It is also argued that stories are important in children's emotional development. There are famous psychoanalytic interpretations of fairy stories in terms of children's need to resolve their Oedipus crisis or their penis envy, notably Bettelheim's *The Uses of Enchantment* (1978). Since these resolutions are normally of unconscious feelings and problems, it is again hard to demonstrate that stories have the "uses" claimed. Stories may also model emotions more directly, as they illustrate their characters' behaviour. Hayward (1980) told a slightly simplified version of *Watership Down* to her class of 4-year-olds, and later observed a little boy with aspirations to toughness and bravado bump his head, and instead of crying say "Miss Hayward, I've hurt myself bad, but don't worry, I'm Bigwig the strongest rabbit – I'm brave like Bigwig".

Stories obviously commonly *evoke* emotions – like play, they provide a relatively risk-free and controllable form of being frightened, excited and exhilarated.

Children begin to understand the form of stories quite early in their experience of them. They are not as dependent on temporal order as Piaget (1969) suggested. Given a logically structured story (his were ill-formed) they make inferences and build up a coherent shapely sequence of events even at the age of 4 (Mandler & Johnson, 1977; Wimmer, 1980;). They develop "story grammars" just as they develop "scripts" of familiar events in their lives. Although their initial re-telling of stories contains mainly surface events, probing with "why" questions elicits much inference about the characters' motives and intentions. Young children's limitations may be attributed to lack of world knowledge and memory problems rather than to lack of an ability to make inferences and other logical connections (Trabasso, & Nicholas, 1980). As children encounter more stories they gain both more "real world" knowledge and more knowledge of the conventions of stories. They begin to appreciate the distancing, reassuring opening "Once upon a time"; they expect there to be good characters who triumph over their troubles and bad characters who get their due come-uppance; they know that foxes are "sly" and witches are "wicked". Traditional stories create a world simpler than the child's own but not entirely unlike it, so that they can try an alternative "reality" just as they do in play.

SKILLS OF LEARNING FROM TEXT

Being literate becomes increasingly important as one progresses through the educational system, both because of the possibilities of gathering, rearranging, comparing and passing on knowledge which it provides, and because it is one of the commonest social "measures" of intellectual adequacy. As we have seen, reading involves many different levels of cognitive processing. Reading a text in order to *learn* from it requires the use of comprehension and study skills.

Comprehension

Collins and Smith (1982) describe some of the important comprehension skills necessary for dealing with written information. The first group are concerned with *monitoring* comprehension, that is checking whether the text is being understood, being aware of a breakdown in understanding and taking appropriate action to remedy it. The reader may fail to comprehend text at the level of a particular word, phrase or sentence, or at the level of fitting bits of text together. Children have limited vocabulary and general knowledge, compared with adults, and may make over-simple assumptions about grammar. When acting out the *spoken* sentence "The cat was bitten by the dog", for example, they proceed as if the passive sentence had the subject-verb-object order characteristic of simple active declarative sentences. Similar problems may be found in many early readers: unusual grammar upsets the child's comprehension. Unusual vocabulary items may puzzle the child too, but they are probably more easily clarified, and children often enjoy grand long words. However, children may have more marked comprehension problems than adults, even at the simplest levels. Ellen Markman suggests that they have major problems over comprehending the integration of separate bits of text into a consistent whole. They often do not notice, she says, what are to the adult glaring inconsistencies or omissions in verbal material, for example incomplete instructions about how to play a game (Markman, 1979; Robinson & Robinson, 1983).

Children's comprehension of text, then, runs into difficulties and the problem arises of how to solve them. Possible strategies include ignoring the uncomprehended words or passage; waiting to see if its meaning later becomes clear; guessing, the guess being confirmed or disconfirmed later; re-reading the immediate problem passage or the larger part of the text in which it occurs; seeking outside help, from peer, teacher, dictionary or another text. Which of these strategies the child uses will depend on the task requirements; casual reading uses the simpler strategies at the beginning of the list, while detailed mastery of difficult texts requires much more re-reading, analysis and comparison of different sources. Which strategy is used will also depend on the characteristics of the reader, and in the case of the very young reader on how he or she is being taught to read. However new reading is, the child has used skills very much like many of these for several years while trying to understand spoken language. The most obvious skill to be applicable to written language but not so readily to spoken language is re-reading, both because spoken words are much more ephemeral and because requests for repetition of an uncomprehended utterance often produce a rephrasing of what was said, not a verbatim repetition. Guessing, ignoring and seeking outside help (sometimes from the same sources) are however well practised strategies. Children, like all who are relatively ignorant or novices, must rather often fail to "comprehend". It is, however, a question of some interest to identify what and when they know *that* they don't know, and what and when they know *why* they don't know.

Collins and Smith (1982) point out that as well as guessing at the meaning of particular words or phrases, the reader will guess about the meaning of more global aspects of the text. Guesses will be made, or hypotheses constructed, about matters like what sort of story this is, what will happen in this situation, who are the "goodies" and who the "baddies", and so forth. (In many cases authors consciously use these hypotheses either to support the plausibility of their narrative [as in romantic novels] or to mislead the reader in a sequence of bluff and double-bluff (as in "who-dun-nits"). Jane Austen's presentation of Mr Darcy and Mr Wickham in *Pride and Prejudice* is a particularly brilliant example of both uses.) Again, children beginning to read will have developed strategies of making sense of stories or events in terms of broad hypotheses which define what this sort of story is likely to be about, or what happens in this sort of event. Schank and Abelson (1977) called the latter "scripts". Careful observation of young children at home shows that they both use and seek to clarify "scripts" (e.g. Tizard & Hughes, 1982; Tizard et al., 1984) and it has been argued that this use is a major opportunity for the development of reasoning (Mills & Funnell, 1983). Children's experience of stories gives them something like "scripts" for stories, as their filling-in of the frame "Once upon a time . . . and then they all lived happily ever after" shows (e.g. Applebee, 1978).

REFERENCES

Applebee, A. (1978). *The child's conception of story.* Chicago; University of Chicago Press.

Banks, M. S. & Salapatek, P. (1983). Infant visual perception. In M. M. Haith & J. J. Campos (Eds.), *Handbook of Child Psychology* (Vol.2). New York: Wiley.

Bettelheim, B. (1978). *The uses of enchantment.* Harmondsworth: Penguin.

Bryant, P. E. & Bradley, L. (1980). Why children sometimes write words which they do not read. In U. Frith (Ed.), *Cognitive processes in spelling*, London: Academic Press.

Bryant, P. E. & Bradley, L. (1985). *Children's reading problems.* Oxford: Blackwell.

Chall, J. S. (1983). *Stages of reading development*. New York: McGraw Hill.

Clark, M. M. (1976). *Young fluent readers*. London: Heinemann.

Clay, M. (1979). *Reading: The patterning of complex behaviour*. Heinemann.

Collins, A. & Smith, E. E. (1982). Teaching the process of reading comprehension. In D. K. Detterman & R. J. Sternberg (Eds.), *How and how much can intelligence be increased?*. Norwood, N.J.: Ablex.

Crowder, R. G. (1982). *The psychology of reading: An introduction*. Oxford: OUP.

Downing, J. (1979). *Reading and reasoning*. Edinburgh: Chambers.

Ellis, A. W. (1984). *Reading, writing and dyslexia: A cognitive analysis*. London: Lawrence Erlbaum Associates Ltd.

Francis, H. (1982). *Learning to read: Literate behaviour and orthographic knowledge*. London: George Allen & Unwin.

Frith, U. (1980). Reading and spelling skills. In M. Rutter (Ed.), *Scientific foundations of developmental psychiatry*. London: Heinemann.

Hayward, C. (1980). *Literary theme development in the nursery classroom*. Unpublished M.ED. thesis, University of Bristol.

Heath, S.B. (1982). What no bedtime story means: Narrative skills at home and at school. *Language in Society, 11,* 49–76.

Heath, S. B. (1983). *Ways with words*. Cambridge: Cambridge University Press.

Liberman, I.Y., Shankweiler, D., Liberman, A., & Fowler, C. (1977). Phonetic segmentation and reading in the beginning reader. In A. S. Reber & D. L. Scarborough, (Eds.), *Toward a psychology of reading*. New York: Wiley.

Mandler, J. M. & Johnson, N. S. (1977). Remembrance of things parsed: Story structure and recall. *Cognitive Psychology, 9,* 111–151.

Markman, E. M. (1979). Realising that you don't understand: elementary school children's awareness of inconsistencies. *Child Development, 50,* 643–655.

Mills, M. & Funnell, E. (1983). Experience and cognitive processing. In S. Meadows (Ed.), *Developing thinking*. London: Methuen.

Morton, J. (1969). Interaction of information in word recognition. *Psychological Review, 76,* 165–78.

Morton, J. (1980). The Logogen model and orthographic structure. In U. Frith, (Ed.), *Cognitive processes in spelling*. London: Academic Press.

Piaget, J. (1969). *The child's conception of time*. London: Routledge & Kegan Paul.

Robinson, E. J. & Robinson, W. P. (1983). Communication and metacommunication: quality of children's instructions in relation to judgements about the adequacy of instructions and the locus of responsibility for communication failure. *Journal of Experimental Child Psychology, 36,* 305–320.

Rumelhart, D. (1977). Toward an interactive model of reading. In S. Dornic (Ed.), *Attention and performance, VI*. Hillsdale, N.J.: Lawrence Erlbaum Associates Inc.

Saxton, M. (1978). *Louisa May: A modern biography of Louisa May Alcott*. London: Andre Deutsch.

Schank, R. C. & Albelson, R. (1977). *Scripts, plans, goals, and understanding*. Hillsdale, N.J.: Lawrence Erlbaum Associates Inc.

Schieffelin, B. B. & Cochran-Smith, M. (1984). Learning to read culturally: Literacy before schooling. In H. Goetman, A. Oberg, & F. Smith (Eds.), *Awakening to literacy*. London: Heinemann.

Smith, F. (1978). *Reading*. Cambridge: Cambridge University Press.

Steedman, C. (1982). *The tidy house*. London: Virago.

Stubbs, M. (1980). *Language and literacy: The sociolinguistics of reading and writing*. London: Routledge & Kegan Paul.

Teale, W. H. (1984). Reading to young children: Its significance for literacy development. In H. Goelman, A. Oberg, & F. Smith (Eds.), *Awakening to literacy*. London: Heinemann.

Tizard, B. & Hughes, M. (1984). *Young children learning* London: Fontana.

Tizard, B., Hughes, M., Pinkerton, G., & Carmichael, H. (1982). Adults' cognitive demands at home and at nursery school. *Journal of Child Psychology and Psychiatry, 23,* 108–117.

Tizard, J., Schofield, W., & Hewison, J. (1981). Collaboration between teachers and parents in assisting children's reading. *British Journal of Educational Psychology, 52,* 1–5.

Trabasso, T. & Nicholas, D. W. (1980). Memory and inferences in the comprehension of narratives. In F. Wilkening, J. Becker, & T. Trabasso, (Eds.), *Information integration by children.* Hillsdale, N.J.: Lawrence Erlbaum Associates Inc.

Tucker, N. (1981). *The child and the book.* Cambridge: Cambridge University Press.

Wells, C. G. (1981a). Some antecedents of early educational attainment. *British Journal of Sociology of Education, 2,* 181–200.

Wells, C. G. (1981b). Pre-school literacy related activities and success in school. In D. R. Olson (Ed.), *The nature and consequences of literacy.* Cambridge: Cambridge University Press.

Wells, C. G. (1985). *Language development in the pre-school years.* Cambridge: Cambridge University Press.

Wimmer, H. (1980). Children's understanding of stories: Assimilation by a general schema for actions of coordination of temporal relations? In F. Wilkening, J. Becker & T. Trabasso (Eds.), *Information integration by children.* Hillsdale N.J.: Lawrence Erlbaum Associates Inc.

Yule, W. & Rutter, M. (1985). Reading and other learning difficulties. In M. Rutter & L. Hersov, (Eds.), *Child and adolescent psychiatry: Modern approaches.* Oxford: Blackwell.

Zipes, J. (1983). *Fairytales and the art of subversion.* London: Heinemann.

Author Index

Subject Index

APPENDIX

The authors of Chapter 15, A.N. Perret-Clermont and N. Bell, have kindly provided us with the following list of references in order to bring their material up to date to October 1987:

This chapter has now been published in:
De Corte, E., Lodewijks, H., Parmentier, R., & Span, P. (Eds.) (1987). *Learning and instruction.* Oxford: Pergamon Press and Leuven University Press.

Other papers referred to in Chapter 15, now published in De Corte et al. (1987), are:
Bennett (1985); Gilly (1985); Pontecorvo (1985).

Also now published is Perret-Clermont & Brossard, cited originally as "in press". The full reference is as follows:
Perret-Clermont, A.N. & Brossard, A. (1985). On the interdigitation of social and cognitive processes. In R. Hinde, A.N. Perret-Clermont and J. Stephanson-Hinde (Eds.), Social relationships and cognitive development. London: Clarendon Press.

The authors have also provided some additional references to work published since the original paper was presented, which they think will be of assistance.

Dinello, R. & Perret-Clermont, A.N. (Eds.) (1987). *Psychopedagogie interculturelle.* Delval: Coussett-Fribourg.

Schubauer-Leoni, M.L. & Perret-Clermont, A.N. (1985). Interactions sociales dans l'apprentisage de connaissances mathématiques chez l'enfant. In G. Nugny (Ed.), *Psychologie sociale du dèveloppement cognitif.* Berne: P. Lang.

Schubauer-Leoni, M.L. (1986). Le contrat didactique: Un cadre interprêtatif pour comprendre les savoirs manifestés par les élèves en mathématiques. *European Journal of Psychology of Education, 1,* 139-153.

Light, P. & Perret-Clermont, A.N. (1986) Social construction of logical structures or social construction of meaning? *Dossiers de Psychologie,* University of Neuchàtel, no. 27.

Light, P. & Perret-Clermont, A.N. (in press) Social context effects in learning and testing. In *Cognition and social worlds* (working title). Oxford: Oxford University Press.